D1481903

# Modern Methods of Data Analysis

# Modern Methods of Data Analysis

edited by
John Fox
J. Scott Long

SAGE PUBLICATIONS
*The International Professional Publishers*
Newbury Park   London   New Delhi

*For information address:*

SAGE Publications, Inc.
2111 West Hillcrest Drive
Newbury Park, California 91320

SAGE Publications Ltd.
28 Banner Street
London EC1Y 8QE
England

SAGE Publications Pvt. Ltd.
M-32 Market
Greater Kailash I
New Delhi 110 048 India

Printed in the United States of America

Library of Congress Cataloging-in-Publication Data

main entry under title

Modern methods of data analysis / edited by John Fox and J. Scott
    Long.
        p.    cm.
    Includes bibliographical references.
    ISBN 0-8039-3366-5
    1. Mathematical statistics.   I. Fox, John 1947-      .   II. Long,
    J. Scott.
QA276.M595    1990
519.5 – dc20

                                                        89-27842
                                                        CIP

**SECOND PRINTING, 1990**

# CONTENTS

# INTRODUCTION

John Fox
J. Scott Long

During the last 30 years there has been a revolution in the way that statisticians think about data analysis. The success of this revolution can be conveniently dated by the publication in 1977 of John Tukey's monumental work *Exploratory Data Analysis* (hereafter, EDA). The seeds of the revolution were sown in a series of papers written by Tukey, his colleagues, and his students. The direction for the revolution was clearly specified in Tukey's 1962 paper *The Future of Data Analysis*. The changes proposed in this seminal paper reflect the realization that analyzing data to learn about a substantive problem involves more than the formal tools of mathematical statistics.

Tukey argues that exploratory analysis is a necessary step in solving many problems, with graphical methods often playing a central role. *Spotty data* or outliers are frequently critical to developing an understanding of the process under study. Typical problems fail to satisfy the assumptions often made by classical statistical methods. As a consequence, Tukey expressed a desire to test these assumptions and to develop methods that require less restrictive assumptions. Resampling methods, such as jackknifing, and robust and resistant statistical estimators illustrate this thrust. Tukey maintained, finally, that many prob-

AUTHORS' NOTE: Lowell H. Hargens provided useful comments on an earlier draft of this chapter.

7

lems require iterative solutions, rather than more convenient single-step solutions.

While Tukey's EDA emphasizes hand computations, even to the extent of drawing figures without a ruler, his future of data analysis repeatedly points to the computer as the means to realize his recommendations. Indeed, current practices of data analysis are impossible without cheap computing. Thus the revolution in computing is an essential component of the revolution in data analysis. The availability of $10,000 microcomputers that have approximately the same computational power as the state-of-the-art mainframe of 20 years ago has spurred advances in data analysis. Statistical software has also evolved significantly, if not quite as dramatically as the hardware. As a consequence, computations that required extraordinary effort and significant expense in the relatively recent past can now be accomplished cheaply and conveniently.

Independent of the guidance provided by Tukey's program of data analysis, the availability of cheap computing has had a major impact on how data are analyzed. When card sorters and mechanical calculators were the major tools for statistical analysis, sophisticated work might have included one or two regressions, each with two or three independent variables. For a large data set, the computations could keep a research assistant occupied for an entire summer. The availability of the computer makes it possible to accomplish the same thing within minutes or even seconds.

Although access to cheap and powerful computers involves obvious savings in time, it has two common adverse consequences. First, researchers become increasingly removed from their data. It is impossible to use a card sorter for statistical analysis without gaining some feel for the univariate distributions of the data. The histogram was literally and physically available in a stack of cards. Computers, in contrast, make it possible to do many multivariate analyses without any consideration for the simple distributional characteristics of the data. Anyone who has served as a statistical consultant can recount tales of disaster resulting from failure to screen data. Although these problems are not necessarily consequences of using a computer, they are frequently products of the availability of cheap computing and sophisticated multivariate methods.

Other, more subtle problems also result from ignoring the data. Consider, for example, the four scatterplots from Anscombe (1973)

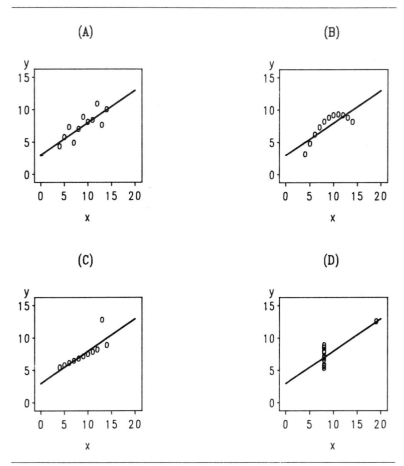

Figure 1. **Four data sets producing identical least squares regression out-**
**puts, including regression coefficients, standard error of the re-**
**gression, correlation, and coefficient standard errors.**
SOURCE: From Anscombe (1973). Reprinted by permission of the American Statistical Association.

shown in Figure 1. The data in these graphs were cleverly contrived to
produce identical standard linear regression outputs, including the intercept, slope, correlation, and standard errors. In cases like this, pictures are worth more than words. Data analysts who ignore such pictures
do so at their own peril, a lesson that has yet to be learned by many
social scientists who imprudently employ statistical methods in their
research.

A second abuse of computational power involves the sheer volume of analysis that can be done with little thought. Scanning a correlation matrix for "significant" findings, throwing dozens of variables into a stepwise regression, and other similar mechanical practices grew more common as they became easier.

While computers can encourage the abuse of data, the development of exploratory data analysis and the renewed interest in graphical methods are important countervailing influences. On-screen graphics make the close examination of data through univariate and bivariate displays fast, simple, effective, and — importantly — enjoyable. Three-dimensional computer graphics for data analysis are appearing as well. Methods of identifying outliers facilitate the search for incorrect and spotty data. New diagnostic techniques address the potentially problematic assumptions of classical statistical methods such as linear least-squares regression analysis. Thus, although modern methods of data analysis include increasingly sophisticated statistical models, they satisfy the basic need to examine the data closely and to question the assumptions of the model.

These characteristics of modern data analysis are reflected in several themes that run through this book. First, there is an emphasis on graphical data analysis. Graphical methods play central roles in the chapters by Spence and Lewandowsky, Fox, Goodall, De Veaux, Monette, and Bollen and Jackman. A second theme is intensive computation. Although it is possible to do good data analysis by hand, as evidenced by many of the methods introduced by Tukey, all of the chapters in this book (with the exception of Spence and Lewandowsky's treatment of graphical perception) present techniques that are quite unthinkable without the assistance of a computer. The intersection of graphics and computers is itself a centrally important development of the past decade. A third theme of the book is regression analysis, which is at the heart of applied statistics, and which is addressed in the chapters by Goodall, De Veaux, Monette, Bollen and Jackman, Berk, Stine, Little and Rubin, and Dubin and Rivers. Finally, the sampling characteristics of data are considered in the chapters by Stine, Little and Rubin, and Dubin and Rivers.

Spence and Lewandowsky's chapter on graphical perception shows how the tools of experimental psychology can be applied to the study of visual presentation of data. They review work in the area, some of it their own, and contribute a novel perspective.

Fox presents a variety of distributional displays, from the simple to the more sophisticated. These displays are useful in their own right for data analysis and presentation and as components of other displays and techniques. Some of the methods described in Fox's chapter are employed by other authors in this text.

Goodall deals with smoothing of series and scatterplots. These methods for extracting systematic information from noise enhance our ability to perceive and interpret the information in graphical displays. Again, they are important partly for their application in areas such as diagnostics.

The chapter by De Veaux describes the ACE algorithm, a computationally intensive nonparametric method for multiple regression analysis. He also considers how the information from ACE may be used to select relatively simple linearizing transformations of the data in regression analysis.

Monette's chapter describes how advanced three-dimensional computer graphics and elliptical geometry can be applied to least-squares multiple regression. This approach offers a remarkably clear and deep understanding of many of the properties of regression analysis, as well as being a powerful tool for analyzing data. It is difficult to develop a full appreciation of the power of these methods without color and motion.

Bollen and Jackman survey some of the most useful methods for diagnosing problems in linear least-squares regression, including outliers, influential data, and nonlinearity. They show how diagnostics can help to improve an otherwise problematic statistical analysis.

Berk takes up the topic of robust estimation in linear regression. He explains how one class of robust estimators, called M-estimators, corrects some of the potential deficiencies of least-squares estimation.

Stine's chapter introduces bootstrapping, which is a resampling method for estimating sampling variation empirically without making strong distributional assumptions about the structure of the data. Stine shows how bootstrapping can be applied to several important problems, including regression analysis.

Little and Rubin survey recent work, much of it their own, on the thorny issue of missing data in statistical analysis. They explain how missing data can compromise an otherwise adequate analysis, and they present better methods of estimation in the presence of missing data than are typically employed in social research.

Dubin and Rivers take up the closely related topic of selection bias in regression analysis. In addition to describing methods of estimation that correct for selection bias in linear regression, they develop analogous techniques for logit and probit models. Social scientists have become sophisticated in their use of statistical methods for analyzing data, routinely employing variants of the general linear model for quantitative data, for example. Yet much, and perhaps most, data analysis in the social sciences embodies a textbook caricature of statistics in which a statistical model is specified for a set of data, the model is fit to data, its parameters are tested, and the results are interpreted. If the results seem suitable, the investigator looks no further; if there is a problem, such as an unreasonable estimate, the model may be discarded or, more typically, respecified. These statistical models, however, make strong assumptions about the sampling, distributional, and functional structure of the data, assumptions that are not treated as problematic by the researcher.

Taken together, the chapters of this book seek to move the standard of statistical analysis and presentation in the social sciences toward a more accurate and sensitive representation of data. The tools exist and are becoming increasingly convenient. It is time that social scientists took them up and applied them in earnest to their work.

## REFERENCES

Anscombe, F. J. (1973). Graphs in statistical analysis. *The American Statistician, 27,* 17-22.

Tukey, J. W. (1962). The future of data analysis. *Annals of Mathematical Statistics, 3,* 1-67.

Tukey, J. W. (1977). *Exploratory data analysis.* Reading, MA: Addison-Wesley.

# 1

# GRAPHICAL PERCEPTION

Ian Spence
Stephan Lewandowsky

## INTRODUCTION

### A Historical Perspective

The pie chart, the bar graph, the line graph, and the scatterplot form the foundation of modern statistical graphics, allowing the display of numerical data in forms radically different from the original tabulation. Although this transformation from table to graph is a profound one, familiarity has dulled our appreciation of its importance. The re-expression of data in pictorial form capitalizes on one of the most highly developed human information processing capabilities — the ability to recognize, classify, and remember visual patterns. As Kosslyn (1985, 1989) has observed, graphs are effective precisely because they exploit the natural perceptual, cognitive, and memorial capacities of human beings.

Most graphs are simple, but their invention was neither simple nor obvious; the idea did not occur to the Greeks or Romans, nor even to the great seventeenth-century mathematician-experimenters such as Newton and Leibniz. Because almost all statistical graphs are Cartesian in nature, the principal tool for their invention has been available only

AUTHORS' NOTE: This research was supported by grant A8351 from the Natural Sciences and Engineering Research Council of Canada to I. Spence and also by grant G1779 from the Natural Sciences and Engineering Research Council of Canada to R. Baecker, A. Fournier, P. Muter, D. Olson, and I. Spence. We wish to thank Linda Tilley for preparing the figures. Correspondence should be addressed to Ian Spence, Department of Psychology, University of Toronto, Toronto, Ontario, Canada M5S 1A1.

13

since Descartes' *La Géométrie* which was published in 1637. The new analytical geometry was of interest to natural philosophers and engineers, who used it to explore the behavior of mathematical functions and sometimes to display theoretical relations among physical variables. The German natural philosopher Johann Heinrich Lambert devised a variety of elegant graphical procedures for the display of physical data, most of which were published posthumously in his *Pyrometrie* of 1779. Lambert used bivariate function graphs to analyze physical data such as monthly variations in soil temperature or the expansion of heated rods, often assessing the validity of a hypothesis by visual inspection of the graph. Ironically, he may also be responsible for the first bad graph in print, having fit the data on the expansion of heated rods with a negatively accelerated curve when a straight line would have been adequate (Tilling, 1975, p. 203).

It was William Playfair, a Scottish engineer turned economist, who invented most of the popular statistical graphs in use today, including the histogram, the pie chart, and the line graph (Playfair, 1786, 1801). As a boy, Playfair was instructed in Cartesian geometry by his older brother John, who was later to become professor of mathematics and natural philosophy at the University of Edinburgh. While in his early twenties, William was involved in the production of charts summarizing the performance of steam engines at the engineering company of Boulton and Watt, in Birmingham. James Watt himself had developed an automatic method for producing indicator diagrams that showed the variation of pressure with volume in steam engines, as well as the relationship between steam pressure and boiling point. Thus William Playfair had the technical background necessary for the invention of statistical graphs, but it was only after his move to London and his increasing involvement in the world of trade and commerce that he devised several graphical methods for the display of economic data, the most notable examples of which appeared in *The Commercial and Political Atlas* of 1786, and *Statistical Breviary* of 1801. Among them was the by-now-familiar graph showing the national debt skyrocketing out of control (see Figure 1.1). Now in its third century, this graph is no less pertinent today.

It took some time for graphs to become widely used in scientific reporting. Shields (1937) and Tilling (1975) have surveyed the major scientific publications and have shown that there was no general use of graphs of any kind until the nineteenth century. Then progress was initially slow. Even scientifically trained readers had to learn how to

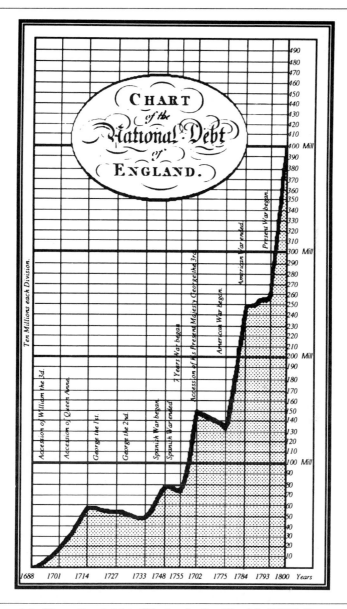

Figure 1.1 The national debt of England, after Playfair (1786). Because the original does not photograph well, this version has been computer enhanced, but is otherwise virtually identical.

cope with the new methods: The Royal Society, for example, requested that the automatically recorded graphs of an early weather clock be "reduce[d] into writing . . . that thereby the Society might have a specimen of the weather-clock's performances before they proceed to the repairing of it" (Hoff & Geddes, 1962; also cited in Tilling, 1975). Not only lack of familiarity but also the technical difficulty of producing graphs was a deterrent to their use. Before the refinement of photographic techniques, the production of a graph in a book or journal was a difficult and time-consuming process that was avoided whenever possible.

For some historical background on the development of statistical graphics and for a survey of various areas of application, the reader may consult Funkhouser (1937), Royston (1956), Tilling (1975), MacDonald-Ross (1977), and Beninger and Robyn (1978). Wainer and Thissen (1981) and Cleveland (1985) summarize for recent developments.

### The Power of Pictorial Displays

Human beings are well equipped to recognize and process visual patterns. Much of the processing power of the human brain is dedicated to handling visual information, and few would dispute the claim that vision is the dominant human sensory modality. When data are presented in a visual display, we can often comprehend subtleties that would be invisible were the data in tabular form.

One spectacular example of the importance of the graph as a tool for scientific discovery is the Hertzsprung-Russell (H-R) diagram, which is sufficiently celebrated to be included in many nonscientific dictionaries of the English language (see, for example, Random House, 1987). In 1913, in an address to the Royal Astronomical Society, H. N. Russell presented, for the first time,[1] a diagram that plotted the absolute magnitude (or brightness) of stars as a function of their spectral class (or temperature). The plot was complex enough to require a 700-word description (Russell, 1913, pp. 324-325), yet a single glance is enough to perceive the pattern that has inspired modern theories of stellar evolution. A computer-enhanced version of Russell's original diagram is reproduced in Figure 1.2, and a more recent variant is shown in Figure 1.3. The horizontal axis represents spectral class, which is related to the surface temperature of the star, with hot and blue at left and cool and red at right. The vertical axis shows absolute magnitude, or brightness, with the brightest stars at the top.

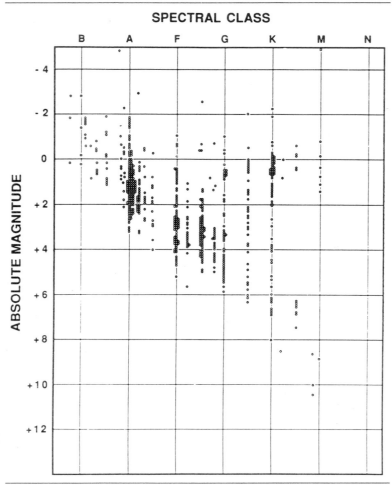

**SPECTRAL CLASS**

Figure 1.2 One of the three digarams from Russell (1914). Because the original is of poor quality, this version has been computer enhanced, but is otherwise virtually identical.

Theories of stellar evolution describe the movement of stars in the H-R diagram as their surface temperature and brightness change over the millennia. Stars are born bright, coalescing from interstellar clouds of hydrogen in the vicinity of the *giants*, before moving downwards and to the left to reach the stable region known as the *main sequence*, where they spend most of their lives. The position on the main sequence

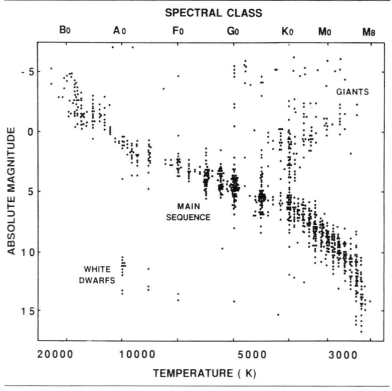

**Figure 1.3   A modern Hertzsprung-Russell diagram.**

depends on the mass of the star; our sun, a relatively small star, lies about one third of the way up the main sequence. In middle to old age, most stars move from the main sequence upward and to the right, becoming *red giants*; in the last stages, many become *dwarfs* at lower left.

One may speculate that the formulation of this theory was possible only after graphing the data. Indeed, the Danish astronomer Ejnar Hertzsprung had previously tabulated the same data in 1905, and in eight years was unable to conceive the theory of stellar evolution proposed by Russell. Hertzsprung (1905, 1907) contributed the terms giants and dwarfs and was aware of the existence of different stellar sequences, which he presented in tabular form, but his writings reveal that his concept of the data was inferior to Russell's.

Similar examples abound, though few are as fundamentally important as the Hertzsprung-Russell diagram. Tilling (1975) reproduced some wonderful early illustrations from the work of J. H. Lambert and J. D. Forbes. A contemporary example was given by Cleveland (1985), who discussed time series involving the concentration of atmospheric carbon dioxide where short-period cycles superimposed on long-term trends become immediately apparent when plotted, but are less easy to discern in tabular form.

## The Psychology of Graphical Perception

It is curious that, despite their importance, we know very little about how graphs and charts are processed. We do not know much about the perceptual, psychophysical, and cognitive processes that are invoked during the examination of a graph. We do not know if people remember information better when they examine one kind of graph as opposed to another. We often rely on intuition to guide us in deciding whether a graph is good or bad, and we do not know how damaging bad graphs are. Several authors have recommended methods of use and construction (e.g., Schmid, 1983; Tufte, 1983), and have offered guidelines on choosing graphs, but the advice generally lacks an empirical foundation; there have been only a few experimental studies of how people use graphs, and most of these are not known to the average practitioner.

### Communication and Analysis

Graphs are used in two fundamentally different ways: to communicate information to an audience and to analyze data. The first use is public and represents the majority of graphs seen. Graphs used to communicate are usually well crafted and represent the final stage in the process of analyzing data. Because they usually contain summary statistics rather than the original data, the total number of points displayed is often quite small. Moreover, because they are intended for an audience that is generally less expert than their author, presentation graphs necessarily tend to be simple in form and content; as Kosslyn (1985) has noted, if a display is unfamiliar, it becomes a problem to be solved rather than an aid to understanding. By contrast, the analysis of data is a private activity involving the production of many graphs that are seen only by their creator before being discarded. While graphs used for communication tend to be simple, graphs used for analysis may be quite detailed and sometimes even complicated or esoteric, containing most, if not all, of the original data. Whereas presentation graphs are mainly intended for the display of discovered patterns, graphs used for analysis are predominantly tools for the detection of important or unusual features in the data.

## COMMUNICATION

### Displaying Proportions and Percentages

Many data sets consist of frequencies, proportions, or percentages that, when tabulated, form small, uncomplicated tables that are relatively easily comprehended. Nonetheless, graphs are often favored for the presentation of such data and constitute the majority of statistical graphs seen by the lay person: Pie charts, bar charts, and tables are used to display percentage or proportional data. For many years the use of pie charts was frowned on by statistical experts, based on psychophysical evidence (see Baird, 1970, for a review) that judgments of area, angle, and arc length are less accurate than judgments of length. Hence the bar chart was favored; Eells (1926) may be consulted for some early references that champion the bar chart and disparage the pie chart, and Macdonald-Ross (1977) gives a more recent review that also discourages use of the pie chart. Notwithstanding this advice, since its invention by Playfair in 1786, many graphmakers have preferred the pie chart to report their data.

A critical review of the existing evidence suggests that the prejudice against the pie chart is unfounded. More than 60 years ago Walter Eells (1926) showed, by experiment, the superiority of the pie chart over the bar chart: He presented drawings of a number of pie charts and horizontally divided bar charts to subjects who estimated the percentages associated with the components. The results showed that the magnitude estimation was performed more accurately and quickly when the data were in pie chart form. Eells's paper drew a barrage of hostile fire, with the first shots coming from von Huhn (1927) and Croxton (1927). Thereafter, several empirical studies (Croxton & Stein, 1932; Croxton & Stryker, 1927; Culbertson & Powers, 1959; Peterson & Schramm, 1955) failed to settle the question of superiority, although none showed the pie chart to be inferior. In spite of these results, modern commentators (for example, Macdonald-Ross, 1977; Tufte, 1983; Wainer & Thissen, 1988) continue to advocate the bar chart in preference to the pie chart.

Most experiments have required subjects to make estimates of the magnitudes of graphical elements. If the sole intention is to communicate precise numerical magnitudes to the observer, however, perhaps the data should remain in tabular form (see Ehrenberg, 1975, 1977). The power of a graph lies in its ability to make the comparison of quantities easier. Such questions as the following are not uncommon: "Does Ford enjoy a larger market share than Toyota?" or "Do Mercedes and BMW together have a larger share of the market than Volkswagen?" Spence and Lewandowsky (in press) conducted an experiment in which subjects examined either a pie chart, a bar chart, or a table, as shown in Figure 1.4. The experimental task was to decide which of two components, or combinations of components, was the greater. Subjects were asked questions like "Which is larger, A or B?" or "Which is larger, A or B+C?" and so forth. The results, summarized in Figure 1.5, show that the pie chart enjoys an advantage for more complicated judgments (involving pairs of components) and is on a par with the other displays for simpler ones. Note that tables are competitive only when the required judgment is a simple one; this corroborates an earlier finding of Feliciano, Powers, and Kearl (1963), who showed bar charts to be superior to tables.

On the face of it, the findings quoted above are at variance with research that has sought to find the psychophysical function relating variables like physical extent, area, or volume to their perceived magnitudes. Macdonald-Ross (1977), for example, has suggested that a power function of the form

$$\text{Perceived area} = \text{Physical area}^{0.86}$$

provides an adequate description of the psychophysical function relating the perceived areas of circles to their physical areas, whereas an exponent of unity is appropriate for judgments of length. In other words, areas are systematically underestimated whereas line lengths are not, apparently forcing the conclusion that we should prefer the bar chart to the pie chart. Since the available evidence does not support the traditional prejudice against the pie chart, a closer examination of the role of traditional psychophysics is needed.

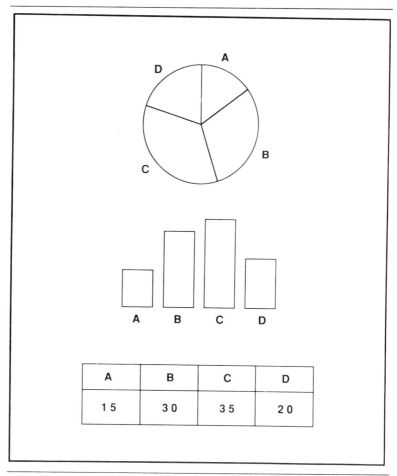

Figure 1.4  Sample stimuli from the experiment comparing the pie chart,
the bar chart, and the table.

## The Psychophysics of Graphical Elements

Various investigators have used psychophysical methods to examine
how accurately subjects judge the constituent parts of graphs. In a series
of experiments (Cleveland, 1985; Cleveland & McGill, 1984a, 1986)
perceptual judgments of six basic stimuli were examined: (1) position
along a common scale, (2) position along nonaligned scales, (3) length,
(4) angle, (5) slope, and (6) area. Cleveland and McGill distinguish (1)

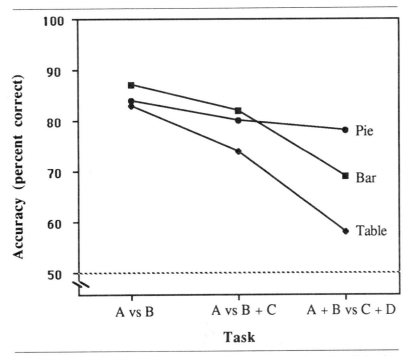

**Figure 1.5** Accuracy (percent correct judgments) as a function of display type (pie chart, bar chart, or table) and task complexity (A vs. B, A vs. B+C, and A+B vs. C+D).

and (2) from (3), claiming that these do not require the estimation of length explicitly, but rather the relative positions of points. Most graphs require one or more of these kinds of judgments. Judging the relative lengths of bars in a bar graph requires judgments of length, or position with reference to a common scale, whereas comparing segments in a divided bar chart requires judgments of length, or position with reference to nonaligned scales. Comparing proportions in a pie chart involves the judgment of angle and possibly area, whereas slope judgments are required to assess trend in line graphs. In the Cleveland and McGill experiments, subjects judged the sizes of stimuli relative to a designated standard. For example, the subject might be asked to say what percentage the area of one circle was of the area of a second one. This procedure was repeated for several different types of displays. Judgments were most accurate when position was judged along a common scale, followed by judgments of length and position on non-

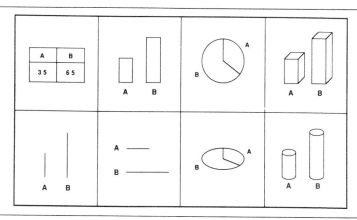

Figure 1.6 Various graphical elements used to display proportions and percentages.

aligned scales. Judgments of slope and angle were performed less accurately, and area was least accurately judged. These results, where comparable, are consistent with those of Croxton and Stein (1932), who conducted an early experiment comparing how well bars, circles, and cubes were judged.

Spence (in press) examined the speed and accuracy with which subjects judged the visual elements that make up pie charts, bar charts, and several variants, and also estimated the power function exponents for each element. Figure 1.6 shows examples of the elements used: pie chart segments, disk segments, bars, boxes, cylinders, horizontal and vertical lines, and table elements (that is, numbers). Disks are frequently seen in the popular press: A disk chart is like a pie chart but with the pie rotated about the east-west axis so that it looks elliptical rather than circular. Boxes and cylinders are often used in three-dimensional bar charts, usually with bases of the same size and varying only in height. The elements were presented in pairs (as in Figure 1.6) by computer, and subjects were required to judge the size of each element relative to the whole. The underlying power function exponent, and the average percentage error, for this task are easily derived. The results, based on a total 96 subjects, each of whom provided 300 judgments, are shown in Table 1.1. As can be seen, the differences among the various elements are not large. An exponent of unity and an average percentage error of zero would represent perfect performance. Most elements have associated exponents that differ little from unity,

**Table 1.1 Power Function Exponents, Average Absolute Accuracies, and Latencies for Several Graphical Elements**

| Graph Element | Bar | Pie | Disk | Box | Cylinder | Line(V) | Line(H) | Table |
|---|---|---|---|---|---|---|---|---|
| Exponent | 1.0 | 1.0 | 1.0 | 0.9 | 0.9 | 0.9 | 0.9 | 1.1 |
| Error (percentage) | 2.8 | 2.5 | 4.1 | 3.2 | 3.3 | 3.8 | 3.2 | 2.4 |
| Latency (seconds) | 5.5 | 6.6 | 6.1 | 5.9 | 5.4 | 7.6 | 8.7 | 8.6 |

SOURCE: Spence (in press).

and even though the average is slightly less than one, for all practical purposes we may consider the relation between the subjective judgments and physical reality to be linear for all elements.

Independent of the magnitude of the exponent, variation was found in the average percentage error: Disk elements are hardest to judge accurately, followed by the table elements (numbers). Interestingly, the pie chart elements were judged at least as accurately as anything else and, in particular, were not judged less well than the bar chart elements.

Spence's (in press) results are interesting in light of the recommendation of one influential modern commentator (Tufte, 1983) that graphical elements should not contain extraneous dimensions. In Spence's experiment, there was no loss of accuracy associated with the addition of extraneous dimensions by moving from one dimension (lines) to two dimensions (bars and pie slices) and then to three apparent dimensions (boxes and cylinders). Indeed, subjects were able to make the judgments about as accurately with the higher dimensional elements, and they were able to do so more quickly. It must be emphasized that these results apply to stimuli with a common base size; one should not expect judged accuracies, or exponents, to be comparable when base size is also varied (Croxton & Stein, 1932). If base size is held constant, subjects attend to length when judging the sizes of bars, boxes, or cylinders, and so it is not surprising that accuracy is comparable across the three dimensionalities. With pie slices, most subjects make angle judgments, which are essentially unidimensional (Cleveland & McGill, 1984a; Eells, 1926; Simkin & Hastie, 1987; Spence, in press).

Thus the addition of extra dimensions is not harmful, *provided that base size remains constant*. The presence of irrelevant dimensions makes for a more attractive display that is processed more quickly, with no concomitant loss in judgmental accuracy, provided the extra dimensions are purely decorative and carry no information.

## Displaying Time-Series or Grouped Data

When values of a single variable are plotted against time, the questions most often asked concern particular quantities ("How many XY widgets did our company produce in October?") or the overall trend in the data ("Did the production of XY widgets increase throughout the financial year?"). Culbertson and Powers (1959) showed that a series of individual bars (either horizontally or vertically oriented) is superior to a line graph if specific quantities must be estimated. The reverse pattern — an accuracy and speed advantage for the line graph over bars — was obtained in an experiment by Schutz (1961a) in which subjects had to identify global patterns in the data and predict future trends. In addition to being faster and more accurate, Schutz's subjects said they preferred working with a line graph as opposed to a series of bars. Based on a second study, Schutz (1961b) recommended that when several time series (in the experiment he varied their number from two to four) are to be compared simultaneously, all variables should be shown as multiple lines in a single graph, rather than as individual lines in separate panels. Schutz (1961b) also provided an empirical confusion matrix for a number of possible plotting symbols for each line in the graph.

Sometimes the constituent components that make up a datum are available; for example, a company's overall profit consists of revenues from several different sources, and one may wish to graph the individual components in addition to the total. A *segmented* or *divided* graph can represent the total by one graphical element (for example, a bar in a bar chart) with subdivisions representing the constituent components. In a *grouped* graph, on the other hand, separate graphical elements originating from a common baseline are used to represent both the components and the total. Culbertson and Powers (1959) found a consistent advantage for grouped over segmented graphs, independent of the particular choice of graph. A grouped bar chart was superior to a divided bar chart, and a grouped line graph (where each line is drawn with reference to the abscissa as baseline) outperformed a segmented line graph (where each line is drawn with the line below as a baseline).

## Labeling Graphical Elements

An important, but largely ignored, part of graph making is labeling. Should the groups represented by bars or segments be identified directly, by printing a label on the graphical elements, or should a legend be used to permit more extended, but less direct, labeling? Culbertson and Powers (1959) concluded that labels placed directly on the graphical elements are preferable to legends. They used graphical elements differentiated by cross-hatching, and either a key was used to associate each cross-hatching pattern with a label or that label was printed directly onto the graph. A more recent study by Milroy and Poulton (1978) corroborated the earlier finding and furthermore showed that the disadvantage associated with using a legend is independent of its location. Subjects were slower in answering questions about time-series data when lines in the graph were identified by a legend, even if the legend was placed *within*, as opposed to below, the axes of the graph.

## Perceptual Distortions

Things are not always what they seem to be. The visual system sometimes presents a distorted view of reality, particularly in situations incorporating some aspect of embeddedness. Witness the famous Müller-Lyer illusion in which two lines, terminated by inward or outward facing arrows, have exactly the same physical length, but appear to be of different lengths. In other geometrical illusions, the apparent size of identical objects can appear to differ depending on whether surrounding objects are bigger or smaller — a circle surrounded by large circles appears smaller than an identical circle surrounded by small circles. There are many varieties of the vertical-horizontal illusion where a vertical line appears to be longer than an identical horizontal line drawn at right angles to the vertical line. Matlin (1988) discussed these and other visual illusions.

There are very few studies that examine the role of perceptual distortions in the reading of graphs. The work of Poulton (1985) is an exception: He has investigated illusions similar to the classical Poggendorf illusion (sloping lines occluded by vertical bars look misaligned, appearing more horizontal than they actually are). Poulton's experiments suggest that the relationship of sloping lines to the vertical and horizontal axes of graphs can produce reading errors that increase with distance from the axes. To mitigate this bias, he proposed that graphs should show all four axes (not just two) and that all axes be calibrated. In an informal survey of leading journals in psychology, however, Poulton (1985) found that graphs with calibrations on all four axes were relatively rare; in most journals less than 15% of articles with graphs used four calibrated edges, and no journal exceeded 55%.

## Memorability of Graphs

Communicators hope that their message will not only be readily comprehended by the audience, but will also be remembered. William Playfair (1786) believed that one of the chief benefits of using graphical displays was as an aid to memory: "On inspecting any of these charts attentively, a sufficiently distinct impression will be made to remain unimpaired for a considerable time, and the idea which does remain will be simple and complete, at once including the duration and the amount" (Playfair, 1786, p. xiv). Playfair's conviction is supported by a large body of evidence from the experimental psychology of memory. For example, in a particularly impressive demonstration of human cognitive ability, Standing, Conezio, and Haber (1970) showed subjects 2,560 different pictures. Each picture was seen only once, for less than 10 seconds, but subjects were able to recognize correctly approximately 2,000 of the pictures for up to four days after studying them. Many other experiments have confirmed our extraordinary capacity to remember pictorially presented information, and have demonstrated that memory for pictures is superior to memory for text (e.g., Bevan & Steger, 1971; Shepard, 1967). Paivio (1974) summarized several studies and concluded that there is at least a 10% advantage in recall for pictures over words or sentences.

Although such data strongly support Playfair's assertion that graphs, like pictures, are well remembered, there has been little empirical work investigating how well different graphs are remembered. In some early studies, Washburn (1927a, 1927b) compared line graphs and bar charts with various kinds of textual presentation and found that numerical information was better remembered when presented in a graph than when embedded in text. In fact, Washburn recommended that if more than two numbers are to be communicated, textual presentation should be avoided. He also found that line graphs lead to better memory for nonspecific overall trends than bar charts, whereas bar charts lead to better retention of simple comparisons between data points.

Although their stimuli often lack the meaningfulness inherent in statistical graphs, cognitive psychologists have discovered basic principles that may be of use to graphmakers. Rock, Halper, and Clayton (1972), for example, showed subjects an outline drawing of a random shape with internal lines connecting points on the outline. A short time after presentation, subjects were given separate recognition tests for the overall figure, the outline, and the internal lines. Even though they could be differentiated when presented on their own, the internal lines fared poorly on the recognition task. Performance was good only for the outline of the figure. This suggests that subjects, when following their own viewing and encoding strategies, pay more attention to the outline of a figure than on its internal configuration. Although Rock et al.'s (1972) findings need to be extended to graphical stimuli, they appear to suggest that the outline, not the internal configuration, of a graph should convey the most important features of the data. By implication, data presented in a bar chart — provided it is not segmented — may be remembered more successfully than those presented in a pie chart.

In another experiment, Mandler and Parker (1976) asked subjects to remember complex visual scenes consisting of a collection of common objects. Information about the relative vertical arrangement of those objects was generally better retained than information about the horizontal relation among objects, suggesting that important information in graphs be arranged vertically as opposed to along the horizontal axis. Again, specific experiments with graphs are needed.

In a series of experiments examining the role of memory with graphical stimuli, Tversky and Schiano (in press) found that subjects remember almost symmetric curves as being more symmetrical than they actually were. This probably reflects the fact that, since we often view symmetric objects off center, we have a tendency to correct our perception toward symmetry. Thus, if the important thing is the departure from symmetry, it may be better to display the deviations rather than the asymmetric curve itself. Tversky and Schiano (in press) also found that memory for the slope of lines is distorted toward the 45° diagonal (in a graph with equal length axes). In other words, steep slopes are remembered as being less extreme than they actually were, and shallow slopes are recalled as being steeper. This finding was replicated for patterns of points not joined by lines: Subjects drew the best-fitting line from memory and generally drew lines with slopes closer to the imaginary 45° line. Tversky and Schiano (in press) suggested that, in addition to the vertical and horizontal axes, the $Y = X$ line is an important perceptual anchor.

Memory for information in graphs may be helped by the application of mnemonic strategies. It is known that memory for simple words is

improved considerably when subjects are instructed to form an interacting mental image of the study items (Wollen, Weber, and Lowry,
1972). For example, memory for the word pair *piano-cigar* is improved
if a mental image is formed of, say, a cigar resting on a piano keyboard
(as opposed to forming two separate images of a piano and a cigar). By
extension, if ways can be found to construct graphs that encourage and
facilitate the formation of interacting images, memory for such graphs
should be improved. Because the meaningfulness of a stimulus correlates highly with ease of imagery (Paivio, Yuille, & Madigan, 1968),
one may speculate that a graph composed of meaningful graphical
elements would be better remembered than a standard chart: Consider,
for example, a bar chart showing annual incomes, in which drawings of
a tall lawyer and a short professor form two of the bars. As we note in
the next section, however, at least one vocal and influential modern
commentator pooh-poohs the use of graphs containing pictograms.

*Chart Junk and the Data Ink Ratio*

One of the earliest experimental graphs, by James Watt in a patent
of 1782, depicts a curve on a ruled rectangle relating pressure and
volume in a steam engine. The graph is "picturesquely framed by a
longitudinal section of a steam-engine" (Shields, 1937). The practice
of adding extraneous decoration to graphs has persisted to this day and
is especially common in popular publications. We see articles on increases in air travel containing illustrations that show passengers walk-
ing up the steeply tilted wing of a smiling airliner, where the tilted wing
actually forms a line graph. Or, in a bar chart devoted to some aspect
of government activity, the bars are replaced by piles of documents on
a civil servant's desk.

Edward Tufte (1983), in one of the most influential and delightful
modern books on graphical technique, abhorred this custom, calling the
embellishment *chart junk*, and advised data analysts to go to the opposite extreme, namely to include nothing in the graph that is not abso-
lutely necessary for the display of the data. Tufte advised maximizing
the *data ink ratio*; that is, the ratio of printer's ink used for data to the
ink used for other parts of the graph. No empirical evidence exists to
support Tufte's presumption that maximizing the data ink ratio is
desirable. Indeed, as noted previously in the section on the psychophysics of graphical elements, it is possible to add extraneous material
without impairing perception of the graph (Spence, in press).

Graphs that lack chart junk and have a high data ink ratio, like the examples in Tufte (1983), sometimes violate well-known perceptual principles. For example, when axes are not connected to form a frame around a scatterplot, or when boxplots retain the whiskers but dispense with the box, the graph does not form an easily comprehended gestalt (Kosslyn, 1985). Moreover, the graphs presented by Tufte as examples of good graphical practice are rather stark and minimalist. In our opinion, people are more likely to be drawn to attractive, appealing graphs and, conversely, be repelled by dry, sterile depictions of the data, devoid of even the slightest decoration. If a graph is not examined, it might as well not have been drawn. Moreover, we speculate that a decorated graph may be better remembered than a minimalist chart, an issue not considered by Tufte (1983).

Undoubtedly, at a certain point, the addition of "non-data ink" serves no useful purpose, and may actually be harmful, but it is difficult to know when this point has been reached on the basis of introspection alone. Is accuracy impaired by certain forms of decoration and not others? Does embellishment draw the eye to a graph and cause it to linger longer? Does ornamentation enhance memorability? John Fox (personal communication, October 1988) has suggested that decoration inside the graph boundary may be more harmful than outside, and Tufte (1983, p. 59) made a similar point. More empirical work on the influence of adding extraneous decoration is required.

## ANALYSIS

Graphs used for data analysis should "force us to notice what we never expected on see" (Tukey, 1977, p. vi). Although it is difficult, if not impossible, to provide general guidelines for achieving this ideal, one piece of advice given by Cleveland and McGill (1984a, 1985) should be heeded: The important aspects of the data should be represented by physical features that require simple perceptual judgments. For instance, if the focus is on the difference between two functions, a single line showing the difference should be drawn, rather than the two original functions. If the slope or rate of change of a function is most important, plot the rate of change rather than the original data.

The ability to interpret graphs depends on previous training and experience. Most people have had sufficient exposure to line graphs, bar charts, histograms, and the like, but it is probably safe to say that only those with university training in statistics have been exposed to stem-and-leaf diagrams, boxplots, rootograms, and quantile-quantile plots. Although each of these has its place in the analysis of data by trained personnel, care should be exercised when data are displayed to less sophisticated audiences. Perhaps a histogram should be used to communicate the shape of a distribution, rather than a stem-and-leaf diagram or a boxplot. A similar caution applies to the use of logarithmic axes, response surface plots, contour plots, and other devices that may be unfamiliar to a lay audience.

## Univariate Displays

Univariate displays are used mainly to examine the distribution of a variable. Historically, histograms or frequency polygons were the preferred forms, but in recent years stem-and-leaf diagrams, boxplots, and rootograms (Tukey, 1977) have been widely used, and the use of density estimators has been advocated by some statisticians (see, for example, Silverman, 1986). Also, quantile-quantile plots (Wilk & Gnanadesikan, 1968) have become popular for examining both single distributions and pairs of distributions. See Chapter 2 in this volume for a discussion of many of these displays.

Boxplots and stem-and-leaf diagrams, in particular, have enjoyed great popularity, but it may take time for data analysts to become thoroughly familiar with the perceptual characteristics of these displays. For example, each of the two partitions of the box always contains the same proportion of observations (25%), which may mislead under some circumstances. If the distribution is skewed, the smaller rectangle corresponds to the greater density of points, but since there is no direct way of indicating density, it is possible that inexperienced observers may misinterpret the smaller area as corresponding to fewer observations, thus becoming confused about the direction of skew. Perhaps the standard boxplot should be enhanced to contain density information — for example, by differential shading of the two box partitions, or by using one of the schemes presented by Benjamini (1988).

Broersma and Molenaar (1985) found that subjects were able to judge the relative sizes of the standard deviations of two distributions, displayed as either a stem-and-leaf diagram or a boxplot, with the former display leading to a slightly more accurate performance. When asked which distribution had the greater skewness or kurtosis, subjects performed no better than chance. Thus it seems that the stem-and-leaf display is to be preferred for judging spread, but neither it nor the boxplot are particularly effective when judgments of skewness or kurtosis must be made.

Wainer (1974) has examined the utility of the hanging rootogram (Tukey, 1972). A rootogram is a histogram constructed using the square-root transformed variable, and a hanging rootogram is one in which the bars, instead of "standing up" from the abscissa, are hanging from a theoretical distribution (e.g., a normal curve). Thus residuals can be compared with reference to a common level by judging how far below the abscissa they extend, or how short they fall from the abscissa. Wainer found that skewness and kurtosis are more accurately judged with a hanging rootogram than with a normal rootogram, in line with Cleveland and McGill's recommendation that important information should be accessible by comparing position along a common scale.

## Scatterplots

Even though they are scarce in the popular press (Tufte, 1983, p. 83), statistical graphs that show the relation between two or more variables are common in scientific publications (Tufte, 1983, p. 85). The bivariate scatterplot, which shows an unabridged picture of the data, is one of the most useful graphs for data analysis.

Unlike summary statistics, such as the correlation coefficient, the scatterplot provides a direct and complete picture of the relation between two variables. The same numerical value of a correlation coefficient may be obtained from dramatically different configurations (Anscombe, 1973) and may be greatly affected by a few outlying observations (see the introduction to this book). The scatterplot is immune to such distortions and limitations, but its usefulness depends on the observer's ability to perceive and interpret the graph correctly. Previous training and experience are important, and seasoned analysts are likely to interpret the scatterplot somewhat differently than novices. In one application, where scatterplots were admitted as evidence in a court of law, there is reason to believe that some of the participants were unable to perceive the correct correlational pattern in the data (Bobko & Karren, 1979), thus possibly affecting the outcome of the trial. This underscores the importance of understanding how people, at all levels of expertise, perceive data presented in scatterplots.

When we examine a scatterplot, we often mentally imagine a "best-fitting" line that summarizes the trend. Mosteller, Siegel, Trapido, and Youtz (1981) investigated how well subjects could estimate the regression line from a point cloud, and found that they concentrated on the perpendicular rather than the vertical distances from the line, tending to choose a line closer to the first principal component than to the regression line. Since the two lines are generally similar unless the vertical variability in the data is high, and since subjects' estimates were within 10% of the actual values on the average, this may not represent a serious shortcoming. Recently, Collyer (1988) replicated Mosteller et al. (1981).

There is more data on how people estimate correlations from scatterplots. In several experiments (Bobko & Karren, 1979; Cleveland, Diaconis, & McGill, 1982; Collyer, 1988; Strahan & Hansen, 1978; Wainer & Thissen, 1979) subjects were presented with scatterplots containing a point cloud of somewhere between 16 (Collyer, 1988) and 200 (Cleveland et al., 1982; Strahan & Hansen, 1978) observations. The experimental task was to estimate the sample correlation. Using data from bivariate normal distributions, with equal variances on both variables and without outliers, the consistent finding was that people underestimate correlations over a wide range. Both statistically unsophisticated subjects (Strahan & Hansen, 1978) and statistical experts (Bobko & Karren, 1979) provide estimates that are below the actual values. Not surprisingly, exceptions occur at the extreme ends of the range: People are quite accurate with correlations near unity or zero.

Because people often underestimate the correlation in a scatterplot, can some other characteristic be identified that predicts performance more accurately? Bobko and Karren (1979), among others, suggested that estimates are generally closer to the square of the correlation ($r^2$) than to the correlation itself. Collyer (1988) noted three other easily computed quantities that people might use as an aid to estimating the correlation: the *balloon rule* (the ratio between the height of a point cloud at its center and its total height at the extremes), the *axis ratio* (the ratio of the lengths of the major and the minor axes), and the *area ratio* (the ratio of the area of the point cloud to that of the smallest rectangle enclosing the cloud). Although a systematic comparative investigation of these four summary statistics is lacking, the data of Cleveland et al. (1982), Collyer (1988), and Strahan and Hansen (1978) all conclude that $r^2$ is a reasonably good predictor of people's estimates of correlation. This is perhaps not surprising since $r^2$ is the proportion of variance accounted for when one variable is used to predict the other.

Cleveland et al. (1982) demonstrated that when the size of the point cloud relative to the size of the scales is decreased, subjects tend to judge the correlations more accurately. That is, their estimates increase with a decrease in point cloud size, thereby reducing the perceptual bias and approximating the true value more closely. Even with a rather small point cloud, however, no instances of subjects overestimating correlations are reported.

Most of the studies mentioned above involved point clouds with equal means and variances on both variables, implying that the regression slope was identical to the correlation coefficient; if the variances are unequal, the regression slope is not equal to the correlation. Bobko and Karren (1979) compared novice subjects' judgments when the true correlation was a constant 0.6, but the slopes were either 0.28 or 1.28, and found that judgments were virtually identical for both slopes, but slightly below the estimates obtained in the equal variance case. The results suggest that even novice subjects can distinguish the correlation from the slope of the regression line.

If subjects can discriminate a regression line and a correlation, might this imply that different cognitive processes underlie each judgment, and if so, are the processes independent? In an interesting experiment, Collyer (1988) required subjects to position what they thought was the best-fitting regression line, and also to estimate the correlation for the same point clouds. He found that after controlling for the true coefficient of determination, subjects' estimates of correlation were virtually independent of the goodness of fit of the regression lines. Collyer concluded that the two types of judgment probably involve independent cognitive processes.

Another important topic is the effect of outliers in the data. It is well known that even a single outlying observation can have a dramatic effect on the correlation, and several robust numeric estimators have been proposed to limit the undue influence of aberrant data points. Wainer and Thissen (1979) presented subjects with scatterplots in which a sample from a bivariate parent population was contaminated by observations drawn from a second population with different parameter values. Subjects were better estimators of the correlation in the parent population, regardless of the level of contamination, than two robust numeric estimators. People are capable of disregarding apparent outliers when viewing a scatterplot. In contrast to previous experiments, subjects in Wainer and Thissen's study were also very accurate judges of correlation when the data were not contaminated, probably reflecting the success of a short training phase prior to presentation of the experimental stimuli. Whereas training may have removed the bias for uncontaminated stimuli, it was unlikely to have been responsible for the robustness of subjects' judgments. Bobko and Karren (1979) also found that subjects can disregard outliers, even without prior training on "clean" point clouds.

The data on the perception of scatterplots form a straightforward picture: Human observers are conservative judges of correlation, tending to estimate the square of the correlation rather than the correlation itself. They are uninfluenced by large changes in regression slope, and, if outliers are present, they exhibit less bias in their estimates of correlation than some robust numerical estimators. Reducing the size of the point cloud, relative to the axes, will lead to less conservative — and therefore more accurate — judgments, as will even limited training.

### Discriminating Strata

Multiple groups, or strata, are often shown together in a single scatterplot to allow comparison of different subgroups with respect to a common set of variables. Baade (1944), for example, plotted two strata, representing different classes of stars, in a single Hertzsprung-Russell diagram, revealing differences in their evolutionary history. Baade used different shadings to differentiate his strata, but other options are available. Partly because they require no special equipment, alphabetic characters have often been the preferred symbol type. Other possibilities include different shapes (for example, circles vs. squares vs. triangles), different amounts of fill (open circles vs. filled circles vs. half-filled circles), or different colors (red vs. green vs. yellow circles). Some examples are shown in Figure 1.7. The reader may use crayons to color the as-yet-undifferentiated circles of panel 1. An observer must be able to discriminate the strata, if the display is to be effective, and intuitive impressions that some types of symbols are easier to discriminate than others are strong. Cleveland and McGill (1984b) have proposed a rank ordering of symbol types, suggesting that the use of different colors produces optimal performance, followed by amounts of fill, then different shapes, and finally letters.

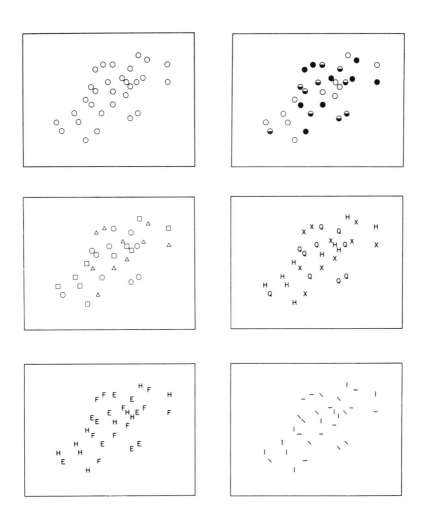

**Figure 1.7 Several different ways of coding strata in scatterplots. The circles in the first panel are undifferentiated and may be colored using crayons.**

Lewandowsky and Spence (1989) investigated the effects of various symbol types. Subjects had to decide which of two strata had the higher apparent correlation. With no restrictions imposed on the time to respond, symbol type had a large effect on speed of responding, but little effect on accuracy. Responding was fastest when strata were coded using circles of different colors and slowest with confusable letters, whereas different shapes, varying amounts of fill, and discriminable letters all produced the same intermediate performance. When processing time was restricted by removing the stimulus after brief exposure and requiring subjects to respond immediately, regardless of how confident they felt of their decision, large differences in accuracy were observed, exactly paralleling the latency differences.

Thus use of symbols of different colors is recommended. It is necessary to remember, however, that more than 8% of males and some 1% of females have difficulty distinguishing color, most commonly along the red-green dimension. If color deficiency is thought to present a problem, or if color is unavailable, discriminable letters are the second preferred choice because, compared to shapes or amounts of fill, they offer a mnemonic without loss in performance. Cleveland and McGill (1984b) have argued against the use of letters to code strata, but Lewandowsky and Spence (1989) showed that one must distinguish between confusable and discriminable sets of letters. The former should not be used, but use of the latter — letters with few shared perceptual features — is comparable to using either shapes or amounts of fill. Table 5 in Lewandowsky and Spence (1989) may be used as an aid to choosing appropriate letters.

Lewandowsky and Spence (1989) observed accuracy effects only when processing time was restricted. Thus it may seem that the choice of symbol type is not very important when designing graphs for publication because the reader may be expected to take as much time as necessary to view the graph. Unrestricted processing time is an ideal that is rarely approached in practice, however. In many contexts, we frequently read and study under the pressure of deadlines and often devote minimal time to an examination of accompanying graphs. If we are looking at a transparency or slide during a lecture, the viewing time is under the control of another. For many reasons, viewing times in real life are seldom truly unrestricted, and results with restricted processing times are therefore more relevant to practical application than may first appear.

## Large Samples and Extra Variables

The number of observations to be represented in a scatterplot is sometimes so large that the point cloud becomes dense. With a sufficiently large number of data points, the symbols for the points may overlap, and visual assessment of the density of the point cloud is impaired. Cleveland and McGill (1984b) proposed the use of "sunflowers" for this high-density situation. The plot area is divided into small regions, and the data falling in each region are represented by a single sunflower, whose salience increases with the number of points. A single data point is shown by a dot, whereas a large number of points forms a dense asterisk (or sunflower), with a smooth gradient between these extremes. If equipment constraints prohibit the construction of sunflowers and overlap of plotting symbols cannot be avoided, Cleveland and McGill recommended the use of open circles (as opposed to squares or triangles) because they maintain their individuality even with a considerable degree of overlap. Although no direct empirical support exists for these recommendations, they are in line with well-known perceptual principles.

How should measurements on a third variable be represented in a scatterplot? For example, if ozone concentration in the atmosphere and solar radiation are plotted in the plane, and temperature is another variable of interest, how should temperature be represented? Possible choices include the size of plotting symbol (e.g., large circles for high temperatures, small ones for low temperatures), orientation of the plotting symbol (e.g., lines drawn at various orientations), or a perspective drawing of the data using a third axis. Wainer and Thissen (1981) discussed these and various other static display schemes.

A recent article by Huber (1987) encouraged the use of dynamic displays, which allow the observer to rotate the three-dimensional point cloud, and a computer program that performs three-dimensional spins is widely available (Donoho, Donoho, & Gasko, 1986). Huber (1987) suggested that this kind of dynamic interaction with the display is essential to identify residuals, assess goodness-of-fit, or detect heteroscedasticity.

Young (1989) described a dynamic display that can show six-dimensional structures. His program, called VISUALS, is more versatile than procedures that merely rotate a three-dimensional point cloud. Although both rotation and translation are possible, VISUALS begins with a three-dimensional space formed by any three of six variables, and then moves smoothly through a sequence of linearly interpolated spaces, finally arriving in the three-dimensional space formed by the remaining variables. The procedure is interactive, and it is possible to apply various constraints and perform several operations, such as spinning, translating, or labeling and highlighting subsets of points, at any stage. Principal component analysis may be applied initially to reduce the dimensionality to six in situations where the number of original variables exceeds six. During the interpolation between the two 3-D spaces, it is possible to compute a "residual" space. This is the 3-D space orthogonal to the current space that has maximal variation on its dimensions. Young claimed that since you can always move to the subspace containing the most variation, getting lost in hyperspace is less likely!

Recently, Cleveland and McGill (1988) presented an edited collection of papers on the topic of dynamic displays (also see Chapter 5, this volume). Although intriguing, the utility and relative merit of such techniques is unknown in the absence of empirical evaluations.

### Smoothing

Cleveland and McGill (1984b) advocated smoothing of scatterplots to assist in detecting the shape of the point cloud in situations where the error in the data is substantial, or where the density of points changes along the abscissa. They defined a smooth function based on the robust average of data points within vertical sections of the plot. The width of the vertical sections, and their overlap, may be adjusted. Cleveland and Kleiner (1975) presented some examples of scatterplots that are readily interpreted after smoothing has been performed. Two additional smooth functions, based on upper and lower semi-midmeans, can be drawn to indicate spread. Cleveland and McGill (1984b) claimed that this type of smoothing is essential for the proper interpretation of residual plots and presented illustrative examples (Cleveland & Kleiner, 1975; also see Chapter 3, this volume).

Although Cleveland and his coworkers have presented numerous interesting — and intuitively compelling — examples of smoothed scatterplots, and even though many data analysts find the use of smoothing helpful, a final verdict on the benefits of the technique must await empirical adjudication. Notwithstanding, two problems should be pointed out. First, Cleveland and McGill's (1984b, p. 821) contention that the interpretation of plots is ineffective without smoothing overstates the case because there are no objective data showing that people benefit from the use of smooth functions. Second, and perhaps more important, it is unclear what is being estimated when these functions are fitted. No well-defined parametric function is employed, and the use of different, arbitrary fitting procedures could easily yield markedly dissimilar functions.

## MULTIVARIATE DISPLAYS

When the data have more than two or three dimensions, graphical presentation becomes increasingly difficult: The two dimensions of the plane cannot accommodate extra variables in the conventional Cartesian fashion, and some other representation is required. Consider the problem of displaying a number of economic indices for various different countries. Table 1.2 shows data taken from the World Development Report (The World Bank, 1988), consisting of measurements of eight variables related to the state of a country's development.

How should a graphical representation encode the values of the eight variables for each country? Many display techniques assign a separate symbol, or icon, to each country, with the components of the icon representing the values of the eight variables. Figure 1.8 illustrates several possible icons (a profile, a star or polygon, a glyph, and a face) to represent the economic data for a single country, in this case Australia. Data values are scaled relative to the largest value for that variable across countries, and the magnitude of the icon element corresponding to that largest value is arbitrary. The ordering of the variables in three of the icons is: GNP, Area, Population, School, Food, Tourists, Radios, Life Expectancy — from the left for the profile and glyph, and clockwise from 12 o'clock for the star. Table 1.3 shows the assignment of variables for the face.

Three of the icons share an important feature: Variables map into the lengths of graphical components. In the profile, the value of a variable is represented by the length of a bar. In a star or polygon (Siegel, Goldwyn, & Friedman, 1971), the bars are replaced by circular rays emanating from a common origin, and in a glyph (Anderson, 1980), the rays are replaced by whiskers extending from a circle. The remaining icon differs in unique and important ways. The cartoon face represents

**Table 1.2 Eight Economic Indices for Twelve Countries**

| Country | Population (millions) | Area (1000km²) | GNP/cap (US dollars) | Life Expectancy | Radios/ 1,000 | Tourists (1,000s) | Food | School |
|---|---|---|---|---|---|---|---|---|
| Canada | 25.6 | 9976 | 14120 | 76 | 758 | 12854 | 3404 | 98 |
| United States | 241.6 | 9363 | 17480 | 75 | 2133 | 20441 | 3632 | 99 |
| Haiti | 6.1 | 28 | 330 | 54 | 21 | 167 | 1906 | 48 |
| Brazil | 138.4 | 8512 | 1810 | 65 | 355 | 1420 | 2575 | 78 |
| Austria | 7.6 | 84 | 9990 | 74 | 475 | 14482 | 3479 | 80 |
| Iceland | .24 | 103 | 13410 | 77 | 593 | 78 | 3122 | 100 |
| Spain | 38.7 | 505 | 4860 | 76 | 274 | 25583 | 3325 | 97 |
| United Kingdom | 56.7 | 245 | 8870 | 75 | 986 | 12499 | 3210 | 96 |
| Gambia | .77 | 11 | 230 | 43 | 120 | 37 | 2217 | 34 |
| India | 781.4 | 3288 | 290 | 57 | 56 | 1305 | 2031 | 54 |
| Malaysia | 16.1 | 330 | 1830 | 69 | 415 | 1050 | 2569 | 77 |
| Australia | 16.0 | 7687 | 11920 | 78 | 1159 | 944 | 3044 | 89 |

NOTES: Food is avarage available calories/day/person; School is percentage enrollment of children aged 6 to 17.
SOURCE: The World Bank (1988).

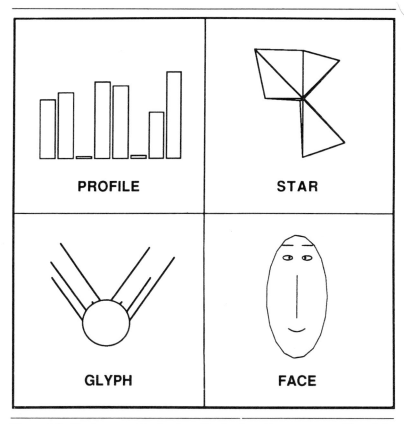

**Figure 1.8** Various methods for displaying the same multivariate observation.

the data by varying the shape or size of facial features: The area of the face, curvature of the mouth, or slant of the eyes represent different variables. Faces as data displays were introduced by Chernoff (1973), capitalizing on the observation that people are skilled at perceiving and remembering even small variations in human faces.

Although the icons shown in Figure 1.8 require the data analyst to assign the graphical components to particular variables, some other techniques perform this assignment automatically, without intervention on the part of the graph designer. The tree display (Kleiner & Hartigan, 1981), for example, exploits the fact that variables in a data set are often correlated: Each icon consists of a tree, whose topology is determined by the results of a hierarchical cluster analysis. Clusters are represented by branches of the tree, and distance between variables by angles between the branches, whose lengths represent the magnitudes of individual variables. Thus, unlike the displays shown in Figure 1.8, trees represent the relations between variables as well as their individual magnitudes.

Andrews's (1972) display also does not require explicit assignment of variables to components: Each multivariate observation vector is represented by a linear combination of sine and cosine functions, whose coefficients are determined by the values of the variables. Andrews's plots are useful in detecting clusters because the functions for related observations tend to be close together and in phase. Owing to the composite nature of each point's function, however, it is not possible to observe the effects of a single variable in isolation.

## Use of Multivariate Displays

Multivariate displays are used to find clusters of related data points and to detect outlying or atypical points. Examples of their use may be found with data in areas as diverse as Soviet foreign policy (Wang & Lake, 1978), mineral analysis (Chernoff, 1973), craters on the moon (Pike, 1974), psychiatric personality profiles (Mezzich & Worthington, 1978), and airline profits (Kleiner & Hartigan, 1981). Figure 1.9 shows the sample economic data from Table 1.2, using stars (left panel) and Chernoff faces (right panel). Consider the faces: Even without knowledge of the assignment of variables to components (those are given in Table 1.3), the deep division between Third World countries (Haiti, Brazil, The Gambia, India, and Malaysia) and the other nations is immediately apparent. Similarly, when told that a country's area is represented by the size of the face, the reader will immediately be able to distinguish large from small countries. Also, the incongruous nature of India is readily apparent; the size of the population correlates with how "football-like" a face is, and India's 780 million people is clearly atypical in this set of countries.

The reader will probably find the faces more memorable than the stars. The happy smile of the United States, reflecting the highest GNP per capita in the sample, is not difficult to remember. Faces are also probably more appealing than stars, but are faces a more effective mode of presentation? Possibly because of their intuitive appeal, much of the empirical work on multivariate displays has involved faces. Research

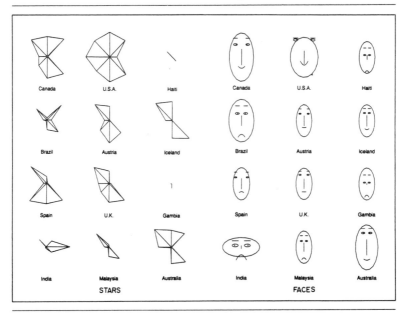

Figure 1.9 The multivariate economic data displayed using stars (left panel) and Chernoff's faces (right panel).

has ranged from evaluating the perceptual salience of individual facial features to comparing the effectiveness of faces to that of other techniques.

### Empirical Work

One major advantage of faces is their inherent meaningfulness: It takes little effort to learn to recognize the rich nations in Figure 1.9 by their smiles. Jacob (1978) has shown that subjects, without training or knowledge of variable-to-component mapping, can match a face to verbal personality profile with reasonable accuracy. The almost self-explanatory nature of faces is negated by inappropriate assignment, however, such as representing GNP by curvature of the mouth, with poor countries smiling broadly, while the rich present sad and stern faces. Although such an assignment could be learned, it nullifies one of the advantages of using faces.

Independent of meaningfulness, facial features also differ in perceptual salience. A variable may be more noticeable if represented by the

**Table 1.3  Assignment of Variables to Components of Chernoff Faces**

| Variable | Component |
|---|---|
| Population | Shape of face |
| Area | Size of face |
| GNP/cap | Curvature of mouth |
| Life expectancy | Length of nose |
| Radios/1,000 | Location of eyes |
| Tourists | Separation of eyes |
| Food supply | Location of mouth |
| School enrollment | Location of pupils |

curvature of the mouth rather than by the height of the eyebrows. Chernoff and Rizvi (1975) compared different random permutations of feature-to-variable assignments and found that subjects' error rate in a clustering task varied by up to 25%, depending on the particular assignment. Huff and Black (1978) showed that clustering performance is improved if the rank order of importance of variables matches the perceived order of importance of facial features. A study by De Soete and De Corte (1985) used a pairwise comparison technique to identify the features that render faces most discriminable: The most salient was the curvature of the mouth, followed by half-face height, half-length of eyes, and length of the eyebrows. The least discriminable features were the position of the center of the mouth, separation and slant of eyes, and the height of the eyebrows. The use of these features to code variables should be avoided.

Another problem inherent in Chernoff's original faces, but one whose effect has not been investigated empirically, is that there are dependencies among the features: When some take on extreme values, others may lose their perceptual effectiveness (Bruckner, 1978). In Figure 1.9, for example, the extreme values of population and GNP for India lead to the curious situation of the mouth extending beyond the outline of the face. While this may emphasize the outlying nature of the observation, it also renders the display less face-like, with possible adverse consequences. Flury and Riedwyl (1981) have provided a modified set of faces that eliminates the problem of dependence and may therefore be preferable to Chernoff's original scheme.

Assuming that care is taken when variables are assigned to features and that extreme values do not lead to distortions, how effective is the face as a data display in comparison to other methods? Comparative studies have revealed that faces are more easily memorized. Jacob (1976, 1978) showed that faces form more memorable stimuli in a paired-associate learning task than polygons, glyphs, or arrays of digits. Moreover, it appears that people prefer working with faces rather than with profiles or polygons. When icons must be sorted into clusters of related observations, subjects have said that using faces makes the task much easier (Mezzich & Worthington, 1978). The evidence is more equivocal when sorting accuracy is measured: Although subjects in Jacob's (1976) experiment were twice as accurate with faces than with either polygons or arrays of digits, Mezzich and Worthington (1978) found no advantage for faces over profiles and polygons. In the latter study, the best results were obtained with Andrews' function plots.

## THEORIES OF GRAPHICAL PERCEPTION

### *Need for Theory*

Good empirical work rarely proceeds in the absence of theory. The perception of graphs is no exception, and so far there have been several major attempts to build formal descriptions (Bertin, 1983; Cleveland & McGill, 1984a; Kosslyn, 1989; Mackinley, 1987; Pinker, 1981). These analyses complement each other, rather than compete, because each has taken a different view. Bertin chose a taxonomic approach that, because of its extensive scope, is the most difficult to categorize and describe. Cleveland and McGill focused on the psychophysical or judgmental aspects of human graphical processing. Mackinley was concerned with the specification of an automatic presentation tool, and as such, his description falls into the realm of artificial intelligence. Nevertheless, he contributed several important psychological insights. The most "cognitive" theories of graph perception to date have been put forward by Pinker (1981) and by Kosslyn (1989). Whereas Pinker focused on the processes presumed to underlie the encoding of graphs, Kosslyn formulated a scheme to analyze graphs and assess how they conform to basic cognitive and perceptual principles.

## Bertin

Bertin's (1983) work is, without doubt, the most ambitious of the theoretical monographs. In some 400 pages, Bertin developed a comprehensive taxonomy of graphical components and the properties of the perceptual system. We focus on only two of his contributions and refer the reader to the original for many other novel ideas.

Bertin introduced a grammar for the description of graphs. Any graph can be unambiguously reduced to, and subsequently reconstructed from, a description that relies on a small number of grammatical elements. Elements consist of symbols that record the type of variable (continuous or discrete), how it is plotted (in a circular fashion, as in a pie chart, or in a linear fashion, as in a bar chart), whether or not it is cumulative, and so forth. An unambiguous description of this type permits efficient storage and transmission of graphical information, and may facilitate predicting performance if the psychological correlates of each symbol can be established. Without experimentation, however, the utility of Bertin's grammar is unknown.

Bertin emphasized the importance of the type of question that an observer is likely to ask of a graph. He suggested that, for a given data set, there is a finite number of questions that may be asked, and that each question, in turn, may be characterized by the "level of reading." The level of reading corresponds to the degree of detail and ranges from elementary ("What is the value of X at Y?") to global ("What is the trend of Y over the entire period?"). Although the intention is admirable, Bertin's taxonomy is not exhaustive. For example, one important function of graphs is to facilitate the detection of outliers, and this purpose is not accommodated by his taxonomy.

## Cleveland

Cleveland and his associates at Bell Laboratories are largely responsible for the current resurgence of interest in the perception of statistical graphs, emphasizing the need for more empirical research and for a theory of graphical perception. In several articles and one book, they have made an impressive beginning, concentrating mainly on psychophysical issues, similar to those considered by Mudgett (1930), Croxton and Stein (1932), and Spence (in press). Their work has made considerable use of two laws from sensory psychophysics, namely Weber's Law and Stevens's Law.

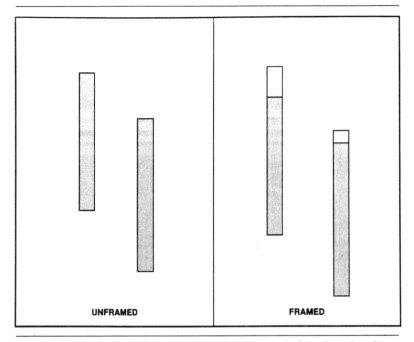

**Figure 1.10** The effect of framing on the perception of the lengths of two nonaligned bars.

Weber's Law (1834) states that the amount by which the intensity of a physical stimulus must be increased in order for the difference to be detected by an observer is a constant fraction of the intensity of the original stimulus. Put another way, sensory discrimination is relative and depends on the magnitude of the stimulus intensity. If a stimulus with intensity $I$ is increased by an amount $dI$, such that this is the smallest increase noticed, then the ratio $dI/I$ is constant for all values of $I$. A large stimulus value requires a large increment for the difference to be detectable, whereas a small stimulus value requires a small increment. So, for example, if the length of two nonaligned bars must be compared, the task is made easier by framing the bars with rectangles of equal length, so that the easier comparison may be made using the shorter of the two lengths (see Figure 1.10).

Cleveland and McGill (1984a) also made extensive use of Stevens's Law, which states that the perceived magnitude of a stimulus is a power function of its physical magnitude (see the section on the psychophysics of graphical elements). The exponent of the power function depends on the nature of the stimulus, the nature of the task, and also varies from individual to individual. Generally, experimental studies (Baird, 1970) show the exponent for length to be in the region of 1.0, for area about 0.8, and for volume about 0.6. This implies that judgments of linear extent are made more accurately than judgments of area or volume, which are systematically underestimated, with the effect greatest for volume. Thus Cleveland and McGill (1984a) recommended that lengths be used, as opposed to areas or volumes, to represent magnitudes wherever possible. In general, experimental results have shown this to be sound advice, although, as noted in the section on psychophysics, if the extra dimensions carry no information but are merely introduced as decoration, no harm is done.

### Mackinley

Mackinley (1987) has developed a highly formalized description of how graphs should be constructed. He has incorporated his theoretical results in a computer program that is capable of automatically generating graphs that satisfy two criteria: expressiveness and effectiveness. Expressiveness, roughly stated, relates to whether a representation properly communicates the information. Are the data faithfully transmitted by the graphical language? Does the representation imply anything false about the data? Mackinley has stated his criteria for expressiveness in algebraic terms, and his computer program implements these criteria when attempting to construct a graph. The notion of effectiveness acknowledges that there may be several representations that correctly express the data, but that some graphs more effectively exploit the perceptual and cognitive capacities of the observer. Mackinley drew heavily on the work of Bertin (1983) and Cleveland and McGill (1984a) for data that define effectiveness, and proposed extensions to the Cleveland rank ordering of the ease of making basic perceptual judgments to include elements like gray level, color saturation, color hue, texture and shape. Like Bertin (1983), Mackinley considered the questions to be asked of a graph important and discussed the effectiveness of communication in relation to the different kinds of questions that may be posed.

## *Kosslyn and Pinker*

Kosslyn (1989) presented a scheme for the analysis of displays to detect features that may make the graph difficult to understand. The concentration is on four major constituents of the display: the background, the framework, the specifier, and the labels. The background is blank in most displays, but could consist of a photograph or some other kind of decoration. The framework represents the entities being related, and in most graphs is formed by the axes. The specifier is the means by which the data are conveyed to the observer, perhaps by lines, curves, or bars. Finally, the labels are the letters, numbers, words, and phrases intended to aid interpretation.

Kosslyn advised subjecting each of these constituent parts to three different levels of analysis, which he calls syntactic, semantic, and pragmatic. The goal of the analysis is to determine whether certain "acceptability principles," derived from known perceptual and cognitive principles, are satisfied. At the syntactic level, the properties of graph elements are considered. Are distinct elements discriminable? Are there visual distortions? Are elements ordered and grouped appropriately, consonant with the perceptual capacities of human beings?, and so on. The semantic level of analysis is concerned with interpretation of qualitative and quantitative relations and assesses the meaning that is intended. The pragmatic level of analysis acknowledges the intended purpose of the display and examines the conveyed meaning, as opposed to the literal meaning.

A graph could fail to satisfy acceptability principles at the semantic level but still convey its meaning satisfactorily, given a particular purpose. For example, most people find line graphs better for the portrayal of interactions than bar graphs, when the explanatory variable is categorical, even though the use of a line may be said to imply continuity of the explanatory variable. The bar graph may be correct at the semantic level, but the line graph is superior at the pragmatic level. Alternatively, the meaning may be clear at the semantic level, and yet the graph may mislead. Huff (1954) catalogued several ways in which this may be done — for example, by truncating scales or changing the type of scale to make differences look larger or smaller. The important point here is that, although the graph may convey accurate information using appropriate elements, it misleads nonetheless, most often by design, but sometimes accidentally.

Pinker (1981) proposed a conceptually related model of graph perception that focuses on the psychological processes presumed to be responsible for the encoding and understanding of graphs. The model divides the comprehension process into distinct stages: First, visual encoding processes provide a *structural description*, or relatively unrefined internal representation of the graph. This structural description conforms to various perceptual principles, such as the gestalt laws of organization, that guide visual encoding. Second, the *conceptual message*, or interpretation of the data, is derived from the structural description by invoking a schema, or processing template. The observer is assumed to have schemata appropriate to most common graphs, and a matching process activates the most suitable schema. In the final stage, various *interrogation* and *message assembly* processes replace variables in the schema with specific data values extracted from the structural description of the graph. These latter processes are assumed subject to conscious control and are tailored to the question asked of the graph.

Although speculative, Pinker's model proposes a psychological analysis that goes beyond a mere quantitative description of the data. The utility of this class of model is reinforced by a recent analysis (Simkin & Hastie, 1987) that provides a detailed, although ad hoc, account of how people estimate magnitudes from bar charts and pie charts.

### Directions for Empirical Research

There are no areas in which we have enough data. Although we know a fair amount about the psychophysical aspects of graphical perception (Cleveland & McGill, 1984a, 1986; Lewandowsky and Spence, 1989; Spence & Lewandowsky, in press), much remains to be learned. More psychophysical work will allow us to say whether the concerns expressed by Tufte (1983), regarding what he considers to be dubious practice, are indeed legitimate. Psychophysical results can also assist in the syntactic analysis of graphs (Kosslyn, 1989) and will be useful in evaluating Bertin's (1983) taxonomy.

We know even less about cognitive aspects, in particular the role of short- and long-term memory, in the processing of graphs. Ideally, we should design graphs to maximize the probability of their being well remembered. There is much that can be accomplished here. Of course, as Kosslyn (1989) and Simkin and Hastie (1987) have done, it is possible to generate plausible hypotheses based on existing data and theory from cognitive psychology, but ideally such conjectures should be investigated by empirical work.

## NOTE

1. The reprint of Russell's address to the Royal Astronomical Society, the first published account that refers to the Hertzsprung-Russell diagram, mentions a "slide shown on screen" (Russell, 1913, p. 324), but does not reproduce the graph. A later paper (Russell, 1914), based on a talk presented within six months of the original address, includes three diagrams, and we conjecture that one of these, shown in our Figure 1.2, was Russell's original graph.

## REFERENCES

Anderson, E. (1960). A semi-graphical method for the analysis of complex problems. *Technometrics, 2,* 387-392.

Andrews, D. F. (1972). Plots of high-dimensional data. *Biometrics, 28,* 125-136.

Anscombe, F. J. (1973). Graphs in statistical analysis. *American Statistician, 27,* 17-21.

Baade, W. (1944). The resolution of Messier 32, NGC 205, and the central region of the Andromeda Nebula. *Astrophysical Journal, 100,* 137-146.

Baird, J. C. (1970). *Psychophysical analysis of visual space.* New York: Pergamon.

Beninger, J. R., & Robyn, D. L. (1978). Quantitative graphics in statistics: A brief history. *American Statistician, 32,* 1-11.

Benjamini, Y. (1988). Opening the box of a boxplot. *American Statistician, 42,* 257-262.

Bertin, J. (1983). *Semiology of graphics.* Madison: University of Wisconsin Press.

Bevan, W., & Steger, J. A. (1971). Free recall and abstractness of stimuli. *Science, 172,* 597-599.

Bobko, P., & Karren, R. (1979). The perception of Pearson product moment correlations from bivariate scatterplots. *Personnel Psychology, 32,* 313-325.

Broersma, H. J., & Molenaar, I. W. (1985). Graphical perception of distributional aspects of data. *Computational Statistics Quarterly, 2,* 53-72.

Bruckner, L. A. (1978). On Chernoff faces. In P.C.C. Wang, (Ed.), *Graphical representation of multivariate data* (pp. 93-122). New York: Academic Press.

Chernoff, H. (1973). The use of faces to represent points in k-dimensional space graphically. *Journal of the American Statistical Association, 68,* 361-368.

Chernoff, H., & Rizvi, H. M. (1975). Effect on classification error of random permutations of features in representing multivariate data by faces. *Journal of the American Statistical Association, 70,* 548-554.

Cleveland, W. S. (1985). *The elements of graphing data.* Monterey, CA: Wadsworth.

Cleveland, W. S., Diaconis, P., & McGill, R. (1982). Variables on scatterplots look more highly correlated when the scales are increased. *Science, 216,* 1138-1141.

Cleveland, W. S., & Kleiner, B. (1975). A graphical technique for enhancing scatterplots with moving statistics. *Technometrics, 17,* 447-454.

Cleveland, W. S., & McGill, R. (1984a). Graphical perception: Theory, experimentation, and application to the development of graphical methods. *Journal of the American Statistical Association, 79*, 531-553.

Cleveland, W. S., & McGill, R. (1984b). The many faces of a scatterplot. *Journal of the American Statistical Association, 79*, 807-822.

Cleveland, W. S., & McGill, R. (1985). Graphical perception and graphical methods for analyzing scientific data. *Science, 229*, 828-833.

Cleveland, W. S., & McGill, R. (1986). An experiment in graphical perception. *International Journal of Man-Machine Studies, 25*, 491-500.

Cleveland, W. S., & McGill, R. M. (Eds.). (1988). *Dynamic graphics for statistics.* Belmont, CA: Wadsworth.

Collyer, C. E. (1988, November). *Perceiving scattergrams: Visual line fitting and direct estimation of correlation.* Paper presented at the annual meeting of the Psychonomic Society, Chicago, IL.

Croxton, F. E. (1927). Further studies in the graphic use of circles and bars II: Some additional data. *Journal of the American Statistical Association, 22*, 36-39.

Croxton, F. E., & Stein, H. (1932). Graphic comparison by bars, squares, circles and cubes. *Journal of the American Statistical Association, 27*, 54-60.

Croxton, F. E., & Stryker, R. E. (1927). Bar charts versus circle diagrams. *Journal of the American Statistical Association, 22*, 473-482.

Culbertson, H. M. & Powers, R. D. (1959). A study of graph comprehension difficulties. *Audio-Visual Communication Review, 7*, 97-100.

De Soete, G., & De Corte, W. (1985). On the perceptual salience of features of Chernoff faces for representing multivariate data. *International Journal of Man-Machine Studies, 9*, 275-280.

Donoho, A. W., Donoho, D. L., & Gasko, M. (1986). *MACSPIN™: A tool for dynamic display of multivariate data.* Monterey, CA: Wadsworth.

Eells, W. C. (1926). The relative merits of circles and bars for representing component parts. *Journal of the American Statistical Association, 21*, 119-132.

Ehrenberg, A.S.C. (1975). *Data reduction: Analyzing and interpreting statistical data.* New York: John Wiley.

Ehrenberg, A.S.C. (1977). Rudiments of numeracy. *Journal of the Royal Statistical Society, Series A, 140*, 277-297.

Feliciano, G. D., Powers, R. D., & Kearl, B. E. (1963). The presentation of statistical information. *Audio-Visual Communication Review, 11*, 32-39.

Flury, B., & Riedwyl, H. (1981). Graphical representation of multivariate data by means of asymmetrical faces. *Journal of the American Statistical Association, 76*, 757-765.

Funkhouser, H. G. (1937). Historical development of the graphical representation of statistical data. *Osiris, 3*, 269-404.

Hertzsprung, E. (1905). Zur Strahlung der Sterne. *Zeitschrift fuer wissenschaftliche Photographie, Photophysik und Photochemie, 3*, 429-442.

Hertzsprung, E. (1907). Zur Strahlung der Sterne II. *Zeitschrift fuer wissenschaftliche Photographie, Photophysik und Photochemie, 5*, 86-107.

Hoff, H. E., & Geddes, L. A. (1962). The beginnings of graphic recording. *Isis, 53*, 287-324.

Huber, P. J. (1987). Experiences with three-dimensional scatterplots. *Journal of the American Statistical Association, 82*, 448-453.

Huff, D. (1954). *How to lie with statistics.* New York: Norton.

Huff, D. L., & Black, W. (1978). A multivariate graphic display for regional analysis. In P.C.C. Wang (Ed.), *Graphical representation of multivariate data* (pp. 199-218). New York: Academic Press.

Jacob, R.J.K. (1976). The face as a data display. *Human Factors, 18,* 189-200.

Jacob, R.J.K. (1978). Facial representation of multivariate data. In P.C.C. Wang (Ed.), *Graphical representation of multivariate data* (pp. 143-168). New York: Academic Press.

Kleiner, B., & Hartigan, J. A. (1981). Representing points in many dimensions by trees and castles. *Journal of the American Statistical Association, 76,* 260-269.

Kosslyn, S. M. (1985). Graphics and human information processing. *Journal of the American Statistical Association, 80,* 499-512.

Kosslyn, S. M. (1989). Understanding charts and graphs. *Applied Cognitive Psychology, 3,* 185-225.

Lambert, J. H. (1779). *Pyrometrie.* Berlin: Babey Houde und Spener.

Lewandowsky, S., & Spence, I. (1989). Discriminating strata in scatterplots. *Journal of the American Statistical Association, 84,* 682-688.

Macdonald-Ross, M. (1977). How numbers are shown: A review of research on the presentation of quantitative data in texts. *Audio-Visual Communication Review, 25,* 359-407.

Mackinley, J. D. (1987). Automatic design of graphical presentations (Doctoral dissertation, Stanford University). Ann Arbor, MI: University Microfilms International.

Mandler, J. M., & Parker, R. E. (1976). Memory for descriptive and spatial information in complex pictures. *Journal of Experimental Psychology, 2,* 36-48.

Matlin, M. W. (1988). *Sensation and perception* (2nd ed.). Boston: Allyn & Bacon.

Mezzich, J. E., & Worthington, D.R.L. (1978). A comparison of graphical representations of multidimensional psychiatric diagnostic data. In P.C.C. Wang (Ed.), *Graphical representation of multivariate data* (pp. 123-142). New York: Academic Press.

Milroy, R., & Poulton, E. C. (1978). Labelling graphs for improved reading speed. *Ergonomics, 21,* 55-61.

Mosteller, F., Siegel, A. F., Trapido, E., & Youtz, C. (1981). Eye fitting straight lines. *American Statistician, 35,* 150-152.

Mudgett, B. D. (1930). *Statistical tables and graphs.* Cambridge, MA: Riverside Press.

Paivo, A. (1974). Spacing of repetitions in the incidental and intentional free recall of pictures and words. *Journal of Verbal Learning and Verbal Behavior, 13,* 497-511.

Paivio, A., Yuille, J. C., & Madigan, S. A. (1968). Concreteness, imagery, and meaningfulness values for 925 nouns. *Journal of Experimental Psychology Monograph Supplement, 76*(1), Part 2.

Peterson, L. V., & Schramm, W. (1955). How accurately are different kinds of graphs read? *Audio-Visual Communication Review, 2,* 178-189.

Pike, J. (1974). Craters on Earth, Moon and Mars: Multivariate classification and mode of origin. *Earth and Planetary Science Letters, 22,* 245-255.

Pinker, S. (1981). *A theory of graph comprehension* (Occasional paper No. 15). Massachusetts Institute of Technology, Center for Cognitive Science, Cambridge.

Playfair, W. (1786). *The commercial and political atlas.* London: Corry.

Playfair, W. (1801). *Statistical breviary.* London: Wallis.

Poulton, E. C. (1985). Geometric illusions in reading graphs. *Perception and Psychophysics, 37,* 543-548.

Random House. (1987). *Dictionary of the English language* (2nd ed.). New York: Author.

Rock, I., Halper, F., & Clayton, T. (1972). The perception and recognition of complex figures. *Cognitive Psychology, 3*, 655-673.

Royston, E. (1956). Studies in the history of probability and statistics: III. A note on the history of the graphical presentation of data. *Biometrika, 43*, 241-247.

Russell, H. N. (1913). "Giant" and "dwarf" stars. *The Observatory, 36*, 324-329.

Russell, H. N. (1914). Relations between the spectra and other characteristics of the stars. *Popular Astronomy, 22*, 275-294.

Schmid, C. F. (1983). *Statistical graphics.* New York: John Wiley.

Schutz, H. G. (1961a). An evaluation of formats for graphic trend displays. *Human Factors, 3*, 99-107.

Schutz, H. G. (1961b). An evaluation of methods for presentation of graphic multiple trends. *Human Factors, 3*, 108-119.

Shepard, R. N. (1967). Recognition memory for words, sentences, and pictures. *Journal of Verbal Learning and Verbal Behavior, 6*, 156-163.

Shields, M. C. (1937). The early history of graphs in physical literature. *American Physics Teacher, 5*, 68-71.

Siegel, J. H., Goldwyn, R. M., & Friedman, H. P. (1971). Pattern and process in the evolution of human septic shock. *Surgery, 70*, 232-245.

Silverman, B. V. (1986). *Density estimation for statistics and data analysis.* London: Chapman & Hall.

Simkin, D., & Hastie, R. (1987). An information-processing analysis of graph perception. *Journal of the American Statistical Association, 82*, 454-465.

Spence, I. (in press). The visual psychophysics of graphical elements. *Journal of Experimental Psychology.*

Spence, I., & Lewandowsky, S. (in press). Displaying proportions and percentages. *Applied Cognitive Psychology.*

Standing, L., Conezio, J., & Haber, R. N. (1970). Perception and memory for pictures: Single-trial learning of 2560 visual stimuli. *Psychonomic Science, 19*, 73-74.

Strahan, R. F., & Hansen, C. J. (1978). Underestimating correlation from scatterplots. *Applied Psychological Measurement, 2*, 543-550.

Tilling, L. (1975). Early experimental graphs. *The British Journal for the History of Science, 8*, 193-213.

Tufte, E. R. (1983). *The visual display of quantitative information.* Cheshire, CT: Graphics Press.

Tukey, J. W. (1972). Some graphic and semigraphic displays. In T. A. Bancroft (Ed.), *Statistical papers in honor of George W. Snedecor* (pp. 293-316). Ames: Iowa State University Press.

Tukey, J. W. (1977). *Exploratory data analysis.* Reading, MA: Addison-Wesley.

Tversky, B., & Schiano, D. (in press). Perceptual and conceptual factors in distortions in memory for graphs and maps. *Journal of Experimental Psychology.*

von Huhn, R. (1927). Further studies in the graphic use of circles and bars I: A discussion of Eells' experiment. *Journal of the American Statistical Association, 22*, 31-36.

Wainer, H. (1974). The suspended rootogram and other visual displays: An empirical validation. *American Statistician, 28*, 143-145.

Wainer, H., & Thissen, D. (1979). On the robustness of a class of naive estimators. *Applied Psychological Measurement, 4*, 543-551.

Wainer, H., & Thissen, D. (1981). Graphical data analysis. *Annual Review of Psychology, 32*, 191-241.

Wainer, H., & Thissen, D. (1988). Plotting in the modern world: Statistics packages and good graphics. *Chance, 1*, 10-20.

Wang, P.C.C., & Lake, G. E. (1978). Application of graphical multivariate techniques in policy sciences. In P.C.C. Wang (Ed.), *Graphical representation of multivariate data* (pp. 13-58). New York: Academic Press.

Washburn, J. N. (1927a). An experimental study of various graphic, tabular and textual methods of presenting quantitative material. *Journal of Educational Psychology, 18*, 361-376.

Washburn, J. N. (1927b). An experimental study of various graphic, tabular and textual methods of presenting quantitative material. *Journal of Educational Psychology, 18*, 465-476.

Weber, E. H. (1834). *De pulsu, resorptione, auditu et tactu: Annotationes anatomicae et physiologicae.* Leipzig: Koehler.

Wilk, M. B., & Gnanadesikan, R. (1968). Probability plotting methods for the analysis of data. *Biometrika, 55*, 1-17.

Wollen, K. A., Weber, A., & Lowry, D. (1972). Bizarreness versus interaction of mental images as determinants of learning. *Cognitive Psychology, 3*, 518-523.

The World Bank. (1988). *World development report.* Washington, DC: Author.

Young, F. W. (1989). Visualizing six-dimensional structure with dynamic statistical graphics. *Chance, 2*, 22-30.

# 2

## DESCRIBING
## UNIVARIATE DISTRIBUTIONS

### John Fox

This chapter presents a variety of univariate distributional displays, some of which are very simple, and most of which are graphical. These univariate displays serve several important functions: (1) We often need to understand the distribution of a variable or to present the distribution effectively. (See, for example, the use of density estimation in Chapter 8, this volume.) (2) Examining data closely is an essential prelude to careful data analysis and statistical modeling. Even where theories are mathematically concrete — a relative rarity in the social sciences — sensitivity to anomalous, unexpected, and problematic data is a hallmark of good data analysis: Such data often herald interesting findings and can compromise an otherwise adequate analysis. (3) The examination of univariate distributions plays a role in more sophisticated statistical methods, such as the analysis of residuals and other diagnostic statistics in regression (e.g., Chapter 6, this volume).

This chapter opens with a treatment of stem-and-leaf displays, simple histograms constructed directly from the digits of numerical data. The second section introduces letter values, which are summary values selected from the data themselves, and boxplots, schematic distribu-

AUTHOR'S NOTE: I am grateful to Michael Friendly, Scott Long, and Valerie Preston for helpful comments on a draft of this chapter, and to Bob Stine for his insightful observations on a number of the methods discussed here.

tional graphs constructed from the letter values. The third section presents one-dimensional scatterplots and index plots. The fourth section describes the empirical distribution function of the data, quantile plots, and quantile-comparison plots for comparing the observed data to a theoretical reference distribution, such as the normal distribution. The fifth section deals with estimating the probability-density function of a population by nonparametrically smoothing the histogram of a sample drawn from the population. The sixth section shows how simple transformations can be used to make data distributions more symmetric. Each of these sections ends with a short discussion of extensions to the methods presented in that section, references to the literature, and suggestions for further reading. The seventh section briefly discusses how the methods presented in this chapter can be implemented using standard statistical software. A final section of recommendations summarizes some of the relative advantages and disadvantages of the displays described in the chapter.

A word to the sophisticated reader: Please do not be put off by the simplicity of the material in this chapter, especially in the earlier sections. Although I have made an effort to ground these methods in statistical theory, the stress is on construction and interpretation of the displays. Even the treatment of density estimation, with minor exceptions, should be accessible to readers with a modest background in mathematics and statistics. Nevertheless, these are *useful* techniques, well worth incorporation in our daily data-analytic practice. Simply pass over the topics that are familiar.

## STEM-AND-LEAF DISPLAYS

The stem-and-leaf display is a type of histogram that cleverly records the data values in the display. This graph is especially useful for small- to medium-size batches of data containing from about 20 to 200 data values.[1] The stem-and-leaf is a good choice of initial display when computation is to be done by hand because it is simple to construct and it sorts the data values almost painlessly. Quite apart from its ease of construction, which is a smaller consideration when data are analyzed with the help of a computer, the stem-and-leaf display is useful because it shows the data values themselves; gives a good impression of the center, spread, and shape of the distribution; and draws attention to unusual values. Nevertheless, the stem-and-leaf display shares the general limitations of histograms (see the fifth section).

Table 2.1 reports the mean level of education, mean level of income, and percentage of female incumbents in 102 occupations drawn from the 1971 Canadian Census. The table also gives the rated prestige of each occupation.[2] Figure 2.1 shows a stem-and-leaf display of mean education for the 102 occupations.

To construct the display:

1. Examine the data and decide how many digits to retain. Then truncate the data values to the right of the last retained digit. All but the last digit form the *stem*, while the last retained digit becomes the *leaf*. It is possible, of course, to round rather than truncate the data, but truncation is simpler when computation is accomplished by hand and, more importantly, truncated numbers are easier to locate among the original list of data values. As will become apparent presently, the point of division of stems from leaves implicitly selects the width for the *bins* of the display.

For the education data, leaves represent the tenths' place. Consequently, for the first few observations:

|            | stem | leaf |
|------------|------|------|
| 13.11 →    | 13   | 1    |
| 12.26 →    | 12   | 2    |
| 12.77 →    | 12   | 7    |
| 11.42 →    | 11   | 4    |

Were there negative data values, these would be handled similarly. Note that when the data straddle zero, there are both −0 and +0 stems, which ensures that each stem represents a bin of equal width, here 1.0. Data values of precisely 0.0 can be divided equally between the two zero stems.

2. Write a list of possible stems from the smallest to the largest, here 6 through 15. Place each leaf to the right of the stem to which it belongs.

3. Sort the leaves on each stem into ascending order: 0 through 9 for positive stems; 9 through 0 for negative stems.

4. Two annotations are shown on the stem-and-leaf display in Figure 2.1, indicating how the data values are to be read from the display.

5. The column of *depths* to the left of the stem records the cumulative count from the closer end of the batch. To calculate these depths, first find the depth of the *median* (M):

*(text continues on page 65)*

**Table 2.1  Mean Level of Education (years), Mean Level of Income (dollars), Percentage of Women, and Rated Prestige for 102 Canadian Occupations in 1971**

| Occupation | Abbreviated Title | Mean Education | Mean Income | Percent Women | Prestige |
|---|---|---|---|---|---|
| 1113 | Government administrators | 13.11 | 12351 | 11.16 | 68.8 |
| 1130 | General manager, other senior officials | 12.26 | 25879 | 4.02 | 69.1 |
| 1171 | Accountant, auditor, other finance | 12.77 | 9271 | 15.70 | 63.4 |
| 1175 | Purchasing officers, nat. whlsl. ret. | 11.42 | 8865 | 9.11 | 56.8 |
| 2111 | Chemists | 14.62 | 8403 | 11.68 | 73.5 |
| 2113 | Physicists | 15.64 | 11030 | 5.13 | 77.6 |
| 2133 | Biologists, related scientists | 15.09 | 8258 | 25.65 | 72.6 |
| 2141 | Architects | 15.44 | 14163 | 2.69 | 78.1 |
| 2143 | Civil engineers | 14.52 | 11377 | 1.03 | 73.1 |
| 2153 | Mining engineers | 14.64 | 11023 | 0.94 | 68.8 |
| 2161 | Surveyors | 12.39 | 5902 | 1.91 | 62.0 |
| 2163 | Draughtsmen | 12.30 | 7059 | 7.83 | 60.0 |
| 2183 | Systems analysts, computer programmer rl. | 13.83 | 8425 | 15.33 | 53.8 |
| 2311 | Economists | 14.44 | 8049 | 57.31 | 62.2 |
| 2315 | Psychologists | 14.36 | 7405 | 48.28 | 74.9 |
| 2331 | Social workers | 14.21 | 6336 | 54.77 | 55.1 |
| 2343 | Lawyers, notaries | 15.77 | 19263 | 5.13 | 82.3 |
| 2351 | Librarians, archivists | 14.15 | 6112 | 77.10 | 58.1 |
| 2391 | Education vocational counsellors | 15.22 | 9593 | 34.89 | 58.3 |
| 2511 | Ministers of religion | 14.50 | 4686 | 4.14 | 72.8 |
| 2711 | University teachers | 15.97 | 12480 | 19.59 | 84.6 |
| 2731 | Elementary and kindergarten teachers | 13.62 | 5648 | 83.78 | 59.6 |
| 2733 | Secondary school teachers | 15.08 | 8034 | 46.80 | 66.1 |

*(continued)*

61

**Table 2.1** continued

| Occupation | Abbreviated Title | Mean Education | Mean Income | Percent Women | Prestige |
|---|---|---|---|---|---|
| 3111 | Physicians, surgeons | 15.96 | 25308 | 10.56 | 87.2 |
| 3115 | Veterinarians | 15.94 | 14558 | 4.32 | 66.7 |
| 3117 | Osteopaths, chiropractors | 14.71 | 17498 | 6.91 | 68.4 |
| 3131 | Nurses, grads, except supervisors | 12.46 | 4614 | 96.12 | 64.7 |
| 3135 | Nursing aides, orderlies | 9.45 | 3485 | 76.14 | 34.9 |
| 3137 | Physio, occupational, other therapists | 13.62 | 5092 | 82.66 | 72.1 |
| 3151 | Pharmacists | 15.21 | 10432 | 24.71 | 69.3 |
| 3156 | Medical lab technologists, technicians | 12.79 | 5180 | 76.04 | 67.5 |
| 3314 | Advertising, illustrating artists | 11.09 | 6197 | 21.03 | 57.2 |
| 3337 | Radio, TV announcers | 12.71 | 7562 | 11.15 | 57.6 |
| 3373 | Athletes | 11.44 | 8206 | 8.13 | 54.1 |
| 4111 | Secretaries, stenographers | 11.59 | 4036 | 97.51 | 46.0 |
| 4113 | Typists, clerk typists | 11.49 | 3148 | 95.97 | 41.9 |
| 4131 | Bookkeepers, accounting clerks | 11.32 | 4348 | 68.24 | 49.4 |
| 4133 | Tellers, cashiers | 10.64 | 2448 | 91.76 | 42.3 |
| 4143 | Elect. data processing equip. opr. | 11.36 | 4330 | 75.92 | 47.7 |
| 4153 | Shipping, receiving clerks | 9.17 | 4761 | 11.37 | 30.9 |
| 4161 | Library, file clerks | 12.09 | 3016 | 83.19 | 32.7 |
| 4171 | Receptionists, info clerks | 11.04 | 2901 | 92.86 | 38.7 |
| 4172 | Mail carriers | 9.22 | 5511 | 7.62 | 36.1 |
| 4173 | Mail, postal clerks | 10.07 | 3739 | 52.27 | 37.2 |
| 4175 | Telephone operators | 10.51 | 3161 | 96.14 | 38.1 |
| 4191 | Collectors | 11.20 | 4741 | 47.06 | 29.4 |
| 4192 | Adjustors, claim | 11.13 | 5052 | 56.10 | 51.1 |
| 4193 | Travel clerks, tkt. stn., frt. agt. | 11.43 | 6259 | 39.17 | 35.7 |

| | | | | | |
|---|---|---|---|---|---|
| 4197 | General office clerks | 11.00 | 4075 | 63.23 | 35.6 |
| 5130 | Supervisors, sales occs., commod. | 9.84 | 7482 | 17.04 | 41.5 |
| 5133 | Commercial travelers | 11.13 | 8780 | 3.16 | 40.2 |
| 5137 | Sales clerks, commodities | 10.05 | 2594 | 67.82 | 26.5 |
| 5143 | Newsboys | 9.62 | 918 | 7.00 | 14.8 |
| 5145 | Service station attendants | 9.93 | 2370 | 3.69 | 23.3 |
| 5171 | Insurance salesmen, agents | 11.60 | 8131 | 13.09 | 47.3 |
| 5172 | Real estate salesmen | 11.09 | 6992 | 24.44 | 47.1 |
| 5191 | Buyers, wholesale, retail, trade | 11.03 | 7956 | 23.88 | 51.1 |
| 6111 | Firefighting occs. | 9.47 | 8895 | 0.00 | 43.5 |
| 6112 | Policemen, detectives, govt. | 10.93 | 8891 | 1.65 | 51.6 |
| 6121 | Chefs, cooks | 7.74 | 3116 | 52.00 | 29.7 |
| 6123 | Bartenders | 8.50 | 3930 | 15.51 | 20.2 |
| 6141 | Funeral directors, embalmers, rel. | 10.57 | 7869 | 6.01 | 54.9 |
| 6147 | Babysitters | 9.46 | 611 | 96.53 | 25.9 |
| 6162 | Laundering, dry cleaning occs. | 7.33 | 3000 | 69.31 | 20.8 |
| 6191 | Janitors, charworkers, cleaners | 7.11 | 3472 | 33.57 | 17.3 |
| 6193 | Elevator operating occs. | 7.58 | 3582 | 30.08 | 20.1 |
| 7112 | Farmers | 6.84 | 3643 | 3.60 | 44.1 |
| 7182 | Farm workers | 8.60 | 1656 | 27.75 | 21.5 |
| 7711 | Rotary well drilling, rel. occs. | 8.88 | 6860 | 0.00 | 35.3 |
| 8213 | Baking, confection mkg., rel. occs. | 7.54 | 4199 | 33.30 | 38.9 |
| 8215 | Slaughtering, meat cutting, canning | 7.64 | 5134 | 17.26 | 25.2 |
| 8215 | Slaughtering, meat cutting, etc. | 7.64 | 5134 | 17.26 | 34.8 |
| 8221 | Fruit, veg. canning, presv. pck. | 7.42 | 1890 | 72.24 | 23.2 |
| 8267 | Textile weaving occs. | 6.69 | 4443 | 31.36 | 33.3 |
| 8278 | Occs. in laboring, etc., textile | 6.74 | 3485 | 39.48 | 28.8 |
| 8311 | Tool, die making occs. | 10.09 | 8043 | 1.50 | 42.5 |
| 8313 | Machinist, mach. tool setting-up | 8.81 | 6686 | 4.28 | 44.2 |

*(continued)*

**Table 2.1** continued

| Occupation | Abbreviated Title | Mean Education | Mean Income | Percent Women | Prestige |
|---|---|---|---|---|---|
| 8333 | Sheet metal workers | 8.40 | 6565 | 2.30 | 35.9 |
| 8335 | Welding, flame cutting occs. | 7.92 | 6477 | 5.17 | 41.8 |
| 8513 | Motor veh. fabricating, assmb. occs. | 8.43 | 5811 | 13.62 | 35.9 |
| 8515 | Aircraft fabricating, assmb. occs | 8.78 | 6573 | 5.78 | 43.7 |
| 8534 | Electronic equip. fab. assmg. | 8.76 | 3942 | 74.54 | 50.8 |
| 8537 | Radio, TV service repairmen | 10.29 | 5449 | 2.92 | 37.2 |
| 8563 | Sewing mach. opr., textiles | 6.38 | 2847 | 90.67 | 28.2 |
| 8581 | Motor veh. mechanics, repairmen | 8.10 | 5795 | 0.81 | 38.1 |
| 8582 | Aircraft mechanics, repairmen | 10.10 | 7716 | 0.78 | 50.3 |
| 8715 | Railway sectionmen, trackmen | 6.67 | 4696 | 0.00 | 27.3 |
| 8731 | Electrical pwr. linemen, rel. occs. | 9.05 | 8316 | 1.34 | 40.9 |
| 8733 | Construction electricians | 9.93 | 7147 | 0.99 | 50.2 |
| 8780 | Foremen: other constr. trades occs. | 8.24 | 8880 | 0.65 | 51.1 |
| 8781 | Carpenters, related occs. | 6.92 | 5299 | 0.56 | 38.9 |
| 8782 | Brick stone masons, tile setters | 6.60 | 5959 | 0.52 | 36.2 |
| 8785 | Painters, paperhangers, rel. occs. | 7.81 | 4549 | 2.46 | 29.9 |
| 8791 | Pipe fitting, plumbing, rel. occs. | 8.33 | 6928 | 0.61 | 42.9 |
| 8798 | Occs. in laboring, other constr. | 7.52 | 3910 | 1.09 | 26.5 |
| 9111 | Air pilots, navigators, flt. engnrs. | 12.27 | 14032 | 0.58 | 66.1 |
| 9131 | Loco. engineers, firemen | 8.49 | 8845 | 0.00 | 48.9 |
| 9171 | Bus drivers | 7.58 | 5562 | 9.47 | 35.9 |
| 9173 | Taxi drivers, chauffeurs | 7.93 | 4224 | 3.59 | 25.1 |
| 9313 | Longshoremen, stevedors, frt. handlers | 8.37 | 4753 | 0.00 | 26.1 |
| 9511 | Typesetters, compositors | 10.00 | 6462 | 13.58 | 42.2 |
| 9517 | Bookbinders, related occs. | 8.55 | 3617 | 70.78 | 35.2 |

SOURCE: Census of Canada (1971, Volume 3, Part 6, pp. 19-1 – 19-21) and personal communication from B. Blishen, W. Carroll, and C. Moore.

64

```
n  = 102
Leaf Unit = 0.10

  1 | 2 = 1.2

  depth

      7      6 |  3666789
     20      7 |  1345555667899
     34      8 |  12333445567788
     44      9 |  0124446899
    (10)    10 |  0000025569
     48     11 |  0000011233444456
     32     12 |  022234777
     23     13 |  1668
     19     14 |  123445667
     10     15 |  0022467999
```

**Figure 2.1 Stem-and-leaf display for mean education (in years) of 102 Canadian occupations in 1971.**

$$d(M) = (n + 1)/2$$

where *n* is the number of data values. As is no doubt familiar, if *n* is even and, hence $d(M)$ is not an integer, then we average the two data values at depth $d(M) - 1/2$ to find the median. For example, $d(M) = (102 + 1)/2 = 51.5$. Next, count in toward the median from each end of the batch to record the depth at each stem; the leaf count for the stem containing the median is also shown, enclosed in parentheses to indicate that it is not a depth. As a check, the sum of the depths on the stems closest to the median and the count at the stem containing the median equals *n*. For the example, $44 + (10) + 48 = 102✓$.

At times, some data values are sufficiently far from the rest to make their direct display awkward. An example is shown in Figure 2.2, which displays mean income for the 102 Canadian occupations: Some occupations have values considerably larger than the others. We could accommodate these values by using 1,000s rather than 100s for the leaf digit, but to do so would lose resolution in the part of the display containing most of the data: 89 of the 102 values would be on the zero

**(A) Using 100s for the leaves**

```
n = 102
Leaf Unit = 100
1 | 2 = 1,200

depth
  2    0 | 69
  4    1 | 68
  9    2 | 34589
 24    3 | 001114445667799
 38    4 | 00123345666777
(14)   5 | 00111245567899
 50    6 | 112345568999
 38    7 | 01445789
 30    8 | 000122347888888
 15    9 | 25
 13   10 | 4
 12   11 | 003
  9   12 | 34
  7   13 |
  7   14 | 015
  4   15 |
  4   16 |
  4   17 | 4
  3   18 |
  3   19 | 2
  2   20 |
  2   21 |
  2   22 |
  2   23 |
  2   24 |
  2   25 | 38
```

**(B) Omitting empty stems**

```
n = 102
Leaf Unit = 100
1 | 2 = 1,200

depth
  2    0 | 69
  4    1 | 68
  9    2 | 34589
 24    3 | 001114445667799
 38    4 | 00123345666777
(14)   5 | 00111245567899
 50    6 | 112345568999
 38    7 | 01445789
 30    8 | 000122347888888
 15    9 | 25
 13   10 | 4
 12   11 | 003
  9   12 | 34
  7   14 | 015
  4   17 | 4
  3   19 | 2
  2   25 | 38
```

**(C) Collecting unusually large values on a high stem**

```
n = 102
Leaf Unit = 100
1 | 2 = 1,200

depth
  2    0 | 69
  4    1 | 68
  9    2 | 34589
 24    3 | 001114445667799
 38    4 | 00123345666777
(14)   5 | 00111245567899
 50    6 | 112345568999
 38    7 | 01445789
 30    8 | 000122347888888
 15    9 | 25
 13   10 | 4
 12   11 | 003
  9   12 | 34
  7   13 |
  7   14 | 01

      high   145, 174, 192, 253, 258,
```

**Figure 2.2  Stem-and-leaf displays for mean income (in dollars) of 102 Canadian occupations in 1971.**

stem. An alternative is to omit empty stems (as in Figure 2.2B), but to do so gives a potentially misleading impression of the distribution of data values. A generally more satisfactory alternative is to collect unusually large values on a special *high* stem (as in Figure 2.2C). The rule employed here to identify unusual values is explained in the second section.

In constructing a stem-and-leaf display, it is sometimes the case that using the units' place for the leaf digit produces a display with too few stems, while using the tenths' place produces too many stems. Consider the stem-and-leaf display for occupational prestige given in Figure 2.3A. Here, using tenths for leaves would produce 74 stems. It is possible to compromise by dividing each of the coarser stems into two or five parts, as in Figures 2.3B and 2.3C, respectively. In Figure 2.3B, the stems marked "*" take leaves 0 through 4; those marked "." take leaves 5 through 9. The scheme in Figure 2.3C is similar, with the letters *t*, *f*, and *s* representing the English names of the leaf digits to which they correspond: *t*wo, *t*hree; *f*our, *f*ive; *s*ix, *s*even.

Although the selection of number of stems is reasonably made impressionistically, it helps to have a rule for guidance, and it is indeed essential to have such a rule when the method is programmed for a computer. Too few stems produce a display lacking in detail; too many stems are confusing and produce unstable bin counts. Generally, we can accommodate more stems when the batch is large than when it is small, but the number of stems should increase less quickly than the size of the batch: The standard error of a bin proportion, for example, is inversely proportional to the square root of the sample size. Let $n^*$ represent the number of data values, excluding those to be shown on high and low stems. Then $S = [10 \times \log_{10} n^*]$ is a reasonable upper bound for the number of stems, and $[2\sqrt{n^*}\,]$ produces a reasonable target value for small $n^* \leq 50$. The square brackets $[\cdot]$ indicate the integer part of the enclosed quantity. Note that $2\sqrt{n^*} = 10 \times \log_{10} n^* = 20$ for $n^* = 100$, which is approximately the upper bound to be applied to the illustrative data set, for which $n = 102$. This rule is satisfied for Figures 2.2C and 2.3B, but it suggests that the stems in Figure 2.1 could each be divided into two parts, thus achieving the upper bound of 20 stems. The resulting display, which can be drawn by the reader, appears reasonable, if slightly rough.

The limit $S$ for the number of stems can also be used to suggest the point of division between stems and leaves. Let $R$ represent the range

(A) Using units for the leaves

```
n  = 102
Leaf Unit = 1.0
1 | 2 = 12

 depth
   2      1 | 47
  20      2 | 000133555666788999
  41      3 | 0234455555556677888888
 (19)     4 | 0011122223344677789
  42      5 | 00011113445677889
  25      6 | 02234666788899
  11      7 | 22233478
   3      8 | 247
```

(B) Dividing each stem into two parts

```
n  = 102
Leaf Unit = 1.0
1 | 2 = 12

 depth
   1     1* | 4
   2     1. | 7
   8     2* | 000133
  20     2. | 555666788999
  25     3* | 02344
  41     3. | 5555555667788888
 (13)    4* | 0011122223344
  48     4. | 677789
  42     5* | 0001111344
  32     5. | 5677889
  25     6* | 02234
  20     6. | 666788899
  11     7* | 222334
   5     7. | 78
   3     8* | 24
   1     8. | 7
```

(C) Dividing each stem into five parts

```
n  = 102
Leaf Unit = 1.0
1 | 2 = 12

 depth
   1     1f | 4
   2     1s | 7
   2     1. |
   6     2* | 0001
   8     2t | 33
  11     2f | 555
  15     2s | 6667
  20     2. | 88999
  21     3* | 0
  23     3t | 23
  32     3f | 445555555
  36     3s | 6677
  41     3. | 88888
  46     4* | 00111
  (6)    4t | 222233
  50     4f | 44
  48     4s | 6777
  44     4. | 89
  42     5* | 0001111
  35     5t | 3
  34     5f | 445
  31     5s | 677
  28     5. | 889
  25     6* | 0
  24     6t | 223
  21     6f | 4
  20     6s | 6667
  16     6. | 88899
  11     7* |
  11     7t | 22233
   6     7f | 4
   5     7s | 7
   4     7. | 8
   3     8* |
   3     8t | 2
   2     8f | 4
   1     8s | 7
```

Figure 2.3  Stem-and-leaf displays for prestige scores of 102 Canadian occupations.

of the data. Rounding $R/S$ up to the next power of 10 produces a suggested bin width. Rounding up to a power of 10 times 1, 2, or 5 allows for stems divided into five or two parts.

For the income data, for example, we have $n^* = 102 - 5 = 97$, from which $S = [10 \times \log_{10} 97] = 19$. The range of the data, disregarding the five high values, is $14{,}163 - 611 = 13{,}552$. Thus $R/S = 13{,}552/19 = 713$, which rounds up to $1 \times 10^3$, suggesting 1,000s for stems (as in Figure 2.2C).

An alternative formulation focuses on bin width rather than on number of stems, and raises issues of sampling and estimation. We return to this question in the fifth section on density estimation.

Stem-and-leaf displays convey a variety of distributional information, but like all histograms they should not be overinterpreted. Figure 2.1, for example, suggests that there may be three modes to the distribution of mean education in the 102 occupations, but is it unclear to what extent this impression is dependent on bin width, bin location, and "chance fluctuation" in the data. Nevertheless, the three modes make some sense here, corresponding roughly to grade school, high school, and university levels of education. Density estimation, discussed in the fifth section, will address this issue more definitively. Figure 2.2 shows clearly the positive skew in the income distribution of the occupations, though the apparent mode near $8,000 seems curious.

### References and Further Reading

The stem-and-leaf display was introduced by Tukey (1972) and is described in detail in his seminal text on exploratory data analysis (Tukey, 1977). The version presented here is from Velleman and Hoaglin (1981). An extensive discussion of rules for determining number of stems, including those given above, appears in Emerson and Hoaglin (1983).

## LETTER-VALUE DISPLAYS AND BOXPLOTS

Letter values are judiciously chosen quantiles selected from among the data values themselves. Quantiles are values cutting off fractions of the ranked scores. Letter values summarize several important characteristics of the distribution of the data, including center, spread, skewness or symmetry, and shape. We shall see later (the sixth section) that letter values are also useful for selecting a transformation to make the data more symmetric. Boxplots depict graphically some of the information in the letter values, and also show unusual data values.

To define letter values, we first order our data from smallest to largest: $x_{(1)}, x_{(2)}, \ldots, x_{(n)}$. Note that the unordered data are denoted $x_1$, $x_2, \ldots, x_n$. If the $x$'s are a sample from some population, then the $x_{(i)}$'s are termed the *order statistics* of the sample. Many robust, outlier-resistant, and nonparametric statistical procedures are based on order statistics.

As for the stems in the stem-and-leaf display (the first section), the *depth* of each data value is its position relative to the nearer end of the batch, that is, the smaller of $i$ (the count from the bottom) and $n + 1 - i$ (the count from the top). For example, for the contrived batch 1, 9, 14, 6, 7, with $n = 5$:

| $i$ | $x_{(i)}$ | $n + 1 - i$ | depth |
|-----|-----------|-------------|-------|
| 1   | 1         | 5           | 1     |
| 2   | 6         | 4           | 2     |
| 3   | 7         | 3           | 3     |
| 4   | 9         | 2           | 2     |
| 5   | 14        | 1           | 1     |

Note that the *extremes*, 1 and 14 in the example, are located at depth 1.

Recall that the depth of the median is $d(M) = (n + 1)/2$. Here, $d(M) = (5 + 1)/2 = 3$, so $M = 7$. The median divides the ordered batch into two parts of equal size: When $n$ is odd, as here, each "half" includes the median and consists of $(n + 1)/2$ scores; when $n$ is even, each half consists of $n/2$ scores. The *hinges* or *fourths* are located at the middle of each of these halves of the data. The hinges are one way of defining *quartiles* of an empirical distribution employing, as we shall see presently, a simple interpolation rule.

To find the depth of the hinges, calculate

$$d(H) = \frac{([d(M)]+1)}{2}.$$

Recall that the square brackets mean truncation to an integer. For the small example, then, $d(H) = ([3] + 1)/2 = 2$, and consequently $H_L = 6$ and $H_U = 9$, where the subscripts $L$ and $U$ denote "lower" and "upper," respectively. If $d(H)$ has a fractional part, then we average the values at depths $d(H) - 1/2$ and $d(H) + 1/2$. The term "hinge" is motivated by the pattern produced by folding the ordered values at the median and fourths; thus, for example,

Given that *n* is sufficiently large, we can proceed in this manner to define *eighths* (*E*), *sixteenths* (*D*), and subsequent letter values (*C*, *B*, *A*, *Z*, *Y*, *X*, . . . ), each of which lies midway between the previous letter value and the closer extreme:

$$d(M) = (n + 1)/ 2.$$
$$d(H) = ([d(M)] + 1)/ 2.$$
$$d(E) = ([d(H)] + 1)/ 2.$$
$$d(D) = ([d(E)] + 1)/ 2.$$

.

.

.

The process continues until we arrive at the extremes of the batch at depth 1. If, in the next-to-last step, letter values are produced at depth 1.5, then these values are only reported if there are no letter values at depth 2, since the values at depth 1.5 are simply averages of the values at depths 2 and 1. Notice that the letter values are quantiles concentrated in the tails of the batch, and that there are more letter values in a large batch than in a small one.

The average of each pair of letter values, called a *midsummary* (e.g., mid-hinge, mid-eighth), contributes information about the center and symmetry of the distribution. The differences between the letter-value pairs, called *spreads* (e.g., hinge-spread, eighth-spread), contribute information about dispersion and shape.

All of these quantities can be shown conveniently in a *letter-value display*, such as that given in Table 2.2 for the occupational income data. A more compact display may be produced by showing only the median, hinges, and extremes (a *five-number summary*), or median, hinges, eighths, and extremes (a *seven-number summary*).

**Table 2.2  Letter-Value Display for Mean Income of 102 Canadian Occupations in 1971**

|       | Depth | Lower |      | Upper | Midsummary | Spread |
|-------|-------|-------|------|-------|------------|--------|
| n =   | 102   |       |      |       |            |        |
| M     | 51.5  |       | 5930 |       | 5930       |        |
| H     | 26    | 4075  |      | 8206  | 6141       | 4131   |
| E     | 13    | 3155  |      | 10013 | 6584       | 6858   |
| D     | 7     | 2594  |      | 14032 | 8313       | 11438  |
| C     | 4     | 1890  |      | 17498 | 9694       | 15608  |
| B     | 2.5   | 1287  |      | 22285 | 11768      | 20999  |
| A     | 1.5   | 764   |      | 25594 | 13179      | 24829  |
|       | 1     | 611   |      | 25879 | 13245      | 25268  |

If the data distribution is symmetric, then corresponding letter values are equidistant from the median, and consequently the midsummaries coincide with the median. Alternatively, a consistent trend in the midsummaries, such as in Table 2.2, indicates skewness: An upward trend is symptomatic of positive skew, a downward trend of negative skew.

If the distribution is roughly symmetric, then the observed spreads can be compared with the corresponding theoretical spreads of a symmetric reference distribution, such as the normal or Gaussian distribution. As is well known, the inter-quartile range of the unit-normal distribution $N(0,1)$ is 1.35, since the quartiles are located at $\pm0.675$. Other theoretical letter-value spreads can be determined in a similar manner; some are shown in Table 2.3.

For a general normal distribution $N(\mu, \sigma^2)$, the letter-value spreads in Table 2.3 are read as multiples of the standard deviation $\sigma$. It follows from this observation that dividing the empirical letter-value spreads by the theoretical unit-normal values produces several estimates of $\sigma$, if indeed the data are drawn from a normal distribution. Under this circumstance, then, the different estimates should be similar. An increasing trend in the estimates for successively higher letter values is indicative of tails heavier than those of the normal distribution. This is a potentially useful observation, since heavy-tailed distributions can wreak havoc on the efficiency of common statistical estimators: least-squares regression, for example. Additionally, $\hat{\sigma} = H$-spread/1.35 is a good robust estimator of spread that behaves well in the presence of

**Table 2.3  Letter-Value Spreads for the Unit-Normal (Gaussian) Distribution**

| Letter Values | Single-Tail Probability | Spread |
|:---:|:---:|:---:|
| H | 1/4 | 1.3490 |
| E | 1/8 | 2.3007 |
| D | 1/16 | 3.0682 |
| C | 1/32 | 3.7255 |
| B | 1/64 | 4.3078 |
| A | 1/128 | 4.8351 |
| Z | 1/256 | 5.3201 |
| Y | 1/512 | 5.7713 |
| X | 1/1024 | 6.1945 |
| W | 1/2048 | 6.5944 |
| V | 1/4096 | 6.9742 |

outliers and retains meaning for distributions that are roughly normal in the center but that depart from normality in the tails.

Boxplots provide a schematic graphical summary of some important features of a distribution, including its center; rough symmetry or skewness; overall spread and spread of the central portion of the data; rough behavior of the tails; and unusual observations. Boxplots for the education and income levels of the 102 Canadian occupations appear in Figure 2.4.

A boxplot is constructed from a five-number summary according to the following procedure:

1. Lay off a scale that accommodates the extremes of the batch.

2. Locate the median and hinges. Draw a box connecting the hinges; draw a line within the box to mark the median. Note that the length of the box is the hinge-spread. The mean, which need not appear in the central box, may optionally be marked with an $X$ or some other convenient symbol.

3. Two sets of *fences* are used to identify unusual values, but do not appear directly on the plot. Define a *step* as $1.5 \times H$-spread. Then the *inner fences* are located one step beyond the hinges

$$f_L = H_L - 1.5 \times H\text{–spread}$$

$$f_U = H_U + 1.5 \times H\text{–spread}$$

**(A)**

**(B)**

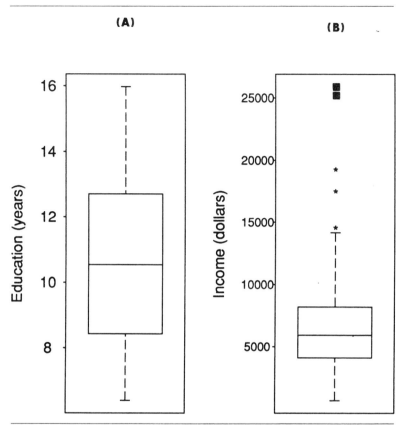

Figure 2.4  Boxplots for 102 Canadian occupations in 1971. (A) Mean education, (B) mean income.

and the *outer fences* are two steps beyond the hinges

$$F_L = H_L - 3 \times H\text{--spread}$$

$$F_U = H_U + 3 \times H\text{--spread}.$$

Values beyond the inner fences are termed *outside* and are shown
individually with asterisks; values beyond the outer fences are termed
*far outside* and are shown with filled squares. Of course, other pairs of

symbols, such as empty and filled circles, may also be used to mark outside and far-outside values.

4. On each side of the central box, draw a dotted line (called a *whisker*) either to the most extreme value on that side or to the most extreme value that is still inside the inner fence. This score is called the *adjacent value*.

A rough justification for the location of the fences is derived from the normal distribution. Here, $1.5 \times H$-spread $= 1.5 \times 1.349\sigma = 2.0235\sigma \simeq 2\sigma$. Thus, in the unit-normal distribution, the inner fences are located at $Z = \pm2.698$, and the outer fences at $Z = \pm4.698$ (recall that the quartiles are at $\pm0.675$). From a standard normal-distribution table, the area beyond $Z = 2.698$ is .00349, and beyond $Z = 4.698$ is about $3 \times 10^{-6}$. Because we want to identify unusual values in either tail, the expected proportion beyond the fences is twice these single-tail values: roughly 1/100 beyond the inner fences and 1/100,000 beyond the outer fences.

These calculations are for a theoretical normal distribution and require upward adjustment when applied to a finite sample, even one drawn from a normal population. More importantly, in a sample of $n$ independently drawn observations from a normal population, the *expected numbers* of outside and far-outside values are on the order of $n/100$ and $n/100,000$, respectively. Moreover, in a skewed or symmetric heavy-tailed distribution, these numbers would be much larger. Consequently, outside — and even far-outside — values are not necessarily "outliers," in the sense of not belonging with the rest of the data. These values are certainly worth a closer look, however, which is why they are displayed individually: Unusual data values are often interesting as well as potentially problematic.

Examining Figure 2.4A, the distribution of education seems reasonably symmetric, especially in its central portion where the hinges are roughly equidistant from the median. The longer upper whisker, however, indicates a slight positive skew in the tails. There are no outside values. Note that the multiple modes, which were discernible in the stem-and-leaf display (Figure 2.1), are missed by the boxplot. Figure 2.4B, the boxplot for income, shows the extreme asymmetry of the tails of the income distribution, though it also reveals that the central half of the data is not far from symmetric. There are three outside values (veterinarians, osteopaths and chiropractors, and lawyers and notaries), and two far-outside values (physicians and surgeons, and general managers and other senior officials). These outside values are, however, consistent with the positive skew of the distribution.

*References and Further Reading*

Letter-value displays, boxplots, and fences were introduced by Tukey (1972, 1977). Tukey, however, employed the term *schematic plot*, reserving boxplot for a simpler display in which the whiskers always extend to the extremes. Further discussion of many theoretical aspects of letter values may be found in Hoaglin (1983), including a justification of the simple rounding rule for finding letter-value depths; the use of fences for identifying unusual values; and the efficiency of letter-values in capturing distributional information. Particularly valuable and interesting treatments of variations in boxplots, including their use in comparing distributions across batches, may be found in Velleman and Hoaglin (1981), Emerson and Strenio (1983), McGill, Tukey, and Larsen (1978), and Benjamini (1988). Their compactness makes it possible to incorporate boxplots into other, more complex graphical displays such as the axes or margins of scatterplots: See, for example, Tufte (1983). Note that the rule developed in this section to identify outside values was employed (following Velleman & Hoaglin, 1981) in the first section to define high and low stems in stem-and-leaf displays.

## ONE-DIMENSIONAL SCATTERPLOTS AND INDEX PLOTS

The methods treated in this and the next section are distinguished from those in the remainder of the chapter in that they do not depend on arbitrary grouping or summarization of essentially continuous observations. One-dimensional scatterplots and index plots are the simplest displays considered here: They are, in effect, direct geometric representations of the data values.

A one-dimensional scatterplot is constructed by arraying points representing the observations along an axis. Illustrative plots for occupational education and income levels appear in Figure 2.5. When many data points coincide, or nearly coincide, interpretation of the plot is hampered. This problem is partly addressed by employing open circles or vertical lines as plotting symbols, rather than filled dots, as in Figures 2.5A and 2.5C. Even more separation is achieved by adding a small vertical random component (*jittering*) to each plotted point, a strategy employed in Figures 2.5B and 2.5D. When there are precisely replicated values, these can be stacked vertically as an alternative to jittering. If,

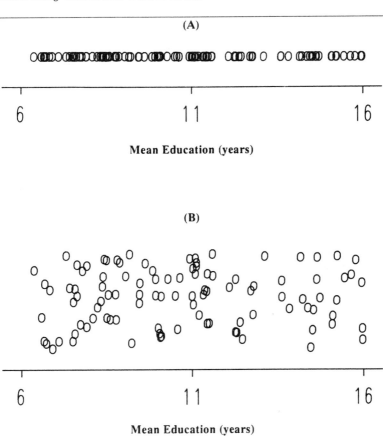

Figure 2.5 One-dimensional scatterplots for mean education (A and B) and mean income (C and D) of 102 Canadian occupations in 1971. The one-dimensional scatterplots in panels (B) and (D) are jittered vertically by a small random quantity.

of course, the variable in question is discrete, then the stacked plot is simply a histogram with the data values represented individually.

It is often difficult to extract distributional information from a one-dimensional scatterplot, but the display does a good job of revealing the range of the data and may show concentrations of values. The three modes of the education distribution are apparent in Figure 2.5 only after

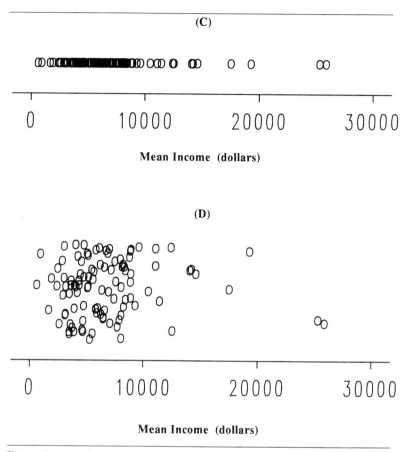

**Figure 2.5  continued**

close examination, and would likely have been missed had we not
looked first at the stem-and-leaf display of Figure 2.1. The skew of
income distribution is clear, however. Because of their compactness,
one-dimensional scatterplots may be used in the margins of other
displays, such as the density estimators discussed in the fifth section.

An index plot is a scatterplot of the values of a variable against the
observation index 1, 2, . . . , $n$, or against some other identifier, such as
a name or code. When the observations are ordered in time, index plots
are called *time series plots*, and data points are conventionally connected by line segments to suggest trend. Although they do not provide

Mean Income

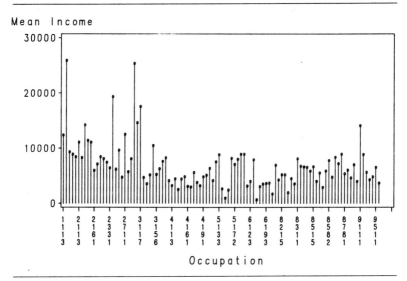

Occupation

**Figure 2.6   Index plot for mean income of 102 Canadian occupations in 1971.**

a good sense of distribution, index plots offer a useful link to the observations and are often helpful in conjunction with other displays in which the identity of the observations is lost.

An illustrative index plot for occupational income level is shown in Figure 2.6. The census code for every fifth observation appears below the horizontal axis. For a smaller data set, the observations could be ranked according to their scores, with an identifier displayed for each observation. Here the horizontal axis would become impossibly crowded unless the size of the plot were increased, and to rank the observations without showing all of the identifiers would render the plot uninformative. The vertical line to each point helps to connect the value of the observation to its index.

### References and Further Reading

One-dimensional scatterplots, jittering, and stacking are described by Chambers, Cleveland, Kleiner and Tukey (1983). Cleveland (1985) presents a thorough discussion of index plots, which he terms *dot charts*.

## QUANTILE AND QUANTILE-COMPARISON PLOTS

The methods of this section are based on the *empirical cumulative distribution function* (*ecdf*), which is defined by

$$\hat{F}(x) = \frac{\#(x_i \leq x)}{n}$$

where #(•) signifies a count. $\hat{F}(x)$ is thus a *stair-step* function, which is zero to the left of the smallest observation $x_{(1)}$, increases $1/n$ at each order statistic, and is one to the right of the largest observation $x_{(n)}$.

Although this definition of $\hat{F}(x)$ has the advantage of simplicity, it has the disadvantage of producing cumulative proportions of zero and one, which make it difficult to compare the *ecdf* to certain theoretical probability distributions, such as the normal distribution. An alternative is to define quantiles corresponding to each order statistic $x_{(i)}$ in such a manner as to avoid values of zero and one. We can, for example, "divide" each observation at its value, conventionally taking half the observation below and half above. This convention produces a cumulative proportion of $0.5/n$ at $x_{(1)}$; of $1.5/n$ at $x_{(2)}$, . . . , and of $(n - 0.5)/n$ at $x_{(n)}$. More generally, at the order statistic $x_{(i)}$, we have the proportion $f_i = (i - 0.5)/n$, so $x_{(i)}$ is the $f_i$ quantile of the data.

Defining quantiles corresponding to the order statistics $x_{(i)}$ by $f_i = (i - 1/2)/n$ is simple, but not the only reasonable possibility. Other common choices are $i/(n + 1)$, which corresponds to letting the order statistics dissect the $x$-line into $n + 1$ regions of equal probability; and $(i - 1/3)/(n + 1/3)$, which compromises between the two other rules, and which is justified by estimation considerations. The last rule also corresponds to the definition of letter values (the second section), which are selected quantiles.

Quantile plots for occupational education and income are shown in Figure 2.7. Steep regions of the plots correspond to concentrations of data values. A skew, in contrast, is represented by a long plateau in one tail, as in Figure 2.7B for income.

Quantile plots are very effective for locating the median, quartiles, and other quantiles of a distribution. It is also possible to use these plots for comparison by superimposing a reference theoretical cumulative distribution function on the observed quantiles. Comparison is better served, however, by plotting observed against theoretical quantiles, since this latter type of comparison does not require estimation of the

**(A)**

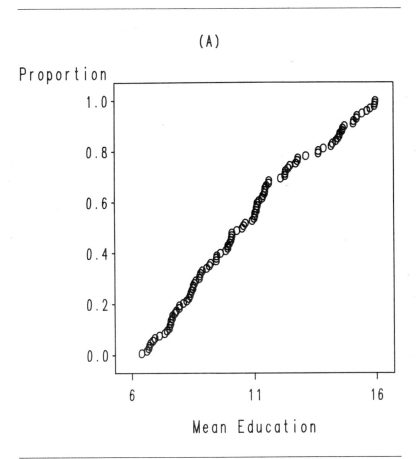

Figure 2.7 Quantile plots for 102 Canadian occupations in 1971.

parameters of the theoretical distribution (e.g., the mean and variance for a normal reference distribution).

Let $x_{(i)}$ give the order statistics of a sample, and $f_i = (i - 1/2)/n$ the corresponding conventional cumulative proportions, as before. Let $F(z)$ represent the comparison cumulative distribution function, usually the unit-normal distribution $N(0,1)$. Then $z_i = F^{-1}(f_i)$ is by definition the $f_i$ quantile of the comparison distribution. Graphing $x_i$ against $z_i$ completes the quantile-comparison plot. Note that the comparison distribution $F$ must be strictly increased to be invertible. By not grouping

(B)

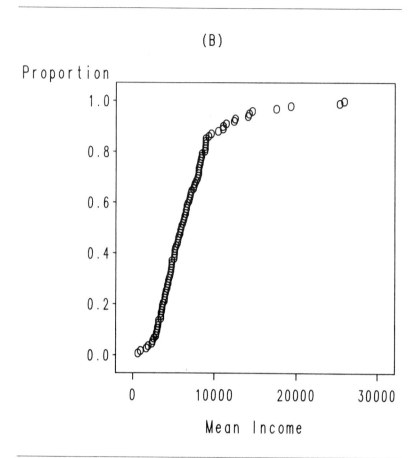

Figure 2.7  continued

observations into bins, the quantile-comparison plot retains information in the tails of the distribution, where data are generally sparse, but which are important for checks of distributional assumptions of classical methods of estimation.

If the $x_i$ are in fact drawn from the reference distribution $F$, then — within sampling error — the quantiles of the two distributions are the same, $x_{(i)} = z_i$, and the quantile-comparison plot is linear through the origin with a slope of one. If, alternatively, the two distributions differ only by a scale factor $\sigma$, then $x_{(i)} = \sigma z_i$, and the plot is still linear through the origin, but with slope $\sigma$. If the distributions differ only in location, then $x_{(i)} = \mu + z_i$, and the plot is linear with nonzero intercept $\mu$ and unit slope. Finally, if the distributions are identical in shape but differ in location and spread, then $x_{(i)} = \mu + \sigma z_i$.

A byproduct of these observations is that, when the comparison distribution $F$ is the unit-normal distribution, the intercept of the plot (given by the median of the $x$'s) estimates $\mu$, and the slope of a line fit to the plot estimates $\sigma$. A simple but effective estimate of slope is the hinge-spread of $x$ divided by the distance between the quartiles of the unit-normal distribution ($H$-spread/1.349), an estimator familiar from the second section.

Because linearity in the quantile-comparison plot is indicative of similarity in shape, departures from linearity represent differences in shape. Judging departures from linearity is assisted by plotting a reference line. A line may either be fit by eye, attending to the central portion of the data, or by estimating $\mu$ and $\sigma$ as explained above. Judgment can be further enhanced by plotting residuals from the linear fit (as in Figure 2.9 below).

Probability plots are, of course, subject to error: Even if the $X_i$ are a random sample from the distribution $F$, the relationship between $x_{(i)}$ and $z_i$ will not be perfectly linear. Estimated approximate standard errors for the quantiles of a sample from a normal distribution are given by

$$\hat{SE}(X_{(i)}) = \frac{\hat{\sigma}}{\phi(z_i)} \sqrt{\frac{f_i(1 - f_i)}{n}} \qquad (2.1)$$

where $\phi(\cdot)$ is the unit-normal density, and $\hat{\sigma}$, an estimate of the standard deviation of $X$, is the slope of the plot. Consequently, error indicators at $\hat{x}_{(i)} \pm 2 \times \hat{SE}$ assist in the interpretation of the quantile-comparison plot.

Some illustrations are given in Figure 2.8, for samples of size $n = 20$, 50, and 100 drawn from a normal distribution with mean 100 and standard deviation 10; for a sample of size $n = 100$ from the heavy tailed $t$-distribution with two degrees of freedom; and for a sample of size $n = 100$ from the positively skewed $\chi^2$ distribution with four degrees of freedom. In each case, the comparison distribution is the unit normal. Normal quantile-comparison plots for the occupational education and income data are given in Figures 2.9A and 2.9B. Departures from the

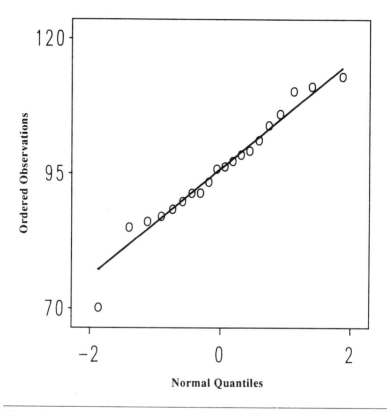

**Figure 2.8  Illustrative normal quantile-comparison plots. (A) A sample of size $n=10$ from $N(100, 10^2)$.**

linear fits are shown in the residual plots in panels C and D of Figure 2.9. The small plus signs in these graphs give two standard-error limits on each side of the fitted line. Note that education has shorter tails than a normal distribution, especially on the left, but the multiple modes are not clearly resolved in the plot. The positive skew in the income distribution is apparent.

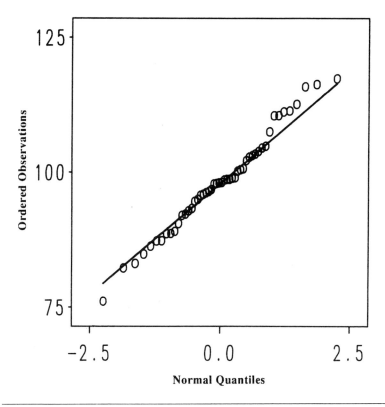

Figure 2.8   continued. (B) A sample of size *n* = 50 from *N* (100, 10²).

### *References and Further Reading*

Chambers et al. (1983) present a thorough discussion of quantile plots and of quantile-comparison plots, called *quantile-quantile plots*. The term *quantile-comparison plot* is adapted from Cleveland (1985), who employs *percentile-comparison plot*. Both Chambers et al. and Cleveland also show how quantile-comparison plots may be used to compare two empirical distributions, as opposed to comparing an empirical distribution with a theoretical reference distribution. An exten-

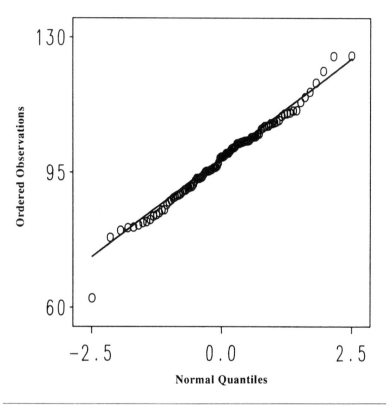

**Figure 2.8  continued. (C) A sample of size** $n$ **= 100 from** $N\,(100,\,10^2)$**.**

sive review of probability-plotting methods may be found in Wilk and Gnanadesikan (1968) and in Gnanadesikan (1977). Daniel and Wood (1980) present many examples of normal quantile-comparison plots for randomly generated data, which are useful for developing a sense of sampling variation in these displays; of course, readers can simply generate their own examples of this type. Equation (2.1) for the standard error of the observed quantiles of a sample from a normal distribution

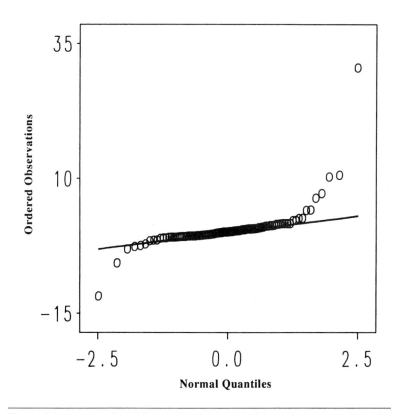

**Figure 2.8   continued. (D) A sample of size *n* = 100 from the heavy-tailed *t* (2).**

is adapted from Chambers et al. (1983), who take the basic result from Kendall and Stuart (1977).

Using $(i - 1/3)/(n + 1/3)$ to define quantiles corresponding to the order statistics was suggested by Anscombe and Tukey (1963) and by Tukey (1977). Hoaglin (1983) explains the connection between this rule and letter values, while Mage (1982) presents a detailed discussion of alternative rules.

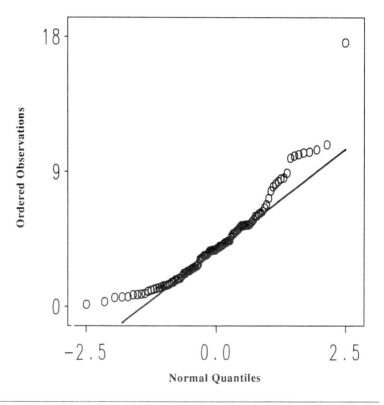

Figure 2.8 continued. (E) A sample of size $n$ = 100 from the positively skewed $\chi^2(4)$.

## DENSITY ESTIMATION (SMOOTHING HISTOGRAMS)

A distribution is more easily understood as a density function $f(x)$ than as a cumulative distribution function $F(x)$, since densities are the continuous analog of proportions. Formally, the density function is the derivative of the cumulative distribution function, so that areas under the density function

**(A)**

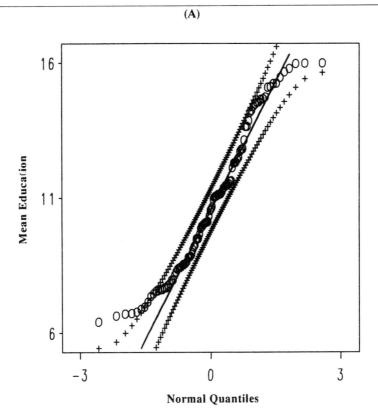

Figure 2.9 Normal quantile-comparison plots for mean education (A) and mean income (B) for 102 Canadian occupations in 1971. Residuals from the linear fits are given in panels (C) and (D). The small plus signs show two-standard-error limits around the fitted line.

$$\int_{x_0}^{x_1} f(x)\, dx = F(x_1) - F(x_0)$$

read off as probabilities, $\Pr(x_0 \leq X \leq x_1)$.

Because the *ecdf* for a sample is a discontinuous stair-step function, it is not suitable for directly estimating a smooth density. The methods developed in this section provide sample estimates of $f(x)$ that smooth

**(B)**

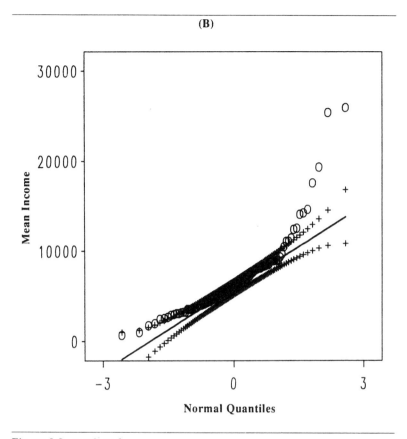

**Figure 2.9 continued**

out roughness and irregularities in the data. Alternatively, these methods can be construed as descriptive smoothers of the familiar histogram.

The histogram of a sample is a crude estimator of the probability density from which the sample is drawn. We define $m$ bins covering the data, each of width $2h$ and with origin $x_0$. Here, $h$ is the *half*-width of the bins to conform to the usage below. The end points of the bins are therefore

$$x_0, x_0 + 2h, x_0 + 4h, \ldots, x_0 + m(2h).$$

A particular observation[3] $X_i$ falls in bin $j$ if

**(C)**

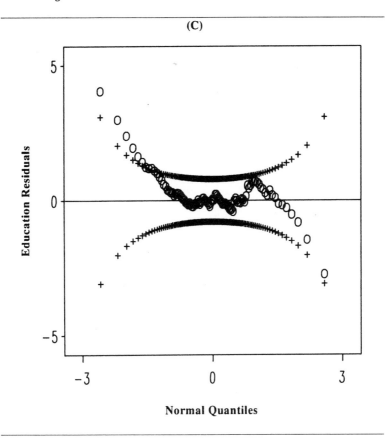

Figure 2.9  continued

$$x_0 + (j - 1)2h \leq X_i < x_0 + j(2h).$$

Note that an observation falling on a bin boundary is placed in the higher bin.

The *histogram density estimator* is given by

$$\hat{f}_H(x) = \frac{\#[x_{\hat{0}} + (j - 1)2h \leq X_i < x_0 + j(2h)]}{n(2h)}$$

for $x$ located in bin $j$. The numerator counts the number of observations in the bin, while dividing by $n(2h)$ ensures that the total area enclosed

**(D)**

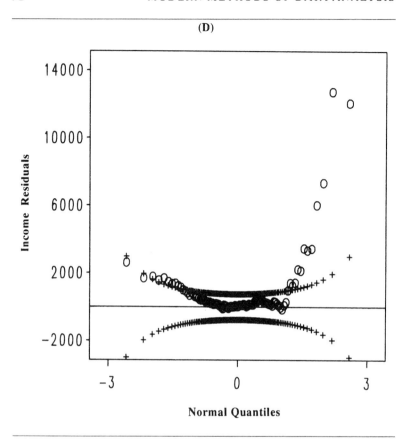

Figure 2.9  continued

by the histogram is one. In practice, we usually ignore the denominator, scaling the vertical axis so that the height of the bars represents frequency or percent.

There are several problems with the histogram as a density estimator or even as a simple descriptive representation of the distribution of a batch.

1. The result is dependent on the origin $x_0$. Consider, by way of example, the two histograms shown in Figure 2.10, for data on the infant mortality rates per 1,000 live births of 101 countries.[4] These histograms differ only in their origins: The bars of the histogram in Figure 2.10A are five units to the left of those in Figure 2.10B, but the bin width is

20 in both cases. Admittedly, $x_0 = -5$ in Figure 2.10A corresponds to a negative infant mortality rate, but this characteristic does not account for the differences between the two histograms. The two histograms convey different impressions of the distributions of infant mortality: Figure 2.10B, for instance, appears clearly bimodal, while the second mode in Figure 2.10A is less clearly defined. Sophisticated data analysts learn partly to discount chance variation in histograms, but naive consumers of statistical graphs are likely to fix on such characteristics. Drawing histograms with alternative origins can be a sobering exercise, however, even for relatively experienced researchers.

2. The histogram density estimator is discontinuous or rough, with jumps at the ends of most of the bins. These discontinuities are primarily a function of the arbitrary bin locations and the discreteness of the data rather than of the population that was sampled.

3. If the bins are narrow enough to capture detail where density is high, typically in the center of the distribution, they may be too narrow to avoid noise where density is low, typically in the tails. Although it is possible to employ variable-width bins, the resulting histograms are subject to misinterpretation, since the height and the area of the bars no longer are proportional: If, for example, bar height represents relative frequency, then bars for wide bins will have disproportionately large areas.

4. The result is dependent on the width of the bars: Recall the illustrations in the first section for stem-and-leaf displays.

In the remainder of this section, each of these problems will be addressed, producing successively more sophisticated — and generally adequate — density estimators.

The density may be thought of as the limit of a histogram bar, centered at $x$, as the half-width $h$ of the bar goes to zero:

$$f(x) = \lim_{h \to 0} \left[ \frac{1}{2h} Pr(x - h < X < x + h) \right].$$

A *simple density estimator* substitutes the sample proportion in a small region (called a *window*) around $x$ for the probability, scaling the estimate so that the total area under $\hat{f}(x)$ integrates to one:

$$\hat{f}_S(x) = \frac{1}{2h} \times \frac{\#(x - h < X_i < x + h)}{n}.$$

**(A)**

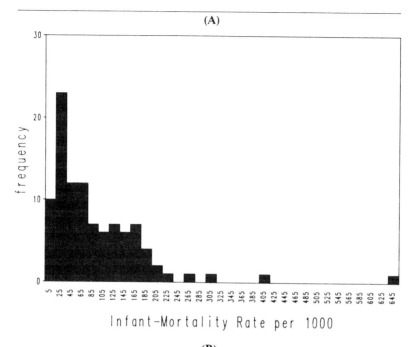

Infant-Mortality Rate per 1000

**(B)**

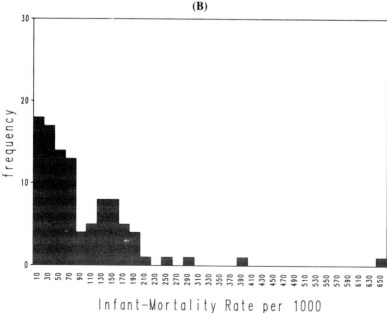

Infant-Mortality Rate per 1000

Figure 2.10   Two histograms for the infant-mortality rates of 101 countries circa 1970. (A) Origin $x_0 = -5$, (B) origin $x_0 = 0$.

SOURCE: Leinhardt and Wasserman (1979).

The simple estimator is, therefore, like a histogram using bins of width 2*h* but no fixed origin.

The simple estimator may also be written employing a *weight function S*:

$$\hat{f}_S(x) = \frac{1}{nh} \sum_{i=1}^{n} S\left[\frac{x - X_i}{h}\right]$$

(2.2)

$$\text{for } S(z) = \begin{cases} \frac{1}{2} \text{ if } |z| < 1 \\ 0 \text{ otherwise} \end{cases}.$$

Note that *z* simply represents the argument of the weight function. This alternative, and equivalent, definition will be useful below when we develop more sophisticated density estimators.

Figure 2.11 shows a simple density estimate for the infant mortality data. A one-dimensional scatterplot appears at the bottom of this figure. Although the simple estimator is rough, with a discontinuity as each data value $x_i$ enters the moving window, the two modes of the distribution show up clearly. Note that the density estimate has not descended to zero at $X = 0$: Were we to continue to the left, there would be nonzero estimates at negative infant mortality rates and, therefore, the portion of the graph shown does not enclose an area of one. In general, the simple density estimator integrates to one between $x_{(1)} - h$ and $x_{(n)} + h$; it provides zero density estimates outside of this range. The possibility of obtaining nonzero density estimates for impossible *X*-values, which is not usually a serious problem as long as our interest is descriptive, also characterizes the more sophisticated methods presented in this section.

As shown in equation 2.2, the simple estimator in effect sums equal-width rectangles centered at the observations $X_i$. The roughness of the estimator is produced by the square corners of the weight function *S*. The *kernel density estimator* smooths out the data by using rounded lumps rather than rectangles:

$$\hat{f}_K(x) = \frac{1}{nh} \sum_{i=1}^{n} K\left[\frac{x - X_i}{h}\right]$$

(2.3)

Density

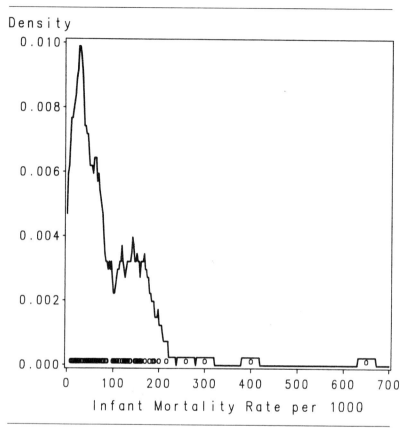

Figure 2.11  Simple density estimate for the distribution of infant mortality
           rates, window half-width $h = 10$. A one-dimenstional scatter-
           plot of the infant mortality rates of the 101 countries is shown
           at the bottom of the density estimate. The plotted discontinuit-
           ies are not quite vertical because the density estimate was
           evaluated only at a finite number of $x$-values.

where the *kernel function K* is some smooth, symmetric probability
density; thus

$$\int_{-\infty}^{\infty} K(z)\, dz = 1$$

ensuring that $\hat{f}(x)$ encloses an area of one.

In formal estimation of a density function $f(x)$, the *mean-squared error* of the estimator at a particular $x$ is defined by

$$\text{MSE}_x(\hat{f}) = E\left\{[\hat{f}(x) - f(x)]^2\right\}$$

and the *mean integrated* (i.e., total) *squared error* is

$$\text{MISE}(\hat{f}) = E\left[\int_{-\infty}^{\infty}[\hat{f}(x) - f(x)]^2\,dx\right]$$

$$\int f\,\text{MSE}_x(\hat{f})\,dx.$$

Let $\mu(x) = E[\hat{f}(x)]$. Then

$$\text{MSE}_x(\hat{f}) = E\left\{[\hat{f}(x) - \mu(x)]^2\right\} + [\mu(x) - f(x)]^2$$

$$= \text{Var}[\hat{f}(x)] + \left\{\text{bias}[f(x)]\right\}^2.$$

Consequently, MISE is the sum of integrated variance and integrated bias.

Intuitively, a good kernel function should minimize bias by assigning greater weight to observations close to the $x$ value at which the density is being estimated. A familiar choice of $K$ is the normal or Gaussian kernel $K_G$. Alternatively, minimizing MISE leads to the maximally efficient *Epanechinkov kernel*:

$$K_E(z) = \begin{cases} \dfrac{3}{4\sqrt{5}}\left[1 - \dfrac{z^2}{5}\right] & \text{for } |z| \le \sqrt{5} \\ 0 & \text{otherwise.} \end{cases}$$

The Gaussian kernel has 95% relative efficiency, however, and even a rectangular kernel, producing the simple density estimator, has 93% relative efficiency. These three kernels are compared in Figure 2.12. All of the kernel estimates in this chapter use the Gaussian kernel.

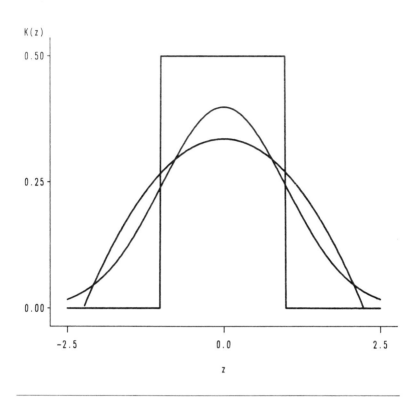

Figure 2.12   Comparison of the rectangular, Gaussian ("bell-shaped") and
Epanechinkov ("egg-shaped") kernels.

Figure 2.13 illustrates how the kernel estimate of equation 2.3 results
from summing individual kernels located at the observations. The
density estimates in this figure are calculated from an artificial "sample" of $n = 10$ observations: 6.9, 7.2, 7.3, 8.0, 9.0, 11.2, 11.4, 11.9, 12.0,
and 12.2. Of course, one would not in a real application calculate a
density estimate from so small a sample. The individual observations
appear in the one-dimensional scatterplot at the bottom of each density
estimate. The individual kernels, shown as light curves, are normal
distributions centered at the observations, each with standard deviation
$h$ and with height scaled down by the factor $1/n$. The density estimate,
shown as a heavy curve, simply sums the heights of the individual

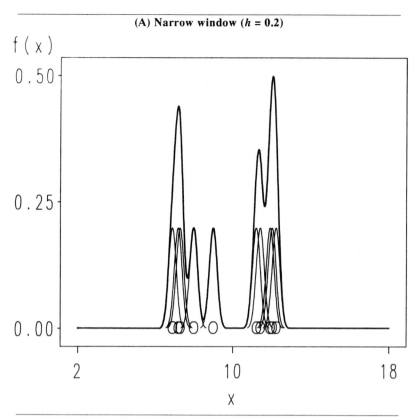

**(A) Narrow window ($h = 0.2$)**

Figure 2.13 How the kernel estimator works for an artificial, small sample
of size $n = 10$. The kernel estimate (heavy curve) sums the
individual kernels (light curves) centered at the observations.
The observations are shown as circles in the one-dimensional
scatterplot at the bottom of the display estimate. Note that for
clarity the vertical (density) scales are different in the three
graphs.

SOURCE: Adapted from Silverman, *Density Estimation*, 1986. With permission, Chapman & Hall.

kernels over each $x$ value. Note that the smoothness of the density
estimate varies directly with the window width, which is narrowest in
panel A and widest is panel C.

A kernel estimate for the infant mortality data appears in Figure 2.14.
The lumps to the right are images of the kernel centered at unusually

**(B) Medium window ($h = 0.8$)**

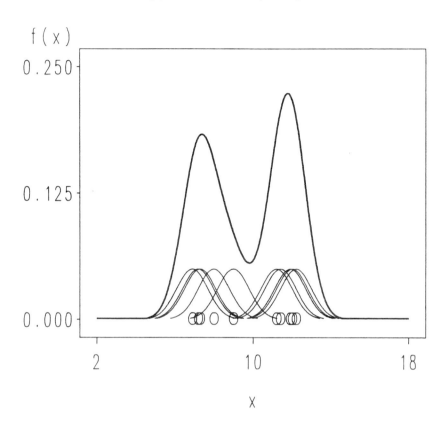

Figure 2.13   continued

large observations; this lumpiness demonstrates that the kernel estimator does not solve the problem of fixed widow width.

The *adaptive kernel estimator* adjusts the window width so that it is narrower where the density is high and wider where density is low, thus retaining detail where data are plentiful and eliminating noise where they are sparse. Since we do not know $f(x)$ beforehand — if we did, there would be no problem of estimation — it is necessary to start with a preliminary density estimate, such as that provided by the fixed kernel method, $\hat{f}_K(x)$. Then, evaluating this initial estimate at each observation

**(C) Wide window (*h* = 1.8)**

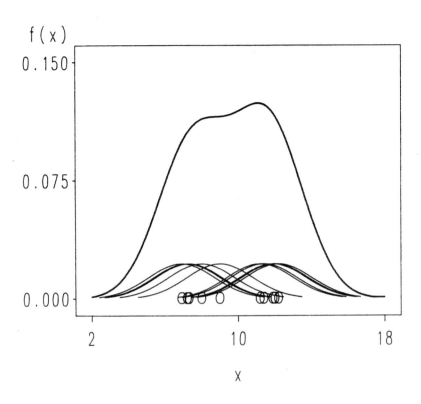

**Figure 2.13  continued**

$X_i$, calculate *local window factors* $w_i$ that are inversely related to density:

$$w_i = \left[ \frac{\tilde{f}_g}{\hat{f}_k(X_i)} \right]^{1/2}$$

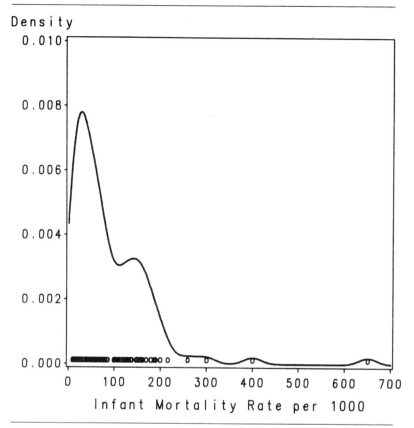

Figure 2.14  Kernel density estimate for the distribution of infant mortality rates, window half-width $h = 20$.

where $$\tilde{f}_g = \left[ \prod_{i=1}^{n} \hat{f}_K(X_i) \right]^{1/n}$$

is the geometric mean of the $\hat{f}(X_i)$, and thus the weights have a product and geometric mean of one. Using the weights, calculate the adaptive-kernel estimator:

$$\hat{f}_A(x) = \frac{1}{nh} \sum_{i=1}^{n} \frac{1}{w_i} K \left[ \frac{x - X_i}{w_i h} \right].$$

Note that applying the weights to $h$ produces a geometric-mean window half-width of $h$. The factor $1/w_i$ is required to adjust for varying window width, ensuring that the total area under the density estimate is one. Although this process can be iterated, using $\hat{f}_A$ to recalculate weights, iteration generally produces little change in the estimated density.

An adaptive-kernel estimate for the infant-mortality data is shown in Figure 2.15. Compared with the fixed-kernel estimate (Figure 2.14), using a similar average window width, the adaptive estimator shows more asymmetry and greater separation of the modes; the unusual observations to the right are smoothed out into a long tail.

The determination of window width remains arbitrary, but some guidance can be provided by statistical theory. A wide window produces small variance because many values are averaged and atypical data are smoothed out, but relatively large bias if, as is typical, values are averaged over a nonlinear portion of the density — an extreme example is a discontinuity. The trick is to pick $h$ so that the trade-off of bias against variance is favorable. It is generally not possible to optimize the window width without knowledge of the shape of the underlying density. Of course, if we knew the shape of the distribution, we would prefer to estimate the density parametrically.

The following method, for a Gaussian kernel, is based on minimizing the MISE for an underlying normal density, with some adjustment for robustness. The method works reasonably well for other distributions, however, as long as they are not highly skewed and do not have widely separated modes; in these cases, too large a value of $h$ is provided, resulting in over-smoothing — for example, loss of separation of multiple modes or loss of detail in the portion of the distribution opposite the skew.

Let

$$s = \min \left[ \left[ \frac{\sum (x_i - \bar{x})^2}{n - 1} \right]^{1/2}, \frac{H\text{-spread}}{1.349} \right]$$

and set

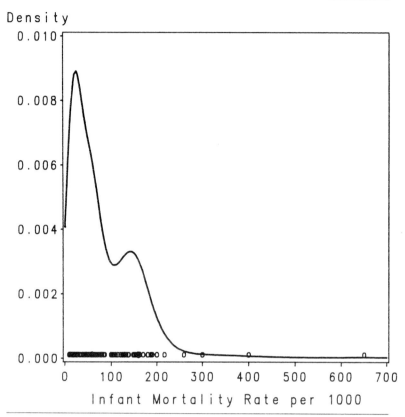

**Figure 2.15** Adaptive-kernel density estimate for the distribution of infant mortality, (average) window half-width $h$ = 20.

$$h = \frac{0.9s}{n^{1/5}}. \qquad (2.4)$$

Note that $s$ is the smaller of two estimates of $\sigma$ in a normal distribution: the usual estimate and one based on the hinge-spread (and familiar from Section 2). The estimator $S$, consequently, is reasonably efficient for a normal distribution, but robust against heavier tails than in the normal distribution. The window half-width $h$ is proportional to the scale of the data $s$, as is sensible, and declines slowly with increasing sample size.

Applied to the infant mortality data, which are skewed and bimodal, equation 2.4 produced a window half-width of $h = 27.7$. The corresponding adaptive-kernel estimate, shown in Figure 2.16, appears over-smooth compared with that produced by the narrower $h = 20$ (Figure 2.15).

A reasonable general procedure is to start with the window determined by equation 2.4, adjusting this value impressionistically, usually downward, until a reasonable balance of smoothness and detail is achieved: Select the smallest window width that does not produce unacceptable roughness in the estimated density. Figure 2.17 shows some adaptive kernel estimates for the occupational education and income data discussed earlier. The multiple modes of the education distribution and the skewness of the income distribution both suggest window widths smaller than optimal for a normal density. The three modes of the education distribution show up clearly in the display. The skewness of the income distribution is also clear, and there is a suggestion of bimodality (see also the stem-and-leaf displays for income and education in Figures 2.1 and 2.2).

### References and Further Reading

The presentation in this section owes a substantial debt to Silverman (1986) who gives an excellent general account of nonparametric density estimation. Briefer general sources are Wegman (1972) and Tarter and Kronmal (1976). These treatments give more theoretical detail than is found in this section. The weight function for the adaptive kernel and the rule for determining window width is adapted from Silverman, who uses the term *window width* for my *half width*. These sources also describe other methods for adapting to varying data density, including so-called *nearest-neighbor* estimators, which base the density estimate at each $x$ on a constant fraction of the data closest to that $x$. There are also other methods for selecting window width and for dealing with bounded data, such as the infant mortality rates, which are bounded by zero and 1,000.

## TRANSFORMATIONS

Transformation or re-expression of variables serves several important purposes in data analysis, including producing approximate sym-

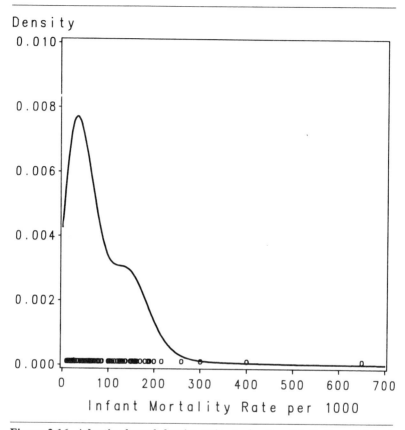

Figure 2.16  **Adaptive-kernel density estimate for the distribution of infant mortality, using the "optimal" window size for Gaussian data, $h = 27.7$.**

metry in a univariate distribution, the focus of the present section; equalizing spreads prior to comparing levels across several batches; linearizing relationships between variables; and eliminating interactions. These goals, indeed, often coincide. After introducing the family of power transformations, I shall discuss how these transformations may be employed to make a skewed distribution more symmetric. Finally, I shall briefly consider transformations of proportions and percents.

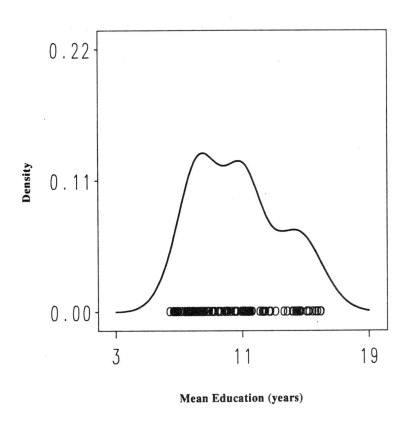

(A)

Window Width *h* = 0.974

Mean Education (years)

**Figure 2.17** Adaptive-kernel density estimates for mean education and mean income of 102 Canadian occupations in 1971. For each variable, the density estimate employing the "optimal" window half-width *h* for Gaussian data appears first.

In transforming a variable, we replace the variable with some generally smooth function of it: $X' = g(X)$. A particularly flexible and useful family of transformations is the *ladder of powers and roots*:

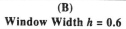

**(B)**
**Window Width $h = 0.6$**

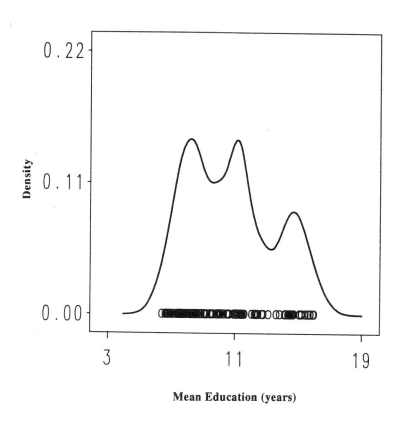

**Mean Education (years)**

**Figure 2.17   continued**

$$
X_p = \begin{cases} \dfrac{X^p - 1}{p} & p \neq 0 \\[3mm] \log_e X & p = 0. \end{cases} \tag{2.5}
$$

Generally, $p$ is a small integer ($-2$, $-1$, $0$, $2$, or $3$) or $\pm 1/2$. Some of these transformations are graphed (along with no transformation, $p = 1$) in

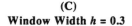

**(C)**
**Window Width $h$ = 0.3**

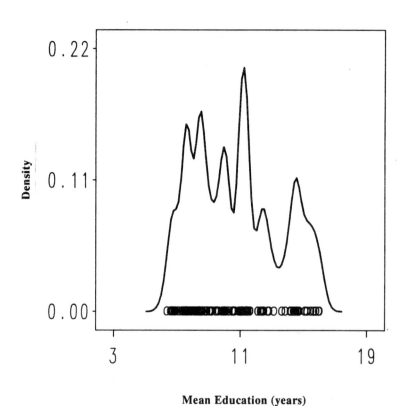

**Mean Education (years)**

---

**Figure 2.17 continued**

Figure 2.18. Note that all of the curves intersect at the point (1,0) and that each has slope one at this point. The zero power, $X^0 = 1$, is not a useful transformation, but the very useful log function fits well into the family of powers, since

$$\lim_{p \to 0} \frac{X^p - 1}{p} = \log_e X .$$

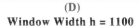

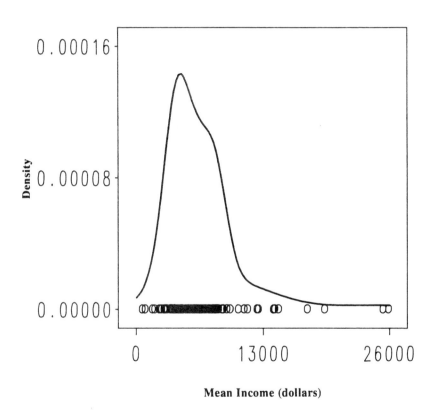

Figure 2.17  continued

Subtracting one and dividing by $p$ is inessential in equation 2.5 because these operations merely change the unit and origin of the transformed scores, though the operations are useful for depicting the unity of the family of power transformations as in Figure 2.18. Dividing

**(E)**
**Window Width h = 700**

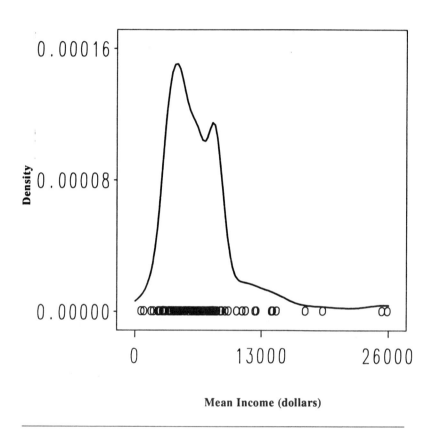

**Mean Income (dollars)**

**Figure 2.17 continued**

by *p* preserves the order of the scores when *p* is negative. Likewise, the base of the log function does not influence the shape of the transformed data. Consequently, we usually use

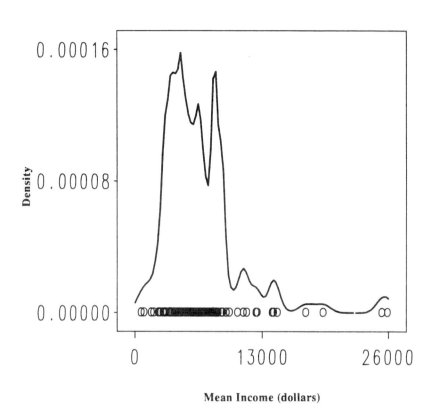

**(F)**
**Window Width h = 300**

Mean Income (dollars)

Figure 2.17   continued

$$X_p = \begin{cases} X^p & & p > 0 \\ \log_{10} X & or \quad \log_2 X & p = 0 \\ -X^p & & p < 0 \end{cases}.$$

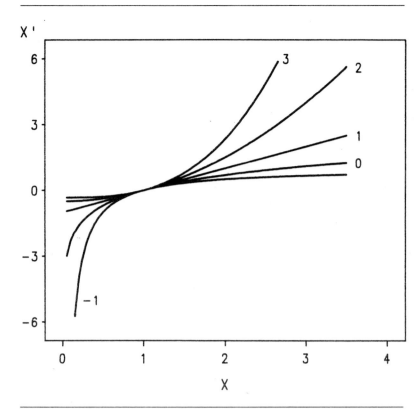

**Figure 2.18  Some members of the family of power transformations. The curve labeled "*p*" is $X' = (X^p - 1)/p$; $p = 0$ is $X' = \log_e X$.**

SOURCE: Adapted from Hoaglin, Mosteller, & Tukey (Eds.), *Understanding Robust and Esploratory Data Analysis.* Copyright © 1983, John Wiley & Sons. Reprinted by permission of John Wiley & Sons, Inc.

Logarithms to base 10 read off in powers of 10, and hence have some familiarity; logs to base 2 are often easily interpretable since an increase of one unit on the log scale represents doubling of the untransformed scores. The minus sign for negative *p* ensures that the order of *X* values is preserved.

Some simple examples are shown in Table 2.4A. Note that large scores are differentially spread out relative to small ones by transformations up the ladder (toward $X^2$), while small scores are spread out more than large ones by transformations down the ladder (toward log *X*).

**Table 2.4 Illustrative Transformations**

(A) Some power transformations.

| $-1/X$ | $\log_{10} X$ | $\leftarrow$ | $X$ | $\rightarrow$ | $X^2$ | $X^3$ |
|---|---|---|---|---|---|---|
| $-1$ | 0 | | 1 | | 1 | 1 |
| $\}1/2^a$ | $\}.30$ | | $\}1$ | | $\}3$ | $\}7$ |
| $-1/2$ | .30 | | 2 | | 4 | 8 |
| $\}1/6$ | $\}.18$ | | $\}1$ | | $\}5$ | $\}19$ |
| $-1/3$ | .48 | | 3 | | 9 | 27 |
| $\}1/12$ | $\}.12$ | | $\}1$ | | $\}7$ | $\}37$ |
| $-1/4$ | .60 | | 4 | | 16 | 64 |
| $\}1/20$ | $\}.10$ | | $\}1$ | | $\}9$ | $\}61$ |
| $-1/5$ | .70 | | 5 | | 25 | 125 |

(B) Descending the ladder of powers to correct a positive skew, pulling in the right tail.

| $X$ | $\rightarrow$ | $\log_{10} X$ |
|---|---|---|
| 1 | | 0 |
| $\}9$ | | $\}1$ |
| 10 | | 1 |
| $\}90$ | | $\}1$ |
| 100 | | 2 |
| $\}900$ | | $\}1$ |
| 1000 | | 3 |

(C) Ascending the ladder of powers to correct a negative skew, pulling in the left tail.

| $X$ | $\rightarrow$ | $X^2$ |
|---|---|---|
| 1.000 | | 1 |
| $\}.414$ | | $\}1$ |
| 1.414 | | 2 |
| $\}.318$ | | $\}1$ |
| 1.732 | | 3 |
| $\}.268$ | | $\}1$ |
| 2.000 | | 4 |

NOTE: [a]The interlinear numbers give the differences between adjacent scores.

To correct a positive skew, therefore, we need to descend the ladder, pulling in the right tail (as in Table 2.4B); to correct a negative skew, we need to ascend the ladder, pulling in the left tail (Table 2.4C).

In applying power transformations, two additional considerations must be kept in mind. First, for the power transformations to be monotone (i.e., to preserve order), the untransformed scores must be all positive. If necessary, we can add a constant, called a *start*, to the data values prior to transforming them (as in Table 2.5A). Second, for power transformations to be effective, the ratio of the largest to the smallest data value must be fairly big, a property that also can be ensured by adjusting the origin of the untransformed scores. See Table 2.5B, where −1970 is employed as a start to produce an effective transformation: Prior to using the start, the ratio of largest to smallest scores is $1975/1971 = 1.002 \simeq 1$; afterwards, this ratio is $5/1 = 5$.

Why should we prefer symmetric distributions? Most estimators of location, including most robust estimators, perform better when applied to symmetric data. By extension, this comment applies as well to regression estimators, though here it is the error distribution that is in question, that is, the conditional distribution of the dependent variable given the values of the independent variables. In fact, it is not obvious what is meant by the location or center of a skewed distribution. Even in a descriptive, univariate context, asymmetry causes poor resolution in the portion of the distribution containing most of the data, since much of the scale of the variable is devoted to the skewed tail.

A frequent negative by-product of transformation, however, is that we lose familiar units, such as dollars and years. At times, the transformed units are directly interpretable; for example, the inverse of distance traveled in a given amount of time is the time required to cover a unit of distance. More commonly, however, transformed values are not directly interpretable: log-dollars, for example. In the latter instance, we may show the original units on displays of the data (e.g., dollars of income as well as log income) or may even prefer the untransformed scale, especially if the scores are not severely skewed. Selecting a scale on which to analyze or present data involves both formal and substantive considerations. Moreover, not every distribution can be rendered approximately symmetric by a power transformation. See, for example, the discussion below of proportions, percents, and rates.

Recall that the letter values of a batch (the second section) provide a useful diagnostic for skewness: An upward trend in the midsummaries indicates positive skew; a downward trend, negative skew. Because power transformations preserve order, the order statistics of a transformed batch maintain their positions; that is, $(X^p)_{(i)} = (X_{(i)})^p$. Consequently, we can simply transform the letter values without returning to the original data.[5]

Table 2.6 shows midsummaries for the original and transformed letter values of the infant mortality data discussed in the fifth section. Because the distribution is positively skewed, we need only examine transformations down the ladder of powers and roots. The log transformation appears to work well, though the pattern of the midsummaries

**Table 2.5  Using Starts for Power Transformations**

(A) To make all scores positive prior to transformation (start = 3).

| $X$ | → | $X^2$ | $(X + 3)^2$ |
|---|---|---|---|
| −2 | | 4 | 1 |
| −1 | | 1 | 4 |
| 0 | | 0 | 9 |
| 1 | | 1 | 16 |
| 2 | | 4 | 25 |

(B) To ensure an effective transformation by increasing the ratio of the largest to the smallest score (start = −1970)

| $X$ | → | $\sqrt{X}$ | $\sqrt{X - 1970}$ |
|---|---|---|---|
| 1971 | | 44.3959 | 1.000 |
| | | }.0113 | }.414 |
| 1972 | | 44.4072 | 1.414 |
| | | }.0113 | }.318 |
| 1973 | | 44.4185 | 1.732 |
| | | }.0113 | }.268 |
| 1974 | | 44.4297 | 2.000 |
| | | }.0113 | }.236 |
| 1975 | | 44.4410 | 2.236 |

for log $X$ suggests a slight negative skew up to $D$ and a slight positive skew thereafter. Here, the square-root transformation fails to correct the positive skew, while inverse square-root overcorrects and produces a negative skew. An adaptive-kernel density estimate for the log-transformed data is shown in Figure 2.19. Three modes now appear in the density plot: a mode slightly to the right of one, corresponding to an infant mortality rate somewhat in excess of 10 on the original scale; a mode to the left of two, corresponding to 100 on the original scale; and another mode to the right of two. The density estimate on the original scale (Figure 2.15) failed to resolve the first two modes. The three groupings of observations are also discernible in the one-dimensional scatterplot at the bottom of the density estimate in Figure 2.19. Note as well that there is no longer a substantial nonzero density estimate at the far left of the graph: Log transformations are frequently useful for data bounded below by zero but unbounded above.[6]

Variables that are bounded below, such as frequency counts and other intrinsically nonnegative quantities, often are positively skewed. Vari-

**Table 2.6 Midsummaries Corresponding to Original and Transformed Letter Values of the Infant-Mortality Rates of 101 Countries**

| Letter Values | Depth | Midsummaries | | | |
|---|---|---|---|---|---|
| | | $X$ | $\sqrt{X}$ | $\log_{10}X$ | $-1/\sqrt{X}$ |
| M | 51 | 60.60 | 7.785 | 1.782 | −0.1284 |
| H | 26 | 77.55 | 8.222 | 1.761 | −0.1426 |
| E | 13.5 | 91.50 | 8.493 | 1.722 | −0.1609 |
| D | 7 | 106.40 | 8.860 | 1.704 | −0.1751 |
| C | 4 | 135.15 | 9.728 | 1.733 | −0.1798 |
| B | 2.5 | 180.08 | 10.947 | 1.775 | −0.1837 |
| A | 1.5 | 267.42 | 13.026 | 1.857 | −0.1811 |
| | 1 | 329.80 | 14.297 | 1.898 | −0.1810 |
| | Trend | ++ | + | 0[−/+] | − |

ables that are bounded both above and below frequently stack up against both boundaries, a condition that does not respond to power transformation. The most common examples are proportions, percents, and rates of incidence; counts, such as test scores, that are bounded above as well as below are disguised proportions and behave similarly.

The stem-and-leaf display in Figure 2.20A, for example, shows the distribution of percent of female incumbents for 102 Canadian occupations, the data for which appeared in Table 2.1. Note that there are many occupations with a very small percentage of women; there are also more occupations with relatively many women than with intermediate percentages.

*Folded logs and roots* often serve to improve the distributional behavior of proportions:

$$\text{Folded-Root}(X) = \sqrt{X} - \sqrt{1-X}$$

$$\text{Folded-Log}(X) = \log X - \log(1-X) = \log\left[\frac{X}{1-X}\right].$$

The folded-log transformation, also and more commonly called the *logit*, is therefore the log of the *odds* $X/(1-X)$. Although the base is irrelevant to the shape of the logit transformation, logs to base two permit relatively easy interpretation, since increasing the logit by one corresponds to doubling the odds. Proportions of $X = 1/2$ translate into

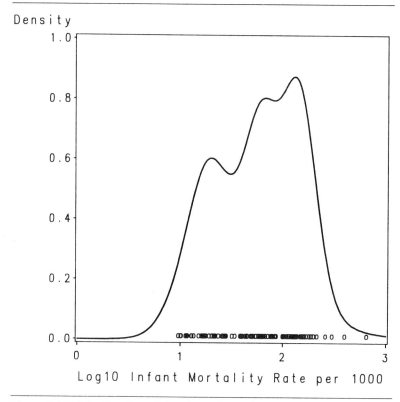

**Figure 2.19** Adaptive-kernel density estimate for the distribution of $\log_{10}$ infant mortality, window half-width $h = 0.15$.

scores of zero for both folded transformations. Since both division by zero and the log of zero are undefined, we need to make special arrangements for data that include proportions of zero or one. A simple device is to replace proportions of zero and one by, say, .001 and .999, or to add a small quantity, say, 1/2, to each of the original frequencies from which the proportions were calculated.

Stem-and-leaf displays for folded-root and logit transformations of the occupational gender-compositional data appear in Figures 2.20B and 2.20C. Both transformations serve to spread out the extremes of the distribution relative to the middle. Here, the logit transformation appears to be more effective.

**(A) Original (untransformed) data**

```
n = 102
Leaf Unit = 1.0
1 | 2 = 12

depth
 44   0 | 0000000000000011111122223333444455556667777899
(15)   1 | 011113335557779
 43   2 | 134457
 37   3 | 0133499
 30   4 | 678
 27   5 | 12467
 22   6 | 3789
 18   7 | 0245667
 11   8 | 233
  8   9 | 01256667
```

**(B) Folded-root transformation**

```
n = 102
Leaf Unit = 0.10
1 | 2 = 1.2

depth
  5  -1* | 00000
 25  -0. | 99999998888888888888
 48  -0s | 7777777777777666666666
(12) -0f | 555555544444
 42  -0t | 3333322222
 32  -0* | 11000
 27   0* | 000011
 21   0t | 2223333333
 11   0f | 455
  8   0s | 6667777
  1   0. | 8
```

**(C) Folded-log₁₀ (logit) transformation**

```
n = 102
Leaf Unit = 0.10
1 | 2 = 1.2

depth
  5  -2. | 99999
 12  -2* | 2111100
 24  -1. | 999987766555
 42  -1* | 444433332222211000
(19) -0. | 999888887777766655
 41  -0* | 444433222211000
 27   0* | 00012333344
 15   0. | 55556679
  7   1* | 013444
  1   1. | 6
```

**Figure 2.20 Stem-and-leaf displays for the distribution of percentage of women in 102 Canadian occupations, 1971.**

119

*References and Further Reading*

The family of powers and roots, including the log function, has a long history of applications in statistics. Box and Cox (1964), for example, use maximum-likelihood methods to select a power transformation of the dependent variable in regression. Box and Tidwell (1962) employ a similar approach to selecting linearizing transformations of independent variables in regression. The term *ladder of powers* is from Tukey (1977), who, along with colleagues, has frequently contributed to the study of transformations (Anscombe & Tukey, 1955; Tukey, 1949, 1957; Tukey & Mosteller, 1977). Emerson and Stoto (1982, 1983) and Emerson (1983) present interesting general treatments of transformations, including a variety of diagnostic displays. Also see Leinhardt and Wasserman (1979).

Folded roots and folded logs are also discussed by Tukey (1977); he called them *froots* and *flogs*. The *arcsine (inverse sine)* transformation is also used in this context, $X' = \text{arcsine } \sqrt{X}$, as is the *probit (inverse cumulative normal)* transformation $X' = \Phi^{-1}(X)$, where $\Phi(\cdot)$ is the unit-normal cumulative distribution function. Logits are now the most common scale on which to analyze probabilities associated with binary data (see, e.g., Fox, 1984).

## NOTES ON COMPUTATION

Most statistical software packages provide some version of the stem-and-leaf display and boxplot, but quality varies. In contrast, letter-value displays are relatively rare. Minitab deserves special mention here because it incorporates the exploratory-data-analysis routines from Velleman and Hoaglin (1981).

One-dimensional scatterplots, index plots, quantile plots, and quantile-comparison plots are easily constructed with standard statistical software. All that is required are facilities for sorting and transforming data; calculating cumulative normal probabilities; and drawing scatterplots and line graphs. Many programs provide these plots directly or incorporate functions that make their construction particularly simple. Some care is required in interpreting quantile and quantile-comparison plots because there is no universal convention about the roles of the axes. BMDP, for example, constructs quantile-comparison plots with normal quantiles on the vertical, rather than the horizontal, axis. All

usable statistical packages incorporate extensive facilities for transforming data.

Sygraph (from Systat), Statgraphics, Stata, and the *S* statistical programming language have particularly impressive statistical graphics
capabilities. Along with *S*, which has many preprogrammed graphical
displays, GAUSS and *APL* are powerful and convenient programming
languages for statistical applications, including graphics.

Kernel density estimation, unfortunately, has not to my knowledge
found its way into any widely distributed statistical computer package.
Nevertheless, the methods discussed in this chapter are easily programmed, either in a general-purpose programming language, or in the
macro languages provided by some statistical software (such as SAS).
Macro execution tends to be slow, however. The fixed-kernel estimator,
for example, may be implemented simply by evaluating equation 2.3
for enough $x$-values to produce a good graph. The plotted points then
may be connected by a method such as spline interpolation (see Chapter 3, this volume). Computation may be speeded by including at each
$x$ only those data values $X_i$ for which the kernel function $K$ is nonzero
or, for the Gaussian kernel, substantially larger than zero. This naive
approach, which can also be applied to the adaptive-kernel estimator,
is practical and reasonably convenient on a fast computer in an efficient
programming language even for $n$ of several thousand. Because the
kernel estimator is a simple convolution of the kernel function with the
data, Fourier methods can be employed to reduce computation substantially. These methods make the kernel estimator feasible for very large
$n$ (see Silverman, 1986, for details). The Fourier approach is sadly not
applicable to the adaptive kernel. The advantage of the adaptive-kernel
over the fixed-kernel method is less pronounced, however, when $n$ is
large because the window width can be made small. Indeed, for very
large $n$, even a histogram will produce a fairly smooth density estimate.

Computations for this chapter were done mostly in *APL*, and partly
with Minitab, SAS, *S*, and SST. Most of the graphs were produced by
SAS/GRAPH, many from *APL* output.

## SOME RECOMMENDATIONS

Stem-and-leaf displays and boxplots are good initial graphs for data
exploration. These displays are quickly constructed and they complement each other nicely: The stem-and-leaf display conveys an impres-

sion of distributional shape, while the boxplot highlights center, spread, skew, and unusual values. For more than about 200 observations, a histogram or density estimate may be substituted for the stem-and-leaf display. Index plots are also helpful for small- to moderate-size samples, and are especially useful when the identity of the observations is meaningful to the researcher. One-dimensional scatterplots often work best in the margins of other displays, such as density estimates.

Letter-value displays are particularly helpful in selecting a monotone transformation to symmetry. Their utility in this context derives partly from the property that the letter values of the transformed batch are simply the transformed letter values.

Quantile plots are typically more useful in data presentation than in data analysis. Quantile-comparison plots, in contrast, are of great value for comparing an empirical to a theoretical distribution because they are capable of highlighting tail behavior, which is frequently problematic. The other displays presented here, with the exception of the letter values, lose information in the tails and are more subject to random fluctuation. Random variation is a potential problem for the interpretation of quantile-comparison plots as well, but it is partially accommodated through the reference distribution: Outliers, for example, stand out not merely as values that are larger or smaller than the rest, but as values that are larger or smaller than expected on the basis of the reference distribution. As we have seen, it is also possible to include information on sampling error in the display.

Of all of methods presented in this chapter, density estimation best captures distributional shape and most clearly presents the distribution as a whole. Disadvantages of the technique include its computational complexity; the potential loss of detail, which is balanced against noise; and the necessity of selecting an essentially arbitrary window width. The last two problems are shared with other histogram-based displays. Paradoxically, although density estimation is a relatively complex method, it produces a good display for data presentation.

It would, finally, be unfortunate to convey the impression that the data displays considered in this chapter are competitors. Each provides a different view of the data, and different views are often complementary.

## NOTES

1. I shall use neutral terms such as *batch* or *data* when I do not wish to imply that the data are an independent sample from some population.

2. These data are drawn from research reported in Fox and Suschnigg (1988). The prestige data were collected by Pineo and Porter (1967) for occupational titles differing slightly from those employed in the Census. I am grateful to Bernard Blishen, William Carroll, and Catherine Moore for sharing the prestige data with me, including the link between Pineo and Porter's occupational titles and those in the Census.

3. Here $X_i$ represents the random observation, which varies from sample to sample, while $x_i$ represents a fixed value in a particular sample.

4. These data are from Leinhardt and Wasserman's (1979) paper on exploratory data analysis. Note that several nations have unreasonably large recorded values of infant mortality. The value for Jamaica (26.2) was misprinted in Leinhardt and Wasserman and is corrected here.

5. This property holds precisely for letter values that correspond to order statistics, but only approximately for letter values that average between adjacent order statistics.

6. As a rate per 1,000, infant mortality is bounded above as well as below (see the following discussion), but while there are many scores close to zero, none approaches 1,000.

## REFERENCES

Anscombe, F. J., & Tukey, J. W. (1955). The criticism of transformations. *Journal of the American Statistical Association, 50*, 566.

Anscombe, F. J., & Tukey, J. W. (1963). The examination and analysis of residuals. *Technometrics, 5*, 141-160.

Benjamini, Y. (1988). Opening the box of a boxplot. *American Statistician, 42*, 257-262.

Box, G.E.P., & Cox, D. R. (1964). An analysis of transformations. *Journal of the Royal Statistical Society, Series B, 26*, 211-252.

Box, G.E.P., & Tidwell, P. W. (1962). Transformation of the independent variables. *Technometrics, 4*, 521-550.

Chambers, J. M., Cleveland, W. S., Kleiner, B., & Tukey, P. A. (1983). *Graphical methods for data analysis.* Belmont, CA: Wadsworth.

Cleveland, W. S. (1985). *The elements of graphing data.* Monterey, CA: Wadsworth.

Daniel, C., & Wood, F. S. (1980). *Fitting equations to data* (2nd ed). New York: John Wiley.

Emerson, J. D. (1983). Mathematical aspects of transformation. In D. C. Hoaglin, F. Mosteller, & J. W. Tukey (Eds.), *Understanding robust and exploratory data analysis.* New York: John Wiley.

Emerson, J. D., & Hoaglin, D. C. (1983). Stem-and-leaf displays. In D. C. Hoaglin, F. Mosteller, & J. W. Tukey (Eds.), *Understanding robust and exploratory data analysis.* New York: John Wiley.

Emerson, J. D., & Stoto, M. A. (1982). Exploratory methods for choosing power transformations. *Journal of the American Statistical Association, 77,* 103-108.

Emerson, J. D., & Stoto, M. A. (1983). Transforming data. In D. C. Hoaglin, F. Mosteller, & J. W. Tukey (Eds.), *Understanding robust and exploratory data analysis.* New York: John Wiley.

Emerson, J. D., & Strenio, J. (1983). Boxplots and batch comparison. In D. C. Hoaglin, F. Mosteller, & J. W. Tukey (Eds.), *Understanding robust and exploratory data analysis.* New York: John Wiley.

Fox, J. (1984). *Linear statistical models and related methods.* New York: John Wiley.

Fox, J., & Suschnigg, C. (1988). *Gender and the prestige of occupations.* Unpublished manuscript, York University Institute for Social Research, Toronto.

Gnanadesikan, R. (1977). *Methods for statistical analysis of multivariate data.* New York: John Wiley.

Hoaglin, D. C. (1983). Letter values: A set of selected order statistics. In D. C. Hoaglin, & F. Mosteller, J. W. Tukey (Eds.), *Understanding robust and exploratory data analysis.* New York: John Wiley.

Hoaglin, D. C., Mosteller, F., & Tukey, J. W. (Eds.). (1983). *Understanding robust and exploratory data analysis.* New York: John Wiley.

Kendall, M., & Stuart, A. (1977). *The advanced theory of statistics* (Vol. 1, 4th ed.). New York: Macmillan.

Leinhardt, S., & Wasserman, S. S. (1979). Exploratory data analysis: An introduction to selected methods. In K. F. Schuessler (Ed.), *Sociological methodology 1979.* San Francisco: Jossey-Bass.

McGill, R., Tukey, J. W., & Larsen, W. A. (1978). Variations of box plots. *The American Statistician, 32,* 12-16.

Mage, D. T. (1982). An objective graphical method for testing normal distributional assumptions using probability plots. *The American Statistician, 36,* 116-120.

Pineo, P. C., & Porter, J. (1967). Occupational prestige in Canada. *Canadian Review of Sociology and Anthropology, 4,* 24-40.

Silverman, B. W. (1986). *Density estimation for statistics and data analysis.* London: Chapman & Hall.

Tarter, M. E., & Kronmal, R. A. (1976). An introduction to the implementation and theory of nonparametric density estimation. *The American Statistician, 30,* 105-112.

Tufte, E. R. (1983). *The visual display of quantitative information.* Cheshire, CT: Graphics Press.

Tukey, J. W. (1949). One degree of freedom for non-additivity. *Biometrics, 5,* 232-242.

Tukey, J. W. (1957). On the comparative anatomy of transformations. *Annals of Mathematical Statistics, 28,* 602-632.

Tukey, J. W. (1972). Some graphic and semigraphic displays. In T. A. Bancroft (Ed.), *Statistical papers in honor of George W. Snedecor.* Ames: Iowa State University Press.

Tukey, J. W. (1977). *Exploratory data analysis.* Reading, MA: Addison-Wesley.

Tukey, J. W., & Mosteller, F. (1977). *Data analysis and regression.* Reading, MA: Addison-Wesley.

Velleman, P. F., & Hoaglin, D. C. (1981). *Applications, basics, and computing of exploratory data analysis.* Boston: Duxbury.

Wegman, E. J. (1972). Nonparametric probability density estimation: I. A summary of available methods. *Technometrics, 14,* 533-546.

Wilk, M. B., & Gnanadesikan, R. (1968). Probability plotting methods for the analysis of data. *Biometrika, 55,* 1-17.

# 3

# A SURVEY OF SMOOTHING TECHNIQUES

Colin Goodall

## INTRODUCTION

A fundamental task in statistics, perhaps *the* fundamental task of data analysis, is to uncover and highlight patterns that are present in data. This is achieved by reducing the distracting effects of noise. Often the investigator has a specific model, that is, a set of possible patterns, in mind. Examples include a linear, straight-line, relationship between two variables, or a sinusoidal annual pattern of increase and decline in a time series of observations. There are many alternative models to consider, but, in any given situation, no guarantee that the model chosen is the right one, or adequately captures the pattern in the data.

Smoothing techniques are a simple approach to uncover patterns in data with a minimum of preconceptions and assumptions as to what those patterns should be. Without any assumptions at all, the possibilities are too broad: As an extreme case, a random-looking string of digits

AUTHOR'S NOTE: I wish to thank David Hoaglin, Frederick Mosteller, and John Tukey for directing me toward writing the forerunner of this chapter several years ago as part of the "Statisticians' Guide Project." I also wish to thank the editors of this volume for their constructive comments, and Richard De Veaux, Michael Phelan, and George Kurian for appreciative remarks on an earlier draft. Special thanks go to John Tukey for numerous comments and discussion over time, and to Susan Lustig for help in preparing the manuscript. The treatment of splines is due indirectly to Doug Bates. All errors remain, of course, my sole responsibility. This work was prepared in connection with research at Princeton University, sponsored by Army Research Office DAAL03-88-K-0045. Software for the smoothing techniques discussed in this chapter is available electronically from the statlib archive. To obtain this software send the message send index to the e-mail address statlib@temper.stat.cmu.edu. For additional details contact the author at colin@jackknife.princeton.edu.

may be an interesting pattern for a cryptographer but certainly not in the context of routine data exploration. The user of smoothing techniques assumes that the most useful relationships between the variables are smooth: an almost continuous curve or surface that does not jiggle too rapidly and may include a small number of steps or transitions.

Our first example is the time series of monthly U.S. housing starts for January 1966 to December 1974. The data, obtained from Construction Reports of the U.S. Bureau of the Census, are included in the distribution of the S package (Becker, Chambers, & Wilkes, 1988). They are readily available, in a powerful computing environment, for analysis using the smoothers discussed here. S readily provides software, data, and graphics capabilities for analyses of this chapter.

Figure 3.1, Panel A, shows the monthly housing starts with the vertical scale in thousands. We expect a strong seasonal, intraannual pattern in the data, as well as a longer-term, interannual pattern that reflects economic trends. One possible model, involving a moderate amount of effort, is to fit a trend plus sinusoid, where the trend is increasing to about June 1972 and then decreasing, and the sinusoid has a period of 12 months. The model is fit by multiple regression using an indicator variable for the sign of the trend and separate sine and cosine carriers. The fit, Figure 3.1, Panel B, turns out to be only a caricature of the pattern in the data, and tells us very little beyond parroting the model. Specifically, the curve is not high enough in Spring 1966, not low enough in Winter 1967, fails to capture the almost linear sequence in Summer 1968, is too high in 1970, and so on. Thus this model, although relatively sophisticated and intuitively appealing, fits the data poorly. We could devise a better model for the trend — for example, the data indicate a step from 1970 to 1971 rather than a gradual longer-term increase — but would still wish to model the seasonal variation as something other than sinusoidal.

The smooth of the housing starts shown in Figure 3.1, Panel C, provides much of the detail and faithfulness to the data lacking in the model-based fit. Housing starts were greater in 1971, 1972, and 1973 than in the other years. Housing starts peaked each year around May, typically declined gradually for several months, and then declined rapidly in the fall to a winter trough. We conclude that the season variation in housing starts is not a simple sinusoid, but reveals a characteristic building season that begins with a spurt in housing starts. The smooth uses the resistant **43RSR2H**, twice smoother, defined in the next section. Briefly, **43RSR2H**, twice involves smoothing the data

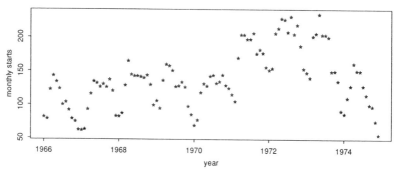

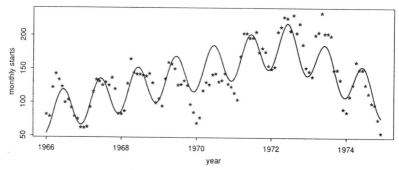

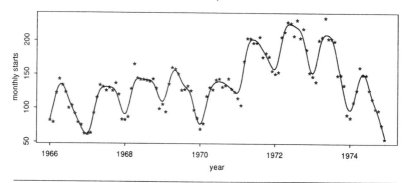

**Figure 3.1**  **The U.S. Census monthly housing start series (A), with parametric fit (B), and interpolation spline of the nonparametric smooth
by 43RSR2H, twice (C).**

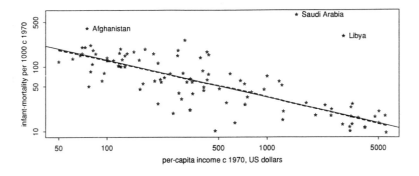

**Figure 3.2   Resistant line (solid) and the default lowess smooth (dashed) for the regression of infant mortality data on per capita income for 101 nations.**

repeatedly by several different running median smoothers. A running median smoother replaces each datum by the median of the current values in a surrounding window. To produce the curve shown in Panel C, an interpolating spline was passed through the smoothed values.

Our second illustration of smoothing is in the regression setting, specifically the relationship between per capita income and infant mortality rate for 101 nations, shown on a log-log scale in Figure 3.2. The data are from Leinhardt and Wasserman (1979). There are three outliers in these data, with unusually high mortality: Afghanistan, Saudi Arabia, and Libya. The solid line shown in Figure 3.2 is the resistant line (Emerson & Hoaglin, 1983; Johnstone & Velleman, 1985) computed from the x- and y-medians of the left, center, and right thirds of the data. To assess the adequacy of this linear fit, we superimpose the default lowess fit (dashed line). The smoother lowess (Cleveland, 1979, 1985) replaces each data point by the fit of a robust line through the surrounding window that contains two thirds of the data. The smooth is surprisingly close to the resistant line, indicating that the large scale pattern in the relationship between infant mortality and per capita income is exactly linear on a log scale and is captured by the resistant line.

The goal of smoothing is to separate the data into a smooth component and a rough component:

$$data = smooth + rough.$$

This is a special case of the equation

$$data = fit + residual$$

found throughout statistical analysis. The rough should contain as little structure as possible. The basic smoothing technique is to replace each observation by an *average* of the surrounding observations. This average may be a mean, a median, or, in the case of lowess, the intercept of a fitted line at the same horizontal coordinate as the observation. The selected observations are those within a *window*, usually centered at the data point. The width of the window (as number of observations or $x$ distance) is called the *span* of the smoother. Local averaging reduces noise while ensuring faithfulness of the smooth to the nearby data and insulating the smoothed value at one part of the data from observations far away. In fact the smoothed values *are* smooth because the windows overlap. The wider the window the greater the averaging and the more correlated are successive smoothed observations. Smoothers with narrow windows are called *light*, those with broad windows are *heavy*. **43RSR2H**, twice is a moderate smoother; the default lowess is a heavy smoother.

These considerations lead us to introduce several families of smoothers. Each family is defined by a particular choice of average, and its members by alternative choices of span. Two such families, discussed in the following section, use means and medians, respectively, and are called the *moving averages*, or *digital filters*, and *running medians*, or *median filters*. Criteria for comparing smoothers are developed in the third section. These include the trade-off between the effectiveness of a smoother in reducing noise and its faithfulness to an underlying pattern in the data (variance vs. bias), the smoother's response to outliers and abrupt changes of level (resistance properties at spikes and steps), and a smoother's ability to attenuate rapidly varying "noise" components in the data while leaving slowly varying "trend" components unchanged (frequency domain analysis).

More sophisticated smoothers involve more than simple averaging of the observations in a fixed-size window. The fourth section includes a description of lowess and smoothing using regression splines.

## DIGITAL FILTERS AND RUNNING MEDIANS

### *Digital Filters*

Digital filters, also called moving averages, take the form of a running weighted mean. For a general introduction, see Hamming (1977) or Cadzow (1987). Let $b$ be the window width, or span of the filter. The *semi-span*, $s$, of the filter is defined to be one half the span, more precisely $b = 2s + 1$ when $b$ is odd, $b = 2s$ when $b$ is even. The $b$ weights $w_{-s}, w_{-s+1}, \ldots, w_{-1}, w_0, w_1, \ldots, w_n$ ($w_0$ omitted when $b$ is even) define the filter. Thus the smooth $S(y)^1$ of the sequence $(y) = y_1, \ldots, y_n$ is the *convolution* of $(y)$ with the sequence of weights, $(w)$. For $n - s \geq i \geq s + 1$,

$$S(y)_i = \sum_{k=-s}^{s} w_k y_{i+k}. \tag{3.1}$$

For example, the running average of 5 has semi-span 2 and weights

$$(w_{-2}, w_{-1}, w_0, w_1, w_2) = (1/5, 1/5, 1/5, 1/5, 1/5).$$

The first few numbers in the housing start series are

81.9 79.0 122.4 143.0 133.9 123.5.

The third value of the smooth sequence is the mean of the first five values, that is, 112.0. The first few numbers of the smoothed sequence (also shown in Figure 3.3A) are

81.9 94.4 112.0 120.4 124.6 120.8.

The first and second values of the smoothed sequence cannot be computed by the convolution with window length 5. Instead, for the first smoothed value we simply copy the first value from the data, 81.9, and

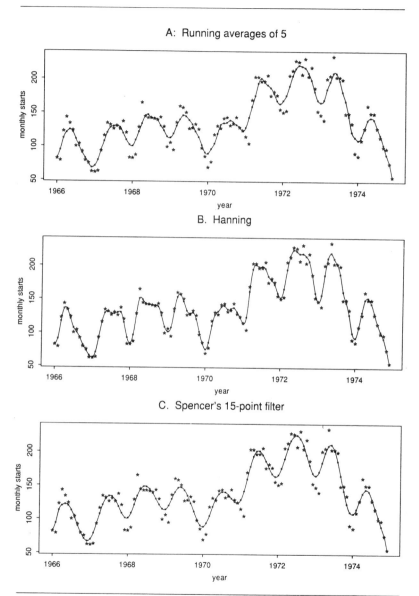

**Figure 3.3  Running averages of 5 (A), Hanning (B), and Spencer's 15-point smooth (C) of the Housing start series.  The smoothed values are denoted by ■'s. An interpolation spline is fit through these points in each panel.**

for the second smoothed value we compute the mean of the first three values of the sequence of data. This is only one alternative of many for dealing with the ends of the sequence; a brief overview is given in the section discussing rules for the ends.

A simple digital filter with unequal weights is the Hanning filter, denoted **H**, which has span 3 and weights

$$(w_{-1}, w_0, w_1) = (1/4, 1/2, 1/4).$$

The first few numbers in this smooth of the housing start sequence (see Figure 3.3B) are

$$81.9\ 90.6\ 116.7\ 135.6\ 133.6\ 120.2.$$

The second value in the smooth is the weighted average of the first three data values, with double weight on the second datum. The subsequent values up to the last in the sequence are computed similarly, and the first and last are copied on as before. Notice that this smooth is a little lighter than the running average of 5 but still fairly effective.

A heavier smooth results from Spencer's 15-point weighted average filter (Kendall & Stuart, 1976). The first 8 of 15 weights are given by

$$(w_{-7}, \ldots, w_0, \ldots) = (-3, -6, -5, 3, 21, 46, 67, 74, \ldots)/320$$

with the remaining weights filled in symmetrically. The smooth also appears in Figure 3.3C. To obtain smoothed values at the ends, the data have been extended by 7 values at each end, by replicating the first and last observation 7 times, respectively.

The three digital filters described here, running average of 5, Hanning, and Spencer's 15-point, are sensible choices from a broad range of possibilities. They illustrate light-moderate, light, and heavy smoothing, respectively.

Some broad guidelines for the choice of weights are the following:

1. The weights must sum to one,

$$\sum_{k=-s}^{s} w_k = 1,$$

in order that the smoother faithfully reproduces the constant sequence, $y_i = a$.

2. The weights must be symmetric, $w_{-k} = w_k$, if the smooth of a sequence is to be the same as the smooth of the same sequence with order reversed. For the infant mortality data this is important because there is no temporal sequence; the order is dictated by the covariate income. On the other hand, an asymmetric filter may be appropriate when we have an autoregressive model or prediction, in mind. For an asymmetric filter the semi-span is

$$s = \max_k \{w_k \neq 0 \text{ or } w_{-k} \neq 0\}$$

3. The weights must be nonnegative, $w_k \geq 0$ for each $k$, if the smooth of any nonnegative sequence is nonnegative. Let $(y_r)$ be the nonnegative spike "basis" sequence that has $y_i = 0$ except that $y_r = 1$, where $r$ is away from the ends of the sequence, that is $s + 1 \leq r \leq n - s$. Suppose $w_k < 0$. Then $S(y)_{r-k} = w_k < 0$. Note that Spencer's 15-point smoother has negative entries, for reasons discussed later.

4. Observations closer to the $i$th should have at least as much weight in determining $S(y)_i$ as more distant observations. Therefore the weights should be monotone decreasing away from the center of the window,

$$w_0 \geq w_1 \geq \ldots \geq w_k$$

and

$$w_0 \geq w_{-1} \geq \ldots \geq w_{-k}.$$

Each filter in the family of running averages has equal weights. The running averages, and also the Hanning filter, satisfy each of the criteria 1-4.

To this point we have discussed filters with odd span, $b = 2s + 1$. The construction of an even-span filter is similar, except that an even-span filter involves a shift of the data sequence by one-half step. Consequently, the sequence shortens from length $n$ to $n - 1$. Even-span filters are most often used in pairs, so that the data sequence and its smooth are back in alignment. The observation that has been lost at each end of the sequence is easily recovered by copying the original datum. However, just as the convolution of the data sequence and the digital filter is the smooth, so we can convolve two digital filters together to obtain a new digital filter that is equivalent to the two filters applied in succession. Mathematically we simply extend the sequence of weights for one filter by zeros in either direction, and then use equation 3.1. For example, the running average of two, (1/2,1/2) applied twice is the smooth of

$$\ldots 0\ 0\ 0\ 1/2\ 1/2\ 0\ 0\ 0\ \ldots$$

by (1/2,1/2), or

$$\ldots 0\ 0\ 0\ 1/4\ 1/2\ 1/4\ 0\ 0\ 0\ \ldots$$

This is identical to the Hanning filter, (1/2,1/4,1/2).

The convolution of digital filters to create new filters is a general purpose mathematical tool that enters also into the definition of Spencer's 15-point smoother. Following Kendall and Stuart (1976), let the notation $[k]/k$ denote the running average of $k$ terms, $[k]/k = (1, \ldots,$ $k$-times, $\ldots, 1)/k$. The Hanning filter is

$$(1,2,1)/4 = [2][2]/4.$$

Spencer's 15-point smoother is

$$[4]^2[5](-3,3,4,3,-3)/320.$$

Note that the span of the convolution of digital filters is the sum of the window widths, less one for every filter after the first. For Spencer's 15-point smoother, $15 = 4 + 4 + 5 + 5 - 3$. Spencer's formula was designed in the era of desktop computing machines for manual computation. The filter includes three narrow-span unweighted averages and a weighted average with small almost equal coefficients (+3's and a 4). The intercept, at the center of the window, of the least-squares fit of a cubic polynomial is a fixed linear combination of the data, that is, a particular choice of weighted average. Spencer's 15-point smoother is an approximation to that linear combination when the data are equally spaced. It also leaves any exact constant, linear, quadratic, or cubic polynomial,

$$y_i = a_0 + a_1 i + a_2 i^2 + a_3 i^3, \qquad (3.2)$$

unchanged. The fit is the required $a_0$ because (1) the constant component is unchanged, $\Sigma w_i a_0 = a_0$, because the weights sum to 1; (2) the linear and cubic components are 0, $\Sigma w_i i = \Sigma w_i i^3 = 0$, because the weights are symmetric and; (3) the quadratic component is 0 by careful choice of weights, $\Sigma w_i i^2 = 0$, with some weights necessarily negative since $i^2 > 0$ for each $i$, $i = -s, \ldots, s$. For additional details of this approach see Kendall and Stuart (1976).

For completeness and clarity we mention two further aspects of digital filters. First, a digital filter need not have finite span. For example, the filter with $w_0 = 1 - \pi^2/3$ and $w_k = w_{-k} = 1/k^2$ ($k \geq 1$) is symmetric with

$$\sum_{-\infty}^{\infty} w_i = 1.$$

This filter has no reality for statistical analysis of a finite data sequence, but is important in a signal processing context where its properties are easily stated in the frequency domain (Hamming, 1977). Second, a digital filter need not *smooth* data. When

$$\sum_{-s}^{s} w_k = 0,$$

that is, the weights sum to zero, the filter is a *differentiator*. For example, $(-1,1)$ computes first differences or finite approximations to the first derivative of the sequence. The convolution of $(-1,1)$ with itself computes second differences, finite approximations to the second derivatives. It is the filter with weights $(1,-2,1)$.

An important property of digital filters is linearity. A smoother $S$ is said to be linear if the smooth of the sum of any two sequences, $(y)$ and $(z)$, say, is the sum of the smooths, that is, if for each $i$

$$S(y + z)_i = S(y)_i + S(z)_i \tag{3.3}$$

where $(y + z)$ denotes the sequence with $i$th term $y_i + z_i$. It is easy to check that a digital filter is linear. Conversely, it is not much harder to check, using spike basis sequences, that any linear smoother is a digital filter, provided we allow a nonstationary definition, that is, the weights may depend on $i$. Linear smoothers are not resistant, however, as we show in the third section. For example, an outlier is smeared across several surrounding data values. This fact is a significant drawback to the use of digital filters in data analysis. As a remedy, we turn to a simple but effective class of *nonlinear* smoothers, namely the running median smoothers. These are resistant, by virtue of replacing the mean in the running average by a median. In place of linearity, equation 3.3, they satisfy only the property of location equivariance, that is,

$$S(y + a)_i = S(y)_i + a \qquad (3.4)$$

where $a$ is a scalar constant.

### *Running Median Smoothers*

Running median smoothers became widely known through Tukey's (1977) text on exploratory data analysis. They are now widespread in both the statistics literature (for example, Velleman & Hoaglin, 1981) and signal processing literature (Cadzow, 1987). Running median smoothers are particularly well suited for rapid hand computation — taking medians is faster and easier than averaging — but software implementations are common also, and easy to program. Of all these smoothers, running medians of 3, denoted **3**, are most prevalent. Progressively heavier smoothers are running medians of 5,7,9, . . . denoted **5,7,9,** . . . The first six numbers in the housing start series and their smooth by running medians of 5 are

81.9 79.0 122.4 143.0 133.9 123.5

81.9 81.9 122.4 123.5 123.5 123.5.

For example, the third smoothed value, 122.4, is the median of 81.9, 79.0, 122.4, 143.0, and 133.9, the first 5 values in the sequence. At the end the span 5 median is not possible. For the second smoothed value the span is stepped down to 3, and the value, 81.9, is the median of 81.9, 79.0, and 122.4. For the end value, Tukey's (1977) extrapolation rule, denoted **E**, is used. An additional "0th" observation is constructed by extrapolating the second and third smoothed values linearly, that is,

$$\hat{y}_0 = 3S(y)_2 - 2S(y)_3. \qquad (3.5)$$

Here $\hat{y}_0 = 3(81.9) - 2(122.4) = 0.9$. The first smoothed value is another median of 3,

$$S(y)_1 = \text{median}(\hat{y}_0, y_1, S(y)_2)$$

$$= \text{median}(0.9, 81.9, 81.9) \qquad (3.6)$$

$$= 81.9.$$

Thus, for the start of the housing sequence, Tukey's rule coincidentally gives the same result, 81.9, as the copy on rule. For additional explanation, Tukey (1977) and Velleman and Hoaglin (1981) may be consulted.

Figure 3.4 shows the smooth of the housing start series by **3, 5** and **9**. With increasing span the approximately flat subsequences are longer and more evident. The shorter span smoothers better preserve the seasonal oscillation, whereas the longer span smoothers better contrast the high level of housing starts in 1971, 1972, and 1973 to the prevailing level in other years. These smooths are relatively unsatisfactory compared with the output of median-based compound smoothers, such as **43RSR2H**, twice (Figure 3.1).

To avoid long flat subsequences, and as explained further in the third section, we prefer to use **3** repeatedly, and sometimes **5**, rather than use long-span running medians. The effective window width of **3** followed by itself, **33**, is 5. However **33**, unlike **5**, gives greater weight to observations closer to the center of the window. A popular smoother is to repeat **3** until there is no further change, denoted **3R**. With the replicate end value rule, or the equivalent (for **3**) copy-on end value rule, there is no further change after at most $(n - 1)/2$ iterations. For the housing start series, only 2 iterations are required. Odd-span running medians do not change the actual data values as a collection, they only rearrange, duplicate, and eliminate individual values, and are therefore called *selectors*. The $i$th smoothed value, $S(y)_i$ is a selection from the set of $y$ values in the window.

Each smoothed value in the output of **3** is the median of itself and the two adjacent values. A running median of 3 leaves a peak or trough comprising two identical observations unchanged. These short flats are prevalent in Figure 3.4A. (Longer flats are prevalent in Figures 3.4B and 3.4C.) To remove the flats, we typically follow **3** or **3R** by one or two iterations of *splitting*, denoted **S**. To split, we divide the data sequence into two separate pieces in the middle of our width-2 peak or trough, smooth each end separately with the end value rule **E**, and then

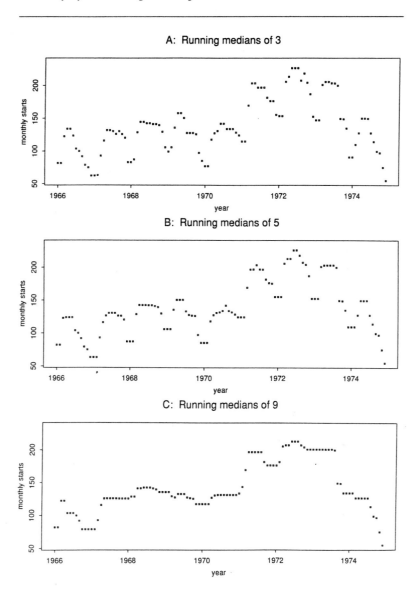

**Figure 3.4  Smoothed values of the 3, 5, and 9 smooths of the housing start data.**

NOTE: There are many flat subsequences, with greater lengths for the running medians with longer span.

glue the parts back together. Figure 3.5A shows both the end value rule and splitting applied to the first four years of the housing start data. The original sequence (∗) is smoothed by **3R** (■) and E and S (o). (The **3R** smooth differs from the **3** smooth, Figure 3.4A, at just 3 of the 48 months.) Peaks and troughs occur at six pairs of months in Figure 3.5A, typically at the seasonal high, April-June, or low, December-January. Splitting does not affect the additional flats that occur as part of monotone subsequences, for example August-September 1968, and a triple trough December 68-February 69.

To split we divide the sequence of ■'s at the vertical dashed lines. We mark the linearly interpolated values by +, with the lines dashed (+ at left) or solid (+ at right). The leftmost dashed line marks the use of E. The effect of splitting is seen in the difference between the ■ (sometimes obscured by ∗ at the same position) and the 0 at each side of each split. Where the two pairs of observations to either side of the peak rise sharply, for example, July-August 1969, then splitting has no effect. If, on the other hand, the surrounding observations are relatively flat on at least one side then that half of the peak will disappear. For example, there is a large change due to splitting at December 1967, and smaller changes at December 1966, June 1967, and May 1968. We may split until there is no further change, denoted **SR**, although Tukey advises it is better to stop with two S's. For the housing start data there is no further change after the first split.

The even-span running median smoothers **2,4,6**, . . . , have a useful role because each smoothed value is the average of the two median data values and smoothing by averaging can take place. We call these *semi-selectors* (Mallows, 1980). The span-2 running median, **2**, is the same as the span-2 running average. Typically, even-span smoothers are used in pairs. A popular choice is **22**, which is the Hanning filter (1/4,1/2,1/4), denoted **H**.

We apply Hanning to the housing start series, already smoothed by **3R,E** and S to remove some of the local irregularities. In Figure 3.5B the original data (∗) are shown, together with the smooth by **3R,E** and S (o). The dotted line shows the result of smoothing the 0 sequence by **H**. We have passed an interpolating spline through the smoothed points. Note that after splitting a running median of 3 will smooth the series further, for example, around May 1967, January 1968, and April 1968. Hanning is just as effective as **3** at this, and in addition lightly smooths the monotone subsequences during the summer and fall months of each year. Monotone subsequences, as well as flat troughs and peaks, are

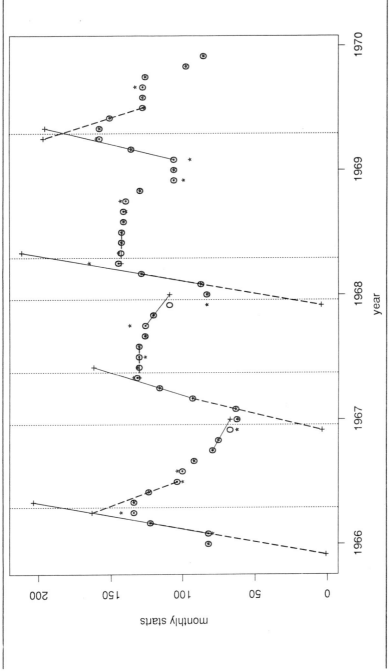

**Figure 3.5A** First 48 months of housing start data, showing the original data (∗), Smooth by 3R (■), smooth by 3R, E, and S (O). The smoothing by 3R (■'s) is split at the vertical dashed lines.

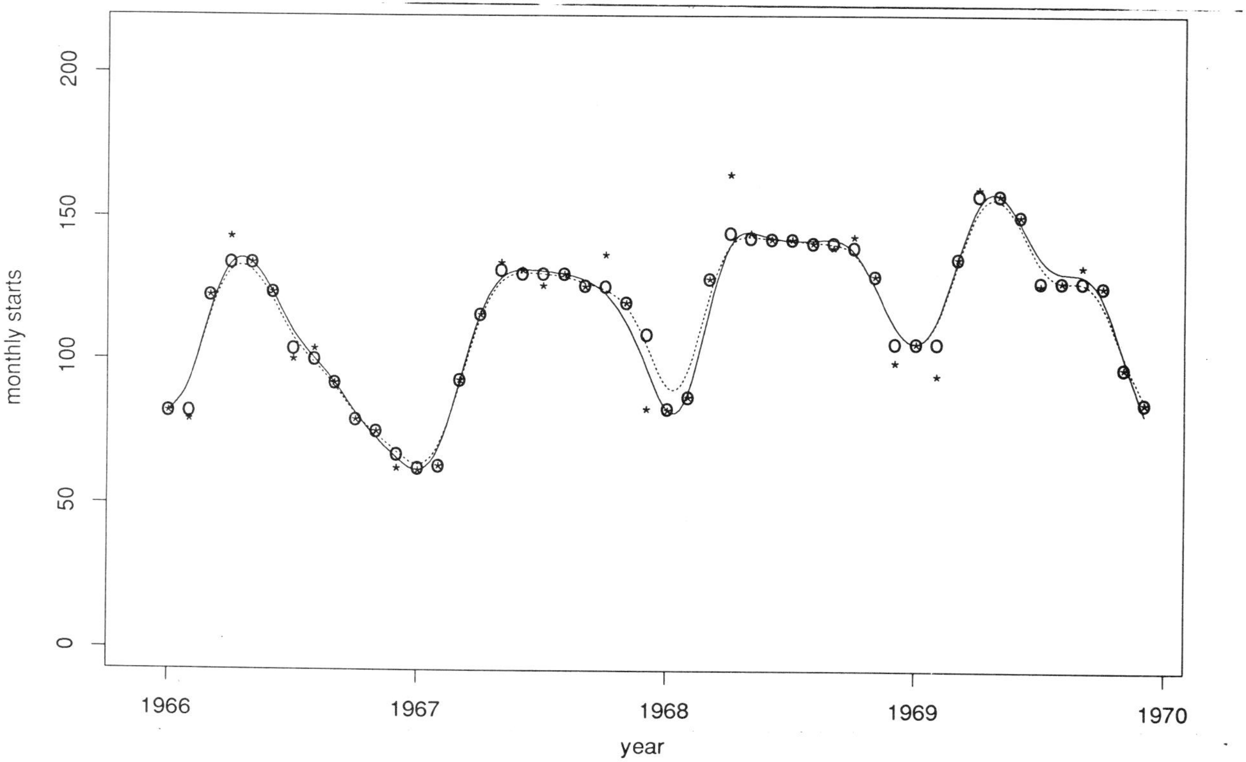

**Figure 3.5B** First 48 months of housing start data, showing the original data (∗), smooth by 3R (■), and splined smooths 3RSSH (dashed curve) and 3RSSH, twice (solid curve).

so-called *root* sequences of running medians, that is, provided that their length exceeds the semi-span of the smoother, they are left unchanged.

Successive running medians do not convolve to a single running median, as do digital filters. A *compound smoother* is a smoother constructed by successive applications of more elemental smoothers; those on the left are applied first. We have constructed the compound smoother for **3RSSH**, step by step, as shown in Figure 3.5. (The **E** step is implicitly included.) Other examples include **53H**, **4253H**, **3RSSH**, and **43RSR2H**. Note that each smoother ends with **H**.

Additional application of the smoother to the rough of the original smooth will tend to uncover additional structure in the data. As is common to many robust and resistant techniques (Hoaglin, Mosteller, & Tukey, 1983), iteration is needed to properly analyze the data. In *twicing* we add the smooth of the original rough to the original smooth, but do not subsequently smooth the sum of smooths. We define

$$S, \text{twice}(y) = S(y) + S(y - S(y)). \tag{3.7}$$

The continuous line in Figure 3.5B is the interpolating spline of the smooth by **3RSSH**, twice. This smooth captures the summer and winter extremes in the series much better than **3RSSH** alone. The difference during winter 1967/1968 is particularly striking. Figure 3.6 shows the pattern in the residuals from **3RSSH**(*'s) and **3RSSH**, twice ($\Delta$'s). The large oscillations in the smooth by **3RSSH** of the first of these sets of residuals (solid line) are almost entirely absent from the smooth, again by **3RSSH**, of the second set (dashed line). Note that the vertical scale of Figure 3.6 is about one fifth of the scale of Figure 3.5.

Twicing may occasionally be carried further, as in

$$S, \text{thrice}(y) = S(y) + S(y - S(y)) + S(y - S(y) - S(y - S(y))). \tag{3.8}$$

Twicing may also be used when $S$ is a digital filter. When $S$ preserves linear, first-order polynomial, sequences (that is, $\Sigma w_i = 1$ and the weights are symmetric), then $S$, twice preserves cubic polynomials. By linearity, however, $S$, twice is a digital filter with weights given by

$$S, \text{twice} = 2S - SS. \tag{3.9}$$

This filter may then be used explicitly, without the need for twicing. For example, **H**, twice is the filter

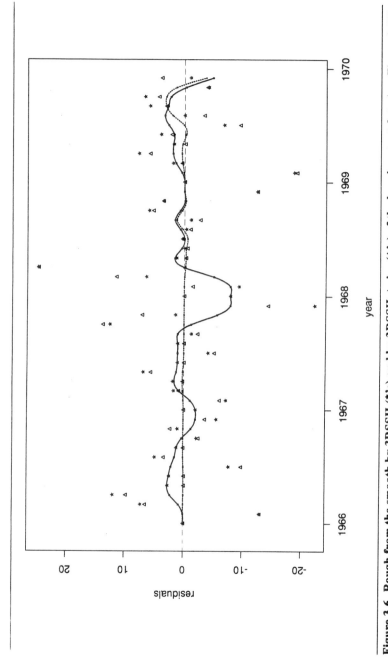

**Figure 3.6** Rough from the smooth by 3RSSH (\*'s) and by 3RSSH, twice (Δ's) of the housing start data (see Figure 3.5B), and the smooths of the roughs by 3RSSH (solid curve and dashed curves, respectively). Considerable additional structure is removed from the original rough by twicing, as is shown by the pattern in the solid curve.

$$2[2][2]/4 - [2][2][2][2]/16$$

$$= (1/2, 1, 1/2) - (1/16, 1/4, 3/8, 1/4, 1/16) \tag{3.10}$$

$$= (-1, 4, 10, -1)/16.$$

Note the negative weights, suggesting that negative weights are needed to minimize erosion, and that guideline 3 of the section on digital filters is overly restrictive.

Recommendations for a bouquet of light and moderate to heavy smoothers include **3R**; **3RSS**, twice; **4253H**, twice; and **3RSSH**, twice. Each involves a number of uses of the copy-on end value rule and **E**. These smoothers have been constructed according to the common sense criteria developed in this section. They have additional theoretical justification, which we touch on in the next section. Above all, however, we recommend these smoothers for their proven effectiveness on many different sets of data when a light to heavy smooth is desired.

### Rules for the Ends

For points close to the ends of the sequence the window extends beyond the ends. There are a variety of approaches to deal with the ends, some of which we have already encountered, but which are summarized here for completeness.

A common approach is to copy the first and last observations, $y_1$ and $y_n$, each $s$ times and extend the sequence. Then $S(y)_i$ may be defined by the equation 3.1 for each $i$, $1 \le i \le n$. We call this the *replicate end-value rule*. As an alternative, according to the *copy-on end-value rule*, we smooth only for $n - s \ge i \ge s + 1$ and use the original unsmoothed data for the $s$ observations at each end. Thus for $1 \le i \le s$ and $n - s + 1 \le i \le n$, $S(y)_i = y_i$.

In some situations, the data may be naturally cyclic, in the sense that $y_1, \ldots, y_n$ are measured around a "clockface," so that $y_1$ and $y_n$ are adjacent. For such data, we can use equation 3.1 for each $i$, when we interpret $i + k$ as the integer between 1 and $n$ equal to $i + k$ modulo $n$. This is the *cyclic end-value rule*. For example, we may wish to compute a seasonal adjustment for housing starts. In assessing economic trends by comparing one month's figures with those of the previous month, we need to take account of the regular intra-annual variation. That is, we

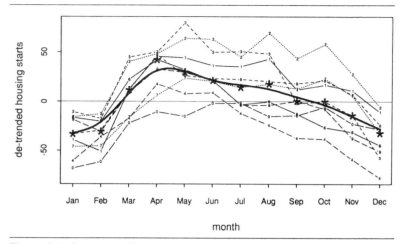

Figure 3.7  Seasonal adjustment: Detrended monthly housing starts, with
individual years (thin lines), median monthly values (∗'s) and
smooth by Hanning (solid curve) with cyclic end-value rule.

must apply a seasonal adjustment. (This difficulty does not arise in
comparing one month's figures with those of the same month in a
previous year.) The seasonal adjustment is the month to month changes
in housing starts, averaged across several years, after removing the
long-term trend. The seasonal adjustments sum to zero, approximately,
and, although based on past data, may be applied to current data. Figure
3.7 shows monthly seasonal adjustments for the housing start series.
First, a long-term trend is fit by the default lowess (not shown in the
figures). It comprises a slight upward trend up to the start of 1972 and
a slight downward trend thereafter. The residuals about this trend are
shown by the broken lines in Figure 3.7, labeled 6-9, 0-4 for the years
1966 and 1974, respectively. As can be seen, the residuals for individual
years tend to be consistently high or low. The median computed for each
month is shown by the ∗'s, and this series is smoothed by Hanning, with
cyclic end-value rule. The results change only in detail with alternative
methods — for example, when the detrending step is omitted — and are
consistent with the month-to-month variation shown in Figures 3.1, 3.3,
3.4, and 3.5. Cleveland and Devlin (1982) describe a comprehensive
procedure, SABL, for seasonal adjustment based on lowess.

A fourth procedure, the *step-down end-value rule,* is to decrease the span of the smoother as necessary close to the ends of the sequence. This rule is common with running median smoothers. In the case of a digital filter, the weights, $w_k$, must be modified. We may truncate the set of weights symmetrically as necessary, and renormalize so that the remaining weights sum to 1. We recommended the step-down rule in conjunction with an *extrapolation* end-value rule, a special procedure for the first and last observations of the sequence. The rule constructs an additional observation, $\hat{y}_0$, beyond the end of the sequence, $y_1$, by linear extrapolation of the current smoothed values $y_2$ and $y_3$. The smooth at the end is then computed from $\hat{y}_0$, $y_1$ and $S(y)_2$, for example, in Tukey's rule as $S(y)_1 = \text{median } (\hat{y}_0, y_1, S(y)_2)$. For equally spaced observations in $x$, the appropriate extrapolation is

$$\hat{y}_0 = S(y)_2 - 2(S(y)_3 - S(y)_2) = 3S(y)_2 - 2S(y)_3. \qquad (3.11)$$

Often, this is good enough for unequally spaced data, also. However Goodall, Stoughton, and Easton (1986) use the $x$ values explicitly,

$$y_0 = S(y)_2 - 2(x_2 - x_1)(S(y)_3 - S(y)_2) / (x_3 - x_2). \qquad (3.12)$$

A fifth alternative is the *omit end-value rule,* which is to simply omit the last $s$ observations from each end of the smoothed sequence and to allow the smoothed sequences to shorten.

The pattern of smoothed values at the ends, and by implication the choice of end-value rule, is very important. Unfortunately, there are no firm guidelines. There is least data at the ends of the sequence, and the smooth tends to behave most erratically there, which may give a misleading impression of the pattern in the data. Even for a sophisticated smoother, a single observation at the end of a sequence can be highly influential. We may also use the ends of the smoothed sequence for extrapolation, but a formal technique for extrapolation may involve other technology, such as exponential-decreasing weights or a Kalman filter. The choice of end-value rule becomes more important as the length of the sequence decreases, and our interest necessarily focuses on the ends as well as the middle of the sequence. The choice is more critical in 2 and higher dimensions, for which the ratio of edge pixels to interior pixels is typically much larger.

In summary, in the signal processing literature the replicate end-value rule is most common for both median filters and digital filters. In

an exploratory data analysis setting, the step-down rule, . . . , **7,5,3**, or
. . . , **6,4,2**, is commonplace, followed, for odd-span smoothers, by
Tukey's extrapolation end-value rule.

## CRITERIA FOR SMOOTHER DESIGN AND EVALUATION

With two families of smoothers under our belts, digital filters and
running medians, we turn now to an overview of the goals of smoothing
and to a more far-reaching discussion of the properties of the two
families. Our criteria for comparing smoothers will be based either on
a statistical model for the data or on the behavior of the smoother at
certain specific, but widely encountered, patterns in data. We first
model the data as the sum of a smooth, but unknown, function and
uncorrelated noise. This allows us to be explicit about the trade-off, in
the choice of smoother, between bias, or faithfulness on the average to
the function, and variance. When the smooth is a low-order polynomial
then we quantify the advantages, for a digital filter of fixed span, of a
monotone decreasing set of weights over flat weights. It is seen that the
bias with even a small quadratic component (small relative to the noise)
is more important than the variance in the smooth. These arguments
extend by analogy to median filters, although the distributional results
are not simple, and to smoothers with different spans.

A frequent set of patterns in data comprises outliers and edges, that
is, spikes and steps. Digital filters and median filters respond quite
differently at these patterns. The *resistant* median filters are preferred
because they eliminate spikes and preserve steps. Digital filters are not
resistant because they are linear.

Another approach uses the decomposition of data into its high-frequency "noise" components and low frequency "signal" components.
An effective digital filter is a low-pass filter: It eliminates the high-frequency components. The nonlinear median filters reduce high-frequency components also, but more selectively. For example, the decomposition of a data sequence containing a step includes both low and high
frequencies, which are collectively preserved by an odd-span median
filter. The choice of view here depends on what is more fundamental in
a particular application: a step or a sinusoidal component.

The section concludes with some broad recommendations on choice
of smoother.

## A Statistical Model

We may regard the smooth simply as an expression of the pattern in the data. There are many alternative expressions of the pattern, each the result of a different smoothing technique. A stronger assumption is that there is a statistical model underlying the data. Then we may regard the smooth as an estimate of that model. However, unlike linear and sinusoidal fits, which are parametric, smoothing is a nonparametric or semiparametric technique. Simple linear regression involves estimating just two parameters, the slope and intercept of an underlying model,

$$y_i = a + bx_i + \varepsilon_i \tag{3.13}$$

where the errors $\varepsilon_i$ are assumed to have mean 0, and may be independent and identically distributed also. For smoothing the analogous model is

$$y_i = f(x_i) + \varepsilon_i \tag{3.14}$$

where $f$ is a smooth function, and we assume similar properties of the $\varepsilon_i$ as for the parametric regression model. The smooth underlying function may be a linear, quadratic, or cubic polynomial in $x$, or a sum of two sinusoids in $x$, but in general it is none of these. There is no natural parametrization of the class of smooth functions $f$, so we call smoothing semiparametric. Estimation of $f$ may be called nonparametric or semiparametric regression. The number of parameters needed to describe $f$ typically exceeds the number of observations. Consequently, inference is difficult.

Not every family of smoothers includes a choice of window width. For example the regression splines (see the fourth section) do not. However, each family of smoothers does include a smoothness parameter, which we denote $\lambda$. A larger $\lambda$ corresponds to a heavier, smoother smooth. Such a smooth will not exhibit much fine-scale variation, but does involve a greater amount of averaging; the local effective sample sizes are larger. When we assume a statistical model equation 3.14, we can discuss the choice of $\lambda$ in terms of a trade-off between bias and variance in estimating $f$.

The bias and variance of the smooth at $x_i$ are, respectively,

$$ES(y)_i - f(x_i) \tag{3.15}$$

where $E$ denotes expectation, and

$$VS(y)_i = E[S(y)_i - ES(y)_i]^2. \qquad (3.16)$$

Large values of $\lambda$ imply high bias — the smooth is less faithful to $f$ — and low variance; small values imply low bias and high variance. This analysis also makes sense when there is *no* function $f$. Then our emphasis is on data summarization; we separate the sequence into a smooth part and a rough part. The rough should contain as little fluctuation in level as possible so that the pattern in the data is contained in the smooth. However the smoothness parameter determines the scale at which we look for fluctuations. Large bias means leaving medium-scale patterns in the rough; large variance means incorporating too much of the fluctuation in the data into the smooth. We discuss specific forms of bias presently.

There are no satisfactory general methods with which to select a smoothing parameter. It is the user who must ultimately decide. Silverman (1986) recommended smoothing, if possible, so that the broad patterns that are obtained in the smooth are interpretable in terms of the associated subject matter, but just lightly enough that there are a few additional wiggles in the data to think about! There are more formal approaches, notably cross-validation (Cleveland, 1979; Wahba, 1979), but these are not completely satisfactory, and it appears impossible to remove the subjective element. Moreover, it is misleading to think in terms of a single smoothing parameter. Instead, there is a vast array of alternative smoothers that differ not only in the characteristic scale but also in the *shape* of patterns in the smooth. These differences are apparent in the alternative smooths of the housing start data. Running medians of 3, 5, and 9 capture a square-cut pattern (Figure 3.4), Spencer's running average a smooth curve (Figure 3.3), and the **3RSSH**, twice (Figure 3.5) something intermediate. These differences are due not only to the weight of the smoothers, but are also characteristic of the class of smoothers to which each smoother belongs.

### Bias Versus Variance with Quadratic (or Cubic) Dependence

A trivial computation shows that when the errors $\varepsilon_i$ in equation 3.14 are uncorrelated and have common variance $\sigma^2$, then the weighted mean $S(y)_i$ at the $i$th observation has variance

$$\sigma^2 \sum_{j=-s}^{s} w_j.$$

The variance is $\sigma^2/k$ for the unweighted average-of-$k$, $[k]/k$. For given span $b = k$ this is the smallest possible variance given the assumptions. For example, the average-of-5 has variance $\sigma^2/5$, the Hanning filter has variance $3\sigma^2/8$ compared to a minimum of $\sigma^2/3 = 3\sigma^2/9$, and Spencer's 15-point smoother has variance $0.193\sigma^2$, which is about three times the minimum of $0.067\sigma^2$.

These comparisons consider only variance, that is, the variability of the smoothed value across repeated samples — if repeated sampling makes sense at all, even conceptually — from the model, equation 3.14. The comparisons do not consider the difference between the average smoothed value, $ES(y)_i$, and the actual value of $f$, $f(x_i)$. For example, if $f$ is nonlinear, with increasing slope, then $ES(y)_i$ will have a positive bias when $S$ is the unweighted running average.

A simple computation makes the difficulties clear. Suppose $f$ is a cubic and the $x_i$'s are equally spaced $x_i = i$. Then $(y)$ may be written

$$y_i = a_0 + a_1 i + a_2 i^2 + a_3 i^3 + \varepsilon_i. \tag{3.17}$$

For the weighted average $(w_{-s}, \ldots, w_0, \ldots, w_s)$ with symmetric weights, $\Sigma w_i = 1$,

$$S(y_0) = a_0 + a_2 \sum_{i=-s}^{s} w_i i^2 + \sum_{i=-s}^{s} w_i \varepsilon_i. \tag{3.18}$$

The bias is

$$a_2 \sum_{i=-s}^{s} w_i i^2.$$

Therefore the mean square error at $x_0$ (bias$^2$ + variance) is

$$(a_2 \sum_{i=-s}^{s} w_i i^2)^2 + \sigma^2 \sum_{-s}^{s} w_i^2. \tag{3.19}$$

We use equation 3.19 to compare Spencer's 15-point smoother to the unweighted average, [15]/15. For the 15-point running average, [15]/15, the bias is $18.67a_2$, but for Spencer's smoother it is 0. Note that this is possible only because some of the weights are negative. Thus, the two mean square errors are

$$348.4a_2^2 + 0.067\sigma^2 \quad \text{(running average)}$$

$$0.193\sigma^2 \quad \text{(Spencer's 15-point).}$$

(3.20)

As we might have predicted, the choice between the two comes down to the relative strengths of the noise and the *symmetric* (relative to the center of the window) nonlinear component (here quadratic) in the signal $f$. A simple summary is the ratio of the sample variance of the symmetric component *in the window* to the noise. Here the ratio is

$$V\{a_2i^2\} / \sigma^2 = 294.7a_2^2 / \sigma^2 = r , \quad (3.21)$$

say, and the respective mean square errors are

$$\sigma^2(0.067 + 1.18r) \quad \text{(running average)}$$

$$\sigma^2(0.193) \quad \text{(Spencer's 15-point).}$$

(3.22)

If the sample variance of $f$, as above, is as little as 11% of the noise (a very small signal variance to noise ratio!) then Spencer's 15-point has smaller mean square error.

As shown in the discussion of twicing in the section on running median smoothers there are many digital filters of differing spans that filter cubic polynomials without change, and therefore, by linearity, have 0 bias. The optimum 15-point smoother, in the sense of giving the least-squares fit to *all* the data in the window for the cubic model equation 3.17 has mean square error $0.151\sigma^2$, compared to $0.193\sigma^2$ for Spencer's 15-point.

These computations demonstrate that a running average, $[b]/b$, with wide span is far from optimum. What of running averages of more moderate span? As we have seen, running medians of 3 are used very often, of 5 often, but of 7 seldom. We may use the procedure above to compare running averages of these orders, specifically,

$$[5]/5 \text{ to } [3][3]/9 = (1,2,3,2,1)/9$$

and

$$[7]/7 \text{ to } [5][3]/15 = (1, 2, 3, 3, 3, 2, 1)/15$$
$$\text{to } [3][3][3]/27 = (1, 3, 6, 7, 6, 3, 1)/27.$$

For the first comparison, with span 5, the mean squares are

$$4a_2^2 + 0.2\sigma^2 \quad \text{(running average)}$$

$$1.8a_2^2 + 0.23\sigma^2 \quad ([3][3] / 9). \tag{3.23}$$

The symmetric-signal variance to noise ratio is $r = 2.5a_2^2/\sigma^2$ and the respective mean square errors are

$$\sigma^2(0.2 + 1.14r) \quad \text{(running average)}$$

$$\sigma^2(0.23 + 0.51r) \quad ([3][3] / 9). \tag{3.24}$$

With $r = 5.4\%$ or greater the weighted alternative has smaller mean square error.

For the second comparison of filters with span 7, the ratio is $r = 14a_2^2/\sigma^2$ and the mean squares are

$$16a_2^2 + 0.14\sigma^2 = \sigma^2(0.14 + 1.14r) \quad \text{(running average)}$$

$$7.1a_2^2 + 0.16\sigma^2 = \sigma^2(0.16 + 0.51r) \quad ([5][3]/15) \tag{3.25}$$

$$4a_2^2 + 0.19\sigma^2 = \sigma^2(0.19 + 0.29r) \quad ([3][3][3]/27).$$

With $r = 3.4\%$, $[5][3]/15$ has smaller mean square error than the running average. With $r = 5.9\%$, $[3][3][3]/27$ has smaller mean square error than $[7]/7$, and with $r = 13\%$, $[3][3][3]/27$ has smaller mean square error than $[5][3]/15$.

In summary, these examples show that even with only a small quadratic component in the data — and *a fortiori* when the quadratic component is larger — the weighted mean with largest weights in the center has smaller mean square error than the running average. The smaller bias term of the former swamps the smaller variance term of the latter. The advantages of filters with monotone-decreasing weights increase as quartic and higher-order symmetric components are added to the signal. Analogous reasoning leads to identical conclusions for median filters. We do not use long-span running medians, but instead build compound smoothers from short-span, 2,3,4, and 5, running medians. The mean square error of a median-based smoother is, of course, not as easy to compute.

In comparing filters with different spans, we may again compare the mean square errors as functions of $a_2^2$ and $\sigma^2$. The heavier smoothers have larger $a_2^2$ coefficients and smaller $\sigma^2$ coefficients. The running average of 15 is poor because of the former. The best of the three span-7 filters, [3][3][3]/27, is comparable to the running average of 5 in both coefficients. The two other span-7 filters have poorer bias but better variance. Quartic and higher-order components become increasingly important as the span of the smoother increases.

Low-order, local polynomial behavior with noise is not the only pattern found in data. Another important pattern is spikes and steps, in other words, outliers and edges. Digital filters and nonlinear smoothers differ significantly in the pattern of the smooth at such phenomena.

### Resistance of Smoothers

There are many different ways to smooth data, with no outright winners. A "good" smoother responds in appropriate ways to specific patterns in the data. One pattern is a spike, or outlier. Panels A1-A4 of Figure 3.8 show spikes of width 1, 2, 3, and 4, respectively, in an otherwise flat sequence. The smoother is *resistant* if outliers have little weight in the final smooth, that is, if the smoother eliminates spikes. A digital filter, for example, the running average of 5, smears each spike, as shown in Panels B1-B4. It is not resistant. In fact no linear filter is resistant, as the sum of smooths of a data sequence decomposed into singleton spikes must equal the smooth of the original data. On the other hand, a running median smoother *is* resistant. A running median of 3 eliminates a single outlier (Panel C1). Heavier smoothers that are resistant tend to eliminate longer sequences of consecutive high or low values. Thus 3 eliminates 1 outlier but not a pair (Panel C2), whereas 7 eliminates 1, 2, or 3 (Panel C3) outliers but not 4 (Panel C4). In general,

$s + 1$ or more successive high values remain high when smoothed by a running median with span $2s + 1$.

An undesirable side effect of smoothing in general and eliminating outliers in particular is erosion: Bumps tend to be flattened and troughs filled in, since the apex of a bump is, in a sense, a spike. The running average of 5 transforms a single outlier to a flat plateau with width 5 and height 0.2. With increasing width of spike (2, 3, 4) the plateau broadens (widths 6, 7, 8) and becomes humped (heights 0.4, 0.6, 0.8). (The total height under the plateau is equal to the number of outliers.) Thus if we choose to regard the spikes of widths 3 and 4 as humps then there is substantial erosion. The running medians are much better: Either the spike is completely eliminated or perfectly preserved. However, real data contain more complex patterns and it would not be wise to adopt a running median in general because it is optimum for the model patterns of Panels A1-A4.

In choosing a more sophisticated smoother, a digital filter with unequal weights, a compound running median smoother, or lowess, we prefer a smoother that incorporates a satisfactory compromise between the competing goals of eliminating outliers and minimizing erosion. Spencer's 15-point smoother (Panels D1-D4) has the same drawbacks as the running average, except that the smearing is more extensive. The spikes are smeared to widths 15, 16, 18, and 18, respectively, including a recoil below 0 that is deeper for the broader spikes. Ignoring the recoil, the patterns in rows B and D are comparable, but Spencer's smoother gives a smoother result.

The smoother **43RSR2H**, twice (Panels E1-E4) eliminates only a single outlier, but does preserve the height, although not the entire extent, of the spikes of 3 and 4. Tukey (1984) remarked that resistance to outliers and minimization of erosion are the two primary obstacles to smoothing for data exploration. The family of compound running median smoothers overcomes both obstacles: The median confers resistance and twicing reduces erosion, as exemplified by **3RSSH**, twice in Figure 3.5B and **43RSR2H**, twice here.

Along with spikes, a second important pattern in a data sequence is a step upward or downward. The step should be isolated, relative to the window width, from other steps so that it is not part of a spike, a monotone subsequence, or simply noise. Panel A of Figure 3.9 shows a model step. A resistant smoother preserves the step, but a smoother that is not resistant will smear the step, from cliff face to hillside. Thus the running average of 5 smears the step to include four intermediate

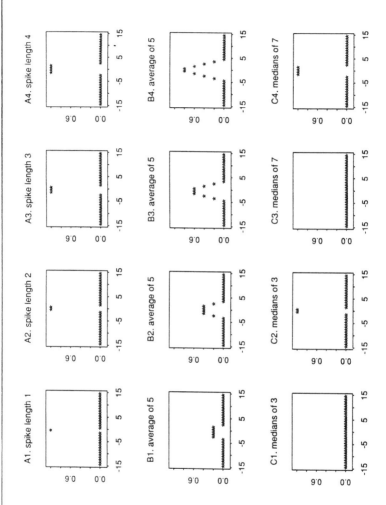

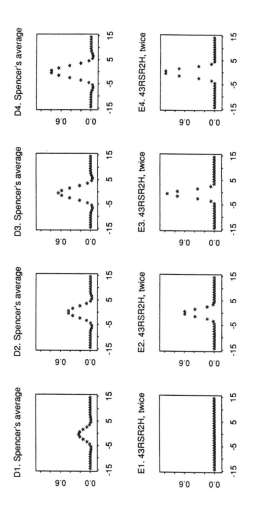

**Figure 3.8** Smooths of spikes of widths 1, 2, 3, and 4 (A1-A4) by the digital filters [5]/5 (B1-B4) and Spencer's 15-point smoother (D1-D4) and by the running medians 3 (C1-C2), 7 (C3-C4) and 43RSR2H, twice (E1-E4).

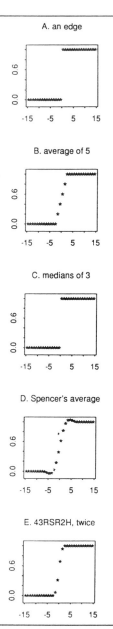

Figure 3.9  Smooths of an edge (A) by [5] / 5 (B), 3 (C), Spencer's 15-point
            smoother (D) and 43RSR2H, twice (E).

values, but the running median of 3 (or 5, or 7, . . . ) leaves the step unchanged. However, a monotone subsequence can be viewed as a sequence of steps, and any smoother that preserves every step will not smooth monotone data. Therefore, as with outlier elimination and erosion, we look for more complex smoothers that compromise effectively at both a step and monotone data. The longer-span digital filter, Spencer's 15-point smoother, smears the step to include 14 values, both intermediate between the original values and outside them in a "Gibb's" overshoot. The resistant compound smoother **43RSR2H**, twice is again particularly effective — there are just four intermediate values.

### *Frequency-Domain Analysis of Smoothers*

We turn now to the role of Fourier analysis in understanding smoothers. For a more thorough treatment see Hamming (1977), Bloomfield (1976), Cadzow (1987), Goodall (1989), Velleman (1980), and Mallows (1980). According to Fourier theory, we can decompose any data sequence into a sum of sinusoidal components at various frequencies. The most common form is the Fourier decomposition into sinusoids with rotational frequencies equally spaced between 0 and 1/2,

$$y_i = \frac{R_0}{2} + \sum_{0 < j \le [n/2]} R_j \cos\left(2\pi \frac{j}{n} i + \theta_j\right) \tag{3.26}$$

where $R_0/2$ is the constant term and $j/n$ the rotational frequency of the $j$th sinusoid, with $R_j$ its amplitude and $\theta_j$ its phase. In a smoothing context the high frequency components may be considered noise. If these are eliminated then we are left with a smooth sequence that is the sum of low frequency components.

For a linear smoother, the smooth of the sum of sinusoids is the sum of smooths of the individual curves. The linear smooth of a single sinusoid with frequency $f$ is a sinusoid with the same frequency $f$ and phase, but different amplitude. The amplitude is multiplied by the *transfer coefficient*, $H(f)$ of the filter at that frequency. The filtered sequence is therefore

$$S(y_i) = H(0)\frac{R_0}{2} + \sum_{0 < j < [n/2]} H(j/n)R_j \cos\left(2\pi \frac{j}{n} i + \theta_j\right). \tag{3.27}$$

The *transfer function*, that is, the collection of coefficients $H(f)$, $0 \leq f \leq 1/2$, is a fixed property of the given digital filter, and does not depend on the data sequence or its length $n$. In fact, for a digital filter with symmetric weights,

$$H(f) = \sum_{-s}^{s} w_k \cos 2\pi fk. \qquad (3.28)$$

Note that if $w_k \geq 0$ for each $k$ then $H(f) \leq 1$, implying attenuation, never amplification. For example, the transfer function of the moving-average filter [7]/7 is

$$H_{[7]/7}(f) = \frac{1}{7} [1 + 2 \cos 2\pi f + 2 \cos 4\pi f + 2 \cos 6\pi f]. \qquad (3.29)$$

Figure 3.10 (dashed curve) shows the transfer function of [7]/7.

Our goal may be a linear smoother with a step transfer function (Figure 3.10, solid curve) that precisely preserves all sinusoids with frequency below a certain threshold, the *pass frequency*, $f_p$, and eliminates all sinusoids with frequency above the pass frequency (Hamming, 1977). This smoother is called the *ideal low-pass filter*. Unfortunately, such a filter, written as a weighted average, has infinite span. Considerable effort has gone into the design of compromise low-pass filters — weighted average smoothers with finite span that tend to preserve low-frequency components and eliminate high-frequency components. The Hanning filter, **H**, is the simplest example.

The transfer function of the running average, $H_{[7]/7}(f)$, is low pass, but has some oscillatory behavior for the larger $f$. Ripples indicate that components of the Fourier decomposition that are close together in frequency are acted on differently by the filter. Thus a particular frequency may be relatively enhanced, leading to artifacts in the smoothed data sequence. We ask that the transfer function of a smoothing filter have long monotone stretches. In fact, in practical applications when smoothing a data sequence, as distinct from many applications in signal processing, we are unsure of a precise pass frequency $f_p$. Instead of a step function, we want the transfer function to be close to 1 near $f = 0$, close to 0 near $f = 1/2$, and to descend monotonically — without ripples — from high to low in a moderately narrow *transition band* for intermediate $f$. Of course, for any finite data sequence we can use the

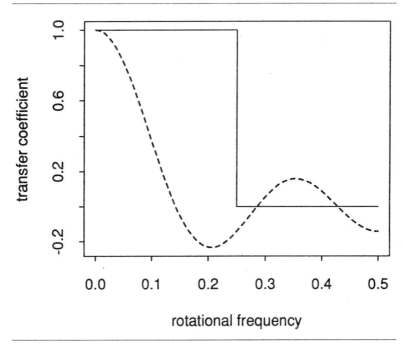

**Figure 3.10  Ideal low-pass transfer function with pass frequency $f_p$ = 1/4 (solid line) and transfer function of [7]/7 (dashed line).**

Fast Fourier Transform (Cooley & Tukey, 1965), apply whichever transfer function we wish, and reconstruct the smoothed sequence. This would not be possible for real-time signal processing.

On the other hand, good smoothers for exploring data are resistant: They eliminate spikes and preserve edges. This means that we must qualify the goal of an ideal low-pass filter, because each of the Fourier decompositions of a spike and an edge contain both low- and high-frequency terms. The infinite range of frequencies in the Fourier decomposition of an edge is, in fact, the same mathematical phenomenon related to the *Gibbs phenomenon*, as the infinite span of the ideal low-pass filter. Resistant smoothers cannot be linear as we have seen. Thus, unlike digital filters, which pass sinusoids unchanged apart from amplitude, resistant nonlinear smoothers exhibit complex behavior when applied to single sinusoids or sums of sinusoids. For example, the smooth of a single sinusoid may contain several frequencies with different phases.

Despite the multiple difficulties, the Fourier analysis of nonlinear smoothers *is* a topic of past and present statistical research. The attraction of this approach is that the properties of the linear smoothers are completely understood in Fourier terms. The properties can be *designed* into linear filters. If we can express a nonlinear smoother as the "closest" linear smoother plus a "pure nonlinear" part (Mallows, 1980), then we may perhaps design the linear part and cogently discuss the benefits and disadvantages conveyed by the pure nonlinear part.

*Fourier analysis and robustness of nonlinear smoothers.* As we have seen, a smoother cannot perfectly preserve low frequencies and annihilate high frequencies, even when the span of the smoother is as large as we like. However, we do tend to prefer resistant smoothers that approximate the ideal low-pass filter. Additional criteria related to the Fourier decomposition are important also. These include the extent of phase shifts, modulation of one frequency in the data to other frequencies in the smooth (transport), and the interference of sinusoids at different frequencies in the data sequence in determining the final smooth. Velleman (1980) compared running-median-based compound smoothers according to these criteria, along with their degree of resistance to spikes, the retention of edges, and the overall robustness to heavy-tailed noise in the sequence. We review his results briefly here. Overall, resistance and robustness are most important to us. Criteria based on the Fourier decomposition are especially relevant when the sequence has a predominant single periodic component, but for resistant smoothing of more complex sequences the Fourier decomposition may not be as informative.

Suppose $y_i = R \cos(2\pi f i + \theta)$ is a sinusoidal data sequence. Then for a linear smoother $S$, with transfer function $H(f)$, the smooth is

$$S(y)_i = H(f)R \cos(2\pi f i + \theta + \phi(f)) \tag{3.30}$$

where the phase shift $\phi$ is 0 if the filter weights are symmetric. For a nonlinear smoother the corresponding expression is much more complex,

$$S(y)_i = H(f, \theta)R \cos(2\pi f i + \theta + \phi(f, \theta)) + E(t). \tag{3.31}$$

The amplitude changes by $H(f,\theta)$ according to both the frequency and phase of the cosine. There is also a phase shift $\phi(f,\theta)$, plus residual terms. The residual $E(t)$ includes the transport of the sinusoid $\cos(2\pi f i + \theta)$ to other frequencies. If the sequence is the sum of two (or more) sinusoids, with frequencies $f_1$ and $f_2$, say, then there is interference. We cannot simply use equation 3.31 twice, take the $f_2$ and $f_1$ components out of the respective $E(t)$ terms, and simplify. The nonlinear smoother is not linear; the results we present below for a single sinusoid are indicative at best for more complex data.

Velleman (1980) described an extensive investigation to estimate the transfer functions $H(f,0)$ at zero phase. The estimates are obtained as the slope coefficient from the simple linear regression of a sinusoidal sequence ($x$-variable) on the smooth of the sequence ($y$-variable), taking care to remove data points from each end of the sequence and its smooth to eliminate end effects. Velleman illustrates the estimated transfer functions for several running median smoothers. The smoothers **3R** and **5** approximate the ideal low-pass filter poorly, with either an irregular ill-defined transfer function or large $\hat{H}$ at high frequencies. However, subsequent smoothing by the Hanning filter is a substantial improvement. The compound smoothers (**3RSSH**; **53H**; **42**; **4253H**, twice; and, best of all, **43RSR2H**, twice) have estimated transfer coefficients that approximate the ideal low-pass filter very well.

A further issue is the extent of transport to other frequencies. In this regard, even-span smoothers are much better than odd-span running median smoothers. Velleman also considered the robustness of the smoother, that is, the recovery of the signal when Gaussian, long-tailed, or spiky noise is added. Velleman concluded that good compound smoothers have close to ideal low-pass characteristics and are robust to noise, resistant to spikes, and preserve edges. His recommendations, in decreasing order, are **4253H**, twice; **43RSR2H**, twice; **3RSSH**; and **53H**, twice. Of these four **4253H**, twice is the best in terms of dependence on phase and transport to other frequencies, and we would improve **3RSSH** by twicing.

## SOME SOPHISTICATED SMOOTHERS

Our previous discussion concerned local fitting of averages, weighted averages, and medians. That approach can obviously be taken further, to other estimates of location, such as any of the $L$- and $M$-estimators described by Rosenberger and Gasko (1983) and Goodall (1983). However, the more profitable course at this point is to broaden our horizons of what a smoother can be, by considering the role of regression.

One approach is to replace the average, mean, or median of the observations in each window by the intercept (at the center of the window) of a regression line or curve fit to the data in the windows. We have seen already that for polynomial regression and equally spaced data this is equivalent to filtering with a specific weighted-average smoother. If the data are unequally spaced, or if greater weight in the regression is given to the observations closer to the center of the window, then this so-called *local weighted polynomial regression smoother* is still equivalent to a running weighted average, but with different weights in each window: The weights are the rows of the hat matrix in regression, $H$: $n \times n$, $\hat{y} = Hy$ (Belsley, Kuh, & Welsch, 1980; Hoaglin & Welsch, 1978; Chapter 6, this volume). Cleveland's *lowess*, discussed in detail below and illustrated in the introduction to this chapter, computes the regressions explicitly. These are usually iterative linear regressions that include both regression weights that decrease as the cube of distance from the center observation and bi-square robustness weights.

A second approach is to fit a polynomial directly to the data. To represent a complex smooth adequately requires a very high-order polynomial, which is numerically unstable. Instead we prefer to fit a low-order, cubic, polynomial piecewise, divided at knots where the second but not the third derivative is continuous. This, the method of splines, is discussed in the section on regression splines for smoothing and interpolation.

A useful property of both lowess and splines is that of interpolation: We can obtain the value of the smooth at any value $x$ within the range of the data.

### Cleveland's Lowess

Cleveland (1979) described robust local-weighted regression estimates, lowess, for smoothing bivariate or time-series data. The basic idea is a simple one: At each $x$ value fit a regression line to the nearby $(x,y)$ observations and take as our estimate $\hat{f}(x)$ the $y$ value of the line at $x$. Unlike the smoothers described to this point, lowess allows $x$ to take *any* value, not necessarily that of an observation. Thus the output of lowess is a smooth curve.

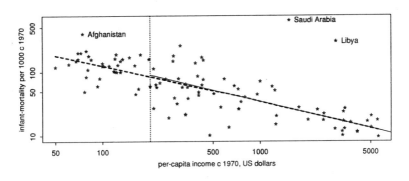

**Figure 3.11  Lowess computations in a window around Libya.**

NOTES: The window around Libya contains the right two-thirds of the data. The local regression line, fit by weighted least squares, is shown solid and the lowess curve dashed (A).

The smoothness parameter of lowess is denoted $f$, the fraction of the data contained in each window. Larger values of $f$ correspond to heavier smooths. For a sequence of length $n$, the exactly $q = [fn]$ observations closest to $x$ are included in the window used to compute $\hat{f}(x)$. The default value of $f$ is 2/3. For the infant mortality data of 101 countries, 67 observations are included in each window. Figure 3.11A shows the window used to estimate $\hat{f}$ at $x = \log 3010$, the $x$ coordinate for Libya. Note that the window is asymmetric about $x$, because Libya is near the end of the range of per capita income.

Two sets of weights are used in fitting the regression line to the data in the window. The *regression weights* are fixed by the $x$ coordinates of the observations. Let $d(x)$ denote the distance to the $q$th nearest neighbor of $x$. If $x$ is itself an observation then we include it as one of the $q$ and consider only the $(q - 1)$ nearest neighbors. The regression weight $w_i$ of the $i$th observation $(x_i, y_i)$ is given by the tricube function

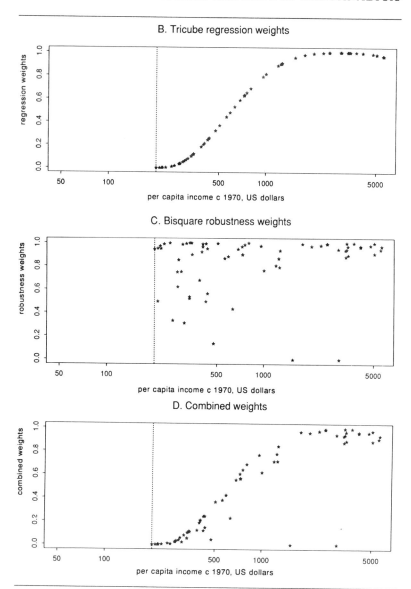

**B. Tricube regression weights**

**C. Bisquare robustness weights**

**D. Combined weights**

*per capita income c 1970, US dollars*

## Figure 3.11   continued

NOTES: The regression weights follow a tricube function with a maximum at Libya (B). The robustness weights are a bisquare function of the scaled residuals about the current lowess curve (C). Libya and Saudi Arabia each have robustness weight equal to zero. The weights used in fitting the regression line are the product of the regression and robustness weights (D).

$$w_i = \left(1 - \left|\frac{x - x_i}{d(x)}\right|^3\right)^3. \tag{3.32}$$

Thus the $q$th, or $(q-1)$st, nearest neighbor determines the scale, $d(x)$, of the tricube function but is given zero weight. Hansen (1989) suggested a modification when most of the $x_i$'s are clustered at distance $d(x)$. Figure 3.11B shows the tricube regression weights for the window in Figure 3.11A.

For resistance, lowess uses a second set of weights, the *robustness weights*. These depend on the residuals from the fitted curve and are bi-square weights

$$w_i^* = \begin{cases} (1 - (r_i/6M)^2)^2 & |r_i| < 6M \\ 0 & |r_i| > 6M \end{cases} \tag{3.33}$$

where $M$ is the median absolute deviation of the $r_i$,

$$M = \underset{i}{\text{median}} \left( \left| r_i - \underset{j}{\text{median}} (r_j) \right| \right).$$

For additional discussion of bi-square weights, see Mosteller and Tukey (1977) and Goodall (1983). We usually refine the robustness weights iteratively over about three iterations. Figure 3.11C shows the robustness weights for the example. Saudi Arabia and Libya have robustness weight zero. The regression line shown in Figure 3.11A is the fit with weights $w_i w_i^*$, the product of the regression and robustness weights (Figure 3.11D). Its value coincides exactly with the lowess curve (dashed line) at $x = \log 3010$, the coordinate for Libya.

Additional exposition of lowess is given by Cleveland (1979), Chambers, Cleveland, Kleiner, and Tukey (1983) and Cleveland (1985). Cleveland, Devlin, and Grosse (1988) and Cleveland and Devlin (1988) describe a generalization of lowess to multiple $x$ variables (surface fitting), termed *loess*. In the latter paper the authors exploit the linear model structure of loess, when robustness weights are not used, to help determine $f$ for the appropriate trade-off between bias and variance.

For the housing start data the default lowess picks out the overall trend and does not reveal the periodicity in the data. Smaller values of $f$ ($f = 0.1$, say) correspond to the compound running median smoothers such as **4253H**, twice. Note that to maintain this approximate equivalence when doubling the number of years of data we would halve $f$.

## Regression Splines for Smoothing and Interpolation

Throughout this chapter we have made assorted references to the model function $f$ and estimating $f$ by fitting a polynomial to the data. The Weierstrass approximation theorem tells us that we can approximate any continuous function on a finite interval arbitrarily well by a polynomial provided that the degree of polynomial can be as large as we need. Thus an alternative to the smoothing techniques discussed here is to fit a single, global, high-order polynomial to the data. It is well known that this approach is inappropriate: The coefficients are unstable, a small change in one datum affects the entire fit, and the extrapolated values, outside the interval of the data, diverge rapidly to infinity.

A different approach, that of splines, is to approximate the model function $f$ by a piecewise, but smooth, low-order polynomial. The most common choice is a piecewise cubic polynomial. We shall assume that choice from here on. We divide the data into subintervals at so-called knots, and fit a cubic polynomial in each subinterval. The knots $y_1, \ldots, y_k$ are chosen such that the data lie between $y_4$ and $y_{k-4}$, inclusive. We also assume, for now, that the knots are distinct. To ensure that the result is smooth, we choose the polynomials so that their values, first derivatives, and second derivatives agree at either side of each knot, apart from the end knots.

As a consequence of these continuity constraints, we cannot fit a cubic polynomial directly in each subinterval by separate regressions. Instead, we note that any piecewise cubic polynomial, $f$, with continuous second derivatives, is expressible as a linear combination of cubic Green's functions (De Boor, 1978; Schumaker, 1981),

$$g(x) = \sum \alpha_j (x - y_j)_+^3 \qquad (3.34)$$

where

$$(x - y_j)_+^3 = \begin{cases} (x - y_j)^3 & x > y_j \\ 0 & x \leq y_j. \end{cases}$$

Notice that each Green's function is nonzero for each $x > y_j$; that is, the Green's function has semi-infinite support $(y_j, \infty)$. A recent technique of Friedman and Silverman (1988) uses the Green's functions directly. The more common approach is that of B-splines. The $k$th B-*spline basis function* is a linear combination of Green's functions at five successive knot points $y_k, y_{k+1}, y_{k+2}, y_{k+3}, y_{k+4}$,

$$Q_k(x) = \sum_{j=k}^{k+4} \beta_j (x - y_j)_+^3.$$  (3.35)

$Q_k(x)$ is a piecewise cubic polynomial with continuous second derivatives at each knot. The linear combination is chosen so that $Q_k(x)$ vanishes outside $[y_k, y_{k+4}]$ ($Q_k(x) = 0$ for $x < y_k$ is obvious) and so that the first and second derivatives vanish at $y_k$ and $y_{k+4}$ ($Q'_k(y_k) = Q''_k(y_k) = 0$ is obvious, taking the derivative from the right). Therefore, any linear combination of B-spline basis functions,

$$g(x) = \sum_{k=1}^{k-4} \gamma_k Q_k(x)$$  (3.36)

is a piecewise cubic with continuous second derivatives at each knot. The B-splines are normalized so that

$$\sum_{k=1}^{k-4} Q_k(x) = 1$$

at each $x$ in $[y_4, y_{k-4}]$. Figure 3.12A shows typical basis functions for the housing start data. The knots are equally spaced at each January 1963-1978, inclusive. Figure 3.12B shows the linear combination

$$(\gamma_1, \ldots, \gamma_{12}) = \begin{pmatrix} -126.8, 159.5, 63.1, 137.5, 143.2, 90.1, \\ 158.1, 190.3, 224.2, 105.9, 171.5, -622.9 \end{pmatrix}$$

of the 12 basis function in Figure 3.12A. This linear combination is computed as the least squares fit, without intercept, of the housing start data to the 12 independent variables (mostly filled with 0's) obtained

A: B-splines with 1 knot each year

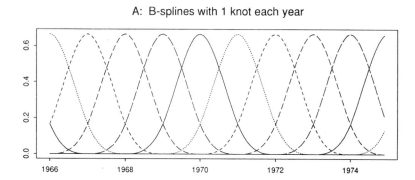

B: Regression spline with 1 knot each year

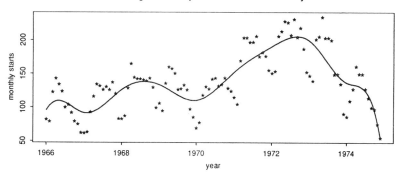

C: Regression spline with 2 knots each year

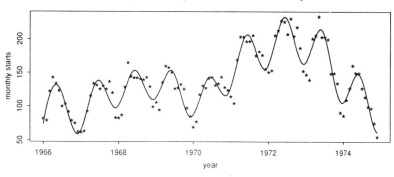

Figure 3.12  **B-spline basis functions with one knot each year (A); regression splines with one (B), two (C), and six (D) equally spaced knots each year; regression spline with three coincident knots each May and one each January (E).**

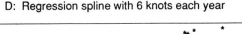

D: Regression spline with 6 knots each year

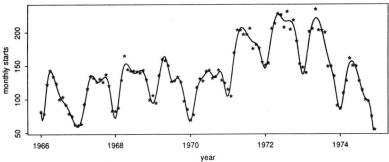

E: Regression spline with 3 coincident knots each May, 1 each December

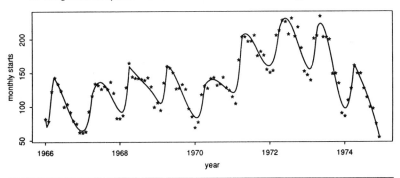

**Figure 3.12 continued**

by computing $Q_k(x)$ for each month, January 1966 through December 1974. This smooth is called a *regression spline* (Wegman & Wright 1983).

The B-spline basis functions comprise a *local basis* for the piecewise polynomials. In this sense the B-spline approach is consistent with our local averaging approach to smoothing. The method is, of course, not resistant, although Lenth (1977) and others have proposed robust versions of splines.

The choice of knots determines the general shape of the fit. Note first of all that the $k$th basis function contributes to the fit at $x$ provided $y_k < x < y_{k+4}$. Therefore there must be 4 knots less than or equal to the smallest $x$ value, and 4 knots greater than or equal to the largest $x$ value. The smoothness of the solution decreases as the number of knots increases. From Figure 3.12B we see that a single knot each year is insufficient to capture the annual variation in housing starts. With a pair of knots each year (Figure 3.12C) the spline includes smooth periodic variation, comparable to Spencer's 15-point smooth (Figure 3.1C). With as many as 6 knots each year (Figure 3.12D) the spline captures the pattern of rapid increase in spring. Finally, with 12 knots each year, one at each data value, the spline interpolates the data with an *interpolation spline*. This is, of course, most useful for making a continuous curve from a discrete but already smooth sequence.

The pattern of equally spaced knots we have selected may not be the best choice; in general we would wish to choose the knot positions and the number of knots carefully (Eubank, 1984, 1988; Wold 1974). The *smoothing spline criterion* (Seber & Wild, 1989; Silverman, 1986; Wegman & Wright, 1983) has this form: Choose *f* to be the function with at least two derivatives that minimizes

$$\sum_{i=1}^{n} [y_i - f(x_i)]^2 + \lambda \int_{a}^{b} (f''(x))^2 \, dx. \qquad (3.37)$$

The first term of equation 3.37 measures the fidelity or closeness of *f* to the data, the second the smoothness of *f*. The smoothing parameter $\lambda$ measures the trade-off between fidelity and smoothness. Large values of $\lambda$ imply a heavier smooth with fewer knots. The solution to equation 3.37 *is* a cubic spline. For this reason, we consider cubic splines only.

Even when restricted to cubic piecewise polynomials, B-splines offer substantial flexibility in the number and placement of knots and also with the possibility that two or more knots may coincide. A knot marks a discontinuity in the piecewise polynomial or one of its derivatives. Where there is no knot, the cubic polynomial and all three derivatives are continuous. Where there is a single knot, the third derivative is discontinuous. Where two knots coincide, the second derivative is discontinuous. Where three knots coincide, the function is continuous, but there may be an abrupt change in slope. Where four knots coincide, the function itself may be discontinuous. Mathematically, we modify equation 3.33 to include Green's functions of progressively *lower* orders at the multiple knot. Figure 3.12E shows the spline smooth of the housing start data with three knots each May and one each January. There is a discontinuity in slope at the start of the summer.

## DISCUSSION

In this chapter we have discussed some of the important smoothing techniques used in data analysis and signal processing. These include digital filters or running weighted averages, running medians, robust local weighted regression or lowess, and spline smoothing by B-splines. The most important factor in the choice of smoother is the degree of smoothness desired. In addition to that discussion, we include three criteria by which to compare smoothers: (1) the trade-off between bias and variance; (2) resistance, that is, elimination of spikes and preservation of edges; and (3) Fourier analysis and low-pass properties.

The first and last criteria provide valuable guidance in choosing between different sets of weights and different combinations of running median smoothers. However, for a versatile tool with which to explore data and uncover systematic patterns in time series, the second criterion is most essential. Running median smoothers offer clear advantages over digital filters. A compound smoother such as **43RSR2H**, twice is both resistant and avoids erosion of bumps and troughs. In the second section we show how a different compound smoother **3RSSH**, twice, is constructed from first principles.

What of more sophisticated, regression-based smoothers, such as lowess and splines? Overall, lowess is a flexible, effective smoother well-suited to everyday use for exploring data. Typically we smooth the data several times, with various *f*. Several potential difficulties are that end effects can be substantial, lowess blurs edges, and the flexibility in choice of *f* can give a misleading sense of security — that all "possibilities are covered."

To elaborate on the last point, although the smoothness parameter *f* may take any value between 0 and 1, the number of observations in each window is an integer, 1,2,3, . . . , or *n*. Therefore the class of lowess smoothers is no larger than the class of simple running median smoothers, **2,3,4**, . . . , **n**. The lowess smoothers are better choices than these simple median smoothers. However, the lowess smoothers are restrictive in terms of the shape of the smooth. Comparison of several smooths that capture the periodic behavior of the housing start series reveals the variety of possible shapes in detail. These are the **43RSR2H**, twice (Figure 3.1C), Spencer's 15-point filter (Figure 3.3C), **3RSSH**, twice (Figure 3.6B), and splines with various choices of knots (Figures 3.12B-3.12E). Splines are a particularly versatile choice. However, even with repeated attempts, it is not certain that we have captured the essential pattern in the housing start data. Thus, although the compound running median smoothers are not readily ordered into a one-parameter family, the use of **3RSSH**, twice, or Velleman's recommendation, **4253H**, twice, or some other choice, may be more generally effective than any single lowess or spline smooth. **3RSSH**, twice is particularly effective in capturing the spring-summer transition housing start data. The other alternatives, including **4253H**, twice give a more rounded result.

There are many other smoothing techniques that are not mentioned here. These include kernel methods (Gasser & Muller, 1979), the supersmoother (Friedman, 1984; Friedman & Stuetzle, 1982), various developments of the resistant technology (Gebski, 1985; Goodall et al., 1986; Tukey, 1984), and the field of spatial smoothers. The interested reader is encouraged to investigate further.

## NOTE

1. Just as $y_i$ is the $i$th element of the sequence $(y)$, so $S(y)_i$ is the $i$th element of the smoothed sequence. The smoother $S$ acts on $(y)$, the entire sequence; therefore we prefer the notation $S(y)_i$ to $S(y_i)$.

## REFERENCES

Becker, R. A., Chambers, J. M., & Wilks, A. R. (1988). *The new S language: A programming environment for data analysis and graphics.* Pacific Grove, CA: Wadsworth and Brooks/Cole.

Belsley, D. A., Kuh, E., & Welsch, R. E. (1980). *Regression diagnostics.* New York: John Wiley.

Bloomfield, P. (1976). *Fourier analysis of time series: An introduction.* New York: John Wiley.

Cadzow, J. A. (1987). *Foundations of digital signal processing and data analysis.* New York: Macmillan.

Chambers, J. M., Cleveland, W. S., Kleiner, B., & Tukey, P. A. (1983). *Graphical methods for data analysis.* Monterey, CA: Wadsworth.

Cleveland, W. S. (1979). Robust locally weighted regression and smoothing scatterplots. *Journal of the American Statistical Association, 74,* 829-836.

Cleveland, W. R. (1985). *The elements of graphing data.* Monterey, CA: Wadsworth.

Cleveland, W. S., & Devlin, S. J. (1982). Calendar effects in monthly time series: Modeling and adjustment. *Journal of the American Statistical Association, 77,* 520-528.

Cleveland, W. S., & Devlin, S. J. (1988). Locally weighted regression: An approach to regression analysis by local fitting. *Journal of the American Statistical Association, 83*, 596-610.

Cleveland, W. S., Devlin, S. J., & Grosse, E. (1988). Regression by local fitting: Methods, properties, and computational algorithms. *Journal of Econometrics, 37*, 87-114.

Cooley, J. W., & Tukey, J. W. (1965). An algorithm for the machine computation of complex Fourier series. *Mathematics of Computation, 19*, 297-301.

De Boor, C. (1978). *A practical guide to splines.* New York: Springer-Verlag.

Emerson, J. D., & Hoaglin, D. C. (1983). Resistant lines for y versus x. In D. C. Hoaglin, F. Mosteller, & J. W. Tukey (Eds.), *Understanding robust and exploratory data analysis.* New York: John Wiley.

Eubank, R. L. (1984). Approximate regression models and splines. *Communications in Statistics: Theory and Methods A, 13*, 433-484.

Eubank, R. L. (1988). *Spline smoothing and nonparametric regression.* New York: Marcel Dekker.

Friedman, J. H. (1984). *A variable span smoother* (Tech. Rep. No. LCS5). Stanford, CA: Stanford University, Department of Statistics.

Friedman, J. H., & Silverman, B. W. (1988). *Flexible parsimonious smoothing and additive modeling* (Tech. Rep.). Stanford, CA: Stanford University, Department of Statistics.

Friedman, J. H., & Stuetzle, W. (1982). *Smoothing of scatterplots* (Tech. Rep. ORION 003). Stanford, CA: Stanford University, Department of Statistics.

Gasser, T., & Muller, H. G. (1979). Kernel estimation of regression functions. In T. Gasser & M. Rosenblatt (Eds.), *Smoothing techniques for curve estimation.* Berlin: Springer-Verlag.

Gebski, V. J. (1985). Some properties of splicing when applied to non-linear smoothers. *Computational Statistics and Data Analysis, 3*, 151-157.

Goodall, C. R. (1983). M-estimators of location: An outline of the theory. In D.C. Hoaglin, F. Mosteller, & J. W. Tukey (Eds.), *Understanding robust and exploratory data analysis.* New York: John Wiley.

Goodall, C. R. (1989). *A survey of smoothing* (Tech. Rep.). Princeton, NJ: Princeton University, Statistics and Operations Research.

Goodall, C. R., Stoughton, C., & Easton, G. (1986). Delineation plots for bivariate data: An example and outline of the method. *Proceedings of the Section on Statistical Graphics, American Statistical Association*, 81-85.

Hamming, R. W. (1977). *Digital filters.* Englewood Cliffs, NJ: Prentice-Hall.

Hansen, K. M. (1989). *Some statistical problems in geophysics and structural geology.* Unpublished doctoral dissertation, Department of Statistics, Princeton University, Princeton, NJ.

Hoaglin, D. C., Mosteller, F., & Tukey, J. W. (Eds.). (1983). *Understanding robust and exploratory data analysis.* New York: John Wiley.

Hoaglin, D. C., & Welsch, R. E. (1978). The hat matrix in regression and ANOVA. *The American Statistician, 32*, 17-22, and *Corrigenda, 32*, 146.

Johnstone, I. M., & Velleman, P. F. (1985). The resistant line and related regression methods. *Journal of the American Statistical Association, 80*, 1041-1054.

Kendall, M. G., & Stuart, A. (1976). *The advanced theory of statistics* (Vol. 3). London: Charles Griffin.

Leinhardt, S., & Wasserman, S. S. (1979). Exploratory data analysis: An introduction to selected methods. In K.R. Schuessler (Ed.), *Sociological methodology 1979*. San Francisco, CA: Jossey-Bass.

Lenth, R. V. (1977). Robust splines. *Communications in Statistics: Theory and Methods, 6*, 847-854.

Mallows, C. L. (1980). Some theory of nonlinear smoother. *Annals of Statistics, 8*, 695-715.

Mosteller, F., & Tukey, J. W. (1977). *Data analysis & regression*. Reading, MA: Addison-Wesley.

Rosenberger, J. L., & Gasko, M. (1983). Comparing location estimators: Trimmed means, medians, and trimean. In D. C. Hoaglin, F. Mosteller, & J. W. Tukey (Eds.), *Understanding robust and exploratory data analysis*. New York: John Wiley.

Schumaker, L. L. (1981). *Spline functions: Basic theory*. New York: John Wiley.

Seber, G. A. F., & Wild, C. J. (1989). *Nonlinear regression*. New York: John Wiley.

Silverman, B. W. (1986). *Density estimation for statistics and data analysis*. London: Chapman & Hall.

Tukey, J. W. (1977). *Exploratory data analysis*. Reading, MA: Addison-Wesley.

Tukey, J. W. (1984). *Thinking about non-linear smoothers* (Tech. Rep.). Princeton, NJ: Princeton University, Department of Statistics.

Velleman, P. F. (1980). Definition and comparison of robust nonlinear data smoothing algorithms. *Journal of the American Statistical Association, 75*, 609-615.

Velleman, P. F., & Hoaglin, D. C. (1981). *Applications, basics and computing of exploratory data analysis*. Boston, MA: Duxbury Press.

Wahba, G. (1979). *How to smooth curves and surfaces with splines and cross-validation*. Proceedings of the 24th Conference on the Design of Experiments, U.S. Army Research Office, Report 79-2.

Wegman, E. J., & Wright, I. W. (1983). Splines in statistics. *Journal of the American Statistical Association, 78*, 351-365.

Wold, S. (1974). Spline functions in data analysis. *Technometrics, 16*, 1-11.

# 4

## FINDING TRANSFORMATIONS FOR REGRESSION USING THE ACE ALGORITHM

### Richard D. De Veaux

The social scientist is often faced with the task of explaining the effect of one or more independent variables (predictors) on a dependent variable (response). The technology of *linear* models is powerful, and it is therefore tempting to propose a simple, empirical model of the form

$$y_i = \beta_0 + \beta_1 x_{1i} + \ldots + \beta_p x_{pi} + \varepsilon_i . \tag{4.1}$$

This model implies that the response, $y_i$, is composed of a systematic component,

$$\beta_0 + \beta_1 x_{1i} + \ldots + \beta_p x_{pi} ,$$

linear in the parameters $\beta_i$, and a random component $\varepsilon_i$. If one is willing to make the assumption that the errors, $\varepsilon_i$, are independently and normally distributed with constant variance, this technology provides efficient estimates of the parameters, confidence intervals for the estimates, and

AUTHOR'S NOTE: I would like to acknowledge the helpful comments of the editors and Rob Tibshirani on an earlier draft of this chapter. I would also like to thank John Fox for providing the data sets used as examples.

confidence intervals for point predictions. For nonlinear models, such a complete machinery is not available.

If the systematic part of the model is known a priori to be intrinsically nonlinear in the parameters, or that the errors are not transformable to be normal, one may have to consider nonlinear regression or generalized linear models. However, it is often possible by transforming some or all of the variables to achieve approximate linearity in the systematic (nonrandom) part of the model. Although the goal of achieving linearity may be at cross-purposes with the goals of transforming the errors to be normal and may have constant variance, the same transformation often brings the analyst closer to all three goals. Additionally, a study of the transformations themselves may aid in the larger goal of understanding the relationships between the predictors and the response. The need for transformation may be driven by any of these problems: nonlinearity, nonnormality, or nonconstant variance (heteroscedasticity). Diagnostics are available for assessing the degree to which a data set exhibits any of these problems (see Belsley et al., 1980, or Fox, 1984).

The goal of this chapter is to introduce the *alternating conditional expectation* (ACE) algorithm, a recently developed nonparametric tool for finding transformations. By using the ACE algorithm, we will find the transformations that maximize the overall multiple correlation, $R^2$, of the response $Y$ with the predictors, $X_1, \ldots, X_p$. We will examine the ACE transformations to see what insights the transformations provide. They may suggest new ways of modeling the dependence of $Y$ on $X_1, \ldots, X_p$. In some cases, it may even be possible to find familiar, closed-form expressions to approximate these transformations. Finally, the ACE procedure can be used as a diagnostic tool for assessing the choice of a model.

The chapter is structured as follows. In the next section, we explain the ACE algorithm and look at its output for simple (one-predictor) regression. In the third section, we review the Box-Cox method for finding closed-form expressions for transformations. This will aid us in interpreting the output from ACE. In the fourth section, we outline the ACE procedure for multiple regression and consider its application to an example from the sociological literature. The fifth section contains caveats and limitations of the ACE procedure. We summarize in the final section.

## THE ACE ALGORITHM

The ACE algorithm (Breiman & Friedman, 1985) provides an automatic way to find the transformation of both the response and the predictors that maximizes the multiple correlation, $R^2$, between $Y$ and the set $X_1, \ldots, X_p$. In this section, we will describe how the algorithm works, what the output of the algorithm consists of, and illustrate its use on two simple linear regression data sets. Readers not interested in the mathematical description of the algorithm may wish to skim the following subsection at first reading and proceed to the next subsection.

### *Theory*

Consider the two variable case, with $Y$ and one $X$. To make things simple, let $Y$ and $X$ be standardized so that they have mean 0 and variance 1. The goal of the ACE algorithm is to find the function of $Y$, $\theta(Y)$, and the function of $X$, $\phi(X)$, so that the correlation of $\theta(Y)$ with $\phi(X)$ is maximized, with the restriction that we keep $\text{Var}(\theta(Y)) = 1$. Maximizing the correlation is equivalent to minimizing the fraction of variance, $e^2$, not explained by a regression of $\theta(Y)$ on $\phi(X)$:

$$e^2(\theta(Y),\phi(X)) \equiv \frac{E\left[(\theta(Y)-\phi(X))^2\right]}{E(\theta^2(Y))} = E\left[(\theta(Y)-\phi(X))^2\right], \qquad (4.2)$$

when $E$ denotes taking expectation. Note that $e^2 = 1 - R^2$ so that minimizing equation 4.2 maximizes $R^2$.

To understand the ACE algorithm solution of equation 4.2, consider first the minimization of (4.2) for $\theta(Y) = Y$. Equation 4.2 becomes

$$e^2 = E(Y-\phi(X))^2. \qquad (4.3)$$

We are looking for the function $\phi(X)$ of $X$, with the smallest mean square error for predicting $Y$. The solution to minimizing (4.3) is to take $\phi(X) = E(Y|X)$, the conditional expectation of $Y$ given $X$. (See, e.g., Rao, 1973, p. 264). In other words, $\phi(X) = E(Y|X)$ is the function of $X$ most correlated with $Y$. If we restrict $\phi(X)$ to be linear, the solution of (4.3) becomes the ordinary linear regression estimator, $\hat{Y} = \phi(X) = \hat{\beta}_0 + \hat{\beta}_1 X$.

If we fix $\phi(X)$, the function of $Y$ minimizing equation 4.2 is:

$$\theta'_1(Y) = E[\phi(X)|Y] . \tag{4.4}$$

To make $\text{Var}(\theta(Y)) = 1$, we divide $\theta'_1(Y)$ by its standard deviation:

$$\theta_1(Y) = \theta'_1(Y) / \sqrt{\text{Var}(\theta'_1(Y))} \tag{4.5}$$

and set $\theta(Y) = \theta_1(Y)$. Now reverse the problem and find the function of $X$ most correlated with $\theta(Y)$. Again, the solution is the conditional expectation of $\theta(Y)$ given $X$,

$$\phi_1(X) = E[\theta(Y)|X]. \tag{4.6}$$

Set $\phi(X) = \phi_1(X)$. We now repeat the process and find $\theta_2(Y)$ by

$$\theta_2(Y) = E[\phi(X)|Y] / \sqrt{\text{Var}(E(\phi(X)|Y))}. \tag{4.7}$$

Set $\theta(Y) = \theta_2(Y)$. By alternating between the conditional expectations (4.6) and (4.7), we iterate until $e^2$ no longer decreases. This is the heart of the ACE algorithm. (To start the algorithm, we let

$$\theta(Y) = Y / \sqrt{\text{Var}(Y)}$$

then proceed to equation 4.6).

Now, if $Y$ and $X$ are random variables, one can in some cases calculate these conditional expectations explicitly (see Buja, 1985). In all practical cases, however, we have only a finite number of observations $(x_i, y_i)$ on $X$ and $Y$. The conditional expectations must be replaced by their data counterparts or estimates. In general, data versions of conditional expectations are smooth functions of the data or data smoothers. We have some choice over how smooth we want the data smoother to be. If we go to the ultimate smoothness, we would take $\phi(X)$ to be linear—i.e., $\phi(X) = \beta_0 + \beta_1 X$, and again, solving (4.3) would result in ordinary linear regression. Instead, we relax the smoothness by taking any of a number of data smoothers. In this chapter, we will use the version of ACE as found in the *Statistics Store* in S (see Schilling, 1985), which uses the supersmoother of Friedman and Stuetzle (1982). It is attractive because of high computing speed and its adaptability to local curvature. For a general discussion of smoothing, see Chapter 3, this volume.

The ACE algorithm can handle variables other than continuous predictors. Included among these are categorical (ordered or unordered) integer and indicator variables. These present no additional complications for the computations. For categorical variables, the ACE transformations can be regarded as estimating optimal scores for each value level of the variable. The extension of ACE to more than one predictor is straightforward. The details are explained in the fourth section.

### Interpreting the Output of ACE

Once the optimal transformations $\theta(Y)$ and $\phi(X)$ are obtained from the empirical ACE algorithm, we can use this information in several ways. Because $\theta(Y)$ and $\phi(X)$ minimize

$$1-R^2 = e^2(\theta,\phi) = E\{[\theta(Y)-\phi(X)]^2\}$$

over all $\theta$, $\phi$ with $E(\theta) = E(\phi) = 0$ and $\text{Var}(\theta) = 1$, we know that $\theta$ and $\phi$ are the optimal set of transformations in the sense of having the highest $R^2$. So, as a first use, while searching for other, possibly simpler, transformations (such as power transformations), we can use the ACE $R^2$ as a benchmark.

The ACE algorithm, as implemented in the *Statistics Store* (Schilling, 1985) is called by issuing the command:

$$\text{result}\leftarrow\text{ace}(\mathbf{x},\mathbf{y})$$

where **x** and **y** are data vectors with $n$ observations each, $(\mathbf{x} = (x_1,\ldots,x_n)^T)$. The output is a structure with seven components, the first five of which will be useful for our purposes: **x**, **y**, **tx**, **ty**, and *rsq*. These are the original **x**, **y**, the transformed **x** and **y**, and the $R^2$ of **ty** on **tx**.

The next step is to examine the ACE transformations themselves. Unfortunately, the output of ACE does *not* contain the functional form for the optimal transformations $\theta(Y)$ and $\phi(X)$. Rather, it contains the vectors **tx** and **ty**, which are the values of the optimal transformations at each data point $(x_i,y_i)$ as found by the empirical ACE algorithm. A look at the plots of **tx** against **x** and **ty** against **y** may give insight into the nature of these (approximately) optimal transformations, and, in the best cases, suggest simple transformations of $X$ and $Y$ to approximate $\phi(X)$ and $\theta(Y)$.

*Example*

To illustrate the use of the ACE algorithm, we first apply it to a synthetic example — i.e., one for which we know the right answer. We let **w** be 100 evenly spaced numbers between 1 and 10, and set

$$v = 1.0 + w + \varepsilon \qquad (4.8)$$

where $\varepsilon$ are 100 randomly generated numbers from $N(0,1)$. A regression of **v** on **w** gave $R^2 = .892$. Suppose that we are given not **w** and **v**, but $x = w^3$ and $y = 1/v$, as data. The correlation of **x** and **y** is $-.346$. A plot of **y** vs. **x** (Figure 4.1) shows obvious nonlinearity.

A data analyst would definitely want to transform **x** and/or **y** before further analysis. We apply the ACE algorithm to **x** and **y** in an attempt to find transformations $f(X)$ and $g(Y)$ for which the model

$$g(Y) = \beta_0 + \beta_1 f(X) + \varepsilon; \qquad \varepsilon \sim N(0,\sigma^2)$$

is reasonable. From equation 4.8 we know that

$$f(X) = X^{1/3} \quad \text{and} \quad g(Y) = 1/Y$$

will recapture equation 4.8 exactly, for which the $R^2$ is .892. The ACE output *rsq* is .896, which matches (actually slightly betters) the $R^2$ for the regression of $1/Y$ on $X^{1/3}$. This tells us that over all transformations of $X$ and $Y$, none will result in a higher $R^2$. To understand the transformations found by ACE, we look at the plots of **tx** vs. **x** and **ty** vs. **y** (Figure 4.2). (Notice that ACE chooses both **tx** and **ty** to have mean 0, and the variance of **ty** is constrained to be 1.) We see that small values of $X$ are mapped to values near 2.0, as are large values of $Y$. Thus, while the correlation of **x** and **y** is negative, the correlation of **tx** and **ty** is positive. In the case of two variables, the ACE algorithm chooses the transformations to have positive correlation.

Both plots in Figure 4.2 exhibit negative curvature (for large values of both $X$ and $Y$, the change in the transformation is smaller than for small values), indicating that the transformations are a smaller power of the data rather than a larger one. If the analyst is familiar with power transformations, he or she may guess that a log transformation for $Y$ and a $-$log transformation for $X$ might approximate the shape of **ty** and **tx**, respectively. In fact, the correlation of $-\log(x)$ with $\log(y)$ is .916 (or

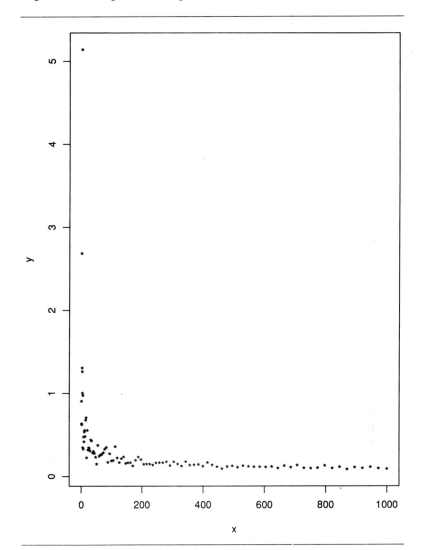

**Figure 4.1 A scatterplot of y versus x with extreme nonlinearity.**

$R^2$ = .839) and a plot of log(y) vs. −log (x) shows approximate linearity. Because the optimal transformations as found from ACE have an $R^2$ = .896, we know, however, that we may have some (although not a great deal of) room for improvement.

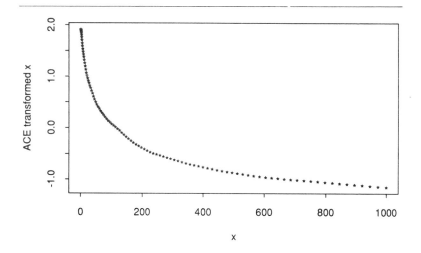

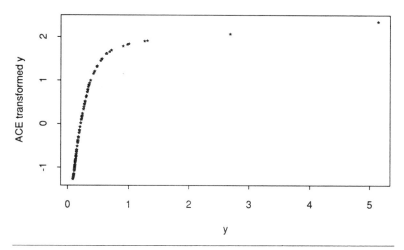

Figure 4.2  The optimal transformations for x and y as found by the empir-
           ical ACE algorithm.

Fortunately, the analyst does not have to guess what transformation
to use. General techniques for finding transformations for two variables
are available. An informal yet very powerful data-analytic approach is
given by Mosteller and Tukey (1977). The use of this method for finding

approximations to the ACE transformations is discussed in De Veaux and Steele (1989). We choose here to concentrate on the more automatic method of Box and Cox (1964) to find these approximations. These approximations will be members of the family of power transformations — roughly all powers of a variable $Z$ with log $(Z)$ used in place of $Z^0$. This will be an appropriate technique if the plots of the ACE transformation are roughly continuous and monotonic (that is, everywhere nonincreasing or nondecreasing, as in Figure 4.2). On the other hand, if the plot shows an extreme discontinuity, this may suggest that the variable is best studied in two separate regimes, while an oscillating pattern may suggest that the variable is periodic. We will explain the Box-Cox procedure in the next section. We defer discussion of more complicated plots to the fourth section in the context of a discussion of Angell's data.

## USING BOX-COX TRANSFORMATIONS TO APPROXIMATE OPTIMAL TRANSFORMATIONS

Our aim in this section is to approximate the ACE transformations $\phi(X)$ and $\theta(Y)$ by power transformations of $X$ and $Y$. In many cases, the plots of the transformed data against the untransformed data are roughly monotone and smooth. If so, we can hope to approximate these curves by closed form expressions, leading us to a simple linear model of the form in equation 4.1. To do this, we use the Box-Cox methodology to estimate the powers of $X$ and $Y$.

Box and Cox (1964) studied the problem of finding the best transformation of $Y$ for the linear model in equation 4.1. They considered taking powers of $Y$, of the form $Y^\lambda$, and regressing $Y^\lambda$ on $X_1, \ldots, X_p$. It is tempting to choose $\lambda$ on the basis of minimum residual sum of squares. However, one can make the residuals smaller just by making the response smaller (by taking square roots of $Y$ if $Y > 1$, for example), so the raw residual sum of squares will not do as a criterion. To fix this, Box and Cox introduced the following family of transformations:

$$Y^{(\lambda)} = \begin{cases} (Y^\lambda - 1)/\lambda\dot{Y} & \lambda \neq 0 \\ (\log Y)\dot{Y} & \lambda = 0 \end{cases} \tag{4.9}$$

where $\dot{Y}$ is the geometric mean of $Y$. This appropriately scales $Y^\lambda$ so that residual sums of squares from a regression of $Y^{(\lambda)}$ on $X_1, \ldots, X_p$, can be compared directly. Let $z_i = y_i^{(\lambda)}$ for $i = 1, \ldots, n$. Box and Cox showed that the maximum likelihood estimate of $\lambda$ occurs where the residual sum of squares

$$S(\lambda, z) = \sum_i (z_i - \hat{z}_i)^2$$

is minimized. They suggested plotting $S(\lambda,\mathbf{z})$ vs. $\lambda$ for various values of $\lambda$ to find $\hat{\lambda}$ graphically. (They also derived approximate confidence intervals for $\lambda$ that we will not need). The plot of $S(\lambda)$ vs. $\lambda$ usually has one minimum, and the optimal $\lambda$ is easily found either from the plot or from a table of $S(\lambda)$ and $\lambda$.

After finding appropriate power transformations for both $X$ and $Y$ ($X^\lambda$ and $Y^\gamma$, say) we assess our approximations by comparing the regression of $\mathbf{y}^\gamma$ on $\mathbf{x}^\lambda$ to the regression of $\mathbf{ty}$ on $\mathbf{tx}$, as found by ACE. We use $R^2$ and diagnostic plots to assess the quality of the regression.

To see this in action, we return to the example of the second section. Recall that $f(X) = X^{1/3}$ and $g(Y) = 1/Y$ are the "right" transformations. We apply the Box-Cox procedure to variables $X$ and $Y$ in turn and estimate $\lambda$ and $\gamma$. We first consider $Y$. We are trying to find an approximation to $\theta(Y)$, so we regard $\mathbf{y}$ as the response and $\mathbf{ty}$ as the predictor. Let $z_i = y_i^{(\gamma)}$ for $i = 1, \ldots, n$. Regress $\mathbf{z}$ on $\mathbf{ty}$ and look at the residual sum of squares $S(\gamma,\mathbf{z}) = \Sigma(\hat{z}_i - z_i)^2$. A table of $S(\gamma,\mathbf{z})$ is presented in Table 4.1 for values of $\gamma$ between $-3$ and $3$ in increments of $0.5$. The minimum occurs at $\gamma = -.05$. For $X$, we let $z_i = x_i^{(\lambda)}$ $(i = 1, \ldots, n)$ and regress $\mathbf{z}$ on $\mathbf{tx}$. Table 4.2 contains $S(\lambda, z)$ for $\lambda$ in $[-1,1]$. The minimum occurs at $\lambda = 0.1$. As a general rule, we find it good practice to try the range of $-3$ to $3$ in increments of $.5$ first. If a minimum does occur, one may want to use a finer grid near the minimum (as in Table 4.2). If $S(\lambda)$ is either always increasing or decreasing, consider powers outside this range. For our approximation purposes, it is often convenient to take the minimum to the nearest $.5$ or $.1$ power. (For more details, the reader is referred to Box and Cox, 1964, or the discussion in Box et al., 1978).

From Tables 4.1 and 4.2, we are led to consider the model

$$Y^{-.5} = \beta_0 + \beta_1 X^{.1} + \varepsilon . \tag{4.10}$$

A plot of $Y^{-.5}$ vs. $X^{-.1}$ shows approximate linearity. A regression of $Y^{-.5}$ on $X^{.1}$ yields an $R^2$ of .889. The plot of residuals vs. predicted

**Table 4.1  Sum of Squares Table for Box-Cox Transformation of $Y$**

| $\gamma$ | $S(\gamma,z)$ |
|---|---|
| −3.0 | 3.13 |
| −2.5 | 1.56 |
| −2.0 | .75 |
| −1.5 | .34 |
| −1.0 | .12 |
| −0.5 | .03 |
| 0.0 | .22 |
| 0.5 | 2.22 |
| 1.0 | 21.7 |
| 1.5 | 246.07 |
| 2.0 | 3238.16 |
| 2.5 | 47654.38 |
| 3.0 | 759284.95 |

**Table 4.2  Sum of Squares Table for Box-Cox Transformation of $X$**

| $\gamma$ | $S(g,z)$ |
|---|---|
| −1.0 | 174562556 |
| −0.9 | 83800459 |
| −0.8 | 40560871 |
| −0.7 | 19750974 |
| −0.6 | 9636488 |
| −0.5 | 4676938 |
| −0.4 | 2229801 |
| −0.3 | 1021621 |
| −0.2 | 432439 |
| −0.1 | 157742 |
| 0.0 | 47208 |
| 0.1 | 27083 |
| 0.2 | 62532 |
| 0.3 | 139360 |
| 0.4 | 255301 |
| 0.5 | 416195 |
| 0.6 | 634838 |
| 0.7 | 931526 |
| 0.8 | 1335944 |
| 0.9 | 1890450 |
| 1.0 | 2655058 |

values is shown in Figure 4.3. From this plot, we see no evidence of heteroscedasticity or other gross violations of linear model assumptions. Although we have not captured the original model

$$Y^{-1} = \beta_0 + \beta_1 X^{.33} + \varepsilon$$

exactly, we have found a reasonable approximation to it in equation (4.10). This model seems to satisfy the three desiderata of linear models (linearity, homoscedasticity, and normality) and captures nearly all of the original $R^2$, .889 out of .896.

We now consider a real data example when the underlying model is unknown. Figure 4.4 shows a plot of 1970 infant mortality vs. per capita income for 101 countries (data are from Leinhardt & Wasserman, 1979, with data for Jamaica corrected). We remove the obvious outliers, Libya and Saudi Arabia, and proceed to apply the ACE algorithm to income and infant mortality. Figure 4.5 shows a plot of the ACE transformed infant mortality vs. ACE transformed income. There is clearly more linearity here, and, in fact, $R^2 = .68$ compared with $R^2 = .27$ for the raw data. Figure 4.6 shows the ACE transformations for income and infant mortality, respectively.

The ACE transformation of income is monotone and fairly smooth. Applying the Box-Cox transformations treating income (**x**) as the response and ACE transformed income (**tx**) as the predictor, we find that the minimum for $S(\lambda)$ occurs at $\lambda = 0$, implying a log transformation. (The approximation is very good; in fact, the correlation of $log(\mathbf{x})$ and **tx** is .996.) Turning to infant mortality, we notice that while the ACE transformation is not perfectly monotone (note the values of infant mortality roughly between 120 and 150 in Figure 4.6), $S(\gamma)$ is also minimized at $\gamma = 0$, and the correlation of $log(\mathbf{y})$ with **ty** is a very respectable .976. A regression of log(infant mortality) versus −log(income) results in an $R^2$ of .66. The plot of log(infant mortality) versus −log(income) with the regression line (Figure 4.7) indicates no obvious problems with the residuals. This plot compares quite closely to the ACE transformed variables in Figure 4.5.

By using the simple model log(infant mortality) $= \beta_0 + \beta_1$ log(income), we have captured most of the optimal $R^2$ (.66 compared to .68). This simple example underscores the power of the methodology. We are led to a sensible transformation by an essentially automatic procedure. In the next section, we extend the discussion to multiple regression.

*(text continues on page 194)*

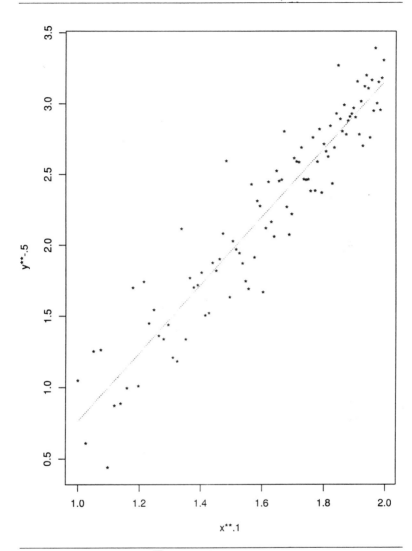

**Figure 4.3** A plot of $1 / \sqrt{y}$ versus $x^{-1}$ with fitted line for model of equation
4.10.

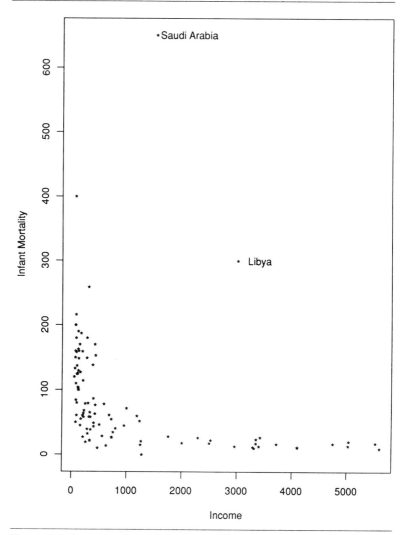

**Figure 4.4  A scatterplot of infant mortality versus per capita income for 101 countries.**

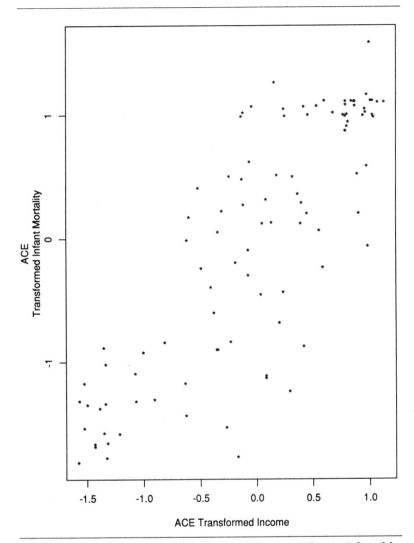

**Figure 4.5  a scatterplot of θ(Infant mortality) versus φ(income) found by ACE.**

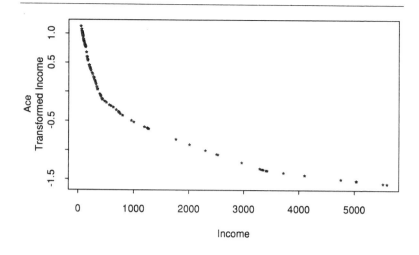

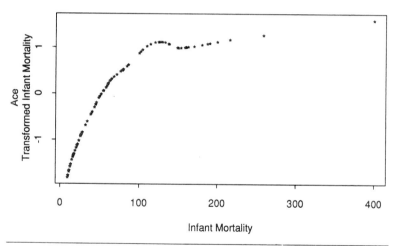

Figure 4.6  ACE transformations of infant mortality and income.

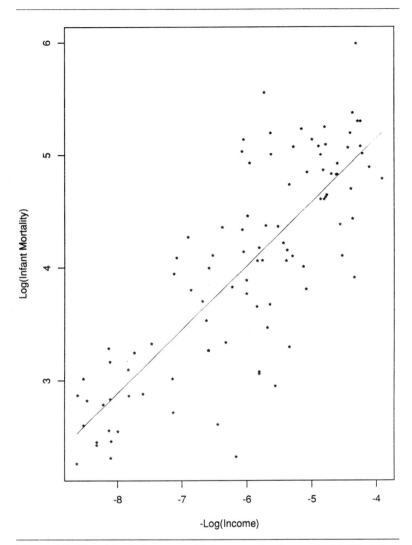

**Figure 4.7 Plot of log(infant mortality) versus –log(income) with fitted line.**

## MULTIPLE REGRESSION

The theory of ACE for more than one predictor variable is a fairly simple extension of the bivariate case. Suppose we have $p$ predictors $X_1, \ldots, X_p$. Set

$$\theta(Y) = Y / \sqrt{\mathrm{Var}\,(Y)}$$

and $\phi_1(X_1) = \ldots = \phi_p\,(X_p) = 0$ to start. Equation 4.6 is replaced by

$$\phi_{k,1}(X_k) = E[\theta(Y) - \sum_{i \neq k} \phi_i\,(X_i)|X_k] \qquad (4.12)$$

for each $k = 1, \ldots, p$. Set $\phi_k(X_k) = \phi_{k,1}(X_k)$ for $k = 1, \ldots, p$. Equation 4.4 is replaced by

$$\theta_1'(Y) = E\left(\sum_{i=1}^{k} \phi_i(X_i)|Y\right). \qquad (4.13)$$

Set the variance of $\theta(Y)$ equal to 1 by

$$\theta_1(Y) = \theta'_1(Y) / \sqrt{\mathrm{Var}\,(\theta_1'(Y))} \qquad (4.14)$$

and set $\theta(Y) = \theta_1(Y)$. Now loop from (4.12) through (4.14) until

$$e^2 = E[\theta(Y) - \sum_{i=1}^{p} \phi_i\,(X_i)]^2 \qquad (4.15)$$

no longer decreases.

Operationally, the full ACE algorithm (as implemented in S in the *Statistics Store*) is called as follows:

$$\text{result} \leftarrow \text{ace}(\mathbf{X}, \mathbf{y})$$

where now $\mathbf{X}$ is an $n \times p$ matrix whose $i$th column contains the $n$ values of the $i$th predictor variable. The output again consists of $\mathbf{X}$, $\mathbf{y}$, $\mathbf{tX}$, $\mathbf{ty}$, and *rsq* where now $\mathbf{X}$ and $\mathbf{tX}$ are $n \times p$ matrices. (There are other options for ACE to be discussed below.)

To interpret the output of the ACE multivariate algorithm, we look at the plots of **ty** vs. **y** and $\mathbf{tx}_i$ vs. $\mathbf{x}_i$ for each $i = 1, \ldots, p$. If appropriate, we approximate each of them by power functions, as explained in the last section. In a multivariate situation, it is not as likely that all variables will have ACE transformations that can be well approximated by power functions. However, the plots may still provide us with valuable information.

As an example, we consider Angell's data on moral integration of non-Southern U.S. cities, as found in Fox (1984). Using the linear model

$$y_i = \beta_0 + \beta_1 x_{1i} + \beta_2 x_{2i} + \varepsilon_i \tag{4.16}$$

where $y_i$ = moral integration, $x_{1i}$ = heterogeneity, and $x_{2i}$ = mobility, we find

$$\hat{y}_i = 21.8 - 0.167x_{1i} - 0.214x_{2i} \tag{4.17}$$

results in an $R^2$ of .42 (see Fox, 1984).

Applying the ACE algorithm to the data, we find the optimal $R^2$ to be .87. This is a profound improvement over the untransformed model. However, our hopes for finding *simple* transformations of $Y$, $X_1$ and $X_2$ to achieve this are dampened a bit by looking at the plots of the ACE transformations in Figure 4.8.

The plot of **ty** vs. **y** shows that the optimal transformation for moral integration is certainly not linear, nor is it even monotone. The ACE transformation is everywhere increasing except for cities with moral integration in the range between roughly 13 and 15. The pronounced dip in the ACE transformation indicates that a different relationship between predictors and response may be operating for these cities. Perhaps these cities should be considered separately. If they are found to represent a particular subclass, it might be useful to introduce an indicator variable for that class. Certainly, one should think hard about this particular group, and why the relationship between predictors and response appears to be different here.

Turning to the ACE transformation of heterogeneity, a striking pattern emerges. For cities with heterogeneity greater than 16 or so, increased heterogeneity implies reduced moral integration. This agrees

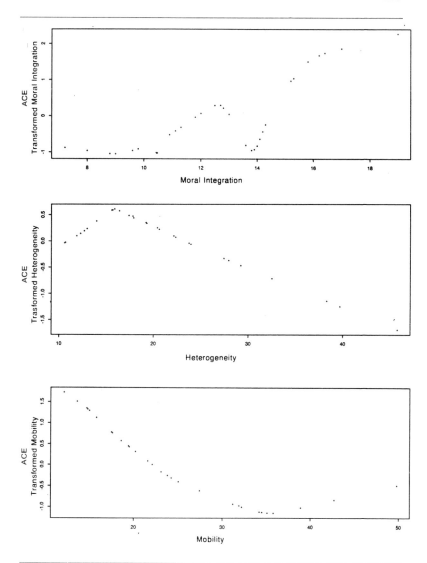

**Figure 4.8  ACE transformations of moral integration, heterogeneity, and
        mobility.**

with the linear model, where the coefficient for heterogeneity is −0.167.
However, for cities with heterogeneity less than 16, the transformation
is increasing, indicating positive correlation with moral integration.

Although this certainly does not indicate a statistically significant positive correlation of heterogeneity with moral integration, it presents an interesting working hypothesis for low heterogeneity cities. Similarly, considering the ACE transformation of mobility, we see a strong negative correlation until mobility reaches 35 or so, at which point the trend stops and even seems to reverse itself. We will return to this observation in the fifth section.

The ACE algorithm has several options that can enhance understanding of complex relationships among variables. One such option is to force some or all of the transformations to be monotonic, avoiding the problems of interpreting transformations such as the moral integration transformation above. The algorithm then finds the optimal transformations under this constraint. This is similar to Kruskal's transformation (see Kruskal, 1965). These optimal monotone transformations are shown for Angell's data in Figure 4.9. As implemented in S, this is achieved by the command

$$result \leftarrow ace(\mathbf{X}, \mathbf{y}, mon = list)$$

where list = (0,1,2) is a list of the variables whose transformations are restricted to be monotone. Positive numbers refer to columns in the $\mathbf{X}$ matrix; 0 refers to the response. (See Schilling, 1985, for more details.)

The monotone transformation of moral integration has three distinct phases (Figure 4.9). It appears linear for values up to 12, constant between 12 and 14, and exhibits strong negative curvature for values greater than 14. The change in direction that we saw above for cities with moral integration between 13 and 15 is now forced to be nondecreasing, resulting in a constant transformation near this range. The monotone transformation of heterogeneity is constant for values up to 16, and linear afterward. For mobility, it is roughly linear until 35, then constant. The transformations suggest that, in general, increased heterogeneity and mobility decrease moral integration, but that there is little additional effect for mobility past 35 or heterogeneity less than 16. The $R^2$ for these transformations is .74.

The complex transformations of the response variable, moral integration, make straightforward interpretation a bit difficult. For this reason, one may wish to find the optimal transformation of the predictors for *linear* transformations of the response. This is an additional ACE option and is in the spirit of generalized additive modeling (see Hastie & Tibshirani, 1986). In S, one sets result $\leftarrow ace(\mathbf{X}, \mathbf{y}, lin=0)$ (see

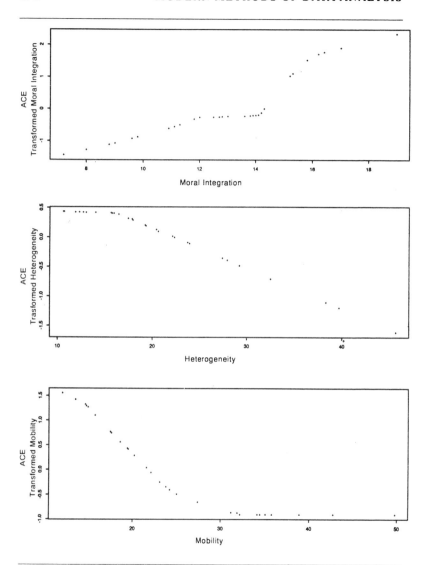

**Figure 4.9  Monotone ACE transformations of moral integration, heterogeneity, and mobility.**

Schilling, 1985). The results for the Angell data are shown in Figure 4.10. The $R^2$ for these transformations is .61, a far cry from the original ACE $R^2$ of .87, but a substantial improvement over the untransformed $R^2$ = .42. The transformation of heterogeneity is monotonic with a slight negative curvature. Applying the Box-Cox transformations to it, we find $S(\lambda)$ minimized at log. The transformation of mobility is more complex, but because the overall pattern is smooth and nearly monotone (with the exception of the two smallest and two largest points), we attempt a Box-Cox transformation and find the minimum to lie in the range $\lambda = -.5$ to $-1$. On the basis of this, we consider two multiple regressions:

$$y_i = \beta_0 + \beta_1 \log(x_{1i}) + \beta_2 / \sqrt{x_{2i}} + \varepsilon_i \qquad (4.18)$$

and

$$y_i = \beta_0 + \beta_1 \log(x_{1i}) + \beta_2 / x_{2i} + \varepsilon_i . \qquad (4.19)$$

The $R^2$ for both models is .54, and the residual plots for each are quite similar. The choice between these models is thus motivated by personal taste and ease of interpretation as much as by any statistical criteria. Because of the relative simplicity of reciprocals as compared with reciprocal square roots, one may prefer equation 4.19. The residual plot for this model (equation 4.19) is shown in Figure 4.11. We see no apparent pattern. To further explore this model, one should consider normal probability plots and other diagnostic tools (see Chapters 2 and 6, this volume).

We can apply ACE once more to the variables in equation 4.19 to assess how optimal our transformations are. The ACE transformations of the variables in equation 4.19 are shown in Figure 4.12. These are quite similar to the original ACE transformations of the untransformed variables (Figure 4.8). Although we have increased $R^2$ from .42 to .54 out of a possible .61 (keeping moral integration untransformed), we still are left with opportunities for improvement. The ACE transformation of log(heterogeneity) again suggests the possibility of two regimes. That is, for the cities with small values of heterogeneity, an increase in heterogeneity may *increase* moral integration, while for most cities, increasing heterogeneity decreases moral integration. We also see a similar effect persisting in the mobility plot. For the few cities with large mobility (small reciprocal mobility), a change in mobility appears to have the opposite effect on moral integration than it does for the rest of the cities. Finally, turning to the response itself, we again see a striking nonlinear transformation in the range of 13 to 15. We cannot

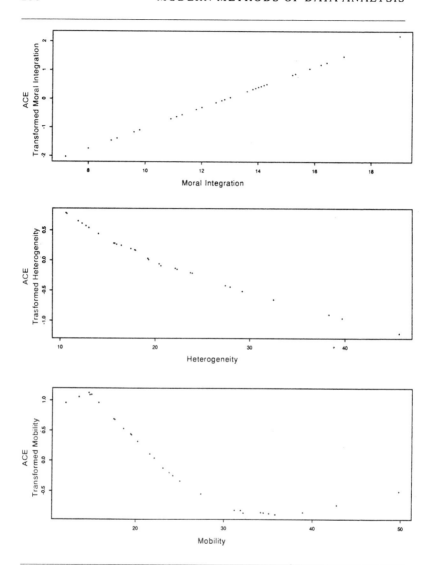

**Figure 4.10** ACE transformations of moral integration, heterogeneity, and mobility where $\theta(Y)$ is restricted to be linear.

hope to achieve the optimal multiple correlation of .87 without a deeper understanding of the relationship of moral integration, mobility, and heterogeneity for cities with moral integration values in that range.

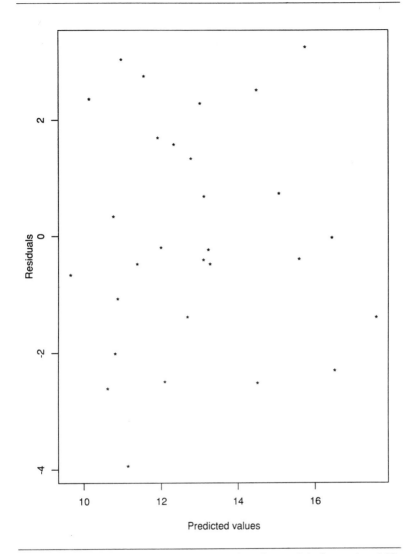

**Figure 4.11  Residuals versus predicted values for model of equation 4.19.**

What have we learned from ACE? First, we know that we can improve the multiple correlation among the three variables by nearly 50% (.42 to .61), at least theoretically, by keeping moral integration untransformed (except linearly). We have found simple transformations

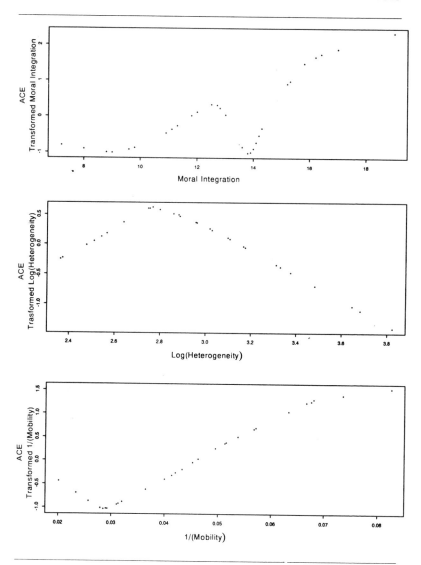

Figure 4.12  ACE transformations of moral integration, log(heterogeneity), and 1/(mobility).

of the predictors by using the Box-Cox procedure for $X_1$ and $X_2$ that achieve an $R^2$ of .54. If we allow arbitrary monotone transformations of all three variables, we can (theoretically) improve $R^2$ to .74. This might be accomplished by, for example, setting heterogeneity to a constant for values below 16, and mobility to a constant for values above 35 (see Figure 4.9). Finally, the optimal transformations have an $R^2$ of .87. To achieve this, it may be necessary to break the cities up into classes (perhaps using indicator variables) and to nonlinearly transform the response. A study of these transformations (Figure 4.8) may lead to greater understanding of the relationships between these variables.

The ACE algorithm is a powerful tool for finding transformations in multiple regression. When relationships among variables are complex, the plots are often not straightforwardly interpretable. However, a study of these plots may lead the investigator to a substantially improved empirical model. It will also give a sense of how much improvement is possible by taking more extreme steps. The procedure is clearly neither completely automatic nor without pitfalls. In the next section, we will discuss some problems, and, where possible, suggest remedies.

## CAVEATS AND LIMITATIONS

As we have seen, the ACE algorithm provides a procedure for estimating optimal transformations in multiple regression. In many cases, utilizing the Box-Cox methodology, one can approximate these optimal transformations by a member of the power transformations, thus providing a simple way to achieve approximate linearity. Even when this is not the case, a study of the plots of the ACE transformations may lead to new insights into the relationships between the response and predictor variables. The benefits of using ACE do not come free, however. In data analysis, no procedure should be used in a completely automatic way. There are problems with the ACE procedure, as well as limits to its usefulness. We discuss some of these in this section.

### *Sensitivity to Extreme Outliers*

One problem with the ACE procedure is inherent in the algorithm itself. Because the algorithm is based on a squared error criterion for minimization, it is highly sensitive to outlying data values and high influence points in the predictor space. As an example of this behavior, we return to the previous nations data example, this time including the outliers Libya and Saudi Arabia. The ACE transformation plots for the full data are shown in Figure 4.13. The transformation indicates a

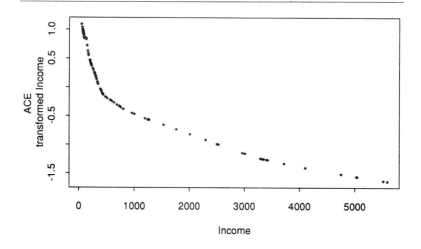

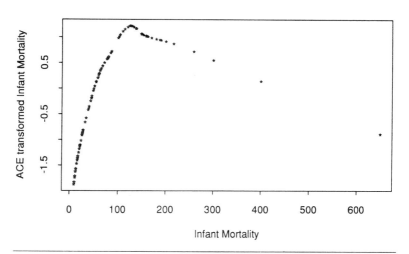

**Figure 4.13  ACE transformations for infant mortality and income, includ-
ing outliers Libya and Saudi Arabia.**

change in the *direction* of the relationship between income and mortality for countries with large mortality rates, indicating that further
increases in income may lead to very low or very high mortality rates!
Comparison with Figure 4.5 shows the sensitivity of the mortality

transformation to the two outliers. Both outliers have large incomes and yet very large mortality rates. Although contemplation of this relationship may lead to the discovery of outliers, we are left with an uncomfortable sense that it is very dangerous to use ACE without a thorough investigation of outliers and influence. The situation in higher dimensional settings is only more precarious. The authors of ACE, Breiman and Friedman (1985), warn that the ACE algorithm "should be used with a great deal of caution in the suspected presence of extreme outliers." Perhaps ACE can be modified to use a less drastic criterion than least squares, but for now, we suggest that the analyst use available methods to detect outliers and high influence points before using the algorithm.

### Normality and Homoscedasticity of Residuals

The ACE transformation is designed to find the transformations that maximize the multiple correlation of the predictors with the response. That is, the *linear* dependence of the response on the predictors is maximized. This is only one of the three goals of an optimal transformation for regression. The others are normality and homoscedasticity of the errors. Fortunately, the principle of universal transformation, discussed in Box and Cox (1964), often comes to our rescue. This principle is an *empirical* observation that the transformations optimal for one criterion are often optimal or nearly so for all three. However, this is certainly not always the case, and, in fact, these three goals may be at cross-purposes. There is no guarantee that the errors in the ACE transformed model will be normally distributed with constant variance. The same is true for the transformations approximating the optimal transformations. Tibshirani (1988) has modified the ACE algorithm in an attempt to achieve a balance between constant variance and maximal linear dependence. The resulting algorithm is called AVAS — additivity and variance stabilization. The syntax of AVAS is nearly identical to ACE, and a program can be obtained from the author (Tibshirani, 1988).

### Sensitivity to Variable Ordering

In the case of multiple predictor variables, Breiman and Friedman (1985) report some sensitivity of ACE to the order in which the predictor variables are entered in the **X** matrix. They suggest trying several orderings once a subset of the predictor variables has been selected.

Recently, Hastie and Tibshirani (1988) have indicated that this sensitivity may be due to the choice of smoother use by ACE and is not inherent in the algorithm itself. For the Angell data set with only two predictors, we found no visually distinguishable differences between the transformations regardless of the order of heterogeneity and mobility.

### ACE as an Automatic Procedure

ACE is sometimes presented as an automatic or fully automated method for finding optimal transformations in multiple regression. The preceding discussion should serve as an indication that while it is fully automatic in maximizing the multiple correlation, the output from ACE should not be blindly trusted as the best overall way to represent the dependence of the response on the predictor variables. Nor is ACE intended to *replace* standard modern regression tools in the data analyst's tool box. The full set of robust regression methods and diagnostic tools such as influence measures, partial residual plots, normal probability plots, added variables plot, etc. (see Belsley et al., 1980; Fox, 1984; and Atkinson, 1985, for discussion of these methods) should be included among the standard set of procedures for any data analyst.

The benefits of a good model lie in its explanatory and predictive power. If possible, a simple explanation of the relationship among variables is preferred to an overly complex one. A model of the form in equation 4.1, linear in the parameters, can be powerful if appropriate. By considering transformations of the predictors and response, we can increase the situations for which such a model is appropriate. The transformation found by the ACE algorithm is optimal for maximizing $R^2$ over all transformations of the predictor and response variables. Finding *familiar* closed-form transformations of these variables that retain most of the correlation of the optimal transformations is useful because of the relative simplicity of these transformations. The scientist may have several choices of these approximating transformations to choose from when presenting an empirical model.

As an example, we return to Angell's data on moral integration of non-Southern U.S. cities. We considered the models of equations 4.18 and 4.19 shown here with the estimated parameter values

$$Y = 19.5 - 4.4 \log(X_1) + 44.9 / X_2 \quad (R^2 = .54) \quad\quad (4.20)$$

$$Y = 13.2 - 4.48\log(X_1) + 62.041/\sqrt{X_2} \quad (R^2 = .54) \quad (4.21)$$

in the fourth section. Looking again at Figure 4.8, we may be tempted to capture the nonlinear nature of the moral integration transformation. The power transformation that best approximates this is $Y^{2.5}$. The model

$$Y^{2.5} = 1404.31 - 518.19\log(X_1) + 17297.51/X_2 \quad (4.22)$$

has an $R^2$ of .56, certainly no worse than those previously considered. Yet because of the $Y^{2.5}$ term, I doubt whether one would be tempted to consider such a model unless it led to *significant* improvement or simplification. If we instead attempt to capture the quadratic appearance of the mobility transformation by using $(X_2-35)^2$ instead of $X_2$, we find

$$Y = 13.91 - 0.18X_1 + 0.015(X_2 - 35)^2 \quad (4.23)$$

has an $R^2$ of .58. Here, heterogeneity and moral integration have been left untransformed, while the dependence on mobility is on how far away it is from 35. Because the coefficient is positive, this model indicates that moving away from 35 in either direction will tend to increase moral integration. This should be taken in the spirit of exploratory rather than confirmatory analysis. At this point, the science of the subject matter must be brought to bear on the model choice. The scientist must decide which model is most informative for his or her purposes, keeping in mind all the while the empirical nature of the model. The ACE algorithm can be instrumental in suggesting model choices for the social scientist.

## CONCLUSIONS

We have shown that the ACE algorithm can be a powerful tool for aiding us in understanding the relationships between predictors and a response and as a tool for guiding us in choosing transformations in a linear model. The Box-Cox procedure provides a method for approximating the ACE transformations by members of the power transformations. In many instances, this will result in powerful linear models with enhanced explanatory and predictive powers as compared with the untransformed variables. In addition, ACE can be rerun on a new set of variables once transformations have been chosen to assess how good the analyst's guess is. Although the results of ACE should not be trusted blindly, we feel that it should be included in the working tools of all scientists engaged in the empirical modeling of social phenomena.

## REFERENCES

Atkinson, A. C. (1985). *Plots, transformations and regressions.* Oxford: Clarendon.

Belsley, D. A., Kuh, E., & Welch, R. E. (1980). *Regression diagnostics: Identifying influential data and sources of collinearity.* New York: John Wiley.

Box, G.E.P., & Cox, D.R. (1964). An analysis of transformations. *Journal of the Royal Statistical Society, B26,* 211-252.

Box, G.E.P., Hunter, W. G., & Hunter, J. S. (1978). *Statistics for experimenters.* New York: John Wiley.

Breiman, L., & Freidman, J. H. (1985). Estimating optimal transformations for multiple regression and correlation. *Journal of the American Statistical Association, 80,* 580-597.

Buja, A. (1985). *Theory of bivariate ACE* (Report no. 74). Seattle: University of Washington, Department of Statistics.

De Veaux, R. D., & Steele, J. M. (1989). ACE guided transformation method for estimation of the coefficient of soil water diffusivity. *Technometrics, 31*(1), 91-98.

Fox, J. (1984). *Linear statistical models and related methods.* New York: John Wiley.

Friedman, J. H., & Stuetzle, W. (1982). *Smoothing of scatterplots* (Tech. Rep. Orion 3). Stanford, CA: Stanford University, Department of Statistics.

Hastie, T., & Tibshirani, R. (1986). Generalized additive models (with discussion). *Statistical Science, 1,* 297-318.

Hastie, T., & Tibshirani, R. (1988). Discussion of "Monotone regression splines," by J. O. Ramsay. *Statistical Science, 3,* 450-456.

Kruskal, J. B. (1965). Analysis of factorial experiments by estimating monotone transformations of the data. *Journal of the Royal Statistical Society, B 27,* 251-265.

Leinhardt, S., & Wasserman, S. S. (1979). Exploratory data analysis: An introduction to selected methods. In K. F. Schuessler (Ed.), *Sociological methodology 1979* (pp. 311-365). San Francisco: Jossey-Bass.

Mosteller, F., & Tukey, J. W. (1977). *Data analysis and regression: A second course in statistics.* Reading, MA: Addison-Wesley.

Rao, C. R. (1973). *Linear statistical inference and its aplications* (2nd ed.). New York: John Wiley.

Schilling, J. M. (1985). *The statistics store.* Murray Hill, NJ: AT&T Bell Laboratories.

Tibshirani, R. (1988). Estimating transformations for regression via additivity and variance stabilization. *Journal of the American Statistical Association, 83,* 394-405.

Tukey, J. W. (1977). *Exploratory data analysis.* Reading, MA: Addison-Wesley.

# 5

GEOMETRY OF MULTIPLE REGRESSION
AND INTERACTIVE 3-D GRAPHICS

Georges Monette

## INTRODUCTION

Within a few years, the graphical power of workstations now used in
computer-aided design and computer animation will be within the reach
of most practitioners of data analysis. The use of interactive 3-D
graphics for the analysis of data and the representation of statistical
concepts opens exciting new realms. For the past three years, my
department (at York University) has used such a workstation for teaching and statistical consulting. Our experiences have spurred us to recast
basic statistical concepts in geometric terms so that we can better
exploit the natural language of the graphics computer: the geometric
figure.

The geometric approach provides a very natural way of representing
concepts in multiple regression. Many perplexing and paradoxical aspects of regression have simple explanations in terms of the shape,
projections, and motions of various geometric figures. An analyst can
visualize the relationships among various models and make inferences
in ways that are more informative and evocative than the traditional
inspection of numerical tables.

This chapter develops the geometry of multiple regression and discusses its use as a way of representing inferential information with 3-D
interactive graphics. I describe a prototype regression program called
vreg whose main purpose is to present the information normally provided by traditional packages (such as PROC REG in SAS) in a form
that exploits interactive 3-D graphics. I conclude with an example of

an application of these methods to the analysis of a data set using linear regression. The graphical approach allowed the rapid identification of observations that were influential in creating the appearance of an interaction between two predictor variables.

## ADVANCES IN GRAPHICS WORKSTATIONS

The popular program MacSpin[1] (McCullough, 1988) already allows the interactive visualization of 3-D point clouds on modestly priced computers. For regression, one would also want to see more complex objects such as fitted surfaces and confidence regions. One would also want to interact graphically with the analysis, not only with the data. For example, it should be possible to see a confidence interval for the height of a regression surface over two variables by pointing with a mouse at the point over which the height is to be estimated.

A new program called Sygraph[2] (Wilkinson, 1988), when combined with AcroSpin[3] (Parker, 1989), allows the interactive rotation of more complex 3-D objects on a personal computer of moderate power. Although the statistical analysis and the 3-D visualization occur in separate programs, it is possible to switch between programs on a fast personal computer rapidly enough that the effect approaches that of a true interactive graphical analysis. Smooth motion of complex objects in perspective is still beyond the reach of today's personal computer and requires specialized hardware to accelerate the recomputation of positions of objects as they move on the screen.

About five years ago, Silicon Graphics began selling its first graphics workstation, the IRIS 1400. At its heart is a pipeline of chips devoted to the extremely rapid multiplication of the $4 \times 4$ matrices with which graphical computations are performed. These machines originally cost about \$50,000. Since then, Silicon Graphics has produced four new lines, each more powerful than the previous, but working on the same basic principle. Other manufacturers, notably Hewlett-Packard, have also marketed similar machines. These machines have been priced beyond the reach of most data analysts, but this is expected to change soon. Silicon Graphics plans to sell a "Personal Iris" for under \$10,000 in 1990. Another imminent development is the marketing of 3-D graphics boards for personal computers. As powerful graphics become more widely available, 3-D graphical representation and visualization will become standard tools of data analysis.

## DYNAMIC GRAPHICS AND GEOMETRY —
## A NEW LANGUAGE FOR STATISTICS

The last decade has seen an explosion of research in statistical graphics. Cleveland (1987) presented a brief discussion and an annotated bibliography containing many recent references to work in dynamic graphics. Instead of presenting a survey of these methods, we will turn to a different question, that of the language of dynamic graphics. With graphics, information is more easily conveyed with geometrical figures than with tables of numbers. How can we translate the information traditionally conveyed by numbers into this geometric language?

Two major works, by Dempster (1969) and Stone (1987), have explored the geometry of statistical inference. This chapter will attempt to translate some of their results into simple geometric terms with explicit references to objects that can be seen in 3-D visualizations. Most linear statistical methods amount to performing operations on ellipsoids: taking shadows (projections), slicing sections, drawing tangent planes, forming the dual ellipsoid, finding conjugate sets of axes, and so on. These operations may sound formidable, but in two or three dimensions they can be easily visualized. The visualizations provide almost intuitive insights into deeper aspects of multiple regression.

We expect that a user with little statistical background can be led to an awareness of statistical concepts far beyond what would have been possible with traditional methods. Experience in teaching and consulting with 3-D graphics has found that they allow the motivated, but statistically untrained, researcher to develop a deeper grasp of slippery issues, such as the relationship between marginal and partial association, collinearity, response surface methods, influence, causal modeling, and so on. The hope is that, with 3-D graphics, we can enrich users' repertoire of statistical concepts and make it easier for them to see how to apply them to their problems.

## VISUALIZING BIVARIATE DATA

If data come from a bivariate normal population, then the first two moments of the data (means, standard deviations, and correlation) contain all the information the data provide about the population. Even with bivariate data that are not normally distributed, it is often true that only the first two moments are needed for a statistical procedure. For example, only the first two moments of the indicator variables in an analysis of variance model are needed to fit the usual model. This is generally true of the $X$ variables in multiple regression under standard assumptions.

There is a very effective visual display of the first two moments of the data in the *data ellipsoid*.[4] The data ellipsoid, whose exact formula is given in Appendix A, is centered at the point of means (the centroid), and its shape reflects the spread and shape of the data. Call the two variables $X_1$ and $X_2$. Figures 5.1A and 5.1B show how the data ellipsoid yields a visual impression of the sample standard deviations, $s_1$ and $s_2$, the correlation $r_{12}$, the slope, $b$, of the regression of $X_2$ on $X_1$, and the residual standard deviation, $s_e$, of the regression of $X_2$ on $X_1$.

This representation is exact if $s_e$, $s_1$ and $s_2$ are defined using the same divisor in the formulas that express them as root mean squares of deviations. For example, in the case of the maximum likelihood estimators for the second moments of a normal model, each sample standard deviation uses the same divisor, $n$, where $n$ is the sample size. With the usual practice of dividing by degrees of freedom ($n - 1$ for $s_1^2$ and $s_2^2$ and $n - 2$ for $s_e$), the statement is only approximately true, but within bounds of *visual resolution* for moderate values of $n$.

In the case of a linear regression model with constant error variance and a random predictor, we have a very simple picture: The marginal variation in $X_2$ is given by the perpendicular *shadow* (onto the vertical axis) of the ellipsoid while the conditional variation is given by the vertical *slice* through the center of the ellipsoid, as shown in Figure 5.1B. The ellipsoid yields similar information on the regression of $X_1$ on $X_2$ by exchanging the roles of the horizontal and the vertical. The duality between shadows and slices of ellipsoids is an underlying theme of the geometric theory of linear models in Dempster (1969) and Stone (1987).

There is an easy way to visualize correlation using the ellipsoid. As shown in Figure 5.2, let $a$ be the height of a line from the horizontal axis through the center of the ellipsoid to the point of vertical tangency on the ellipsoid, and let $b$ be the height from the horizontal line to the highest point on the ellipsoid (or equivalently, from the midpoint to the top of the vertical shadow of the ellipsoid). Then the correlation is $a/b$.

The shadow of the ellipsoid onto the $X_1$-axis is the *standard interval* for $X_1$, by which we mean the interval centered at $\overline{X}_1$ and with width $2s_1$ ($\overline{X}_1 \pm s_1$). Similarly, the standard interval for $X_2$ is obtained by taking the shadow of the data ellipsoid onto the $X_2$ axis.

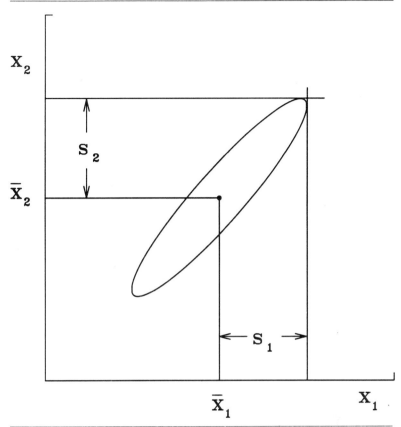

Figure 5.1A The data ellipsoid is centered at the point of means $(\overline{X}_1,\overline{X}_2)$. Its shadow onto the $X_1$ axis is the "standard interval," $X_1 \pm s_1$ and similarly for $X_2$.

If the units for $X_1$ and $X_2$ are drawn so as to have the same length on the plot, then we can say more. The standard interval for any linear combination of $X_1$ and $X_2$, for example, the sum or the difference of $X_1$ and $X_2$, can be obtained by taking the perpendicular shadow of the ellipsoid onto the axis for the new variable. The axis for a linear combination $c_1X_1 + c_2X_2$ is the line passing through the origin and the point $(c_1,c_2)$. See Figure 5.3 and a brief discussion in Appendix B.

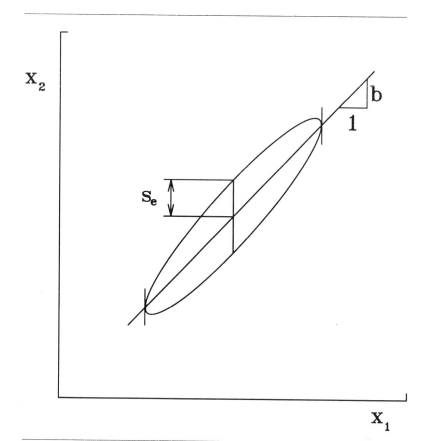

**Figure 5.1B** The line passing through the points of vertical tangency is the least squares line for the linear regression of $Y$ on $X$. Its slope, $b$, is the least squares slope. A vertical slice through the middle of the ellipsoid yields the residual standard deviation.

## FITTING A PLANE

In this section we will consider the linear model with one dependent and two independent, or predictor, variables. We will show how some of the difficulties in understanding this model can be resolved with a 3-D display of the data and regression planes along with a display of confidence ellipsoids and confidence intervals for the regression planes.

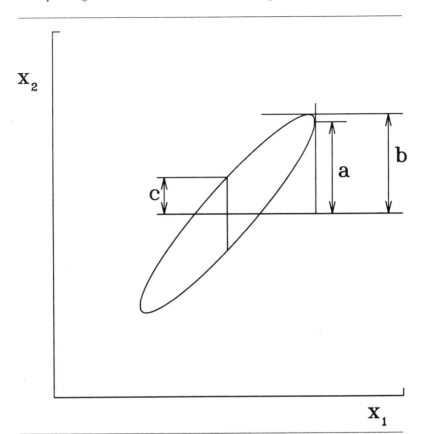

Figure 5.2 The correlation between $X_1$ and $X_2$ is the ratio $a/b$. The correlation is also related to the ratio of the "slice" to the "shadow" of the ellipsiod: $\sqrt{1 - r^2} = c/b$.

With two predictors, $X_1$ and $X_2$, we can fit four linear models.

| Model | Equation |
|---|---|
| 0 | $Y = \text{constant} + \text{error}$ |
| 1a | $Y = \text{constant} + \gamma_1 X_1 + \text{error}$ |
| 1b | $Y = \text{constant} + \gamma_2 X_2 + \text{error}$ |
| 2 | $Y = \text{constant} + \beta_1 X_1 + \beta_2 X_2 + \text{error}.$ |

With these four models we often consider the five hypotheses shown in Table 5.1.

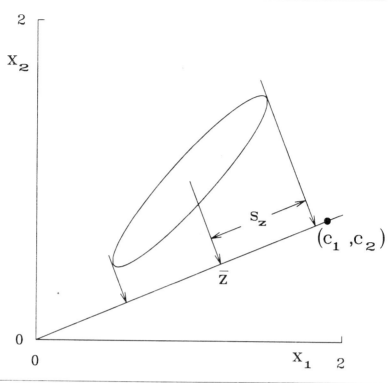

Figure 5.3   The  standard interval for $Z = c_1 X_1 + c_2 X_2$. The scale is determined by noting that at $(c_1, c_2)$ the value of $Z$ is $c_1^2 + c_2^2$. Hence,
if $(c_1, c_2)$ is normalized, the scale for $Z$ is Euclidean distance. See
Appendix B for discussion.

Table 5.1  Linear Models and Hypotheses with Two Predictor Variables

| Model | Variables | Slope parameters | Hypotheses |
|---|---|---|---|
| 0 | none | — | |
| 1a | $X_1$ | $\gamma_1$ | 1a) $\gamma_1 = 0$ |
| 1b | $X_2$ | $\gamma_2$ | 1b) $\gamma_2 = 0$ |
| 2 | $X_1, X_2$ | $\beta_1, \beta_2$ | 2) $\beta_1 = \beta_2 = 0$ |
| | | | 2a) $\beta_1 = 0$ |
| | | | 2b) $\beta_2 = 0$ |

Let $\hat{\gamma}_1, \hat{\gamma}_2$ and $\hat{\beta}_1, \hat{\beta}_2$ denote the least squares estimates of the parameters. If $X_1$ and $X_2$ are uncorrelated, then $\hat{\gamma}_1 = \hat{\beta}_1$ and $\hat{\gamma}_2 = \hat{\beta}_2$. Furthermore, in this case, tests of hypotheses generally give unparadoxical answers. Except for occasional close calls, if we reject hypothesis **2** we are likely to reject at least one of **2a** or **2b**, and vice versa. Also, hypotheses **1a** and **2a** will stand or fall together, as will **1b** and **2b**. Estimates and confidence intervals for $\beta_1$ and $\gamma_1$ will be centered at the same point. The interval for $\gamma_1$ might be wider than that for $\beta_1$ if $X_2$ is quite correlated with $Y$, thus substantially reducing the error variance.

When $X_1$ and $X_2$ are correlated, the situation is more challenging, and it can be difficult to get a grasp on the possible consequences. What is the relationship between $\hat{\beta}_1$ and $\hat{\gamma}_1$? Would it be surprising to reject hypothesis **2** without being able to reject either **1a** or **1b**? Is it possible to have different signs for $\hat{\beta}_1$ and $\hat{\gamma}_1$? What would such a situation say about the data?

A graphical analysis allows a complete answer to all these questions. To illustrate, we will use some imaginary data that a researcher might have gathered in research on the possible effects of coffee consumption. Suppose that we have measured three variables on 20 human subjects:

$X_1$    Daily coffee consumption

$X_2$    Index of occupational stress

$Y$    Index of cardiac damage

Let us imagine that, in reality, there is a strong association between $X_1$ and $Y$, but this association does not reflect a causal relationship. The association occurs because both $X_1$ and $Y$ are *caused* by the construct measured by $X_2$, stress. Further assume that $X_2$ is a highly reliable and valid measure of stress. Figures 5.4A and 5.4B give a partial picture of what the data might look like. We fit model **1a** (Figure 5.5A) to the data and see a strong significant relationship between $Y$ and $X_1$. This model can be shown by drawing a line on a two-dimensional plot of $Y$ and $X_1$. It suits our purposes better to think of this model as being represented by the equivalent least squares plane: the plane that comes closest to the data among planes that are forced to be horizontal in the direction of $X_2$. The fitted model is:

$$Y = 0.45 + 0.56 \times X_1 + 0 \times X_2 + 0.082 \times \text{error}$$

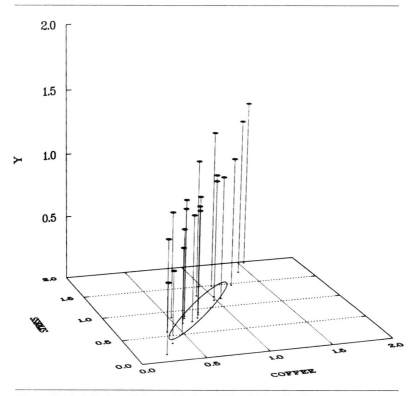

**Figure 5.4A 3-D plot of data with data ellipsoid for $X_1$, $X_2$.**

where *error* represents an error term with mean 0 and standard deviation 1, so that 0.082 is the estimated standard deviation of the error term in the fitted model. The significance of the relationship between $Y$ and $X_1$ is reflected by the 95% confidence interval for $\gamma_1$ shown in Figure 5.5B. Note that $X_1$ and $X_2$ have been generated with an unrealistically high correlation to dramatize the appearance of the figures. The reader applying the techniques of the fourth section will guess that the correlation is near 0.97.

What happens if we include $X_2$ in the model? The best fitting plane for both $X_1$ and $X_2$ is shown in Figure 5.6A. Its equation is

$$Y = 0.459 - 0.187 \times X_1 + 0.588 \times X_2 + 0.052 \times \text{error}.$$

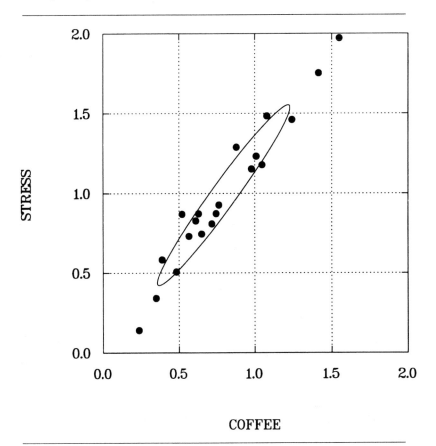

**Figure 5.4B** View of data from "above" a plot of $X_1$ vs. $X_2$ with data ellipsoid. The tilt of the ellipsoid in the $X_1 \times X_2$ plane reflects the correlation between $X_1$ and $X_2$.

Instead of showing a positive slope in the direction of $X_1$, the slope is now negative. One model seems to say that coffee is very bad for you while the other seems to indicate that it is good for you. It is, of course, not hard to fathom the apparent paradox. $\gamma_1$ is the expected change in $Y$ associated with a unit change in $X_1$ when $X_2$ is allowed to vary. In contrast, $\beta_1$ is the expected change in $Y$ for a unit change in $X_1$ when $X_2$ is kept constant. The fact that it is possible, indeed quite unsurprising, for these two coefficients to have different signs is evident when looking at the regression planes for models **1a** and **2**. Observe that both

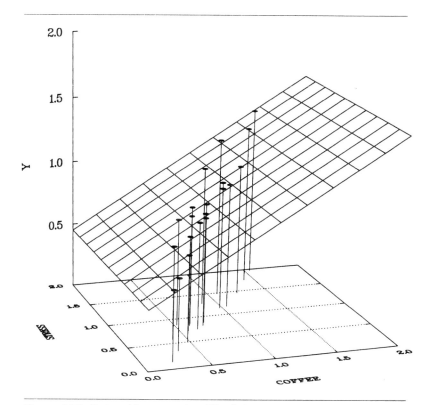

Figure 5.5A Data with regression "line" for $Y$ vs. $X_1$. The "line" is the best-fitting plane among planes constrained to have a slope of zero in the direction of $X_2$.

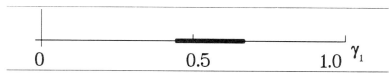

Figure 5.5B 95% Confidence interval for the regression of figure 5.5A.

planes go through the data that is mainly clustered in a cylinder around the *diagonal* line in Figure 5.4A. The tilt of a plane through the data is not well determined by this cylinder. The plane of model **1a** is constrained to have a zero slope in the direction of $X_2$. The plane of model **2** tilts up over $X_2$ resulting in substantially different slopes in the

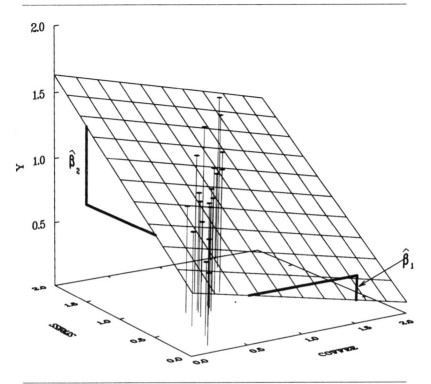

**Figure 5.6A** Fitted plane with both $X_1$ and $X_2$ as predictors. Note negative slope in the direction of $X_1$ in contrast with Figure 5.5A.

directions of the axes $X_1$ and $X_2$. On the other hand, the slopes of the two planes are very similar in a direction in which $X_1$ and $X_2$ increase simultaneously, that is, when moving through the bulk of the data.

## GRAPHICAL INFERENCE

With one parameter, a plot of the confidence interval gives a way of presenting an interval estimate for the parameter. Moreover, the plot allows easy *visual* tests of hypotheses: A hypothetical value can be tested merely by verifying whether it is in the confidence interval or not. With two parameters, the natural extension of the interval estimator is given by an ellipsoid. This is an ellipsoid of *plausible* combinations of values for the two parameters. Any joint hypothesis about the two parameters (e.g., $H_0$: $\beta_1 = 1$ and $\beta_2 = -1$) can be tested visually by verifying whether the hypothetical point, here $(1,-1)$, is inside or outside the ellipsoid. A C% confidence ellipsoid yields $(100\text{-}C)\%$ tests. What if one is interested in a test concerning only one of the two parameters? (e.g., $H_0$: $\beta_1 = 0$). Confidence intervals for each parameter can almost be obtained by taking the shadow of the confidence ellipsoid onto the axis for the parameter — almost, because the shadow of a 95% ellipsoid is indeed a confidence interval, but with confidence level somewhat higher than 95%.[5] To obtain a true 95% interval it is necessary to shrink the ellipsoid slightly to an approximately 85% confidence ellipsoid.[6] We will call this ellipsoid, whose shadows are 95% intervals, the CISE (Confidence Interval Shadowing Ellipsoid). Its shadow onto the $\beta_1$ axis is a 95% interval for $\beta_1$ and, similarly, for $\beta_2$. See Figure 5.6B.

If the units of $\beta_1$ and those of $\beta_2$ are plotted the same size, we can go further. A confidence interval for any linear combination of $\beta_1$ and $\beta_2$ is obtained by taking a perpendicular shadow of the CISE onto the axis for that linear combination. For example, to visually estimate $\beta_1 - 0.5 \times \beta_2$, we draw the axis through the point whose coordinates are the coefficients of the linear combination: $(1, -0.5)$. The perpendicular shadow of the CISE then gives a 95% interval for $\eta = \beta_1 - 0.5 \times \beta_2$. See Figure 5.7A. A natural application when $X_1$ and $X_2$ are commensurable is to compare the two coefficients. The hypothesis that $\beta_1 = \beta_2$ can be checked by projecting the CISE onto the line through the origin with a slope of $-45°$. See Figure 5.7B.

This procedure can be applied to the estimation of the *directional derivative* of the regression surface, that is, the change in height of the surface for a unit[7] step in any specified direction. Observe that $\hat{\beta}_1$, the projection of $\hat{\beta} = (\hat{\beta}_1, \hat{\beta}_2)'$ onto the horizontal axis, is the change in height for a unit step in the horizontal direction. Similarly, $\hat{\beta}_2$ is the change in height for a unit step in the vertical direction. This pattern holds for a unit step in any direction. To form a confidence interval for a unit step in any direction, one merely takes the shadow of the CISE onto the axis that points in the desired directions. See figures 5.8A and 5.8B.

The shadows of the 95% CE itself are not to be neglected. They provide 95% Scheffé confidence intervals with protection against fishing for a one-dimensional hypothesis in a two-dimensional space. This means that if the selection of a direction for a test or confidence interval is inspired by the data, then the shadow of the CE is conservative as a

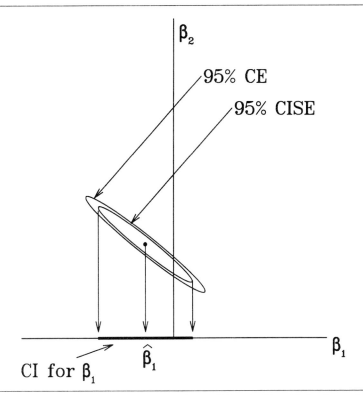

**Figure 5.6B  Outer ellipsoid is the 95% confidence ellipsoid for $\beta_1$ and $\beta_2$ jointly. The inner ellipsoid (CISE) has shadows that produce 95% confidence intervals. Note that the 95% confidence interval for $\beta_1$ shows that the negative value of $\hat{\beta}_1$ does not give evidence that $\beta_1$ is not zero.**

95% interval (i.e., the true coverage probability of the procedure is at least 95%). This interval is exact for the direction toward the point on the ellipsoid closest to the origin if that direction is selected for this reason. See Figures 5.9A and 5.9B. In summary, if the hypothesis is motivated by reasons that existed prior to the examination of the data, one can use the shadow of the CISE, understanding that if there is more than one such hypothesis, the probability of Type I error applies to each individually, not collectively. If a hypothesis is inspired by the data, or if one wants to control the probability of Type I error for a family of

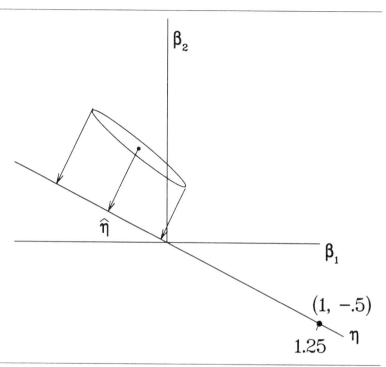

Figure 5.7A Confidence interval for $\eta = \beta_1 - 0.5 \times \beta_2$. The axis for $\eta$ goes through the point $(1,-0.5)$. The scale is determined by the fact that the value of $\eta$ is 1.25 at $(1,-0.5)$.

hypotheses, then the shadow of the CE is a safe procedure — although possibly too safe in some cases.

Some facts emerge clearly from the geometry of the ellipsoid.

1. The direction of steepest ascent of the surface is the direction pointing toward $\hat{\beta}$.
2. If the origin is outside the CE, the direction in which there is the strongest evidence of a nonzero slope (in the sense of the largest lower bound for a confidence interval) is that pointing toward the point on the ellipsoid closest to the origin.
3. Directions in which there is no evidence of a nonzero slope form a cone, which can be constructed by first drawing the cone generated by the ellipsoid (Figures 5.10A and 5.10B) and then rotating this cone ±90°, that is, taking the cone of directions perpendicular to the cone generated by the ellipsoid.

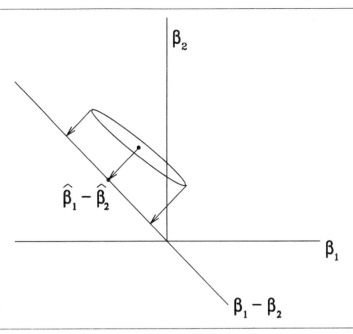

**Figure 5.7B** Test of $H_0: \beta_1 = \beta_2$. Since the shadow of the CISE does not cover the origin, we would reject $H_0$ with a 5% (=100%-95%) test.

4. The cone of directions in which there is evidence of a nonzero slope is the complement of the cone in number 3.

## THE RELATIONSHIP BETWEEN $\beta_1$ AND $\gamma_1$

The CE not only serves to give a fast visual picture of inferences concerning the slope, it also provides deeper understanding of the structure of the data. The shape of the CE is, in a sense, the inverse of the data ellipsoid for the predictor variables $X_1$ and $X_2$. The matrix of the quadratic form defining the CE is the inverse of the matrix for the data ellipsoid. The consequence with two dimensions is that the shape of the CE is simply the 90° rotation of the data ellipse. Note that by *shape* we mean the eccentricity and the orientation, not the size of the ellipse. Compare the data ellipse in Figure 5.4B with the CE of Figure 5.6B.

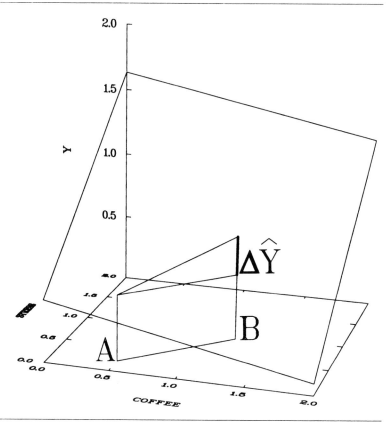

**Figure 5.8A  The directional slope of the fitted plane can be used to measure the change in $\hat{Y}$ when moving a distance of 1 from point A to point B.**

The shape of the CE is of interest for a number of reasons. One that is immediately apparent is to understand the seeming paradox in which one rejects the hypothesis $\beta_1 = \beta_2 = 0$, but cannot reject either of the single hypotheses $\beta_1 = 0$ or $\beta_2 = 0$. One can easily see how such a situation could arise with correlated data, leading to a CE like that of Figure 5.11, where the CE misses the origin, but the shadows of the CISE include it.

The CISE also elucidates the relationship between $\hat{\beta}_1$ and $\hat{\gamma}_1$. While $\hat{\beta}_1$ is obtained by projecting the center of the CISE downward onto the horizontal axis, $\hat{\gamma}_1$ is obtained by projecting the center obliquely along

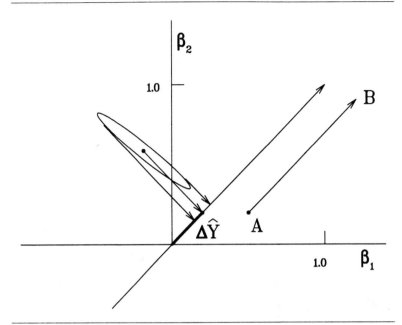

Figure 5.8B An axis is drawn parallel to the segment AB. The projection of
the CISE onto this axis yields a 95% interval for the expected
change in $Y$ when moving from A to B.

a line that passes through the point of horizontal tangency. See Figures 5.12A and 5.12B.

These properties also hold for the true $\beta_1$, $\beta_2$ and $\gamma_1$, $\gamma_2$ under suitable
assumptions about the randomness of $X_1$ and $X_2$. An ellipsoid with the
same shape and orientation as the CE centered at the true point $(\beta_1, \beta_2)$
will have oblique projections onto $\gamma_1$ and $\gamma_2$. This fact provides a
visualization of the property that $\beta_1 = \gamma_1$ if $X_1$ and $X_2$ are uncorrelated
or if $\beta_2 = 0$. A similar property holds for $\beta_2$ and $\gamma_2$ in that $\gamma_2$ is obtained
by taking an oblique projection onto the vertical axis through the point
of vertical tangency.

The oblique projection of the CISE is a *centered inner bound* for the
confidence interval for $\gamma_1$ that arises by fitting model **1a**. By this we
mean that the latter has the same center and is at least as large as the
former. The interval formed by the oblique projection can also be
interpreted as a confidence interval: It estimates the slope of the surface

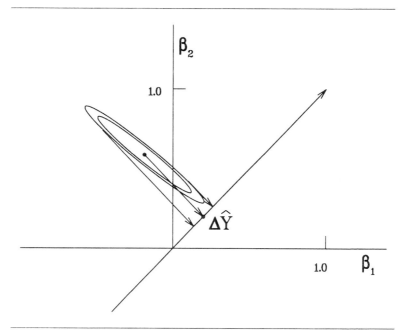

**Figure 5.9A** 95% Scheffé confidence interval for the true slope in the direction given in figure 5.8A. The coverage probability is at least 95% regardless of how the direction was selected for attention.

along a direction parallel to the regression line of $X_2$ on $X_1$. That is, it estimates the expected change in $Y$ for a unit increase in $X_1$ forcing $X_2$ to change by the average change observed in the data. In contrast, the larger interval estimates the expected change in $Y$ for a unit change in $X_1$, allowing $X_2$ to vary as it would in the population from which $X_1$ and $X_2$ form a putative sample. There is, as one would expect, less information about the latter than about the former. An alternative interpretation of the larger interval is that it estimates the expected change in $Y$ for a unit change in $X_1$ if the true value of $\beta_2$ is 0.

Armed with an understanding of these geometric relationships, it is easy to understand and even anticipate *paradoxical data*. A typical configuration yielding significantly different signs for $\beta_1$ and $\gamma_1$ might look like Figures 5.13A to 5.13D. The confidence ellipsoid, in a situation in which neither $\gamma_1$ nor $\gamma_2$ appear significantly different from 0, yet both $\beta_1$ and $\beta_2$ are highly significant, would look like Figure 5.14. At

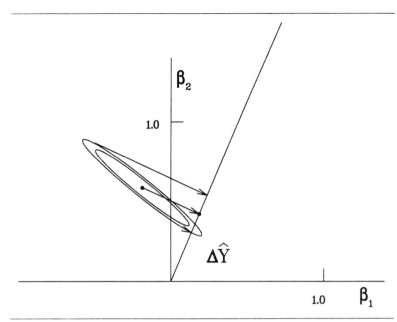

**Figure 5.9B** The Scheffé level is in a sense exact for the slope in the direction of "greatest evidence," i.e., in the direction pointing toward the point on the surface of the ellipsoid that is closest to the origin.

first glance this might seem like a highly contrived and unlikely situation. Upon reflection, however, we see that it is typical of situations in which $Y$ is not so much affected by $X_1$ and $X_2$ individually, but rather by the "residual" of $X_1$ on $X_2$ (or vice versa). Consider, for example, the possible relationship among $Y$ as health, $X_1$ as weight, and $X_2$ as height. In the population as a whole, $Y$ might not be strongly related to $X_1$. But $Y$ might be strongly related to $X_1$ within subgroups that have similar values for $X_2$.

These geometric observations could be viewed as mere curiosities with little relevance for practical data analysis. The power of these devices, when incorporated into a graphical package, is that they elevate to a much higher level (or, more strictly, to a higher dimension) the user's understanding of the potentially complex interrelationships among variables. When the devices are part of the everyday analysis of data sets, this awareness becomes inescapable.

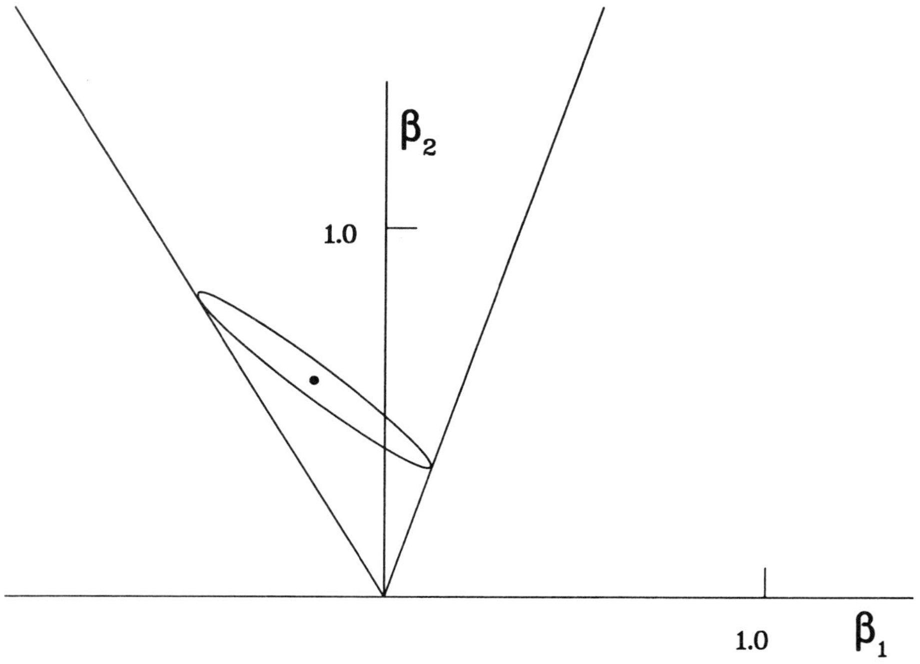

**Figure 5.10A** The cone generated by the confidence ellipsoid can be rotated ±90° to obtain the set of directions in which there is no strong evidence of a nonzero slope.

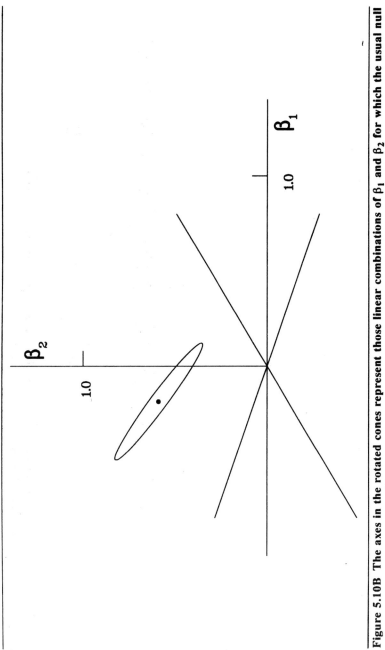

Figure 5.10B The axes in the rotated cones represent those linear combinations of $\beta_1$ and $\beta_2$ for which the usual null hypothesis would be accepted. Axes not in these cones represent linear combinations for which the null hypothesis would be rejected.

231

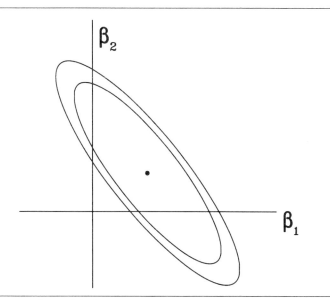

Figure 5.11   CE and CISE that would lead to rejection of hypothesis 2 but
"acceptance" of hypotheses 2a and 2b.

## FITTING CURVED SURFACES

While the ellipsoid provides a powerful adjunct to the analysis of the
regression model with two linear predictor variables, the relative advantage of interactive graphics is much more marked with models
whose regression surfaces are curved. In the usual regression model
with two *independent* variables, we fit a curved surface to the two
variables by adding new *model* variables that are defined as functions
of the original independent variables. For example, $X_1^2, X_2^2$ and $X_1 \times X_2$
can be added to fit a quadratic surface. In the SAS package, among
others, these extra variables are presented as ordinary data to a regression program like PROC REG. To prepare a 3-D display, however, we
must be able to distinguish between independent input variables and
variables that can be taken as functions of other variables. In fact, since
the height of the fitted surface needs to be computed over a range of
values that is different from the observed combinations of values of the
$X_1$ and $X_2$ variables, the program needs to be able to compute the
function over a range of arguments. Hence, the regression program must
be supplied with the algorithm to generate the new variables.

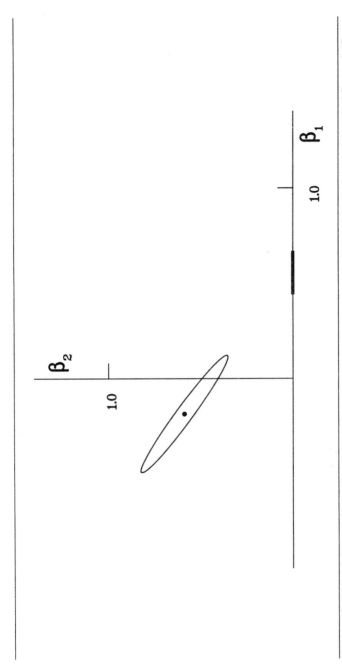

**Figure 5.12A** We combine the CISE for $\beta_1$ and $\beta_2$ shown in figure 5.6B with the confidence interval for $\gamma 1$ of figure 5.5B.

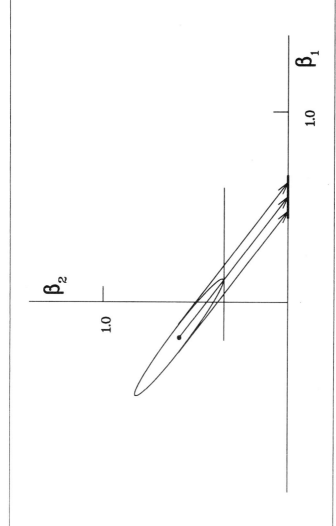

**Figure 5.12B**  The oblique projection of the CISE along a line going through the point of horizontal tangency is an inner bound for the confidence interval for $\gamma^1$. The ratio of the inner interval to the outer is approximately equal to the ratio of the standard deviation of $Y$ adjusted for $X_1$ and $X_2(s_e)$ and the standard deviation of $Y$ adjusted for only $X_1$.

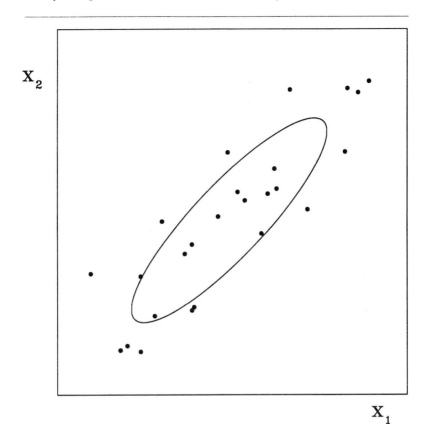

Figure 5.13A  The data ellipse shows a high correlation between $X_1$ and $X_2$. The 90° rotation of this ellipse produces the shape and orientation of the confidence ellipse for the slope of the regression of a variable $Y$ on $X_1$ and $X_2$.

We will distinguish between a set of *true* independent variables, that is, variables that cannot be taken as functions of each other, and variables that can be expressed as functions of these by calling the former *input variables* and the latter *computed variables*. Together, the variables in a model, be they input or computed variables, will be called *model variables*. Note that the $X_0$ dummy variable in a regression with an intercept term is a computed variable in this classification since its value (always 1) is a function (in the mathematical sense) of the input variables.

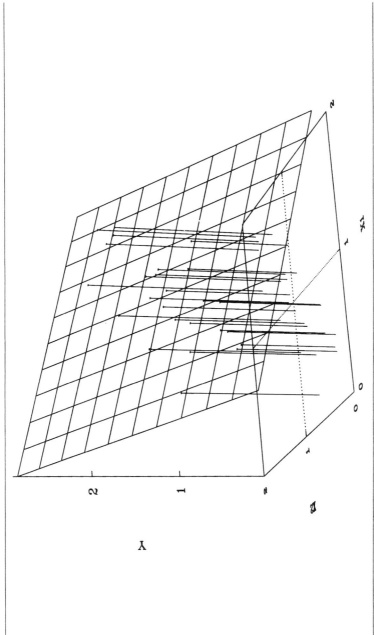

**Figure 5.13B** The fitted plane for the model with both $X$ Variables has a negative slope in the direction of $X_1$.

236

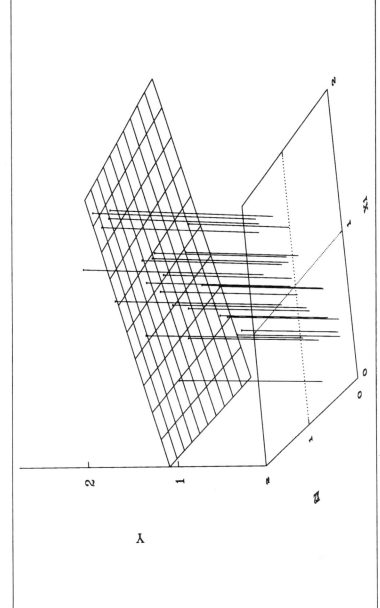

**Figure 5.13C** The line fitting a model with $X_1$ alone has positive slope.

237

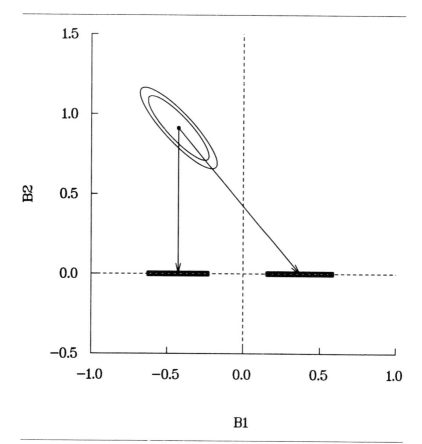

**Figure 5.13D** **The CE and CISE are on one side of the Y axis while the oblique shadow is on the other side, and the CI for $\beta_1$ obtained by taking the downward shadow of the CISE indicates the opposite sign to that shown by the CI for $\gamma_1$.**

The notion of a computed variable is potentially complex. If $Y$ is given as a function of $X$ and the function is one-to-one, then $X$ could also be viewed as a function of $Y$. A sophisticated implementation of a regression program might be able to recognize that certain algorithms are invertible. For our purposes, the operational definition of a computed variable relies merely on explicit variable definition statements.

To clarify these notions, consider a fragment of input code to vreg. Vreg uses a simple input language that mimics SAS, but does not allow

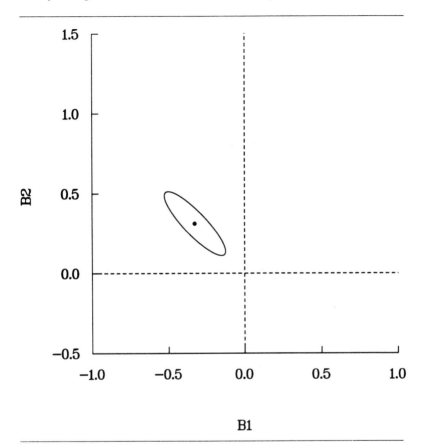

**B1**

**Figure 5.14** With $X1$ and $X2$ as in figure 5.13A but a different slope for the regression plane, the CE and CISE could be positioned as shown above. Projecting the ellipsoid perpendicularly onto the horizontal axis and onto the vertical axis, we see that both $\beta_1$ and $\beta_2$ are significantly nonzero in a regression on both $X_1$ and $X_2$. One can see immediately, however, that the oblique projection onto the horizontal axis through the point of horizontal tangency includes zero. An oblique projection onto the vertical axis through a point of vertical tangency also includes zero. Hence, neither $\gamma_1$ nor $\gamma_2$ can be significantly far from zero.

conditional statements. The IF-THEN-ELSE construct is replaced with the *conditional expression* borrowed from C. The conditional expression has the form

$$Y = exprA \ ? \ exprB : exprC;$$

It is equivalent to the SAS construct

```
IF (exprA) THEN Y = exprB;
ELSE Y = exprC;
```

Consider the following input:

```
input Y in1 in2 in3;
com1 = in1*in2;
com2 = com1**2;
com3 = (in1 > in2) ? com2 : 0;
```

The labels of the variables have been chosen to distinguish between input variables and computed variables.

The model

$$Y = \beta_0 + \beta_1 com1 + \beta_2 com2 + \beta_3 in2 + error$$

can be represented as a surface over the variables in1 and in2, and vreg, when asked to fit such a model, will recognize this fact and generate the fitted regression surface. The computed variable com3 is also a function of in1 and in2. It is not, however, a continuous function of in1 and in2, and a fitted model would be represented by a possibly discontinuous surface. We will discuss later how such a situation can be handled by turning the expression in1 > in2 into a categorical variable that, when treated as an input variable, will generate two surfaces, one for each value of the categorical variable.

The significance of all this is that if a regression model is such that all of its model variables can be expressed as functions of two input variables, then the model can be fitted in three dimensions by showing the graph of the fitted response function.

Let us take a quadratic model as an example of a model that yields a curved surface. Researchers often use the product term in such models to model possible multiplicative interaction between variables. They are then perplexed at the difficulty in interpreting the parameters of the linear terms in the model. The difficulty arises from the fact that the linear terms estimate the directional slopes (the partial derivatives) of the surface over the origin, whereas the slopes of interest are those over the bulk of the data. Vreg provides an interactive estimate of the slope of the surface. The user points with a mouse at a point in the plane of predictor variables and the program displays the confidence ellipsoid for the slopes of the surface over that point. As described above, this ellipsoid can be used to visualize confidence intervals for any directional slope by taking the shadow of the ellipsoid onto a line pointing in the desired direction. This tool allows an *inferential* examination of the surface and helps to distinguish possibly spurious features from those that reflect a property of the underlying process generating the data.

## CATEGORICAL VARIABLES AND ANALYSIS OF COVARIANCE

If, in addition to one or two continuous input variables, one wants to fit one or more categorical variables, the model can be visualized by showing a number of surfaces, one for each combination of possible values of the categorical variables. We will call each combination a *cell* for the model. In regression, categorical variables are handled by generating suitable dummy variables. If we generate a single *cell variable*, $C$, to index the cells of the model, then all dummy variables become computed variables (in the sense of the previous section, above) that can be expressed as functions of the cell variable $C$.

Interaction is modeled by including suitable products of variables. Interactions between the continuous and dummy variables are seen as a lack of parallelism of the fitted surfaces. The statistical significance is checked by producing confidence ellipsoids for the relevant parameters. This approach allows the representation of models with complex unsaturated factorial structures, although the relationships among the resulting surfaces might be challenging to interpret.

## VISUALIZING APTITUDE-TREATMENT INTERACTION

A special application of the approach in the previous section can be made to the problem of aptitude-treatment interaction. Often a treatment might have different effects on different subsets of a target population. For example, a new teaching method might result in an improvement of performance for gifted students but a deterioration for others.

The usual approach to verify the presence of an interaction effect is to test for an interaction term between the aptitude variable, $A$, and the dummy treatment variable, $T$. Calling the response $Y$, we fit the model

$$E(Y) = \beta_0 + \beta_T \times T + \beta_A \times A + \beta_{AT} \times A \times T$$

and check for a significant $\hat{\beta}_{AT}$, which would indicate that the response lines are not parallel for the two treatments. This result in turn implies that the treatments have different effects for different values of $A$. Lack of parallelism, however, is sometimes not, in itself, of great concern. Frequently, the important question is whether the direction of the effect is different for different values of $A$ that occur in the population. Geometrically, this translates into the question of whether the two response lines intersect over a specified range of values of $A$. In this case, we can use the term *strong* interaction. The value of $A$ over which the intersection occurs separates the population into those who might be expected to benefit more from one treatment rather than the other.

With two aptitudes, $A_1$ and $A_2$, we can visualize a response surface (often a plane) for each treatment. Aptitude-treatment interaction can be tested by determining whether the surfaces depart significantly from being parallel. The intersection of the two surfaces, when projected down into the $A_1 \times A_2$ plane, separates values of $A_1 \times A_2$ into regions that might be expected to benefit more from one treatment than from the other. With 3-D graphics we can immediately check the presence of strong interaction by seeing whether the two surfaces intersect over the range of observed values of $A_1 \times A_2$. See Figures 5.15A and 5.15B. The line(s) of intersection are visually projected down to see the location and shape of the two regions. We can interactively estimate the difference in the height of the two surfaces to partition the $A_1 \times A_2$ space into regions in which (a) treatment 1 is significantly (statistically) better than treatment 2, (b) treatment 2 is significantly better than treatment 1, and (c) it is plausible that the two treatments have the same effect. This is a task that is difficult to accomplish without graphics even in the case of simple planar response surfaces.

The approach is easily applied to nonplanar regression models where the ability to graphically view the relative shapes and positions of the regression surfaces is even more important. The surfaces will intersect in curves whose downward projections form the boundaries of regions that have different relative benefits from the treatments. It becomes important to assess the evidence in favor of one treatment or the other

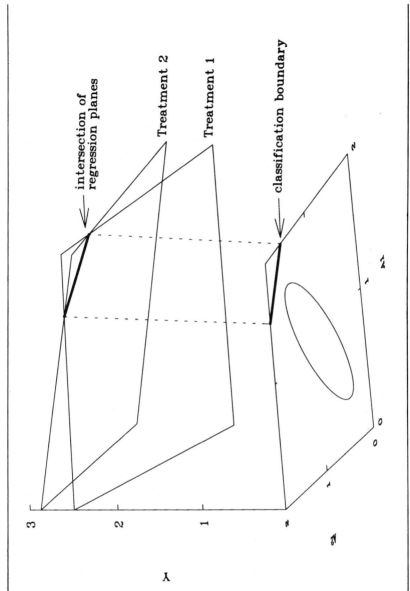

Figure 5.15A  Two regression planes intersect over a line that is to one side of the range of $A_1$-$A_2$.

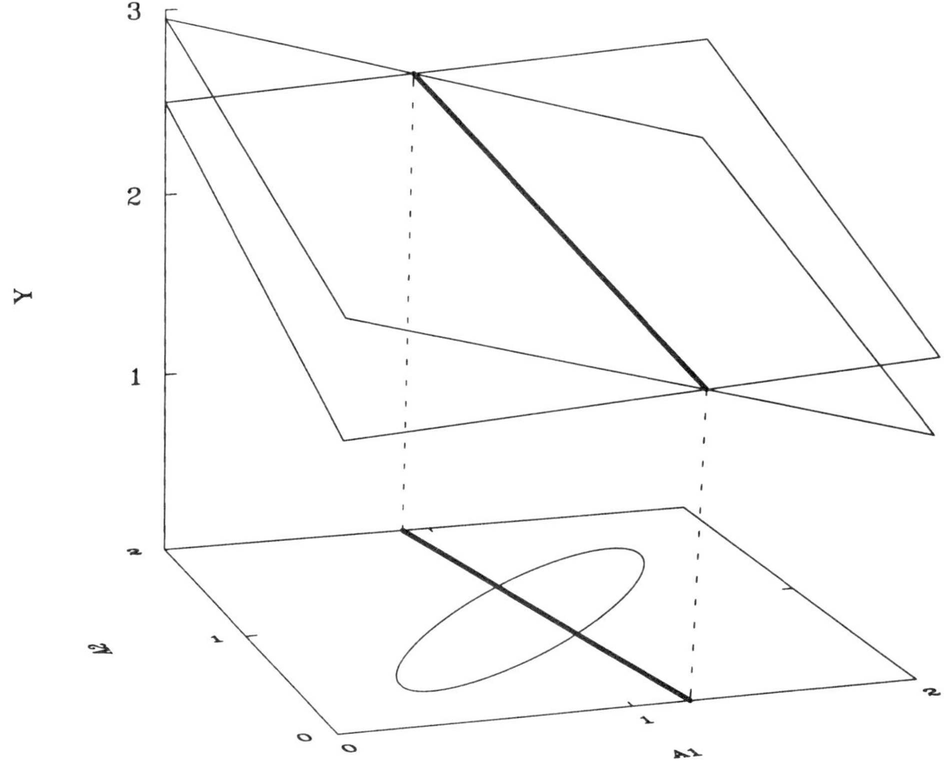

**Figure 5.15B** The intersection of the two regression planes splits values of $A_1$-$A_2$ into two regions according to which treatment is estimated to be the most favorable.

244

at various places in the $A_1 \times A_2$ space. Interactive estimation is invaluable for this purpose.

## OTHER CONTINUOUS VARIABLES

The two- or three-dimensional representation of higher-dimensional data is not a new problem in statistics. In regression models we are typically not just interested in discovering the shape of a point cloud. Methods like principal component regression are expedient, but they lose the orientation of the points with respect to the original axes. These axes define controlling variables of interest, that is, they define the directional slopes that are of interest in the study. Transformation to principal components presents us with a new set of estimable slopes that may not be relevant to the substantive problem. With the following techniques, although limited in application, the controlling function of variables in the model is not lost.

1. Three-dimensional partial regression residual plots (PRP). (For an explanation of two-dimensional partial regression plots, see Chapter 6, this volume.)
2. Discretization, that is, defining a cell variable $C$ such that the additional variables are approximate functions of $C$. Different surfaces are drawn for each value of $C$, but the model variable that is a function of $C$ is an approximation of the original variable.
3. Hot surfaces: Drawing an interactive regression surface over two variables while changing the values of other variables.

In three dimensions, as in two, partial regression plots are sufficient for inference on the parameters of the model displayed through the plots. Suppose a model contains a dependent variable $Y$ and three independent variable $X_1, X_2$ and $X_3$. The PRP for $Y, X_1$ and $X_2$ adjusting for $X_3$ is obtained by taking the residuals of each of $Y$, $X_1$ and $X_2$ regressed on $X_3$ and plotting them in a three-dimensional plot. The CE for the resulting slopes (except for a small adjustment for degrees of freedom) will be the same as the CE for the slopes in the direction of $X_1$ and $X_2$ in the model containing $X_1$, $X_2$, and $X_3$ as predictors.

An effective way of visualizing the effects of controlling for one or more additional variables is to view alternately the *marginal* model with predictors $X_1$ and $X_2$ only and the PRP model adjusting for additional variables. The geometrically imaginative might visualize the CE of the PRP model as the *downward* shadow of a high-dimensional ellipsoid, whereas the CE of the marginal model is the *oblique* shadow in a way that is analogous to the shadows described earlier. A large change from one ellipsoid to the other signifies that the additional variables are potentially important confounding effects.

In discretization, the discrete variable $C$ is not necessarily entered directly in the model. It enters only through variables that are functions of $C$ and that approximate the discretized variable. This allows $C$ to be treated partly as a classification variable in that a separate fitted surface can be drawn for each value of $C$, yet the model can depend on $C$ through variables that are functions of $C$ in an arbitrary way. This allows the modeling of approximate linear, quadratic, or other effects, in a discretized variable.

Suppose that a regression model involves three input variables (through an arbitrary number of computed variables). The fitted regression function cannot be visualized over a pair of the input variables unless the third omitted variable is given a value. With a *hot* surface, one interactively changes the value of the third variable and sees the surface change in response. This approach can be applied to more than one omitted variable and can be seen as a *model-based* version of the technique of brushing (Cleveland, 1987).


## INTERACTIVE INFLUENCE DIAGNOSTICS

What happens if one or a few of our points are wild points that do not come from the population or process about which we want to make inferences? Will a particular point, if it is wild, make a disproportionate difference to the fitted model? Or, more pertinently, to inference about the model? One way of telling is to see the effect on a confidence interval or ellipsoid of either dropping or moving a point. It is potentially misleading to focus exclusively on the effect of dropping a point on an estimator itself. Potentially critical points are easy to pick out for either their large residual from the fitted plane or for their unusual position in the predictor variable space (or both). All measures of influence are based on some combination of these two factors. But no single measure can capture the potential effects of a bad point. Some points will greatly affect the value of estimators, others will perhaps not affect the value, but the shape of confidence ellipsoids. Inference can be affected as much by the latter as the former, a point that is often missed.

Since the CE or CI represents the information for inference concerning a parameter, it would seem that the most informative way of assessing the influence of a point is simply to see what happens to a CE or CI when the point is dropped or moved. With an interactive graphical analysis, points can be dropped or moved at will, and the effects on CEs and CIs can be seen (almost) immediately. Vreg, after having computed the new surfaces, CEs and CIs, allows the user to switch from one fit to the other, thereby gaining an almost animated view of the influence of a point.

## AN EXAMPLE

In this section we consider an example in which graphical analysis led to a quick insight into a data analytic problem. A psychologist, Ginzberg (1987), was seeking to get a better understanding of the relationship between the level of depression, $Y$, among subjects suffering from reactive depression and a variety of other psychological measurements. In the process, she found evidence of an interaction between two of these measurements: *complexity* $(X_1)$ and *fatalism* $(X_2)$. The direction of the interaction was inconsistent with expectations, and the resulting coefficients for the effects of $X_1$ and $X_2$ were difficult to interpret.

The first problem to address in deciding how to view the data in 3-D is what should be done with the other measurements in the study. Two possibilities are to marginalize, that is, to ignore the other variables (Figure 5.16), or to control for them by looking at what in effect is a three-dimensional partial regression plot, a plot of $Y$ adjusted for the omitted variables versus $X_1$ and $X_2$, each also adjusted for the omitted variables (Figure 5.17). We will denote these adjusted variables $\dot{Y}$, $\dot{X}_1$, and $\dot{X}_2$. In passing from one view to the other, one point (to which we will refer as Doug) became more isolated from the bulk of the others. This point, although not very atypical with respect to $Y$ and $X_2$ alone, appeared to have much more unusual values of $Y$ and $X_2$ *relative* to what these values should have been given the values of the omitted variables. In other words, this point displayed an unusual profile, if not unusual values, for the variables themselves.

When the point was identified to the researchers, it turned out that the situation was not entirely unexpected. While the study had intended to focus on reactive depression, Doug had ultimately been given a

*(text continues on page 252)*

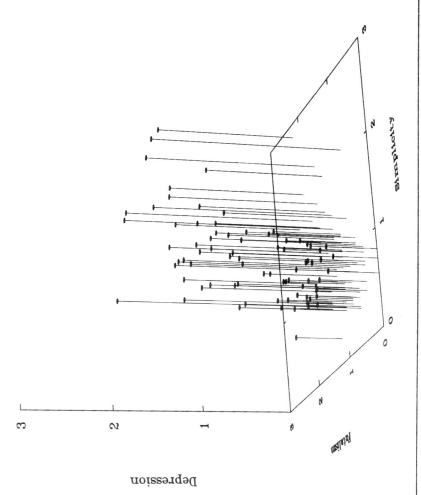

Figure 5.16 Raw data for depression (Beck Scale), simplicity, and fatalism.

248

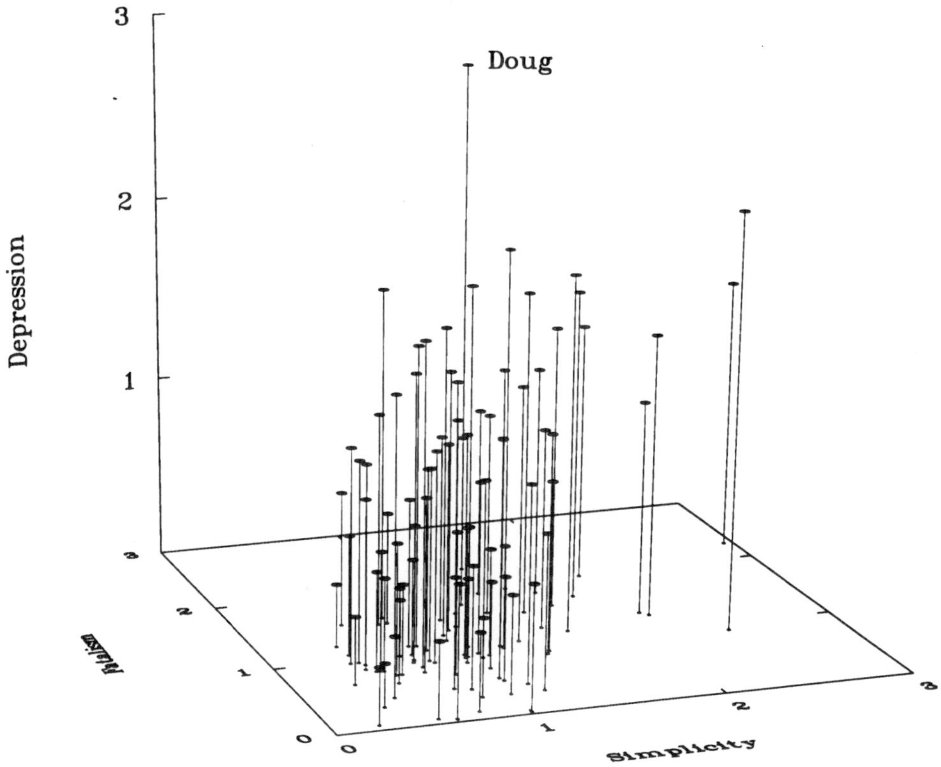

Figure 5.17 Depression, simplicity, and fatalism adjusted for other variables recorded in study.

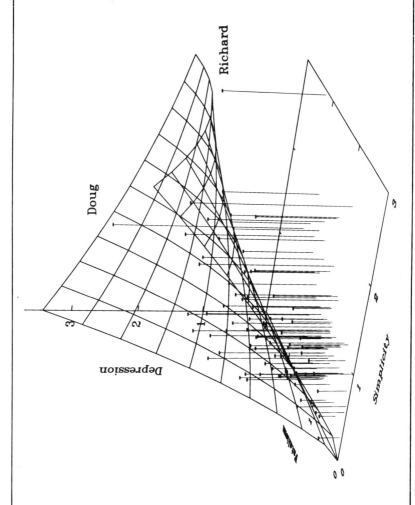

**Figure 5.18A** One outlier, "Richard," appears to be pulling down the tip of the regression surface.

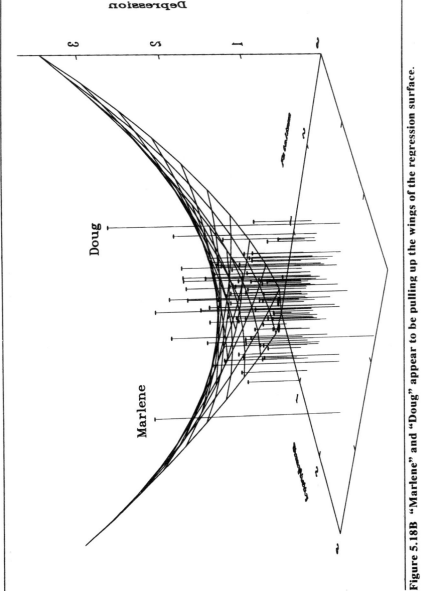

**Depression**

**Figure 5.18B** "Marlene" and "Doug" appear to be pulling up the wings of the regression surface.

251

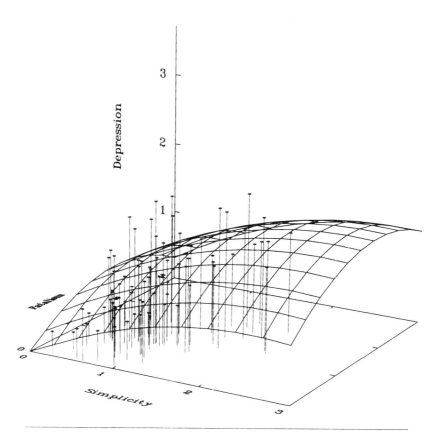

Figure 5.19A **Removing three points causes a large change in the shape of the regression surface. In particular, the new surface does not differ significantly from a plane.**

different diagnosis — *schizo-dissociative* depression — by clinicians who were working independently of the research team.

The presence of interaction between $X_1$ and $X_2$ means that a plane does not adequately represent the regression of $\dot{Y}$ on $\dot{X}_1$ and $\dot{X}_2$ controlling for omitted variables. Although it is impossible to represent the usual multiplicative interaction model (using a product term $X_1 \times X_2$) with a regression surface for $\dot{Y}$ versus $\dot{X}1$ and $\dot{X}_2$, we can generate a curved regression surface over $\dot{X}_1$ and $\dot{X}_2$ to approximate such a model.

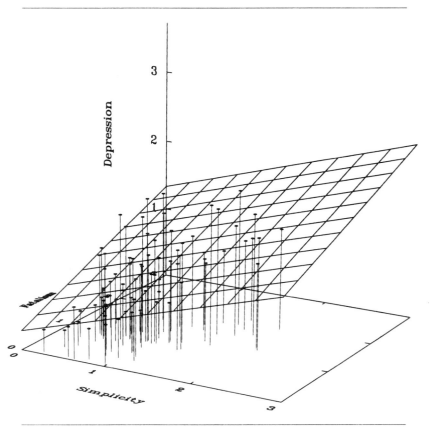

Figure 5.19B  The least squares plane provides a reasonable fit when outlying points are omitted.

In fact, some reflection on the possible nature of processes might convince one that the usual multiplicative term is quite arbitrary, especially in the presence of other controlling variables. Fitting a quadratic model to the residuals $\dot{X}_1$ and $\dot{X}_2$ instead of the raw $X_1$ and $X_2$ allows the modeling of quite reasonable phenomena. Consider, for example, a situation in which $Y$ achieves an optimum for values of $X_1$ and $X_2$ that are consistent with their expected values given other variables, but falls off as $X_1$ and $X_2$ become inconsistent with these other variables. A quadratic model in the residuals $\dot{X}_1$ and $\dot{X}_2$ will model this situation potentially much better than a quadratic model in the raw variables $X_1$ and $X_2$.

Viewing the quadratic model fitting $\dot{Y}$ to $\dot{X}_1$ and $\dot{X}_2$ quickly revealed three outliers in different parts of the $\dot{X}_1$-$\dot{X}_2$ space, which seemed to be pulling the regression surface into its curved shape. See Figures 5.18A and 5.18B. Doug, high in $\dot{Y}$ and $\dot{X}_2$, Marlene, high in $\dot{Y}$ and $\dot{X}_1$, and Richard, low in $\dot{Y}$ but high in $\dot{X}_1$ and $\dot{X}_2$, seemed to be responsible for pulling up the *wings* of the surface while holding the *nose* down. Indeed the removal of these three points results in the surface of Figure 5.19 in which all significant curvature has disappeared. Understanding the role of these three points in creating the appearance of interaction would have been extremely difficult without an interactive 3-D graphical presentation that allows complete perception of the spatial relationships among the points and surfaces.

## NOTES

1. MacSpin is a trademark of $D^2$ Software Inc.

2. Sygraph is a trademark of Systat. Inc. Sygraph was used to produce the figures in this chapter.

3. AcroSpin is a trademark of Acrobits.

4. We will use the word ellipsoid to denote two-dimensional ellipses and higher dimensional ellipsoids.

5. The confidence level is approximately 98.6% for large $n$, and always greater than 96.8%

6. The exact amount depends on error degrees of freedom. With one degree of freedom for error the value is 92.15%, but it quickly decreases toward its limit of 85.35% for large $n$.

7. Units correspond to distance when $X_1$ and $X_2$ are plotted so that their units have the same length. Although units in the $X_1 \times X_2$ space might not have a substantive interpretation when $X_1$ and $X_2$ are not commensurable, the units can be thought of as an arbitrary way of specifying distance in the plane.

## APPENDIX A: THE DATA ELLIPSOID

The data ellipsoid for a bivariate population is centered at the point of means $\mu = (\mu_1,\mu_2)'$ and has a shape that reflects the standard deviations and covariance of the population. For a bivariate normal distribution, the ellipsoid is a contour of the density. The ellipsoid of radius $r$ is the set of $\mathbf{x} = (x_1,x_2)'$ that satisfy

$$[\mathbf{x} - \mu]' \Sigma^{-1} [\mathbf{x} - \mu] \leq r^2$$

where

$$\Sigma = \begin{bmatrix} \sigma_{11} & \sigma_{12} \\ \sigma_{21} & \sigma_{22} \end{bmatrix}$$

is the variance matrix for the population.

A more suggestive way of defining the ellipsoid uses a matrix "square root" of $\Sigma$, which we define to be any $2 \times 2$ matrix $A$ such that

$$\Sigma = AA'. \tag{5.1}$$

Letting $U$ denote the unit disk in the plane, we can write the ellipsoid as

$$E = \mu + rAU.$$

If $y$ is another variable (of dimension one or two in the present context) that is defined as a linear transformation of $x:y = Tx$, then the ellipsoid for $y$ is just

$$F = TE = T\mu + rTAU. \tag{5.2}$$

There are infinitely many matrices $A$ that satisfy equation 5.1. A frequently convenient form is the lower triangular "Cholesky" factorization of $\Sigma$:

$$A = \begin{bmatrix} \sigma_1 & 0 \\ \sigma_{12}/\sigma_1 & \sigma_{2.1} \end{bmatrix} \tag{5.3}$$

where $\sigma_1 = (\sigma_{11})^{1/2}$ and $\sigma_{2.1} = (\sigma_{22} - \sigma_{12}^2/\sigma_{11})^{1/2}$ is, in the standard linear regression case, the standard deviation of the conditional distribution of $X_2$ given $X_1$. It is easy to verify that $AA' = \Sigma$. The columns of $A$ are "conjugate" axes of the ellipsoid $AU$. This means that each column defines a point on the surface of the ellipsoid, and the other column (columns in the general case) is parallel to the tangent of the former. A mathematically more abstract, but powerful, description of the columns of $A$ is that they form an *orthonormal basis* with respect to the inner product $(x,y) = x'\Sigma^{-1}y$.

## APPENDIX B: PERPENDICULAR SHADOWS

The fact that linear combinations of two variables, $X_1$ and $X_2$, can be identified with perpendicular shadows when a graph is Euclidean (in the sense that the units for each axis are drawn with the same length) rests on a simple property of linear combinations. Let $c_1$ and $c_2$ be numbers, not both zero, and consider a variable $Z$ defined by $Z = c_1X_1 + c_2X_2$. Let $L$ be the line through the point $c = (c_1, c_2)$. Now consider all the points $X = (X_1, X_2)$ that yield a given value for $Z$. These points form a line, call it $M$. If the graph is Euclidean, then $M$ is perpendicular to $L$.

The result of this is that the value of $Z$ for any point $X$ can be obtained by dropping a perpendicular to $L$ and reading off a scale on $L$ that give the value of $Z$ for each point along $L$. In this sense $L$ serves as an axis for the variable $Z$ in precisely the same way that the $X_1$-axis serves as an axis for the variable $X_1$. Since the scale on $L$ is linear, we only need to determine one nonzero value, and all the others follow by linearity. An easy value to obtain is that at the point $c = (c_1, c_2)$ itself, where the value of $Z = c_1^2 + c_2^2$. This fact is illustrated in Figures 5.3 and 5.7A.

Note that the Euclidean property is a property of the graph and has nothing to do with the nature of the variables. In particular, a graph can be Euclidean without the variables being commensurable. If a graph is not Euclidean, we can still obtain the value of a linear combination by projecting onto a line. The only difference is that the projection will not be perpendicular, but oblique, in a way that can be determined from the "unit sphere" of the graph.

## REFERENCES

Cleveland, W. S. (1987). Research in statistical graphics. *Journal of the American Statistical Association, 82,* 419-423.

Dempster, A. P. (1969). *Elements of continuous multivariate analysis.* Reading, MA: Addison-Wesley.

Ginzberg, E. (1987). Personal communication.

McCullough, B. D. (1988). *MacSpin graphical data analysis and decision support software, notes for version 2.* Austin: D$^2$ Software.

Parker, D. B. (1989). *AcroSpin, version 2.* Redwood City, CA: Acrobits.

Stone, M. (1987). *Coordinate-free multivariable statistics.* Oxford: Oxford University Press.

Wilkinson, L. (1988). *SYGRAPH.* Evanston, IL: Systat.

# 6

## REGRESSION DIAGNOSTICS:
## An Expository Treatment of
## Outliers and Influential Cases

Kenneth A. Bollen
Robert W. Jackman

Regression analysis is a powerful tool in social research because it helps to identify and summarize relations between variables. The emphasis on generalization is critical: Among the many assumptions that statistical analysis involves is the idea that a minority of observations does not drive the obtained results. We are justly skeptical of empirical results that are unduly sensitive to one case (or to a very small number of observations).

Whether or not regression estimates are sensitive to one or a few cases is in part a function of sample size. In small samples, a few observations can have a major impact on estimates. While less common, this can also happen in very large samples. For instance, Kahn and Udry (1986, pp. 734-737) analyzed a sample of over 2,000 cases in which 8 outliers had a big effect on the coefficient estimates. The same problem can occur in other samples of moderate to large size. Thus it is prudent

AUTHORS' NOTE: This is a revised version of a paper originally published in *Sociological Methods & Research*, Volume 13 (May 1985). We would like to thank Brian Silver, the editors, and the anonymous referees for their comments and to acknowledge support from the National Science Foundation (SES-8112023).

to screen both large and small samples for outliers and influential observations.

If the model is bivariate it is possible to gain some perspective on the robustness of small-sample estimates by examining such items as the univariate distributions of the variables, bivariate scattergrams, and the residuals from the fitted model. As the complexity of the model increases, simple diagnostic checks become more difficult. Most notably, when one is interested in a multiple regression, the examination of bivariate scatterplots is not always an optimal strategy. One alternative is to examine residuals, but even this strategy can be inadequate. For instance, one observation may have sufficiently extreme values on both the response variable and on one or more of the regressors so that it has an overriding effect on the estimates, even though the residual for that observation is small.

Our goal in this chapter is to provide an expository treatment of recent developments in the analysis of outliers and influential data points in the multiple regression framework. The term *influential data point* refers to an observation that, either by itself, or along with other observations, "has a demonstrably larger impact on the calculated values of various estimates (coefficients, standard errors, t-values, etc.) than is the case for most of the other observations" (Belsley, Kuh, & Welsch, 1980, p. 11).

It is useful to distinguish influential cases from outliers. In a most general sense, outliers are observations that are distinct from most of the data points in a sample. This distinctiveness can assume a variety of forms. For example, an outlier may be a case whose residual is large compared to the other residuals from a regression analysis. On the other hand, an outlier may simply be a case with an extremely high or low value on one variable. Yet these kinds of outliers are not necessarily influential cases. An outlier observation can only be called influential when its deletion from the analysis causes a pronounced change in one or more of the estimated parameters. Thus an influential case is a special kind of outlier.

It is also useful to remember that whether or not an observation is an outlier depends on the context of the analysis, that is, the sample of observations, the functional form of the model, the variables included in the model, and so on. An observation that is an outlier in one sample may no longer be an outlier after the sample has been supplemented with additional cases. Similarly, a change in functional form through the transformation of one or more variables may change an observation so that it is no longer an outlier. Alternatively, a case may be an outlier because an important explanatory variable has been omitted from the model — indeed, in such a setting, the outlier may be the most important case in the analysis because it points to this form of specification error. And if the omitted variable is correctly identified and incorporated into the analysis, the former outlier case will no longer have the same status.

That the classification of a case as an outlier depends on the context of the model means that once a case is diagnosed as an outlier in a given analysis, a variety of possible remedial actions is available. The choice among these remedies must be based on substantive knowledge of the model concerned. This is a point that our examples are intended to underscore.

We begin with a brief review of the diagnostics to be employed, which include graphic displays, measures based on residuals, and measures that highlight influential observations. In the main part of the chapter, these diagnostics are applied to two substantive examples from the cross-national literature. As will become clear, we regard these procedures as a major tool in regression diagnostics that provide considerable information on the fit of a model to a given set of data, and therefore on the robustness of a given set of estimates. In this sense, they can be an important guide to understanding.

We also emphasize at the outset, however, that these are not procedures to be employed mechanically; they are an aid to, rather than a substitute for, careful statistical analysis. Indeed, our emphasis on the substantive examples is intended to highlight the variety of problems that the diagnostics can help identify. Without substantive knowledge of a given problem, the diagnostics take us nowhere. Auxiliary information is required before appropriate remedies can be evaluated.

## DIAGNOSTICS

A variety of diagnostic procedures has recently been proposed, and we obviously have to be selective. Our choice of a set of diagnostics is governed by two main considerations. First, we want a graphic display alternative to the traditional bivariate scattergram. Second, we need measures that aid in general outlier detection, and we also need ways of finding out whether these outliers are influential cases. Given these consideration, we review six diagnostic procedures in this section: (1) partial regression plots, (2) the *hat* matrix, (3) studentized residuals, (4)

DFITS$_i$, (5) Cook's D$_i$, and (6) DFBETAS$_{ij}$. Some or all of these procedures are available in standard software packages.[1]

### Partial Regression Plots

In the case of one independent variable ($X$) and one dependent variable ($Y$), the bivariate scattergram of $Y$ and $X$ reveals a great deal. For instance, it can help identify curvilinearity, heteroscedasticity, or extreme observations (outliers). However, as Daniel and Wood (1980, pp. 50-53) showed, the bivariate scattergram is not ideal in the more common situation of multiple explanatory variables.

The partial regression plot is the multivariate analog of the bivariate scattergram that overcomes many of the scattergram's limitations. Like the usual scattergram, it is a plot of two variables. But unlike it, the variables plotted are residual variables. These plots may be simply illustrated using an equation with two explanatory variables. The equation for the population is

$$Y = \beta_0 + \beta_1 X_1 + \beta_2 X_2 + \varepsilon. \tag{6.1}$$

The Ordinary Least Squares (OLS) estimate of equation 6.1 for the sample is

$$Y = b_0 + b_1 X_1 + b_2 X_2 + e. \tag{6.2}$$

A partial plot for each explanatory variable (and the intercept) may be constructed. The partial plot for $X_1$ is formed, in part, from the residuals of the regression of $Y$ on $X_2$. Call these residuals $Y_{\cdot[1]}$. The second set of residuals comes from the regression of $X_1$ on $X_2$. Call these residuals $X_{1\cdot[1]}$. The partial regression plot shows the relation of $Y_{\cdot[1]}$ to $X_{1\cdot[1]}$. In a similar manner, the partial regression plot for $X_2$ relates the residuals from the regression of $Y$ on $X_1$ to the residuals of $X_2$ regressed on $X_1$.

These plots have several well-known properties. First, the regression of $Y_{\cdot[1]}$ on $X_{1\cdot[1]}$ leads to the same regression coefficient (i.e., $b_1$) as the regression coefficient for $X_1$ in the regression of $Y$ on $X_1$ and $X_2$. Second, the residuals from the $Y_{\cdot[1]}$ and $X_{1\cdot[1]}$ regression are equal to $e$ of equation 6.2. Third, the correlation between $Y_{\cdot[1]}$ and $X_{1\cdot[1]}$ is equal to the partial correlation of $Y$ and $X_1$, controlling for $X_2$. Analogous results hold true for the partial regression plot of $X_2$. Among the most important properties of these plots is that they enhance an analyst's ability to see outliers not visible in the ordinary scattergram. Further, curvilinear relations and other possible violations of OLS assumptions are more apparent.[2] For a three-dimensional version of the partial regression plot, see Chapter 5, this volume.

An alternative to the partial regression plot is the partial residual (or component-plus-residual) plot (see Atkinson, 1985; Daniel & Wood, 1980; Larsen & McCleary, 1971; Velleman & Welsch, 1981). We restrict our attention again (without loss of generality) to a model with two explanatory variables, as in equation 6.2 above. The partial residual plot for each $X_i$ is formed by summing $b_i X_i$ and the residuals from equation 6.2 and arraying the result against $X_i$. Velleman and Welsch (1981, p. 236) suggested that the partial residual plot may have a slight edge over the partial regression plot in diagnosing nonlinearities, although they also conclude that the partial regression plot is more helpful in the identification and analysis of leverage points.

Other discussions of these plots are in Belsley, Kuh, and Welsch (1980), Velleman and Welsch (1981), Cook and Weisburg (1982a, 1982b), and Atkinson (1985). One of the attractive practical features of such plots is that they offer a graphic display that is readily generated from most of the available regression computer packages: All that is required is the capacity to save and analyze OLS residuals.

### Hat Matrix

Consider the general linear regression model

$$\mathbf{Y} = \mathbf{XB} + \varepsilon \tag{6.3}$$

where $\mathbf{Y}$ is an $n \times 1$ vector of values for the dependent variable, $\mathbf{X}$ is an $n \times p$ matrix of the explanatory variables (and intercept), $\mathbf{B}$ is a $p \times 1$ vector of regression coefficients, and $\varepsilon$ is an $n \times 1$ vector of disturbances. The number of observations is $n$, the number of columns in $\mathbf{X}$ is $p$, and $\mathbf{X}$ is assumed to be of full column rank. The usual assumptions of OLS regression are made, namely, that $\varepsilon$ is distributed independently of $\mathbf{X}$, $E(\varepsilon) = \mathbf{0}$, and $E(\varepsilon\varepsilon') = \sigma^2 \mathbf{I}$.

The OLS estimator of $\mathbf{B}$ is

$$\mathbf{b} = (\mathbf{X}'\mathbf{X})^{-1}\mathbf{X}'\mathbf{Y}. \tag{6.4}$$

The predicted value of the dependent variable is formed as

$$\hat{Y} = Xb = X(X'X)^{-1}X'Y. \tag{6.5}$$

By defining a new matrix $H$, as $X(X'X)^{-1}X'$, equation 6.5 may be written as

$$\hat{Y} = HY. \tag{6.6}$$

The $\hat{Y}$ (Y-hat) vector equals the observed dependent variable, $Y$, pre-multiplied by the $n \times n$ matrix $H$. In other words, $Y$ is transformed into $\hat{Y}$ with the $H$ matrix. Because of this, $H$ is referred to as the "hat matrix" (Hoaglin & Welsch, 1978, p. 17).

The diagonal elements of $H$, usually called $h_i$ (or $h_{ii}$), are important to regression diagnostics. They possess a number of useful properties. Each $h_i$ gives the "leverage" exerted on $\hat{Y}_i$ by $Y_i$. The $h_i$ value is bounded by $1/n$ and 1 ($1/n \leq h_i \leq 1$).[3] The closer $h_i$ is to $1/n$, the less $Y_i$'s leverage on $\hat{Y}_i$. On the other hand, $\hat{Y}_i$ is completely determined by $Y_i$ when $h_i$ is 1. In general, $h_i$ will fall somewhere between these extremes.

Another property of these diagonal elements is

$$\sum_{i=1}^{n} h_i = p. \tag{6.7}$$

That is, the sum of all $n$ $h_i$ elements is equal to $p$, the number of variables in $X$. From equation (6.7) we can see that the mean (average) value of $h_i$ is $p/n$. Hoaglin and Welsch (1977, p. 18) suggested that $h_i$'s greater than $2p/n$ are worthy of further attention.[4] Observations associated with $h_i > 2p/n$ have high leverage. Belsley et al. (1980, p. 17) found that for small $n$ or small $p$, $2p/n$ tends to be too low. Velleman and Welsch (1981, pp. 234-235) suggested that for smaller $p$ and $n$, $3p/n$ is more appropriate.

It is instructive to consider the simple regression case, $Y_i = b_0 + b_iX_i + e_i$, to gain further insight into the meaning of the $h_i$ elements. The leverage value for the $i$th observation is (Hoaglin & Welsch, 1978, p. 18)

$$h_i = 1/n + (X_i - \overline{X})^2 / \sum_{k=1}^{n} (X_k - \overline{X})^2. \tag{6.8}$$

Equation (6.8) shows that the further $X_i$ is from the mean $\overline{X}$, the larger is $h_i$. The closer $X_i$ is to $\overline{X}$, the less is the leverage of the data point. This illustrates the *distance* interpretation of $h_i$. The same distance interpretation holds for more than a single explanatory variable. The greater the $h_i$ value, the further a case is from the mean of all the explanatory variables.

## Studentized Residuals

In OLS regression, the disturbance of the population, $\varepsilon$, is assumed to have the same variance for each observation ($E(\varepsilon\varepsilon') = \sigma^2 I$). However, the sample residuals, $e_i$, are generally not homoscedastic. Rather, their variance is a function of $\sigma^2$ and $h_i$:

$$\text{var}(e_i) = \sigma^2 (1 - h_i) \tag{6.9}$$

In equation 6.9 we see that those observations with the greatest leverage (the largest $h_i$'s) have residuals, $e_i$, with the smallest variance. Observations with the least leverage have the largest variance.

Because of these differences in the variances of the sample residuals, it is useful to standardize $e_i$. This helps to determine whether the residual is large relative to its variance. Belsley et al. (1980, p. 20) recommended use of studentized residuals (RSTUDENT):

$$e_i^* = e_i / \sqrt{(s^2(i)(1 - h_i))}. \tag{6.10}$$

In equation 6.10, $s^2(i)$ is the sample estimate of the disturbance variance when the $i$th case is removed.

The studentized residuals are useful for several reasons. Unlike the untransformed residuals ($e_i$), the studentized residuals $e_i^*$ have equal variances. Also, in many practical situations, Belsley et al. (1980) suggested that $e_i^*$ is distributed closely to a $t$ distribution with $n-p-1$ degrees of freedom (although like $e_i$, the $e_i^*$'s are not independent). If an observation is identified in advance, then we can select the critical $t$ value at a conventional Type I error of, say, $\alpha = .05$ and test the statistical significance of the $e_i^*$ for that case. However, if we do not specify a case and we compare all the $e_i^*$ to the same critical $t$ value, we will identify too many cases. This is a simultaneous testing problem, where the choice of the Type I error does not take into account the number of tests that are performed. For instance, suppose that we choose a critical $t$ value at $\alpha = .05$. We then compare 10 $e_i^*$'s to this critical value. For independent $t$ tests, the probability that at least one $e_i^*$ exceeds the critical value is .40, not .05. Although the $e_i^*$'s are not independent, this example illustrates the simultaneous testing problem when evaluating all $e_i^*$ in the sample. A Bonferroni adjustment provides a conservative correction for this problem. To maintain an overall significance level of no more than $\alpha$ when performing $n$ one-tailed tests, choose a critical value for $t$ that corresponds to $\alpha/n$. In the more typical case of a two-tailed test for each residual, choose a critical value of $t$ that corresponds to $\alpha/2n$. In the preceding example, to keep $\alpha = .05$ for $n = 10$ and with two-tailed tests, we should choose a critical $t$ value corresponding to $.05/(2)(10) = .0025$. Weisberg (1980, pp. 116-117), Daniel and Wood (1980, pp. 232-233) and Fox (1984, pp. 169-171, pp. 418-427) provided extended $t$ tables for these smaller $\alpha$ levels and further discussion of the simultaneous testing problem for residuals.

Finally, if a dummy variable is coded one for the $i$th observation and zero elsewhere, and a $t$ statistic is computed for the regression coefficient of this dummy variable, the resulting $t$ statistic is equal to $e_i^*$.

Despite these useful properties, caution must be observed in using studentized residuals. Unfortunately, the term studentized residuals is sometimes applied to transformations of $e_i$ other than that described in equation 6.10. For instance, Weisberg (1980, p. 105) forms studentized residuals by using the sample-estimated disturbance variance ($s^2$) including the $i$th case, rather than $s^2(i)$ as in equation 6.10. In this alternative form, the numerator ($e_i$) and the denominator ($\sqrt{s^2[1-h_i]}$) are not independent and are not distributed as a $t$ distribution.[5] Other residuals, referred to as standardized residuals, may be computed in alternative ways, such as $e_i/s$ (Velleman & Welsch, 1981, p. 238). Thus the researcher using statistical packages should be sure to check the formula used to compute the *studentized* or *standardized* residuals.

More important than these issues is that reliance solely on residuals for detecting influential points may be misleading. An observation with a small residual may still be quite influential, in the sense that its removal may seriously affect regression estimates. For example, this would occur in the bivariate case where the bulk of the observations exhibit no association, but a single point distant from the rest of the data pulls the regression line through it. While the residual associated with the observation is small, removal of the observation leads to a radical shift in the regression estimates. For this reason, we should not rely only on residuals.

## *DFITS$_i$ and Cook's D$_i$*[6]

In the two previous sections, we reviewed methods designed to detect observations with high leverage (i.e., large $h_i$ values) and large studentized residuals (i.e., $e_i^*$). However, these two indicators of problem cases need not overlap. We may find observations with large $h_i$ values but small $e_i^*$'s, or vice versa (Hoaglin & Welsch, 1978, p. 20). Ideally, we should employ a measure that is affected by both deviant residuals and extreme leverage points. DFITS$_i$ is one such measure:

$$\text{DFITS}_i = \left( \sqrt{(h_i / [1 - h_i])} \right) \left( e_i / \sqrt{(s^2[i] [1 - h_i])} \right). \quad (6.11)$$

The $\sqrt{(h_i / [1 - h_i])}$ term in equation 6.11 is greatest for points with the greatest leverage. The remaining expression on the right-hand side of equation 6.11 is the formula for the studentized residual discussed in the previous section. Thus, DFITS$_i$ may be affected by large leverage points or by large studentized residuals. As a rough cutoff point, Belsley et al. (1980, p. 28) suggested that DFITS$_i$ greater than $2\sqrt{(p/n)}$ require more investigation.

An alternative, but equivalent, representation of DFITS$_i$ is

$$\text{DFITS}_i = (\hat{Y}_i - X_i b_{(i)}) / \sqrt{(s^2(i)h_i)}. \quad (6.12)$$

The numerator of equation 6.12 is the predicted $Y_i$ value for the full sample minus the $Y_i$ value predicted from the regression coefficients obtained with the $i$th observation omitted. The denominator of equation 6.12 is the standard deviation of the fit, $\hat{Y}_i = X_i b$, with the disturbance variance ($\sigma^2$) estimated by $s^2(i)$. Combining the numerator and denominator, DFITS$_i$ may be interpreted as a scaled measure of the change in fitted $Y_i$ values. A change in any of the regression coefficients for the $X$ variables may affect DFITS$_i$, since the fitted $Y$ values depend on all the regression coefficients.

A popular alternative to DFITS$_i$ is Cook's D$_i$ (Cook, 1977). Like DFITS$_i$ the formula for D$_i$ has several forms. One that is analogous to equation 6.11 is

$$D_i = (1 \,/\, p) \,(h_i \,/\, [1 - h_i]) \,(e_i^2 \,/\, [s^2 \,(1 - h_i)]). \tag{6.13}$$

Among the differences between DFITS$_i$ and D$_i$ is that D$_i$ has a factor of $1/p$ that is absent from DFITS$_i$. And D$_i$ uses $s^2$ while DFITS$_i$ has $s^2(i)$ as the estimator of residual variance. The relation between D$_i$ and DFITS$_i$ is

$$D_i = (1 \,/\, p) \,(\text{DFITS}_i \,[s(i) \,/\, s])^2. \tag{6.14}$$

Equation 6.14 reveals that D$_i$ and DFITS$_i$ have different scales so that we cannot use the same cutoff values for each. D$_i$ is in the metric of an $F$ distribution with $p$ and $n - p$ degrees of freedom. Cook and Weisberg (1982a, p. 345) suggested that D$_i$'s that exceed the 50% point of the $F$ distribution ($df = p, n - p$) are large.[7] This critical value is typically close to one, so this amounts to a cutoff of one for D$_i$. By solving equation 6.14 for DFITS$_i$, we can see that this implies a cutoff of approximately $\sqrt{p}$ for DFITS$_i$ (Velleman & Welsch, 1981, pp. 236-237). For $n > 4$, this creates a higher cutoff value than the $2\sqrt{(p/n)}$ suggested by Belsley et al. (1980, p. 28). It follows that fewer cases would be identified with a cutoff of one for D$_i$ than would be with a cutoff of $2\sqrt{(p/n)}$ for DFITS$_i$. Consensus on the best cutoff is absent. We have found the cutoff of $2\sqrt{(p/n)}$ for DFITS$_i$ to work well in moderate-sized samples. A cutoff of $4/n$ for D$_i$ would be roughly equivalent.

Although DFITS$_i$ and D$_i$ typically rank cases similarly, there are some differences. For example, Atkinson (1985) argued that DFITS$_i$ gives greater weight to outliers than does D$_i$. He also noted that DFITS$_i$ uses $s^2(i)$, the preferable residual variance estimator, while D$_i$ uses $s^2$. Velleman and Welsch (1981, p. 237) suggested that, when all observations save one are on a line, D$_i$ can flag some observations on the line as more influential than the one observation not on the line, while DFITS$_i$ will be infinite for the latter case. For an alternative viewpoint, see Cook (1986).

### DFBETAS$_{ij}$

DFITS$_i$ takes into account changes in all the regression coefficients that result when a single observation is removed. It seems natural to have a measure of how individual coefficients change when a case is omitted. DFBETAS$_{ij}$ is one such measure:

$$\text{DFBETAS}_{ij} = (b_j - b_j(i)) / \sqrt{(s^2(i)\,(\mathbf{X'X})_{ij}^{-1})}. \qquad (6.15)$$

The $i$ subscript refers, as before, to the measure obtained when the $i$th observation is removed. The second subscript, $j$, is needed to index the $j$th component in the $b$ vector. For instance, the regression coefficient associated with the third column of $\mathbf{X}$ would be indexed with $j$ equal to 3.

The numerator of equation 6.15 is the difference in the regression coefficients for the $j$th variable estimated for the full sample and for the sample removing the $i$th observation. The denominator is the estimated standard error of the $j$th regression coefficient, with the disturbance variance $(\sigma^2)$ estimated by $s^2(i)$. The double $j$ subscript indicates the $j$th diagonal element of $(\mathbf{X'X})^{-1}$.

Large positive or negative values of $\text{DFBETAS}_{ij}$ indicate observations that lead to large changes in the $j$th regression coefficient. Belsley et al. (1980, p. 28) suggested a size-adjusted cutoff for $\text{DFBETAS}_{ij}$ of $2/\sqrt{n}$. Alternatively, we can use the generally higher cutoff of one. This will identify cases that shift the regression coefficient estimate at least one standard error.

## SUMMARY

By way of summary to this point, Table 6.1 lists the procedures that we have discussed along with the approximate cutoff criteria for identifying *unusual* cases. We list *low* and *high* cutoffs for the diagnostic statistics. The choice of a cutoff depends on the number of cases in the sample, the number of explanatory variables, and the number of cases highlighted with the low or high cutoff. For instance, if in a large sample the low cutoff leads to a high percentage (e.g., 10% or more) of the cases being flagged and there is no obvious problem with them, then it may make more sense to use the high cutoff. Alternatively, inspection of the diagnostic plots is often helpful in identifying unusual observations. One simple graph is to plot the values of the diagnostic statistics against the case number $(1, 2, 3, \ldots, n)$. This is called an index plot, and it serves to reveal extreme values or gaps in the statistics. Also, a normal probability plot or a stem-and-leaf diagram of the studentized residuals could highlight problem cases whether or not they satisfied the other

**Table 6.1  Approximate Cutoff Points for Identifyint "Unusual" Cases**

| Diagnostic Plots | Cutoff | | |
|---|---|---|---|
| Partial regression plot | Visual inspection | | |
| Partial residual plot | Visual inspection | | |
| Univariate plots of | | | |
| $h_i$, $e_i^*$, DFITS$_i$, D$_i$, & DFBETAS$_{ij}$ | Gaps and extreme values | | |

| Diagnostic Statistics | Cutoff | | |
|---|---|---|---|
| | *low* | | *high* |
| Diagonal of hat matrix ($h_i$) | $2p/n$ | | $3p/n$ |
| Studentized residuals ($|e_i^*|$) ($|$RSTUDENT$|$) | $\alpha/2$ | t distribution (df = $n - p - 1$) | $\alpha/2n$ |
| $|$DFITS$_i|$ | $2\sqrt{(p/n)}$ | | $\sqrt{p}$ |
| Cook's D (D$_i$) | $4/n$ | | 1 |
| $|$DFBETAS$_{ij}|$ | $2/\sqrt{n}$ | | 1 |

NOTE: See text for discussion of cutoffs. For $e_i^*$, the "low" cutoff is for testing a single value of $e_i^*$ and the "high" cutoff is for testing all $n$ values of $e_i^*$ with two-tailed tests.

cutoffs. In samples with many hundreds of cases it is not feasible to examine each diagnostic statistic for each case, and the partial residual plots may be too crowded to be interpreted. Here, too, univariate plots (e.g., histograms) of the diagnostic statistics can quickly reveal cases that are more extreme than the others. See Chapter 2, this volume, for a discussion of univariate displays. We recommend that researchers view these cutoffs as guidelines and not as rigid laws.

Now that we have reviewed these regression diagnostics, it is important to examine their behavior in an empirical setting to gain a practical sense of what we can learn from them. Both of our empirical applications are drawn from cross-national comparative research, and each illustrates a different use for the diagnostics. The first cross-national example centers on the relation between voting turnout and income inequality in industrial societies, while the second is based on an analysis of economic dependency and political democracy.

Typically, published research reports the end product of a long research process rather than showing each step of the analysis that led to the final results. This, of course, presents a distorted picture of how empirical research is actually done. And since we want to show how these diagnostics can be incorporated into the data analysis process, we start with an initial model and proceed step by step toward a more refined end product.[8]

## CASE 1: VOTING TURNOUT AND INCOME INEQUALITY

The effect of democratic political systems and voter participation on the distribution of a society's income has long been of interest to social scientists. Hewitt (1977) and Stack (1979) provide two recent empirical analyses of this relationship. Hewitt selected a sample of industrial democratic societies with varying years of *democratic experience*, and found that democratic experience had no effect on income inequality. Stack criticized Hewitt and suggested that voter turnout in national elections (as a percentage of the adult population) would be a superior measure of democracy. Stack then provided evidence that when turnout statistics are used, they have a significant negative effect on inequality.

Stack's (1979) analysis is useful for an expository point of view for several reasons. First, it employs a multiple regression analysis confined to just two explanatory variables. Second, it is a small-sample analysis based on only 18 countries. Third, examination of at least the simple bivariate scatterplots suggests that Stack's analysis suffers from a severe outlier problem (Jackman, 1980); whether such a conclusion is warranted in light of the more complete diagnostic procedures reviewed above remains an open question.

Following Stack, when inequality is regressed on voting turnout and energy consumption per capita, the estimates (with their $t$ ratios in parentheses) are as follows (Jackman, 1980, Table 1):

$$INEQ = 10.31 - .081TURNOUT - .0003ENCAP. \qquad (6.16)$$
$$(8.9) \quad (5.8) \qquad\qquad (2.1)$$

The overall equation has an $\overline{R}^2$ of .666 and an $F$ ratio of 18.0.[9]

Figures 6.1A and 6.1B display the partial plots for these estimates. The first figure contains the plot for turnout and arrays the residuals obtained from regressing INEQ on ENCAP (vertical axis) against those from the regression of TURNOUT on ENCAP (horizontal axis). The second figure shows the corresponding partial plot for energy consumption. Inspection of these graphs suggests that there are two apparently influential observations in the analysis. Specifically, South Africa ap-

A    TOP20B40

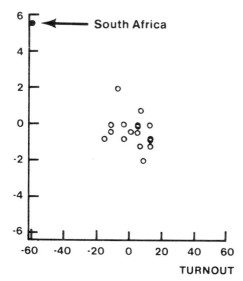

B    TOP20B40

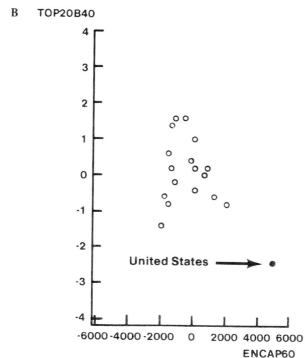

Figure 6.1    Partial regression plots for (A) TURNOUT and (B) ENCAP ($N = 18$).

pears as an extreme outlier in the northwest corner of Figure 6.1A; indeed, it is evident from this figure that South Africa could well be responsible for the negative estimated coefficient for TURNOUT reported above. In a similar but less extreme vein, the United States appears as an influential outlier in the southeast corner of Figure 6.1B that could be largely responsible for the negative estimated coefficient reported above for ENCAP.[20]

To pursue these issues further, Table 6.2 displays the remaining diagnostics by country. Overall, the entries in this table reinforce the conclusions drawn earlier. Looking first at the diagonal elements of the hat matrix (i.e., the $h_i$ in the first column of the table), most of the values are small. However, the $h_i$ for South Africa (.75) is large, while the $h_i$ for the United States (.64) is only slightly smaller. Both figures easily exceed the $2p/n$ cutoff of .33, and, indeed, both are substantially larger than even the more conservative cutoff of $3p/n$ (= .50). Remember that $h_i$ is bounded by $1/n$ and 1 and that a value of 1 means that the fitted value of $Y_i$ is wholly determined by $Y_i$. The $h_i$ values for South Africa and the United States are clearly much closer to 1 than they are to $1/n$.

The second column in Table 6.2 displays the studentized residuals (the $e_i^*$). With $n = 18$, $p = 3$, the low cutoff ($p = .05$) is 2.1. This cutoff assumes that we are testing a specific residual, which we have identified in advance. Because we are examining all residuals, the higher cutoff of 3.6 based on the Bonferonni adjustment is more appropriate for a strict application of significance testing. None of the $e_i^*$'s exceed the high cutoff. The two highest, those for South Africa (2.27) and Argentina (−2.55), exceed the low cutoff. Taken alone, this is weak evidence for an outlier status for these two countries. However, for reasons we discussed earlier it is unwise to rely solely on residuals when searching for outliers.

The $DFITS_i$ are displayed in the third column of Table 6.2. It is clear that those for South Africa and the United States are extreme: Both exceed the $2\sqrt{(p/n)}$ criterion and even the higher cutoff of $\sqrt{p}$. Indeed, the value of 3.89 for South Africa is more than twice the size of even the latter criterion. Thus the $DFITS_i$ figures reinforce the impression from the other diagnostics that these two cases are highly influential. Note also that the $DFITS_i$ for Argentina is larger than the $2\sqrt{(p/n)}$ criterion, although it remains smaller than the $\sqrt{p}$ criterion: This case again seems somewhat influential, but its influence is much smaller than the other two observations. The analysis of Cook's $D_i$ leads to the same conclusions as those for $DFITS_i$.

**Table 6.2 Regression Diagnostics for Estimates in Equation 6.14 $n = 18$**

| COUNTRY | DIAGONAL OF HAT MATRIX $h_i$ | RSTUDENT $e_i^*$ | DFITS$_i$ | Cook's $D_i$ | DFBETAS$ij$ TURNOUT | ENCAP |
|---|---|---|---|---|---|---|
| Argentina | .15 | -2.55[a] | -1.06[a] | .27[a] | .52[a] | .71[a] |
| Australia | .12 | -.25 | -.09 | .00 | -.05 | -.05 |
| Denmark | .09 | .35 | .11 | .00 | .07 | .01 |
| Finland | .09 | 1.43 | .45 | .06 | .16 | -.21 |
| France | .07 | 1.64 | .44 | .06 | -.17 | -.10 |
| West Germany | .08 | .57 | .17 | .01 | .05 | .08 |
| Israel | .12 | -1.25 | -.46 | .07 | -.17 | .26 |
| Italy | .15 | .21 | .09 | .00 | .05 | -.05 |
| Japan | .11 | -1.16 | -.40 | .05 | .05 | .28 |
| Netherlands | .10 | 1.20 | .40 | .05 | .26 | .03 |
| Norway | .07 | -.39 | -.11 | .00 | -.05 | -.01 |
| Puerto Rico | .09 | -.22 | -.07 | .00 | -.00 | .04 |
| South Africa | .75[b] | 2.22[a] | 3.89[b] | 3.99[b] | -3.73[b] | -.74[a] |
| Sweden | .07 | .25 | .07 | .00 | .02 | .03 |
| Trinidad & Tobago | .07 | -.59 | -.18 | .01 | .08 | .08 |
| United Kingdom | .15 | -.06 | -.02 | .00 | .00 | -.02 |
| United States | .64[b] | -1.70 | 2.27[b] | 1.52[b] | -.36 | -2.07[b] |
| Venezuela | .06 | .41 | .11 | .00 | .03 | .00 |
| Cutoff points    Low | .33 | 2.1 | .82 | .22 | .47 | .47 |
| ($n = 18, p = 3$)  High | .50 | 3.6 | 1.73 | 1.0 | 1.0 | 1.0 |

NOTE: [a]Exceeds low cutoff point in absolute value.
[b]Exceeds both cutoff points in absolute value.

Finally, the DFBETAS$_{ij}$ are reported in the fourth and fifth columns of the table for TURNOUT and ENCAP, respectively. These figures show the influence of individual cases on each of the two coefficients (rather than the overall fitted values), and reinforce our earlier reading of the partial plots. The TURNOUT DFBETA for South Africa is −3.73, almost eight times the size of the $2/\sqrt{n}$ cutoff value of .47, nearly four times the higher cutoff of one, and indicates that South Africa has a major effect on the TURNOUT coefficient. The ENCAP DFBETA for the United States is somewhat smaller, but remains over four times the lower cutoff and two times the high cutoff, which suggests that this case substantially influences the coefficient for ENCAP. Note also that both DFBETAS for Argentina are larger than the low cutoff, but much smaller than the two others just discussed.

Taken as a whole, these diagnostics clearly identify South Africa and the United States as problem cases that are substantially influencing the estimates. They also suggest that Argentina behaves somewhat unusually. We can further gauge the impact of these outliers by examining the metric regression coefficients and the $\bar{R}^2$'s generated when each case is dropped. As is evident in Table 6.3, there are several differences between the resulting sets of estimates and those for the full sample in equation 6.16 above. First, South Africa has a substantial influence on the estimates. Removing just this one case drastically reduces both the $\bar{R}^2$'s (from .666 to .083) and the coefficient for TURNOUT (from −.081 to −.035). In fact, with South Africa excluded, the coefficients for both TURNOUT and ENCAP have $t$ ratios considerably less than 2.0.

The United States seems to be the next most influential case. When it is removed, a drastic drop toward zero occurs for the ENCAP coefficient, which has a $t$ ratio of 0.1 (compared to 2.1 in the full sample). The absolute values of the TURNOUT coefficient and the $\bar{R}^2$ marginally increase. The last influential case is Argentina. Removing this case increases the $\bar{R}^2$ from .666 to .769, and leads to a slight increase in the absolute value of the coefficients for TURNOUT and ENCAP.

These regression estimates reinforce the diagnostics reported in Table 6.2. South Africa and the United States are influential cases, with Argentina having lesser effects. Now that these cases have been highlighted, we need to ask, Why are they so influential? Here, we must draw on our substantive and empirical knowledge.

First, consider South Africa and Argentina. If we recall that the sample of countries is supposed to consist of industrial democracies, it

**Table 6.3  Regression Estimates Removing, in Turn, South Africa, the United States, and Argentina [coefficients ($t$ ratios)]**

| Country Removed | Intercept | TURNOUT | ENCAP | $\bar{R}^2$ | $F$ Ratio | $n$ |
|---|---|---|---|---|---|---|
| South Africa | 6.457 (3.2) | −.035 (1.4) | −.0002 (1.6) | .083 | 1.7 | 17 |
| United States | 10.048 (9.1) | −.086 (6.4) | −.00003 (0.1) | .712 | 20.7 | 17 |
| Argentina | 11.130 (10.7) | −.088 (7.2) | −.0004 (3.1) | .769 | 27.6 | 17 |

is rather odd to find South Africa and Argentina included in this group. Although they may meet the criteria for industrialization set forth by Hewitt (1977, p. 450), they did not have democratic political systems in the early 1960s.[11] Examining the other countries in the sample, the same argument can be made for Venezuela, which, in the period to which the analysis refers, was not particularly democratic.

These arguments raise questions about the appropriateness of including South Africa, Argentina, and Venezuela in a sample of industrial democracies, and, indeed, one could make a strong case for excluding these three countries from the analysis. However, for the purpose of further illustrating these regression diagnostics, we do not do this. Instead, we retain Argentina and Venezuela in the sample because of their relatively minor influence on the estimates, but we do provisionally remove South Africa, given its extreme outlier position. We will return to South Africa's influence on the regression estimates shortly.

What other corrective action remains, given that the United States remains an influential data point? Note that the estimates under consideration are based on raw ENCAP figures, that these raw scores are badly skewed, that the ENCAP value for the United States of 8047 is an extreme value (even within this subset of industrial countries) that is over 60% higher than the next value of 4907 for the United Kingdom, and that it is the ENCAP coefficient that is most affected by the inclusion of the United States. This suggests that instead of excluding the United States from the analysis, we might profitably consider a simple transformation of ENCAP to reduce the skewness of its distribution. A natural logarithmic transformation would appear appropriate.

The next step in the analysis is to reestimate the model with South Africa excluded and ENCAP transformed, and then to repeat the diagnostic checks on the revised estimates. With such a procedure, we can withhold judgment on the status of Argentina and Venezuela in the analysis until we examine the revised diagnostics.

The revised estimates are

$$\text{INEQ} = 7.97 - .026\text{TURNOUT} - .359ln\text{ENCAP}. \qquad (6.17)$$
$$(2.0) \quad (1.1) \qquad \qquad (0.9)$$

With $N = 17$ and t ratios in parentheses, this overall equation has an $\bar{R}^2$ of .000 and an $F$ ratio of only 0.8, which is statistically insignificant at any meaningful test level. It is evident that these estimates are similar to the Table 6.3 estimates removing South Africa, but radically different from the full-sample estimates in equation 6.16. Where the equation 6.16 figures indicated that both TURNOUT and ENCAP accounted for about two thirds of the variance in INEQ, the revised estimates in equation 6.17 imply that neither of these two explanatory variables influences INEQ, at least among the relatively wealthy countries under consideration here. Note, too, that the size of the primary coefficient of interest (that of TURNOUT) drops to a third of its original value (from −.0813 to −.0259).

Figures 6.2A and 6.2B display the partial plots for these new estimates: Figure 6.2A shows the revised partial plot for TURNOUT, while Figure 6.2B has the corresponding plot for *ln*ENCAP. Comparing these partial plots with the originals indicates that one case (France) stands a little apart from the other points in Figure 6.2A, and, to a lesser extent, in Figure 6.2B. However, compared to the outlier status of South Africa in Figure 6.1A, and even of the United States in Figure 6.1B, it is evident that France is best seen as a minor outlier in both Figures 6.2A and 6.2B.[12]

Of more significance is the pattern followed by the residuals of Figure 6.2B. Specifically, these indicate that equation 6.17 misspecifies the relation between ENCAP and INEQ, and suggest instead that an inverted U-shaped curve may be more appropriate, even for this relatively wealthy subset of countries. The partial residual plots (not shown) also reveal the same form of curvilinearity. Such a curve was originally proposed by Kuznets (1955) and has been discussed by many others since (e.g., Ahluwalia, 1976). However, Kuznets was concerned

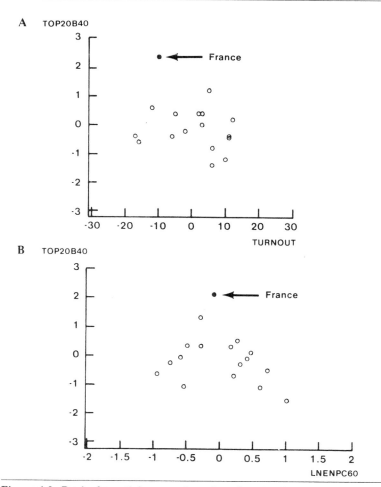

**Figure 6.2  Revised partial regression plots for (A) TURNOUT and (B)**
**            _ln_ENCAP (_N_ = 17).**

with countries at all levels of economic development, and we did not
initially anticipate such a pattern for the wealthier subset of countries
under consideration here.

Accordingly, we estimate a revised model that includes a quadratic
term for _ln_ENCAP, again excluding South Africa.

$$\text{INEQ} = -100.19 - .060\text{TURNOUT} \qquad (6.18)$$
$$(2.9) \qquad (2.7)$$

$$+ 28.094 ln\text{ENCAP} - 1.81(ln\text{ENCAP})^2.$$
$$(3.1) \qquad\qquad (3.1)$$

With $N = 17$ and $t$ ratios in parentheses, this overall equation has an $\overline{R}^2$ of .371 and an $F$ ratio of 4.1, which is statistically significant at the .03 level. Comparing these figures with those in equation 6.17, which are estimated for the same cases, we see that the misspecification of ENCAP suppressed the effects of both TURNOUT and ENCAP, even with South Africa excluded.

The partial plots associated with equation 6.18 are displayed in Figure 6.3: Figure 6.3A has the plot for TURNOUT; Figures 6.3B and 6.3C show the plots for $ln$ENCAP and $(ln\text{ENCAP})^2$, respectively. Compared with the earlier partial plots, those in Figure 6.3 are relatively well behaved. First, there are no extreme outliers, as there were in Figure 6.1, although one case does stand out a little in each of the panels of the figure. The case involved is, again, France. Second, there is no evidence of nonlinearity, which contrasts markedly with the pattern evident in Figure 6.2B. In sum, the plots in Figure 6.3 do not identify any major problems.

The remaining diagnostics are displayed by country in Table 6.4, with the diagonal elements of the hat matrix (the $h_i$) in the first column. All except one are smaller than the $2p/n$ criterion of .47, but the $h_i$ for the United States is larger than even the high cutoff criterion of $3p/n$ (=.71). Evidently, the United States remains a high leverage observation. The second column of Table 6.4 contains the studentized residuals. All cases are lower than the high cutoff of 3.7, and only France exceeds the low cutoff. Thus France is flagged by the partial plots and, to a lesser extent, by the $e_i^*$.

It is interesting that both the United States and France have comparatively large values in the remaining columns of the table. The DFITS$_i$ for both countries are larger than the $2\sqrt{(p/n)}$ criterion of .97, although only the United States has a value that slightly exceeds the larger $\sqrt{p}$ criterion of 2.0. The same pattern is manifested by the country values for Cook's D$_i$. Similarly, both countries have large DFBETAS$_{ij}$ for

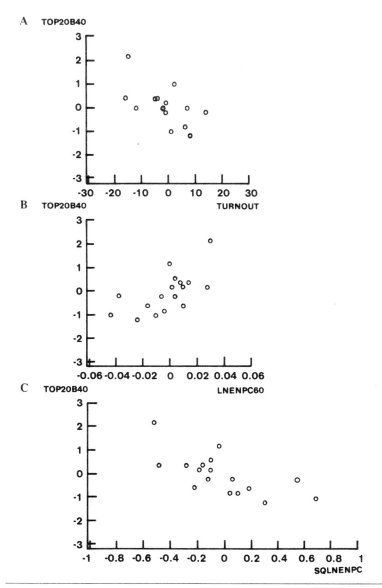

Figure 6.3   Revised partial regression plots for (A) TURNOUT, (B) *ln*ENCAP, and (C) (*ln*ENCAP)$^2$ (*N* = 17).

**Table 6.4 Regression Diagnostics for Estimates in Equation 6.18, $n = 17$**

| COUNTRY | DIAGONAL OF HAT MATRIX $h_i$ | RSTUDENT $e_i^*$ | $DFITS_i$ | Cook's $D_i$ | DFBETAS$_{ij}$ TURNOUT | $ln$ENCAP | $ln$ENCAP$^2$ |
|---|---|---|---|---|---|---|---|
| Argentina | .38 | -1.23 | -.96 | .22 | .54[a] | .16 | -.14 |
| Australia | .18 | -1.13 | -.54 | .07 | .33 | .05 | -.06 |
| Denmark | .15 | -.45 | -.19 | .01 | -.10 | -.04 | .04 |
| Finland | .10 | 1.92 | .63 | .08 | .19 | .04 | -.05 |
| France | .28 | 2.51[a] | 1.57[a] | .44[a] | -1.24[b] | 1.16[b] | -1.16[b] |
| West Germany | .11 | .24 | .09 | .00 | .00 | .03 | -.03 |
| Israel | .23 | 1.08 | -.59 | .09 | -.32 | .33 | -.32 |
| Italy | .43 | 1.52 | 1.33[a] | .40[a] | .93[a] | -.91[a] | .89[a] |
| Japan | .21 | .29 | -.15 | .01 | .02 | .05 | -.05 |
| Netherlands | .16 | .65 | .29 | .02 | .17 | .05 | -.05 |
| Norway | .11 | -1.39 | -.49 | .06 | -.09 | -.23 | .23 |
| Puerto Rico | .12 | .16 | .06 | .00 | -.02 | .01 | -.01 |
| Sweden | .11 | -.24 | -.09 | .00 | -.04 | -.04 | .03 |
| Trinidad & Tobago | .31 | -.85 | -.57 | .08 | .47 | -.37 | .38 |
| United Kingdom | .17 | -.05 | -.02 | .00 | .00 | .00 | .00 |
| United States | .83[b] | .94 | 2.06[b] | 1.07[b] | -.22 | -1.20[b] | 1.24[b] |
| Venezuela | .11 | -.08 | -.03 | .00 | .00 | -.02 | .02 |
| Cutoff points Low | .47 | 2.2 | .97 | .24 | .49 | .49 | .49 |
| ($n = 17, p = 4$) High | .71 | 3.7 | 2.00 | 1.0 | 1.0 | 1.0 | 1.0 |

NOTE: [a]Exceeds low cutoff point in absolute value.
[b]Exceeds both cutoff points in absolute value.

279

*ln*ENCAP and its square, and France also has a large DFBETA$_{ij}$ for TURNOUT. In addition, the diagnostics in the last five columns for Italy are larger than the low cutoff points (but smaller than those for France and the United States). Note, too, that the first three diagnostics do not suggest that Italy is an excessively influential observation.

Taken as a group, then, the diagnostic procedures in Figure 6.3 and Table 6.4 consistently isolate France and the United States as potentially influential cases. What implications does this have for the estimates in equation 6.18? Our own additional analyses indicate that the TURNOUT coefficient is especially sensitive to the inclusion of France. When this case and South Africa are excluded ($N$ = 16), the TURNOUT coefficient drops to –.037 ($t$ ratio: 1.8), which is a drop of about 40% below the corresponding figure in equation 6.16. At the same time, the $\bar{R}^2$ drops by almost one half to .205, with an $F$ ratio of 2.3. (The additional exclusion of the United States does not influence the TURNOUT coefficient.) In contrast, the exclusion of France and the United States produces *ln*ENCAP coefficients of similar magnitude to those in equation 6.16. This seems to suggest that the estimates for *ln*ENCAP in that equation are relatively robust, but that the estimate for TURNOUT is somewhat less reliable.

Two other points about the estimates for the quadratic model are worth noting. First, the parallel estimates with South Africa included ($N$ = 18) are

$$INEQ = -119.49 - .083TURNOUT \qquad\qquad (6.19)$$
$$(3.9) \qquad (8.0)$$

$$+\ 33.556ln\text{ENCAP} - 2.170(ln\text{ENCAP})^2.$$
$$(4.2) \qquad\qquad\qquad (4.3)$$

This equation has a $\bar{R}^2$ of .814 and a highly significant $F$ ratio of 25.8. Thus, even with the revised specification, South Africa remains a highly influential observation, in the sense that excluding it reduces the $\bar{R}^2$ by over one half. However, its impact on the TURNOUT coefficient is less extreme than it was in the original specification, involving a reduction of about 30% (from .083 to .060), and the TURNOUT DFBETA for South Africa is –2.24, which, while large, is smaller than the figure of –3.73 reported in Table 6.2 above. Although we have continued to exclude South Africa given both its influence on the estimates and its distinctive political arrangements, it is clear that its extreme influence on the estimates of equation 6.16 is in part due to the misspecification of ENCAP in that equation.

Second, we should note that inspection of the diagnostics obtained with both South Africa and France excluded indicates that other cases were becoming mildly influential. For example, in addition to the United States, the DFBETAS$_{ij}$ for Italy and Israel exceeded the cutoff points of Table 6.1, although they were of opposite sign. Assuming for the moment that removal of cases is the only remedy for influential cases and that the cutoff points are to be applied mechanically, one might be tempted to repeat the process iteratively, calculating the diagnostics, removing apparently influential cases, recalculating the diagnostics, and so on. We hope that these diagnostics are not misused in this way. For one thing, in a purely practical sense, such a strategy has to generate an increasing number of *influential* observations.

Beyond this, as we have emphasized throughout, these diagnostics are not procedures to be employed mechanically. Additionally, the idea that case removal is the only remedy for apparently influential cases is quite misleading. In fact, case removal is the most severe remedy; sometimes, as in the present example, less severe action such as a change in functional form is optimal, while at other times, no remedy at all is called for.

There are at least three general lessons to be learned from our analysis. First, the diagnostics helped identify problems of sample composition by identifying South Africa and Argentina as influential cases. Neither these two countries nor Venezuela belong in a sample of industrial democracies for the period under investigation, and this is true even though Venezuela did not appear as an outlier. If we take the arguments of Hewitt and Stack seriously, then all three countries should be excluded from the analysis because none was especially democratic during the period under investigation. Alternatively, if we are concerned with a more diverse sample of countries, these cases may in fact be seen as providing useful information rather than as outliers. If this view is correct, then our analyses would suggest a need to obtain data on additional nondemocratic countries to broaden the nature of the sample by ensuring that a reasonable portion of the sample does represent such cases. An important implication is that the status of an observation depends in good part on the substantive definition of the sample (and population) being studied: A case may be an outlier in one setting but not in another.

Second, the diagnostics helped identify a misspecification of functional form. This possibility was indicated by the outlier status of the United States in the earlier part of our analyses. The partial plots, combined with previous research, indicated that the inverted U-shaped relation between level of economic development and inequality suggested in other research held even within the context of an *industrialized* group of countries. Correcting the misspecification increased the fit of the model considerably, and, of more interest, indicated that the misspecification itself was responsible for suppressing some of the effects of voter turnout on inequality. In this example we were fortunate to have prior research to suggest the proper functional form. In most situations we do not have such information and are forced instead to turn to empirical procedures. For instance, the partial regression or partial residual plots can be helpful. Power transformations of the explanatory or dependent variables are often a flexible way of capturing curvilinear relations (see, e.g., Box & Cox, 1964; Tukey, 1977; Chapter 4, this volume).

Third, we hope it is evident from the foregoing that a synergy of statistical diagnostics and substantive knowledge is required. Specifically, the diagnostics did not by themselves somehow magically *show* the problems of sample composition or of misspecification in functional form. Rather, they helped to highlight abnormalities in the data that demanded explanation. In the next section, we will illustrate a different application.

## CASE 2: WORLD SYSTEM POSITION AND POLITICAL DEMOCRACY

World system theory (Chirot, 1977; Wallerstein, 1974) has had a major impact on the analysis of international development. Basic to this view is the division of the world system into three sets of countries: the core, the semiperiphery, and the periphery. The core consists of the industrialized powerful nations, the periphery contains the poor and relatively weak ones, while the semiperiphery is made up of countries in between that seek core status. The problem that our next empirical example addresses is whether peripheral or semiperipheral status has a negative impact on political democracy. The details of the theoretical arguments for such an effect are provided in Bollen (1983): Here we are concerned with the narrower question of whether regression diagnostics help us to analyze the relationship.

Following Bollen (1983, Table 1), when political democracy (POLDEM) is regressed on dummy variables indicating semiperipheral (SEMPER) and peripheral (PER) positions and economic development (*ln*ENCAP), the following results are obtained (*t* ratios in parentheses):

$$\text{POLDEM} = 7.29 + 10.05 ln\text{ENCAP} \tag{6.20}$$
$$\quad (0.5) \quad (5.7)$$

$$- \, 2.71\text{SEMPER} - 6.76\text{PER}.$$
$$\quad (0.4) \qquad\qquad (0.8)$$

With an *n* of 100, this equation has an $\overline{R}^2$ of .453, and an *F* ratio of 28.3.[13]

Given these regression results, it is attempting to conclude that *ln*ENCAP has a positive and significant effect on political democracy, while SEMPER and PER have no meaningful effects at all. But, as we shall see, such a judgment is premature.

Figure 6.4 displays the partial plot for SEMPER and reveals a minimum of three, and perhaps as many as six, outliers. Specifically, Spain, Portugal, and South Africa (represented with black dots in the lower left of Figure 6.4) have large negative values for both axes. These countries would tend to pull the line fitted to these points toward zero. Three less obvious outliers (see the lower right portion of Figure 6.4) are Taiwan, Iraq, and Saudi Arabia. The position of these cases would tend to magnify the negative slope of the line fitted to the data. A similar pattern occurs in the partial plot for PER (not shown here).

In view of both the partial regression plots and the other regression diagnostics (see Bollen, 1983), these six countries appear to be outliers that may influence the regression results.[14] In fact, when these six cases are removed, the regression estimates are

$$\text{POLDEM} = 23.48 + 8.97 ln\text{ENCAP} \tag{6.21}$$
$$\quad (1.9) \quad (6.1)$$

$$- \, 3.90\text{SEMPER} - 17.84\text{PER}.$$
$$\quad (0.6) \qquad\qquad (2.5)$$

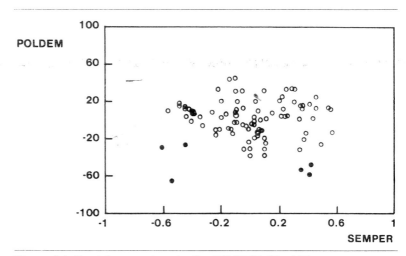

Figure 6.4  Partial regression plot for SEMPER ($N = 100$).

Equation 6.21 has an $\bar{R}^2$ of .610, and an $F$ ratio of 49.4. Note that with the six outliers removed, the coefficient for PER has nearly tripled in size over that reported in equation 6.20 — from −6.76 to −17.84 — indicating the substantial effect of peripheral position compared to core position. The coefficient for SEMPER is larger than in equation 6.20, but still not significant, whereas the $\bar{R}^2$ for equation 6.21 is considerably larger than that for equation 6.20: .610 versus .453. Thus the estimates in equation 6.21 reinforce the impression from the partial plots that these six countries are influencing our assessment of the effects of world system position.

Knowing that our estimates are affected by outliers raises the next question: What should we do with these observations? If we simply leave them in the sample and do nothing, we are left with a distorted picture of the relationship that characterizes the bulk of the countries. If, on the other hand, we remove them from our sample, we are ignoring the fact that half a dozen of our cases are not fitted by the model.

However, this *drop or keep* strategy does not exhaust the potential remedies, and, indeed, oversimplifies the alternatives. It is much more instructive to ask why these countries appear as deviant cases. In the present context, consideration of a number of possible explanations of the outlier behavior suggest classification error as the most probable source of the problem. Specifically, Spain, Portugal, and South Africa were classified by Snyder and Kick (1979) as core countries, but semiperipheral status seems far more reasonable for the period of these data (circa 1965).[15] Similarly, although Taiwan, Iraq, and Saudi Arabia were placed in the semiperipheral category by Snyder and Kick, peripheral status seems more appropriate.

Details on the arguments to support this reclassification of these six countries are reported in Bollen (1983), and we do not restate them here. But we do want to show the results obtained when the same model is estimated with these six countries reclassified on the world system measure. If the reclassification arguments are correct, then these six countries should be less likely to appear as outliers. Equation 6.22 reports the regression estimates after reclassification.

$$POLDEM = 37.69 + 7.23lnENCAP \qquad (6.22)$$
$$(2.6) \quad (4.4)$$

$$- 13.35SEMPER - 25.98PER.$$
$$(1.8) \qquad (3.3)$$

The $\overline{R}^2$ is .507, and the $F$ ratio is 34.9.

Examining the new partial regression plots associated with equation 6.22, Spain is the only country of the six that still exhibits a distinctive pattern. However, the removal of Spain does not substantially change the estimates in equation 6.22. Thus the evidence is consistent with the idea that the six countries were outliers in the original data because of measurement error. Once this error is corrected, negative relations between PER and POLDEM and, to a lesser extent, between SEMPER and POLDEM, are found, leading to quite different conclusions than would be reached from the *naive* original regression estimates of equation 6.20.

Leaving to one side the substantive implications of this example, Case 2 illustrates two additional features of the regression diagnostics. First, and most important, it indicates that the diagnostics can be a useful tool in the analysis of measurement error, since such error may make observations apparently influential. Second, it is evident from this example that a very small minority of observations can be influential even when sample size increases. That one or two cases can be influential with a basic $n$ of 18 may be little cause for surprise, but our second example shows that similar problems can occur with an $n$ of 100.

## CONCLUSIONS

We have focused on a number of diagnostic procedures that provide important information on the robustness of regression estimates, especially those generated from small samples. One could, of course, ignore these procedures and employ a naive form of analysis that involves estimation with no checks for robustness. However, as our examples make clear, such a mode of analysis can lead us to false acceptance or rejection of hypotheses. Consider the relation between economic development and inequality in Case 1 or that between world system position and political democracy in Case 2.

Whereas the analysis of bivariate scatterplots and regression residuals offers some improvement over the naive approach, such analyses have major shortcomings. For example, the bivariate scatterplot between semiperiphery status (a binary variable) and political democracy does not identify the problem suggested by the partial plot in Figure 6.4. Similarly, residuals by themselves do not necessarily help identify influential cases, as is evident, say, from the status of South Africa in Figure 6.1A (an outlier despite its relatively small residual). Compared to these simple procedures, the diagnostics we have discussed provide much more systematic procedures for evaluating the robustness of regression estimates. The question that remains is this: What corrective action should be taken when one or more cases have been identified as influential?

Under certain circumstances, we may be justified in dropping the case(s) involved. However, this involves radical surgery, and can be recommended as a last resort only when there are good substantive reasons for it.[16] Instead of routinely following such a procedure, it is more fruitful to determine why the observation is an outlier. As our examples indicate, there are many different ways that this outcome can occur. In Case 1 we saw that the diagnostics can be helpful in identifying problems of sample composition and of misspecifications of functional form. Case 2 illustrated a way in which the diagnostics helped detect measurement error problems. There are other problems like heteroscedasticity that these diagnostics can help identify. Remember, too, that apparent outliers may be the most important cases of some analyses in the sense that they help identify omitted variables and other forms of specification error. Once detected, corrective action can be taken for problems like these, and such action will typically fall far short of the extreme procedure of case removal.

Other diagnostic procedures in addition to those we have discussed have been proposed (e.g., Atkinson, 1985; Chatterjee & Hadi, 1986; Cook & Weisberg, 1982a).[17] To date, no consensus has emerged on a single optimal way to detect outliers and influential cases. While we have found the techniques discussed here very helpful in our own research, we encourage others not to rule out alternative procedures. We need far more experience with these detection procedures before we can decide which are the most useful.

We also remind the reader that our concern has been exclusively with searching for outliers and influential cases. We largely have ignored the possible presence of other problems such as heteroscedasticity, autocorrelation, or collinearity. Each of these problems has a literature of its own that provides diagnostic devices, tests, and corrections (see, e.g., Beggs, 1988; Belsley et al., 1980; Johnston, 1984).

Finally, as we have stressed throughout, these procedures are an important aid to careful empirical analysis, not a substitute for it. Like other techniques, these can be misapplied to produce a degenerate form of number crunching. Without some substantive knowledge of the problem at hand, any statistical analysis becomes vacuous, concealing more than it reveals.

## NOTES

1. Descriptions of software to compute various diagnostics can be found in Velleman and Welsch (1981, pp. 239-241) and Cook and Weisberg (1982a, pp. 355-356). The most recent versions of SAS, SPSS, and MINITAB have procedures to provide all or some of the regression diagnostics described in this chapter. Our figures were computed using SAS.

2. Partial regression plots are sometimes also referred to as *partial plots, partial-regression leverage plots*, or *added variable plots*.

3. The proof that $1/n \leq h_i \leq 1$ follows from $H$ being an idempotent matrix (i.e., $[X(X'X)^{-1}X'][X(X'X)^{-1}X'] = [X(X'X)^{-1}X']$). Because of this,

$$h_{ii} = \Sigma \, h_{ij}^2$$

$$= h_{ii}^2 + \sum_{i \neq j} h_{ij}^2.$$

This may be rewritten as

$$h_{ii}^2 - h_{ii} + \sum_{i \neq j} h_{ij}^2 = 0$$

The summed term in this expression must be a nonnegative number because all of its components are squared. Thus $h_{ii}^2 - h_{ii}$ must be $\leq 0$. For this latter condition to hold, $h_{ii}$ must be less than or equal to one, and greater than or equal to zero (see Hoaglin & Welsch, 1978, p. 18). Belsley et al. (1980, pp. 66-67) further show that the lower bound is $1/n$.

4. Belsley et al. (1980) show that when the explanatory variables follow an independent multinormal distribution, then $(n - p) [h_i - (1/n)]/(1 - h_i)(p - 1)$ is distributed as $F$, with $p - 1$ and $n - p$ degrees of freedom. For $p > 10$ and $n - p > 50$, the 95% value for $F$ is less than 2. Thus twice the average $h_i$ value $(2p/n)$ is a useful cutoff. As Belsley et al. (1980, p. 17) stated, multinormality and independence are often not found in practice, so this rule must be regarded as an approximation.

5. Weisberg (1980, p. 106) suggested that as a first approximation these transformed residuals may be treated as if they were distributed as standard normal variables.

6. Belsley et al. (1980) referred to this measure as DFFITS. We drop the extra F as suggested by Velleman and Welsch (1981, p. 236).

7. $D_i$ does *not* follow an $F$ distribution. This is merely a way to provide a scale for $D_i$.

8. Of course, this strategy means that significance levels are not fully accurate, which makes replication even more important.

9. Inequality is defined as the ratio of the income received by the wealthiest population fifth to that received by the poorest two fifths. The raw data, which are for around 1960, are listed by country in the Appendix.

10. Note that the extreme scores for these two cases could have been detected from simple histograms for ENCAP and TURNOUT. However, such histograms would not have helped identify the two cases as potentially influential. In addition, observations can be influential without having extreme values on one or more variables.

11. South Africa, in particular, is unique in the way it formally restricts the political participation of an overwhelming majority of its adult population.

12. In this connection, care is needed in the visual comparison of plots such as these. Most obviously, the plotting routines contained in statistical computing packages generally adjust the range of both vertical and horizontal axes to reflect the observed range of the variables being plotted. In our case, the exclusion of South Africa drastically influences the variance of both INEQ and TURNOUT (the standard deviations of both variables are almost halved by the exclusion of this one case). As a result, when comparing Figures 6.1A and 6.2A, it is important to note the changes in both axes: Where the vertical axis in Figure 6.1A ranges from −6 to +6, that in Figure 6.2A ranges from −3 to +3; the range of the horizontal axis is reduced by the same factor when we go from Figure 6.1A to Figure 6.2A. The exclusion of South Africa coupled with the transformation of ENCAP produces parallel differences between Figures 6.1B and 6.2B. These differences need to be borne in mind because it is important that one's visual interpretation and comparison of plots not be influenced unduly by simple changes in the metrics of either or both axes.

13. For this equation, the core is the omitted category of world system dummy variables, so that the coefficients for SEMPER and PER should be interpreted as deviations from the core countries. The $n$ of 100 includes all non-Communist countries with valid data on all variables. To conserve space, we do not display the data here, but they are readily available from the following sources: Bollen (1980) for POLDEM; Taylor and Hudson (1972) for ENCAP; and Snyder and Kick (1979) for SEMPER and PER. The logarithmic transformation of ENCAP (*ln*ENCAP) is used following Jackman (1973).

14. At this point, a comprehensive examination of the DFITS$_i$, RSTUDENTs, and the other diagnostics for each of the 100 countries could be displayed. While these other

diagnostics inform the following analysis, we do not display them by country to save space. Instead, we concentrate on the six cases that are found to be influential. On a more general level, note that as the $n$ increases, so does the number of combinations of potentially influential observations. This again underscores the point that the regression diagnostics cannot be applied mechanically to a set of estimates: Indeed, such routine applications can readily produce numbers that are difficult, if not impossible, to interpret. Instead, the diagnostics can only be used in conjunction with substantive information about the problem at hand.

15. On this point, compare the Snyder and Kick (1979) classification with that of Wallerstein (1976).

16. It is unfortunate that other treatments of regression diagnostics often fail to consider any remedy other than case deletion (e.g., Chatterjee & Wiseman, 1983; Stevens, 1984).

17. As an alternative to these diagnostics, one can use robust regression procedures that are less sensitive to outliers and influential cases (see Weisberg, 1980, pp. 237-238). However, as we have already indicated, outliers and influential cases can provide useful information about model specification problems, so that it is not always optimal to downplay them.

# APPENDIX
## Raw Data for the Inequality Example

| COUNTRY | INEQ. | TURNOUT | ENCAP |
|---|---|---|---|
| Argentina | 2.960 | 61.8 | 1088 |
| Australia | 1.940 | 85.3 | 3918 |
| Denmark | 2.734 | 86.8 | 2829 |
| Finland | 4.441 | 82.1 | 1650 |
| France | 5.653 | 66.5 | 2419 |
| West Germany | 3.435 | 77.6 | 3673 |
| Israel | 1.950 | 84.1 | 1243 |
| Italy | 2.916 | 89.2 | 1135 |
| Japan | 3.007 | 72.3 | 1166 |
| Netherlands | 3.457 | 87.9 | 2691 |
| Norway | 2.440 | 81.9 | 2740 |
| Puerto Rico | 3.693 | 73.3 | 1453 |
| South Africa | 9.410 | 14.3 | 2338 |
| Sweden | 3.143 | 78.1 | 3491 |
| Trinidad & Tobago | 3.888 | 64.7 | 1935 |
| United Kingdom | 2.876 | 72.4 | 4907 |
| United States | 2.296 | 56.8 | 8047 |
| Venezuela | 3.515 | 78.8 | 2623 |

NOTE: These data and their sources are described in Jackman (1980, pp. 344-345).

## REFERENCES

Ahluwalia, M. S. (1976). Inequality, poverty and development. *Journal of Development Economics, 3,* 307-342.

Atkinson, A. C. (1985). *Plots, transformations, and regression: An introduction to graphical methods of diagnostic regression analysis.* Oxford: Clarendon.

Beggs, J. J. (1988, June). Diagnostic testing in applied econometrics. *Economic Record, 64,* 81-101.

Belsley, D. A., Kuh, E., & Welsch, R. E. (1980). *Regression diagnostics: Identifying influential data and sources of collinearity.* New York: John Wiley.

Bollen, K. A. (1980, June). Issues in the comparative measurement of political democracy. *American Sociological Review, 45,* 370-390.

Bollen, K. A. (1983, August). World system position, dependency, and democracy. *American Sociological Review, 48,* 468-479.

Box, G.E.P., & Cox, D. R. (1964). An analysis of transformations (with discussion). *Journal of the Royal Statistical Society (Series B), 26,* 211-246.

Chatterjee, S., & Hadi, A. S. (1986). Influential observations, high leverage points, and outliers in linear regression. *Statistical Science, 1,* 379-416.

Chatterjee, S., & Wiseman, F. (1983, August). Use of regression diagnostics in political science research. *American Journal of Political Science, 27,* 601-613.

Chirot, D. (1977). *Social change in the twentieth century.* New York: Harcourt Brace Jovanovich.

Cook, R. D. (1977). Detection of influential observations in linear regression. *Technometrics, 19,* 15-18.

Cook, R. D. (1986). Comment. *Statistical Science, 1,* 393-397.

Cook, R. D., & Weisberg, S. (1982a). Criticism and influence analysis in regression. In S. Leinhardt (Ed.), *Sociological methodology 1982* (pp. 313-316). San Francisco: Jossey-Bass.

Cook, R. D. & Weisberg, S. (1982b). *Residuals and influence in regression.* New York: Chapman & Hall.

Daniel, C., & Wood, F. S. (1980). *Fitting equations to data: Computer analysis of multifactor data* (2nd ed.). New York: John Wiley.

Fox, J. (1984). *Linear statistical models and related methods.* New York: John Wiley.

Hewitt, C. (1977, June). The effect of political democracy and social democracy on equality in industrial societies: A cross-national comparison. *American Sociological Review, 42,* 450-464.

Hoaglin, D. C., & Welsch, R. E. (1978, February). The hat matrix in regression and ANOVA. *The American Statistician, 32,* 17-22.

Jackman, R. W. (1973, August). On the relation of economic development to democratic performance. *American Journal of Political Science, 17,* 611-621.

Jackman, R. W. (1980, April). The impact of outliers on income inequality. *American Sociological Review, 45,* 344-347.

Johnston, J. (1984). *Econometric methods.* New York: McGraw-Hill.

Kahn, J. R., & Udry, J. R. (1986, October). Marital coital frequency: Unnoticed outliers and unspecified interactions lead to erroneous conclusions. *American Sociological Review, 51,* 734-737.

Kuznets, S. (1955, March). Economic growth and income inequality. *American Economic Review, 45,* 1-28.

Larsen, W. A., & McCleary, S. J. (1971). The use of partial residual plots in regression analysis. *Technometrics, 14*, 781-790.

Lenski, G. (1966). *Power and privilege.* New York: McGraw-Hill.

Snyder, D., & Kick, E. L. (1979, March). Structural position in the world system and economic growth, 1955-1970. *American Journal of Sociology, 84*, 1096-1126.

Stack, S. (1979, February). The effects of political participation and socialist party strength on the degree of income inequality. *American Sociological Review, 44*, 168-171.

Stevens, J. P. (1984, March). Outliers and influential data points in regression analysis. *Psychological Bulletin, 95*, 334-344.

Taylor, C. L., & Hudson, M. C. (1972). *World handbook of political and social indicators* (2nd ed.). New Haven, CT: Yale University Press.

Tukey, J. W. (1977). *Exploratory data analysis.* Reading, MA: Addison-Wesley.

Velleman, P. F., & Welsch, R. E. (1981, November). Efficient computing of regression diagnostics. *The American Statistician, 35*, 234-242.

Wallerstein, I. (1974). *The modern world system: Capitalist agriculture and the origins of the European world economy in the sixteenth century.* New York: Academic Press.

Wallerstein, I. (1976). Semi-peripheral countries and the contemporary world crisis. *Theory and Society, 3*, 461-484.

Weisberg, S. (1980). *Applied linear regression.* New York: John Wiley.

# 7

# A PRIMER ON ROBUST REGRESSION

Richard A. Berk

## INTRODUCTION

For more than two decades, least squares estimation has dominated multivariate analyses in the social sciences. Much like cross-tabulation for an earlier generation, analysis of variance, analysis of covariance, and multiple regression, often extended to multiple equation applications, have become basic tools of the trade. With the more recent interest in latent variables, maximum likelihood estimation procedures also have become popular, but when the normal distribution is invoked, the least squares criterion is still effectively in place. Indeed, maximum likelihood estimation for the full set of generalized linear models may be properly undertaken with iteratively reweighted least squares. These generalized linear models include not just the conventional linear regression, but such popular techniques as logistic regression, probit analysis, and log-linear techniques for contingency tables (McCullagh & Nelder, 1983). In short, the vast majority of estimation procedures currently used in sociology rely on at least the equivalent of a least squares "fit."

It is widely recognized that estimators associated with the least squares principle are especially sensitive to larger residuals. In effect, the estimates produced take particular account of larger "errors." If by a "good fit" one means responding to larger residuals, all may be well. However, if by a good fit one means protecting against larger residuals,

AUTHOR'S NOTE: Thanks go to Jan De Leeuw for helpful comments on an earlier version of this chapter and to Alice Hoffman for help in constructing the difficult tables.

fitting by least squares will often give misleading answers. The mean, for example, rests on a least squares fit and is well known to be misleading for asymmetric distributions with long tails.

In this chapter, I consider M-estimators for regression analysis, which, as one kind of robust location estimator, do not depend on the least squares principle. M-estimators can minimize many different functions of the residuals, not just the sum of their squared values. As a result, M-estimators can weight observations in a variety of ways. Other robust estimators of location share these characteristics, but M-estimators for *robust regression* have excellent statistical properties, may be easily modified for particular problems, and are relatively easy to compute (Hampel et al., 1986; Li, 1985; Wu, 1985; Chapter 2, this volume). Whereas by these criteria M-estimators probably dominate the field,[1] I will not be discussing the full variety of robust regression procedures, many of which have considerable merit. Nor will I tackle in any depth the more general issues associated with robust statistics.[2] Both are well beyond the scope of a single introductory chapter.

In the next section, I provide a broad overview of the issues that motivate the material to follow. In the third section, I briefly consider the formal definition of M-estimators and summarize how M-estimators perform. It cannot be overemphasized that my exposition will be no more than an introduction and that interested readers should consult the references cited. Then, in the fourth and fifth sections, I undertake some data analyses showing how robust regression may be applied. The data in the fifth section are particularly instructive because there are far too few observations to capitalize on the statistical convenience of asymptotic (i.e., large sample) distributions. Finally, in the last section, I extract some general lessons.

## SOME BACKGROUND

Problems with quadratic objective functions are well documented in the statistical literature, and excellent discussions can now be found in a few elementary texts (e.g., Mosteller, Fienberg, & Roarke, 1985, Mosteller & Tukey, 1977).[3] Briefly, there are two generic concerns: diagnosis and cure. Under diagnosis falls a very rich and useful tradition in statistics, including the detection of anomalous observations and determinations of the impact of those observations on one's results (Barnett & Lewis, 1978; Belsley, Kuh, & Welch, 1980; Cook &

Weisberg, 1982; Chapters 5 and 6, this volume). Whereas these diagnostic procedures have been developed from a variety of perspectives and in reaction to a number of particular problems, many speak effectively to the ways in which quadratic objective functions may be inappropriate for certain kinds of data.

Under the heading of cure, there have been two related strategies. On the one hand, there are situations in which observations that are clearly anomalous (*outliers*) result from known measurement errors or known flaws in the execution of a research design. It is then possible either to correct the troublesome data or to delete them. For example, perhaps one's problems derive from the transposition of digits during coding or from the inadvertent aggregation in only some units (e.g., school districts) being studied. In both cases, if the errors cannot be corrected, one may choose to discard the offending observations. I will not consider such options in this chapter, but suffice it to say that one must have a convincing explanation for how the errors were introduced (Barnett & Lewis, 1978; chap. 2; Hampel, Ronchetti, Rousseeuw, & Stahel, 1986; pp. 56-71; Chapter 6, this volume).

On the other hand, there will often be times when it is not clear which observations are anomalous. They may not appear to be dramatically different from the rest of the data, and/or they are not readily explained by any known error in measurement or data collection. Indeed, it is all too easy to forget that improbable events occur; what looks to be a strange data point may be nothing more than the luck of the draw. To further complicate matters, deviant observations may actually carry vital information, perhaps as "ideal" types of the units being studied. In short, as an alternative to fixing the data or discarding it, one needs statistical procedures that in some sense "accommodate" it (Barnett & Lewis, 1978).

More positively, one may decide on substantive grounds that the quadratic objective function is inappropriate. For example, suppose that one is regressing income on education. A least squares fit implies that individuals with unusually high or low incomes will have a disproportionate impact on the estimated regression parameters, especially if such individuals are also unusually high or low in education. Thus graduate students (presumably high in education and low in income) will have a far larger relative impact on the regression fit than, say, assembly line workers or secretaries. Note that more is involved than potential atypicality per se; the impact of any atypicality is magnified by the squaring process. Clearly, it would be useful to have estimation procedures that could provide alternatives to the quadratic objective function. M-estimators are one viable option.

## M-ESTIMATORS OF LOCATION

Drawing on Li (1985, p. 291), the M-Estimator for the vector $\beta$ is based on the objective function $\rho(t)$ and the data $(Y_1, X_1, \ldots, Y_n, X_n)$. It is the value of $\beta$, denoted $\hat{\beta}_m$ that minimizes

$$\sum_{i=1}^{n} \rho(y_i - x_i\hat{\beta}_m) = \sum_{i=1}^{n} \rho\left(y_i - \sum_{j=1}^{J} x_{ij}\hat{\beta}_j\right). \tag{7.1}$$

Equation 7.1 is a generalization of the conventional least squares objective function,[4] with $\rho(t)$ left unspecified. If the residuals are squared (i.e., $\rho(t) = t^2$), one has, as one M-estimator, ordinary least squares. If the absolute value is taken (i.e., $\rho(t) = |t|$), one has the least absolute residual estimator. These and other options specify the *particular* M-estimator being used, to which we will turn shortly.

It is often instructive to consider not just $\rho(t)$, but its derivative $\rho'(t) = \psi(t)$. If the goal is to minimize equation 7.1, taking the derivative of equation 7.1 with respect to $\hat{\beta}_m$, setting the result equal to zero, and solving leads to the desired result. Indeed, in the quadratic case, the intermediate result is the usual normal equations. Thus $\psi(t)$ figures centrally in the production of actual estimates, both in a generalization of the normal equations and as $\omega(t)$, a function of $\psi(t)$ and $t$, used as a weight in iteratively reweighted least squares. More will be said about estimation later.

In addition, the properties of M-estimators are often characterized in part through $\psi(t)$. For example, $\psi(t)$ figures in formal treatments of the *influence function* (e.g., Li, 1985, pp. 298-299), which will be addressed briefly below. In this introductory chapter, however, such uses of $\psi(t)$ are not essential and are discussed only in passing. Most of the central ideas can be addressed through the objective function and a few numerical illustrations.

Figure 7.1 plots the ordinary least squares (OLS) objective function against the values of residuals, called more generally deviation scores.[5] As the quadratic form implies, the weight given to deviation scores increases at an increasing rate as the absolute value of the deviation scores increase.

Figure 7.2 shows the objective function when, instead of squaring the deviation scores, one takes their absolute values. The weights now increase linearly so that the larger deviation scores are given no special importance. While in Figure 7.1 the weights for deviation scores around 4 in absolute value were approaching weights of 6, the weights for those same scores in Figure 7.2 are a little over 3. Using the absolute value as the objective function leads to least absolute residual (LAR) regression and is another type of M-estimator.[6]

Figure 7.3 represents a compromise between least squares and least absolute residual regression. Up to the predetermined absolute value of a deviation score (e.g., |1.5|), the objective function is OLS. Beyond that value, the objective function is LAR. This is the Huber M-estimator.[7]

While LAR regression gives larger deviation scores less weight than ordinary least squares regression, there will be circumstances in which larger deviation scores will stem from suspect observations, and when, therefore, these observations need to be discounted. One discounting method can be seen in Figure 7.4. The bi-square is an M-estimator that weights deviation scores steeply up to some predetermined deviation score value (like the Huber M-estimator just described), at which point weights become constant. That is, beyond that predetermined deviation score value, larger scores are given the same weight as smaller scores.

Figure 7.5 shows a less "severe" discounting M-estimator, the Bell M-estimator. Like the bi-square, at some point increases in residual values do not translate into commensurate increases in weights, but full discounting to constant weights is only approached as a limit. Moreover, the shift to discounting occurs gradually.[8]

## Statistical Performance Criteria

It should be clear from Figures 7.1 through 7.5 that M-estimators provide a rich menu of objective functions. But how can one choose between them? To begin, there is a set of statistical criteria that basically define how a "good" robust estimator should perform.[9]

First, it is clearly desirable for M-estimators to have the usual "large sample" properties of maximum likelihood estimators: consistency and asymptotic normality.[10] The OLS, LAR, and Huber estimators meet these criteria. The bi-square and Bell estimators will as well, as long as the distribution to which they are applied is strongly unimodal. If the

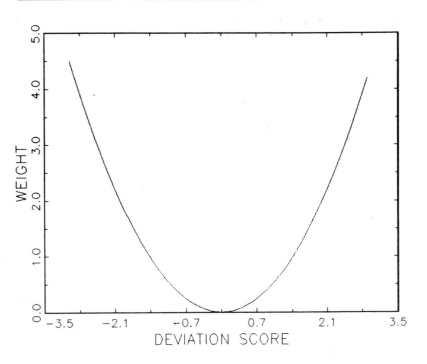

**Figure 7.1  OLS objective function.**

distribution is not strongly unimodal, the bi-square and Bell estimators may or may not be consistent and asymptotically normal, depending on technical considerations beyond the scope of this chapter. However, a good rule of thumb seems to be that the predetermined constant required by these estimators be kept relatively large (Wu, 1985). What this means is that the strong "discounting" of larger deviation scores does not begin until the larger deviations become quite large. Exactly what defines large is a tuning constant that may be manipulated (e.g., deviations larger than two in absolute value).

At the same time, however, it is very easy to make too much of good asymptotic properties. Small- to modest-sized data sets are common in the social sciences (e.g., $N < 200$), especially for large observational units such as organizations, cities, and countries. In samples of this size, it is typically very difficult to make any general statements about the

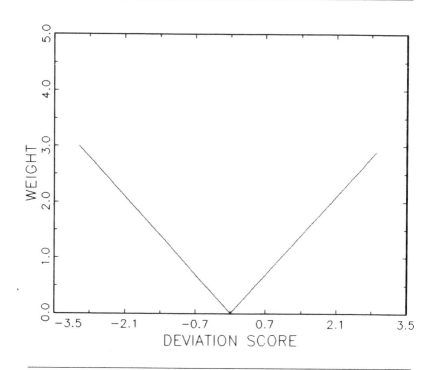

**Figure 7.2  LAR objective function.**

performance of M-estimators without specific assumptions about the distribution of the disturbance term. In short, asymptotic properties are often irrelevant.

Second, good M-estimators should be "resistant." Basically, a resistant estimator is relatively unaffected by a few rather deviant observations or many slightly deviant observations. Drawing heavily on Mosteller and Tukey (1977, pp. 350-352), consider the following 14 observations:

$$-6 -5 -4 -3 -2 -1 -.5 .5 1 2 3 4 5 6 .$$

Imagine another observation $X$ that can be "moved" through the data, beginning with large negative numbers and ending with large positive numbers. For each increment in $X$, one calculates a summary measure

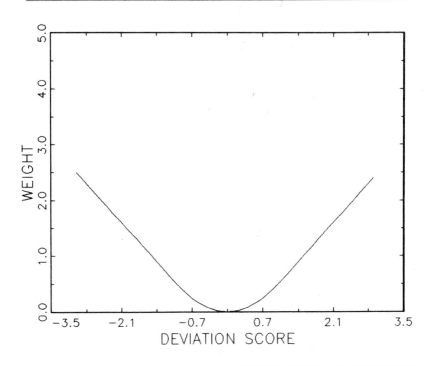

**Figure 7.3  Huber objective function.**

of location, so that it is possible to plot the measure against the changing value of $X$. If the summary measure is the mean, its value will increase in a linear fashion with increases in $X$. If the summary measure is the median, its value will not change until the increasing value of $X$ exceeds −.5, will change linearly between −.5 and .5, and will not change for increased values of $X$ larger than .5. In both cases, the plot of the summary measure against $X$ conveys the degree of resistance. In both cases, one is, in effect, studying an influence curve. Figure 7.6 shows these influence curves for the mean and median.

Because the influence curve of the mean is unbounded, the mean is formally said to lack resistance. That is, the mean can be shifted any arbitrary amount with an arbitrarily large or arbitrarily small value of $X$. This implies that the mean is very vulnerable to anomalies in the data. The median is also formally said to lack resistance because of the sharp

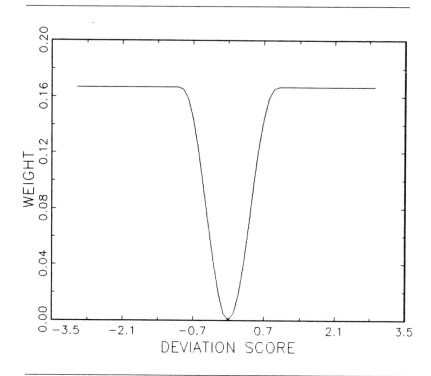

**Figure 7.4  Bi-square objective function.**

shift around the middle value(s) of the distribution. The point in both cases is that the summary statistic is rather easily bounced around when the data do not cooperate. However, because the shift in the median is bounded, the median is usually treated as if it were resistant.

A bit more formally, the influence curve actually shows how much the value of a particular estimator changes in response to infinitesimal changes in the underlying distribution. That is, one is able to examine how the estimate is altered by arbitrarily small changes in distribution. Mathematical statisticians find influence curves extremely useful, but for our purposes the overall message is that LAR, Huber, bi-square, and Bell M-estimators all considered resistant.[11]

Third, good M-estimators should have a high *breakdown point*. The idea of a breakdown point is closely related to the properties of influence curves. Suppose that some number of observations from a sample

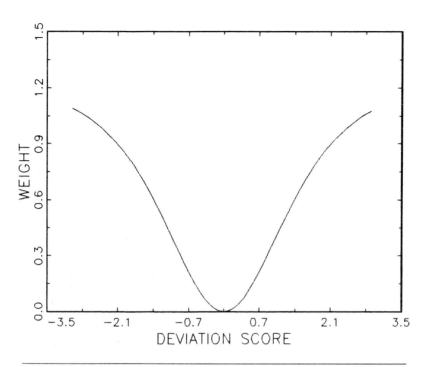

**Figure 7.5  Bell objective function.**

are arbitrarily replaced. Or suppose that to the given sample, some number of new observations is arbitrarily added. The breakdown point of an estimator is the smallest proportion of the sample that may be arbitrarily replaced or added, which may result in the estimate becoming unbounded (i.e., going off "to infinity"). For example, as Figure 7.6 suggests, the mean may be made arbitrarily large by adding a single, sufficiently large observation. In contrast, the median can be made to break down if half of the data is shifted. In practical terms, estimators with high breakdown points do not change dramatically in the face of large disparities between the assumed and actual distribution, including qualitative errors in the shape assumed. For M-estimators of *location*, all but the OLS estimator do quite well; they have relatively high breakdown points.

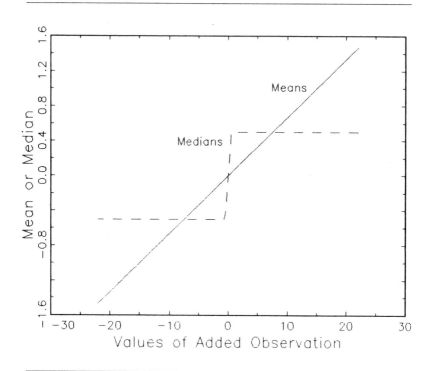

**Figure 7.6  Influence curves.**

The story is somewhat more complicated for *regression* M-estimators. The key idea is that each observation must be evaluated with respect to where it lies in the distribution of the response (dependent) variable *and* the joint distribution of the explanatory (independent) variables. Observations that are outliers on the response variable, and with respect to the joint distribution of the explanatory variables, are particularly problematic.

Consider, for example, the usual bivariate OLS regression. The regression line is fit in two-dimensional space, and outliers are distinguished by their location with respect to the bulk of the bivariate scatterplot. Regression M-estimators can discount the impact of outliers in the *y-direction*, but do not address outliers in the *x-direction*. In an important sense, only half of the problem is solved, even in principle. Thus regression M-estimators have low breakdown points (Rousseeuw

& Leroy, 1987, pp. 68-70). Estimators that discount outliers in both the y-direction and x-direction exist, but there are important trade-offs, which some feel make them problematic. There seems to be, for instance, a nearly inevitable trade-off between a high breakdown point and high efficiency. In any case, these alternatives to M-estimators are beyond the scope of this chapter.[12]

Fourth, good M-estimators are relatively efficient across a range of likely distributions. Recall that efficiency refers to the variance of an estimator's sampling distribution. Also recall that small (or *finite*) sample efficiency is determined by how an estimator performs in a sample of a particular (typically modest) size, while asymptotic efficiency is determined by how an estimator performs in a sample that becomes arbitrarily large. Under certain circumstances, optimal estimators may achieve the smallest standard error that is theoretically possible.

Unfortunately, evaluating the efficiency of M-estimators is complicated. To begin, optimal efficiency can only be achieved, even in theory, with respect to a specific distribution, and an estimator that may be optimal for one distribution may perform poorly for others (Wu, 1985, p. 350). As a fallback position, therefore, one typically focuses on relative efficiency, which is a standardized ratio of sampling distribution variances. Moreover, since it is rare for the data's distribution to be known, it makes sense to pick an M-estimator whose relative efficiency (compared to other M-estimators) is high across a range of possible distributions. In the end, however, the only general conclusion seems to be that the least squares estimator performs worst. That is, even with modest deviations from the normal distribution, relative efficiency falls off dramatically. Among the other M-estimators, overall conclusions depend on the particular set of distributions being considered.[13]

Finally, good M-estimators should be practical: relatively easy to compute, useful for a variety of data problems, and comprehensible to the mere mortals who will have to use them. All M-estimators for robust regression are reasonably practical.

To summarize, a review of statistical criteria for robust regression is primarily an exercise in OLS bashing. Selection among the remaining M-estimators seems too often to be data specific and dependent on judgment calls about the relative importance of different performance characteristics. In particular, there is often a trade-off between the breakdown point and efficiency. Moreover, much of what we know about the performance of M-estimators depends on asymptotic properties, which may be misleading for samples of the size often available to social scientists. An important implication, to which I shall return, is that one may well benefit from trying a variety of approaches and proceeding in a more inductive manner than is commonly recommended (see, for example, Leamer, 1983).

## Substantive Criteria

While it may be difficult to provide general guidance on the choice of an M-estimator from statistical performance criteria alone, there will often be times when choices between different M-estimators can be made on substantive grounds. Recall the earlier example in which income was regressed on education, and the relative importance of data on graduate students was considered. Depending on how one chooses to weight the deviation scores, the regression line estimated can differ substantially. If larger deviation scores are discounted relative to smaller deviation scores, the regression line will more closely summarize the experience of more typical individuals. That is, information from more typical individuals is treated as more important than information from less typical individuals.

If one has reason to suspect that atypicality on the average results from some anomaly, the discounting may make sense. Alternatively, there may be no reason to differentially weight atypical observations; indeed, there may be circumstances when they should be given extra weight. For example, perhaps observations near the center of the scatterplot represent cases in which the available measures failed to record more extreme values. Thus low income individuals may underreport their income for fear of losing eligibility for various kinds of transfer payments; or smaller municipalities with less professional public servants may routinely fail to record incidents, such as reported crimes, that are later aggregated as the official statistics for the locale. The point is that there will be situations in which, on substantive grounds, typical observations may be less credible than atypical ones. Then, the typical observations should be downweighted, or at the very least, not given extra weight. In short, before proceeding it is vital to consider objective functions such as those shown in Figures 7.1-7.5 and decide which makes the most substantive sense.[14]

*Computation*

Regression M-estimators are perhaps most easily computed with any software that contains procedures for iteratively reweighted least squares. SAS, BMDP, GAUSS, and PC-ISP are examples.[15] One begins with conventional OLS estimates and then weights the data (the response variable, the explanatory variables, and the vector of 1's for the intercept) by a function of residuals. The particular function used depends on the M-estimator being employed. OLS is then applied to the weighted data. Again, residuals are calculated, new weights are constructed, and the data are reweighted. OLS is then applied a third time. The OLS estimation and the reweighting is continued until the estimates converge. Table 7.1, reproduced from Li (1985, p. 293), shows for popular M-estimators the objective function $\rho(t)$, the derivative of the objective function $\psi(t)$, and the weighting function $\omega(t)$.

With the exception of OLS and LAR regression, a scale parameter (much like $\sigma^2$ in OLS regression) also needs to be estimated *along with* the usual regression parameters. That is, a scale parameter is required as part of the iteration process; all of the residuals are divided by (i.e., scaled by) the scale parameter. This presents no special difficulties, although there is some debate about what scale parameter estimator should be used. Details can be found in Li (1985, pp. 300-310).

Unfortunately, the issues are far more complicated when one turns to statistical inference. First, just as in the usual formulas for OLS regression, a scale parameter is required for calculation of the standard errors. However, a key motivation for robust regression is concern about outliers, and that same motivation applies to estimates of scale. Hence, one needs a sensible robust scale estimator, and there are many possible candidates. For example, a linear objective function leads to the mean absolute deviation (MAD) scale estimator. Yet there seems to be no consensus about which is best, and the difficulties caused by a number of unresolved technical matters. Second, statistical inference requires that the sampling distribution of the estimates be known. For large samples one can rely on asymptotic normality, but for small samples the sampling distribution is almost certainly not known and may well be a very long way from normal. These and other difficulties make statistical inference for M-estimators problematic (Li, 1985, pp. 300-301; Wu, 1985, pp. 365-363, 367).

Perhaps the best approach, therefore, relies on resampling methods such as the bootstrap (see, in particular, Chapter 8, this volume). The

**Table 7.1 M-Estimators for Regression**

| Estimator | $\rho(t)$ | $\psi(t)$ | $\omega(t)$ | Range of t |
|---|---|---|---|---|
| OLS | $\frac{1}{2}t^2$ | $t$ | $1$ | $\|t\| < \infty$ |
| LAR | $\|t\|$ | $sgn(t)$ | $\dfrac{sgn(t)}{t}$ | $\|t\| < \infty$ |
| Huber[a] | $\frac{1}{2}t^2$ | $t$ | $1$ | $\|t\| \leq k$ |
|  | $k\|t\| - 1/2k^2$ | $k\,sgn(t)$ | $k/\|t\|$ | $\|t\| > k$ |
| Andrews[a] | $A^2[1 - \cos(t/A)]$ | $A\sin(t/A)$ | $A/t\sin(t/A)$ | $\|t\| \leq \pi A$ |
|  | $2A^2$ | $0$ | $0$ | $\|t\| > \pi A$ |
| Biweight[a] (bi-square) | $\dfrac{B^2}{6}\left\{1 - [1 - (t/B)^2]^2\right\}$ | $t[1 - (t/B)^2]^2$ | $[1 - (t/B)^2]^2$ | $\|t\| \leq B$ |
|  | $\dfrac{B^2}{6}$ | $0$ | $0$ | $\|t\| > B$ |

SOURCE: David C. Hoaglin, Frederick Mosteller, and John Tukey (Eds.), *Exploring Data Tables, Trends, and Shapes.* Copyright © 1985, John Wiley & Sons. Reprinted by permission of John Wiley & Sons, Inc.

NOTES: a. The illustrative example ρ-functions and ψ-functions use $k = 1$ for the Huber, $A = 1/\pi$ for the Andrews and $B = 1$ for the biweight.

basic idea of the bootstrap is to treat the data set as a population. Certainly, if the data were sampled properly by probability procedures, the data set will well represent the population, within sampling error. Then, one takes bootstrap samples from the data set by selecting single cases at random *with replacement*. (Each bootstrap sample is the same size as the data set.) From bootstrap sample to bootstrap sample, parameter estimates will vary. In effect, the sampling distribution of the estimator is being empirically generated. Statistical inference then follows naturally. In the application to follow in the fifth section, bootstrapping is employed.

## AN ILLUSTRATION

Before launching into a *real life* application with all of its complexities and uncertainties, a far more simple illustration may perhaps prove useful. In an article on Adolphe Quetelet, Stone (1988) included data on the number of births and deaths by time of day for a particular

**Table 7.2  Births and Deaths in Brussels by the Hour**

| Hour | Births | Deaths | Hour | Births | Deaths |
|------|--------|--------|------|--------|--------|
| 1 | 142 | 228 | 13 | 94 | 257 |
| 2 | 173 | 253 | 14 | 97 | 233 |
| 3 | 130 | 230 | 15 | 88 | 217 |
| 4 | 122 | 242 | 16 | 91 | 237 |
| 5 | 120 | 231 | 17 | 104 | 281 |
| 6 | 111 | 213 | 18 | 100 | 233 |
| 7 | 112 | 217 | 19 | 121 | 204 |
| 8 | 99 | 248 | 20 | 97 | 194 |
| 9 | 88 | 207 | 21 | 133 | 199 |
| 10 | 130 | 228 | 22 | 115 | 220 |
| 11 | 137 | 311 | 23 | 224 | 243 |
| 12 | 48 | 110 | 24 | 4 | 14 |

hospital in Brussels. The number of births by hour covers a 30-year period in the nineteenth century, whereas the number of deaths dates from 1811 to 1822. Table 7.2 shows these data.

Figure 7.7 (constructed with the statistical package STATA) shows the scatterplot for deaths (y) and births (x), along with the univariate boxplot for each. Twenty-two of the observations are clustered and show little association. Two observations (for noon and midnight) are dramatically smaller in both the y-direction and x-direction. With these two included, there is obviously a positive association in the data. It is difficult to know what to make of the two apparent outliers without being a lot more familiar with how the data were recorded and collected. However, since there is no apparent biological reason for the outliers, hospital practice or data collection are implicated.

Table 7.3 shows four regression estimates for the bivariate relationship shown in Figure 7.7. The first is the ordinary least squares estimate. Roughly speaking, there is a one-to-one increase of deaths with births. The intercept is approximately 100. Both coefficients are statistically significant at the (two-tailed) .05 level for a null hypothesis of zero. However, given the small sample and real questions about the disturbance distribution, both tests are probably not very useful. Next (moving to the right) are shown the results for least absolute residual regression. The estimated relationship is, in effect, rotated clockwise: The slope is cut by about 50% and the intercept is increased by about 50%. No standard errors are presented because there is no really convenient way of getting them.[16] Next are shown the Huber regression

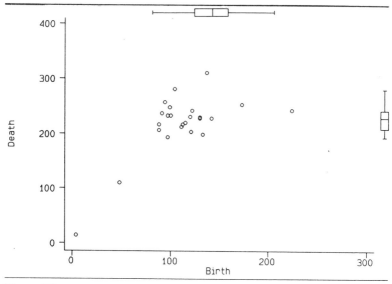

**Figure 7.7**

results and little changes. However, standard errors are provided, and both coefficients are *statistically significant,* if one assumes that the disturbance distribution is normal. In short, both robust regression M-estimators tell a rather different story compared to ordinary least squares.

Recall, however, that regression M-estimators only address outliers in the y-direction. The final column in Table 7.3 shows the results for least median squares regression (calculated with PROGRESS by Rousseeuw & Leroy). Least median squares regression (Rousseeuw & Leroy, 1987) fits the regression line (hyperplane) by minimizing the median of the squared residuals rather than the sum of the squared residuals; that is, the criterion is a robust measure of location rather than a very nonrobust sum. While the details are beyond the scope of this chapter, outliers in both the y-direction and x-direction are taken into account. Note that the estimated relationship is now rotated further in a clockwise direction. Compared to the robust M-estimators, the slope is decreased by about half, and the intercept is increased by about a third. Indeed, there now appear to be virtually no relationships between births and deaths. No standard errors are available. Nevertheless, the

**Table 7.3 Quetelet Birth-Death Data: Results for Three Regression M-Estimators and LMS Regression**

|  | *OLS* | *LAR* | *HUBER* | *LMS* |
|---|---|---|---|---|
| CONSTANT | 114.9 | 159.4 | 169.9 | 195.8 |
|  | (26.31) | * | (18.5) | * |
| COEFFICIENT | .92 | .54 | .47 | .26 |
|  | (.22) | * | (.16) | * |

NOTE: *Standard error not computed.

vulnerability of regression M-estimators to outliers in the x-direction is apparent.

In summary, the illustration makes clear that regression M-estimators can make a difference. However, their small sample properties are typically unknown in just those instances when they are most likely to be needed. In addition, outliers in the x-direction are ignored. We turn now to a far more realistic application.

## AN APPLICATION

While robust regression represents a particular set of estimation procedures, equally important is the underlying data analysis perspective. At each step in the process, from research design to reporting results, one proceeds as if Murphy's Law applies. This means that as many assumptions as possible are made problematic, and, where possible, efforts are made to protect the analysis. This also means being explicit and conservative about what may be learned. As an illustration, I present below an evaluation of an effort in Alameda County, California, to more effectively prosecute narcotics cases (Greenspan, Berk, Feeley, & Skolnick, 1988).

### The Program

On January 10, 1985, Oakland's Assemblyman Elihu Harris introduced legislation in the State Assembly that was intended to coordinate and enhance law enforcement efforts to control drug use in Alameda County. Particular attention was directed toward the courts. The bill assumed that more effective and efficient prosecution of narcotics cases could lead to a reduction in drug crimes and drug-related crimes. A number of interventions were proposed, including an oversight "Targeted Urban Crime Narcotics Task Force" and additional financial support for the county's courts, Prosecutor's office, Public Defender's office, probation department, and crime laboratory. The bill was approved in July of 1985, and program funding became available on October 1, 1985.

For the present purpose, I will focus on whether the legislation made the sanctioning process more effective, and on a particular outcome measure: the number of offenders incarcerated. I will not address the ultimate impact of the program on crime or other kinds of outcomes such as efficiency (e.g., how fast cases were processed). Readers interested in the substantive issues should consult the evaluation completed by Greenspan and her colleagues (1988).

Under the Alameda Program, there were essentially two routes by which drug offenders could be incarcerated. Offenders could be sentenced by the court after a conviction (or pleading) or be sent to prison or jail for having violated probation. For the first route, the state legislation supported the use of a *team approach* to prosecution, in which all drug-related offenses were handled by a specialized group of Deputy District Attorneys, under the direction of a *coordinator*. The team was given sufficient staff to try at least two cases simultaneously.

For the second route, an effort was made to orchestrate better the probation revocation process so that drug offenders who violated the conditions of their probation would be swiftly incarcerated. Offenders found violating a condition of their probation were required either to serve the original sentence imposed or a new sentence if the original sentence had been suspended. One key advantage of incarceration through probation revocation was that the standards of proof are lower than in court trials. This meant that it was often more effective to simply "violate" an offender than to go through the trouble of trying the offender for a new crime. A single member of the drug prosecution team was made responsible for revocation process.

Despite the face validity of the program, it was not at all clear that it would work. For example, the greater use of probation revocation might divert "good" drug cases away from the usual channels. Thus, while revocations might increase, convictions might decline. Alternatively, the District Attorney's office might have to use the additional resources to aggressively pursue a small number of difficult cases, with the bulk of the caseload unaffected. Anticipating such questions, the legislation required a program evaluation.

## The Research Design

The legislative requirement for an evaluation was not matched by a great deal of insight into what a sound evaluation would entail. For a variety of reasons, therefore, the strongest design that could be implemented was an interrupted time series from official statistics. In brief, data on cases processed by the county's court were available from a management information system (called CORPUS) used to monitor the processing of cases forwarded to the District Attorney's office. These data were examined and from tapes provided by the county, a longitudinal file was constructed organizing key outcome variables by quarter. There were 12 quarters of data, with the intervention falling in the eighth quarter. I will focus on the number of drug cases sanctioned over those 12 quarters.

Figure 7.8 shows with a broken line and open squares the time series for the number of drug cases in which the offender was sanctioned (i.e., sent to prison or jail). The number of drug offenders sanctioned by quarter ranges from about 70 to about 350, but there is clearly an upward trend, beginning before the eighth quarter. Moreover, since the steps from arrest to sentence may take months, cases sanctioned in the eighth quarter were largely processed before the program began; that is, program effects on sanctioning should appear after the eighth quarter. And in this case, the trend begins in about the fourth quarter, especially if the downward spike in the eighth is considered aberrant.

Note how one could have been misled by a pretest/posttest design. A comparison between the number of cases sanctioned in the seventh quarter, for example, and the tenth quarter would have revealed a dramatic gain of about 100 cases, but would have neglected the positive trend beginning well before the program was launched. This illustrates simply an important principle in a robust approach: One can reduce dramatically the difficulties faced during data analysis by anticipating possible difficulties in one's research design.

In this instance, the design can be further strengthened by adding a comparison group not subject to the program. Figure 7.8, therefore, also shows a time series for the number of theft cases sanctioned (in which no drug offenses were involved). As with the drug cases, there is a general upward trend, although it seems to begin a bit later.[17] This supports the speculation that there may be no distinct program impact because the increase that both series share must be driven by common or correlated causes.

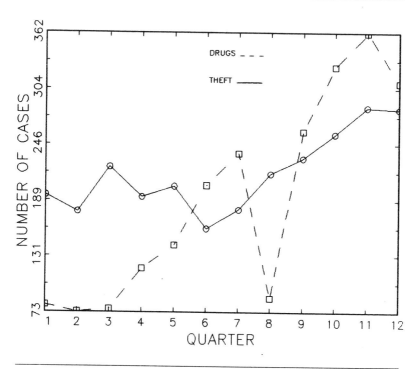

**Figure 7.8  Cases sanctioned.**

The search for common or correlated causes leads directly to a concern with the number of drug and theft cases entering the system; more cases coming in the front door must generate more cases going out the back door. This leads to standardizing the number of sanctioned by the number of arrests. That is, one may control for the number of cases entering the system by simply calculating the proportion of arrests for which sanctions were applied.

Figure 7.9 plots, therefore, the proportion of final dispositions in which sanctions were imposed. The proportions range from a low of about .11 to a high of about .40. Thus, for example, a high of about 40% of the theft dispositions involved incarceration. Perhaps the major conclusion from Figure 7.9 is that the drug series seems to be gaining on the theft series.

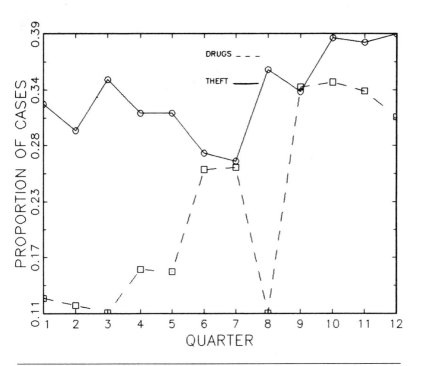

**Figure 7.9  Cases sanctioned.**

Unfortunately, it is still difficult to disentangle the long-term relative gains for the drug series, beginning in the sixth quarter, from gains after the eighth quarter that may be attributable to the program. Inferences are made especially difficult because of the possible outlier in the eighth quarter for the drug time series. Alternatively, the eighth quarter may be reasonably atypical of quarter-to-quarter variation, and the proportions for the sixth and seventh quarters may be atypical. In short, there seems to be unusual variation in the drug time series in the middle of the observational period, but its causes and consequences are unclear. In any case, the importance of visual displays should be apparent; there is no substitute for a careful examination of one's data before statistical analysis is begun.

*Statistical Analysis*

As a way of capitalizing on the information produced by the research design, an outcome variable was defined as the difference between the proportions of drug and theft cases sanctioned. Using proportions standardized for the number of cases overall reaching final disposition controls for the number of cases entering the system, whereas differencing the two time series controls for common or correlated causes.[18] From the perspective of robust data analysis, differencing has the asset of requiring that no parameters be estimated.

As for any time series, there is also reason to be at least suspicious about autocorrelation within the differenced time series. This suggests the need for some kind of autoregressive formulation. Were there more than a suspicion, one might choose to longitudinally difference the (already cross-sectionally differenced) series. However, since "over-differencing" can lead to biases in the analysis of time series data, it is probably more sensible to allow the amount of difference to be an empirical question.

Figure 7.10 shows with a broken line the difference between the standardized drug and theft time series. Using that differenced series as the response (dependent) variable, an OLS model was fitted using one-period lagged values of the response variable and a dummy variable for the treatment, coded 0 through the eighth quarter and 1 thereafter. The lagged response variable was introduced to control for any first order serial correlation, and the dummy variable was introduced to estimate any treatment effects. The solid line in Figure 7.10 represents the *predicted values* from the OLS regression.

Figure 7.10 suggests that there was a treatment effect, and, from the upper panel in Table 7.4, we see that although the autoregressive component is not important, the estimated treatment impact is. The drug series gains 9% on the theft series after the program is introduced (beginning in the ninth quarter). Looking back at Figure 7.9, one can see that a 9% increment is nontrivial, given base sanctioning rates between 11% and 40%. Put another way, about 20% of the pretest final dispositions in drug cases include incarceration. The OLS estimates of the program's effect suggest an increase in that figure to about 30%, or about a 50% relative improvement. However, under the *t* distribution (given the small sample size), the effect is not statistically significant at the .05 level for either a one-tailed or a two-tailed test.

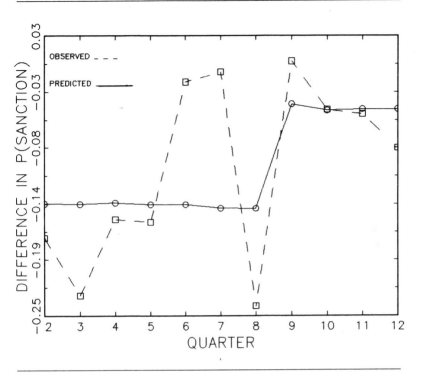

**Figure 7.10  Cases sanctioned.**

There are, however, ample grounds for being uneasy with these results. First, because of the small sample, conventional significance tests require that the disturbance term have a normal distribution. This is formally impossible since the response variable is the difference between two proportions. Indeed, there are not even grounds for assuming that the disturbance term has a symmetric distribution, in part because the drug series has several observations close to zero.

Second, there is no reason to assume that the events making up each proportion are independent. Indeed, given the bureaucratic environment in which the cases were processed, the events are probably clustered by *spells*. That is, there is a spell of great concern about crowded court dockets, followed by a return to business as usual. During a spell of concern, cases are processed faster than at other times, implying serial correlation between the length of time between events and,

**Table 7.4   Regression Analysis for the Impact of the Program**

| | *Ordinary Least Squares Regression* | | |
|---|---|---|---|
| Variable | Coefficient | Standard Error | T Value |
| Intercept | −0.14 | 0.05 | −2.82 |
| Program impact | 0.09 | 0.05 | 1.79 |
| Lagged outcome | −0.03 | 0.29 | −0.09 |
| | *Bootstrapped Least Absolute Residual Regression* | | |
| Variable | Coefficient | Standard Error | T Value |
| Intercept | −0.21 | 0.05 | −4.33 |
| Program impact | 0.16 | 0.06 | 2.68 |
| Lagged outcome | −0.30 | 0.27 | −1.10 |

therefore, the events themselves. While the lagged response variable may well "soak up" any correlations between the proportions over time, any correlation among the events making up the proportions remains a potential problem, which undermines conventional statistical inference.

Third, the very large residuals for quarters six, seven, and eight are grounds for concern. Perhaps the results are being inappropriately dominated by these three quarters. Within the pretest period at least, the data for quarters six and seven look particularly aberrant. In short, there is good reason to worry about the quadratic objective function and a rationale for trying a robust alternative.

A priori, there seems to be no reason for significantly downweighting the larger residuals relative to the smaller ones. That is, there is no reason to suspect that the three largest residuals result from a measurement or design error. This suggests ruling out any of the redescending M-estimators in favor of least absolute residual regression. Recall that the objective function for least absolute residual regression weights the residuals in a linear fashion.

Recall that LAR regression can be easily undertaken with iteratively reweighted least squares (Li, 1985, pp. 305-310). Basically, before each least squares "pass," all of the data for each case (including the column of 1's associated with the intercept) are multiplied by the square root of the inverse of the absolute value of the residual for that case.[19] Unfortunately, it is not clear how best to calculate the standard errors directly (Li, 1985, pp. 300-301), and for these data, the small sample precludes any reliance on a normal asymptotic distribution for the parameter estimates (Amemiya, 1985, p. 75).

In response, the entire procedure was bootstrapped using resampling techniques appropriate for autoregressive time series models (Efron & Tibshirani, 1986, p. 65), but applied to M-estimators (Efron, 1982, pp. 35-36). Bootstrapping has a number of strengths, including the ability to represent all sources of instability, not just those addressed by conventional significance tests. However, it is necessary to assume that one's sample is truly representative of some theoretical population because, in a very real sense, the sample is being treated as a population. In the case of historical data such as these, the best that one can typically do is assert that if the underlying historical process in principle produces a population of realizations with the same properties as those observed in the given sample, the bootstrapped sampling distribution is appropriate. Although this may seem like a long stretch, the same argument basically applies to conventional statistical inference used on historical data. For both, the population is a hypothetical set of realizations from a given historical process.

Table 7.4 reports in the lower panel the LAR regression results based on 1,000 bootstrapped samples (estimated using GAUSS). Note that while the standard errors are basically unchanged, the treatment effect has approximately doubled. This doubling translates into a nearly 100% increase in the proportion of cases sanctioned. Note also that the $t$ value is now well over 2.00. However, while the autoregressive coefficient has increased substantially, it is still not much larger than its standard error.

Taking the point values of all of the regression coefficients seriously for the moment, Figure 7.11 shows the goodness of fit. Clearly, the impact of the residuals for sixth and seventh quarters has been significantly reduced under the linear objective function. The result is lower estimates of the pretest predicted values leading to a larger estimated increment during the posttest period.

Figure 7.12 shows the bootstrapped sampling distribution for the treatment coefficient, based on 1,000 bootstrap samples. The distribution shows some skewing to the right, which, as noted earlier, is not surprising given the distributions of the theft and drug proportions; the right tail and left shoulder are heavy. Yet, because the distribution falls off more quickly on the high end, the mean, mode, and median are about the same (about .16). Ninety-five percent of the estimates fall between .03 and .33, which defines the 95% confidence interval, and 99.2% of

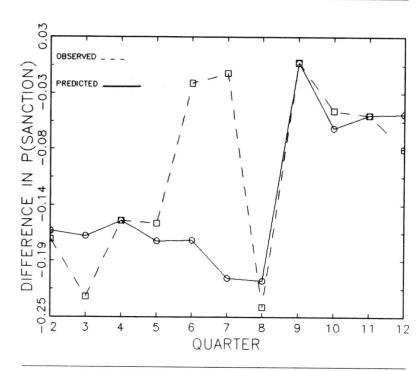

**Figure 7.11  Cases sanctioned.**

the estimates are above 0. Clearly, it is very unlikely that there is no posttest increment.

The story could have been different under conventional inference. If the *t* distribution had been applied (given the small sample size), the 95% confidence interval would have been between −.02 and .30. Under a two-tailed test, therefore, one would have failed to reject at the .05 level the null hypothesis of no treatment effect. However, the treatment effect would have been statistically significant at the .05 level for a one-tailed test.[20]

To summarize, there was ample reason to be suspicious about the OLS estimates. Because of the quadratic objective function, large residuals immediately before the intervention could have been distorting the results. LAR regression, coupled with bootstrapping, led to more plausible estimates of the treatment effect and to the conclusion that

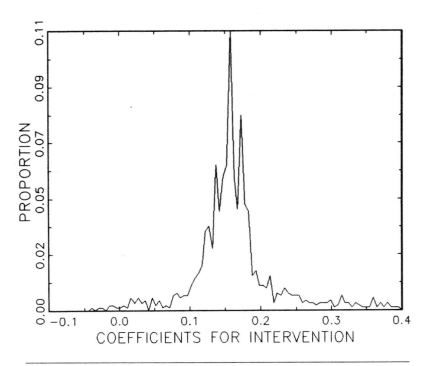

**Figure 7.12  Distribution of estimates.**

sanctioning increased after the program was initiated. At the same time, attribution of cause is always fraught with risk, and it was only after considering a range of other possible explanations for the posttest increase that policy recommendations were made (Greenspan et al., 1988).

## CONCLUSIONS

Choosing a proper regression estimator requires that a pair of complementary judgments be made: What objective function makes substantive sense, and what estimator(s) has the best statistical properties? When the quadratic objective function makes substantive sense and when the normal distribution is closely approximated by the observed disturbance distribution, one has, regardless of sample size, the best of all possible worlds: convenient least squares estimators with excellent statistical properties that match the questions being asked. With large samples, one is able, as a fallback, to capitalize on a number of handy asymptotic properties, even if the observed disturbance distribution is a long way from normal.

However, estimators relying on the quadratic form are fragile, and one may be seriously misled when other objective functions are more appropriate. Moreover, in the presence of outliers, least squares regression may lead one astray. Finally, least squares estimators may be well short of optimal, especially in small samples, if the observed disturbance distribution is not normal.

Given the widespread availability of cheap computing and the relative ease of computing M-estimators, M-estimators should be applied, at least as a supplement to OLS, whenever there is any doubt about OLS. When M-estimators and OLS (which, technically, is also an M-estimator) produce the same substantive story, all may be well. When they differ, the data must be carefully examined for these reasons. It should then be possible to make an informed decision about which set of results is most plausible.

More generally, there is an enormous gap between what sociologists know and what sociologists need to know to use properly the rich set of tools statisticians have provided. To meet the assumptions required for instructive statistical analyses, sociologists must have a reasonably accurate understanding of the substantive phenomena in question and have access to data sets unsullied by significant measurement and design errors. In other words, the data need to be an accurate reflection of some underlying social process whose general properties are known. Stated in these bald terms, it should be apparent that, in principle, almost all quantitative research in sociology is suspect and that statistical analyses of sociological data should be designed from a robust perspective. In practice, this means being very cautious about what may be learned from a given data set and regularly applying techniques that minimize the risk of being seriously misled. Routine application of a robust perspective could dramatically improve quantitative research in sociology.

# NOTES

1. There are, however, important differences of opinion about the relative merits of robust estimators, and as further developments occur, the comparative advantages of different estimators may change. For example, Koenker and Portnoy (1987) have recently proposed a very interesting L-estimator for linear regression that asymptotically is the same as the Huber M-estimator (see below), but, unlike the Huber M-estimator, is scale invariant. For an interesting set of exchanges on such issues, see Draper (1987) and the comments that follow.

2. Fortunately, excellent discussions can be easily found elsewhere (e.g., Hampel et al., 1986; Li, 1986; Wu, 1985). Especially interesting are "generalized" M-estimators (Hampel et al., 1986, chap. 6; Li, 1985; Welsch, 1980) and certain S-estimators (Rousseeuw & Leroy, 1987) that address the impact of deviant values among one's *explanatory* variables as well as the impact of deviant residuals. I will have more to say about this issue below.

3. Since the "objective" of least squares procedures is to minimize the sum of the squared residuals, the function that does this is called an *objective function.*

4. It is also easy to show that M-estimators are a *slight* generalization of conventional maximum likelihood estimators (Hampel, 1986, p. 36). The M in M-estimator refers to its maximum likelihood roots.

5. These were drawn from a rectangular distribution, but any set of values covering a reasonable range would suffice. The distribution of the input to the objective function is irrelevant to the shape of its output.

6. The mean is the location measure that minimizes the sum of the squared deviation scores. The median is the location measure that minimizes the sum of the absolute values of the deviation scores. In effect, therefore, ordinary least squares regression fits a set of conditional means to the data while least absolute value regression fits a set of conditional medians. Consequently, many of the comparative merits of means and medians carry over to the two regression generalizations.

7. Where one sets the cutoff point is basically a judgment call, although there are diagnostics that may help.

8. Both the bi-square and Bell estimators belong to a class of "redescending" estimators because the derivative of the objective function, $\psi(t)$, first increases and then decreases to zero. There are also location estimators that give no weight whatsoever to deviation scores beyond a certain size by literally dropping them from the analysis. However, these are not M-estimators. The "trimmed mean" is one example (Rosenberger & Gasko, 1983, pp. 307-312).

9. The discussion that follows on desirable properties of M-estimators borrows heavily from Wu's excellent exposition (1985, pp. 325-327, 344-356).

10. As with all maximum likelihood estimators, one must assume that for the observed distribution in question (e.g., for the particular response variable), each observation behaves as if it were randomly and independently sampled from a particular distribution. However, this is not as restrictive as it might seem because the independence is *conditional* upon the values of the distribution's parameters and whatever conditioning variables are being used. In the case of linear regression, for example, the independence is found in the disturbance term (not the dependent variable per se), which represents the *conditional* distribution of the dependent variable around the regression hyperplane.

11. Technically, resistance requires that the derivative of the objective function ($\psi(t)$) be continuous and bounded. While the derivative of the objective function for the LAR estimator is discontinuous (at zero), the discontinuity is unimportant in practice.

12. One alternative, *bounded influence regression*, is briefly described in Li (1985, pp. 324-328). A major drawback is that the breakdown point is a decreasing function of the number of explanatory variables; in the very instances when the opportunities for outliers are great, the breakdown point is relatively low (Rousseeuw & Leroy, 1987, p. 13). Another alternative is "least median of squares" regression, which minimizes the median of the squared residuals instead of the sum. While least median of squares regression has a high breakdown point (indeed, it achieves the theoretical maximum of 50%, it gives up some efficiency (Rousseeuw & Leroy, 1987, sect. 4). Still, one must keep in mind that efficiency is calculated with respect to a particular distribution, typically the normal, and the relative efficiencies of estimators can easily change if the assumed distribution is incorrect. An unusually clear exposition of these issues can be found in Rousseeuw and Leroy (1987), and software for their preferred estimators is easily obtained from the authors.

13. Readers with good statistical backgrounds and a particular interest in efficiency might well want to work through Chapter 6 in Hampel et al. (1986). However, it is not clear to me that much of genuine practical significance will be learned.

14. This is especially important in applied work. See, for example, Berk and Cooley (1987) and Berk (1988).

15. Some software have routines designed especially for certain M-estimators. For example, SAS has a procedure for LAR regression, and PC-ISP has procedures for LAR and Huber regression estimators. PROGRESS does least median squares regression and trimmed estimator via weighted least squares.

16. This is because the second derivative of the objective function is not defined. Put another way, the underlying disturbance distribution (the Laplace distribution) is not continuous. Bootstrap methods are employed below.

17. Theft cases were chosen because they are common and in some ways similar to drug cases. But the basic point is that the program was directed at drug cases and not theft cases. Time trends that both share, therefore, cannot be attributed directly to the program.

18. The differencing is identical to inserting into a regression analysis a dummy variable for every time period but one, which is common in analyses of pooled cross-sectional and time series data within an analysis of covariance perspective (Hsiao, 1986, pp. 29-32). It is also closely related to the notion of cointegration for time series data (Granger & Newbold, 1986, pp. 224-226). Note that differencing does not assume a constant disparity between the two series. Shared effects that vary over time are removed.

19. There is a tendency for iteratively reweighted least squares, when applied to LAR regression, to produce one estimated residual very close to zero. Should this cause the software to abort before convergence is reached, a vary small number (e.g., .00001) can be added to each estimated residual.

20. Recall that the events making up the proportions are unlikely to be independent and the proportions themselves are unlikely to be independent. Thus conventional significance tests comparing, for example, the pretest differences in proportions against the posttest differences in proportions (McNemar, 1962, pp. 86-88) would have been technically incorrect and could not have been taken literally. In all fairness, however, almost any reasonable discounting of $t$ values would have suggested a statistically significant treatment effect.

# REFERENCES

Amemiya, T. (1985). *Advanced econometrics*. Cambridge, MA: Harvard University Press.

Barnett, V., & Lewis, T. (1978). *Outliers in statistical data*. New York: John Wiley.

Belsley, D. A., Kuh, E., & Welsch, R. E. (1980). *Regression diagnostics*. New York: John Wiley.

Berk, R. A. (1988). The role of subjectivity in criminal justice classification and prediction methods. *Criminal Justice Ethics, 7*, 35-46.

Berk, R. A., & Cooley, T. F. (1987). Errors in forecasting social phenomena. *Climatic Change, 11*, 247-265.

Cinlar, E. (1975). *Introduction to stochastic processes*. Englewood Cliffs, NJ: Prentice-Hall.

Colin, A. C., & Trivedi, P. K. (1986). Econometric models based on count data: Comparison and applications of some estimators and tests. *Journal of Applied Econometrics, 1*, 29-53.

Cook, R. D., & Weisberg, S. (1982). *Residuals and influence in regression*. New York: Chapman & Hall.

Draper, D. (1987). Rank-based robust analysis of linear models. *Statistical Science, 3*(2), 239-258.

Efron, B. (1982). *The jackknife, the bootstrap and other resampling plans*. Philadelphia: Society for Industrial and Applied Mathematics.

Efron, B., & Tibshirani, R. (1986). Bootstrap methods for standard errors, confidence intervals, and other measures of statistical accuracy. *Statistical Science, 1*, 54-77.

Granger, C.W.J., & Newbold, P. (1986). *Forecasting economic times series*. Orlando, FL: Academic Press.

Greenspan, R., Berk, R. A., Feeley, M. M., & Skolnick, J. H. (1988). *Courts, probation, and street crime: Final report on the targeted urban crime narcotics task force*. Berkeley, CA: Center for the Study of Law and Society.

Hampel, F. R., Ronchetti, E. M., Rousseeuw, P. J., & Stahel, W. A. (1986). *Robust statistics*. New York: John Wiley.

Hsiao, C. (1986). *Analysis of panel data*. New York: Cambridge University Press.

Huber, P. J. (1977). *Robust statistical procedures*. Philadelphia: Society for Industrial and Applied Mathematics.

Huber, P. J. (1981). *Robust statistics*. New York: John Wiley.

Koenker, R., & Portnoy, S. (1987). Comment. *Statistical Science, 3*(2), 259-261.

Leamer, E. E. (1983). Let's take the con out of econometrics. *American Economics Review, 73*, 31-43.

Li, G. (1985). Robust regression. In D. C. Hoaglin, F. Mosteller, & J. W. Tukey (Eds.), *Exploring data tables, trends, and shapes*. New York: John Wiley.

McCullagh, P., & Nelder, J. A. (1983). *Generalized linear models*. New York: Chapman & Hall.

McNemar, P. (1962). *Psychological statistics* (3rd ed.). New York: John Wiley.

Mosteller, R., Fienberg, S. E., & Rourke, R.E.K. (1985). *Beginning statistics with data analysis*. Reading, MA: Addison-Wesley.

Mosteller, R., & Tukey, J. W. (1977). *Data analysis and regression*. Reading, MA: Addison-Wesley.

Rosenberger, J. L., & Gasko M. (1983). Comparing location estimators: Trimmed means, medians, and trimean. In D. C. Hoaglin, F. Mosteller, & J. W. Tukey (Eds.), *Understanding robust and exploratory data analysis* (pp. 297-338). New York: John Wiley.

Rousseeuw, P. J., & Leroy, A. M. (1987). *Robust regression & outlier detection*. New York: John Wiley.

Stone, M. (1988). Quetelet and the poetry of statistical conjecture. *Chance, 1*, 10-16.

Welsch, R. E. (1980). Regression sensitivity analysis and bounded-influence estimation. In J. Kmenta & J. B. Ramsey (Eds.), *Evaluation of econometric models* (pp. 153-167). New York: Academic Press.

Wu, L. L. (1985). Robust M-estimation of location and regression. In N. B. Tuma (Ed.), *Sociological methodology 1985* (pp. 316-388). San Francisco: Jossey-Bass.

# 8

---

# AN INTRODUCTION TO
# BOOTSTRAP METHODS
## Examples and Ideas

### Robert Stine

The bootstrap is an *approach* to estimating sampling variances, confidence intervals, and other properties of statistics. Just as maximum likelihood refers to an estimation strategy rather than to any specific estimator, bootstrapping is a methodology for *evaluating* statistics based on an appealing paradigm. This paradigm arises from an analogy in which the observed data assume the role of an underlying population. As a result, bootstrap variances, distributions, and confidence intervals are obtained by drawing samples from the sample.

Data analysis seeks answers to questions such as "Does a new drug cure more people than the old one?" or "What factors affect how someone votes in an election?" Statistical answers to such questions require models that characterize the random behavior of observed factors. Estimates of the model arise from observed data and lead to description or inference. The importance of the bootstrap lies in this inferential step: The bootstrap gives standard errors and confidence intervals that are typically better than alternatives that rely on untested assumptions. The flexibility of the bootstrap gives the data analyst the freedom to choose statistics whose standard errors would otherwise be difficult to measure. The bootstrap offers reliability and brings new insights to some of the difficult problems of data analysis.

Bootstrap calculations are typically computationally demanding. The bootstrap replaces difficult mathematics with an increase of several orders of magnitude in the computing needed for a statistical analysis. Rather than computing one or two sets of regression coefficients, bootstrapping easily entails several thousand. The computing demands of the bootstrap made such a strategy unthinkable until recently (Efron, 1979a). This trend toward greater use of computers can be expected to continue. As Tukey (1986) put it "In a world in which the price of calculation continues to decrease rapidly, but the price of theorem proving continues to hold steady or increase, elementary economics indicates that we ought to spend a larger and larger fraction of our time on calculation" (p. 74).

### The Key Ideas: Bootstrapping the Mean

The problem of estimating the variance of a sample mean illustrates the basic ideas. This friendly context permits the introduction of new topics without the added complexity of intricate statistical methods. The example also introduces some needed notation.

Probability distributions play a large role in the bootstrap. First let $X = (x_1, x_2, \ldots, x_n)$ denote a random sample of size n from the same population with mean $\mu$ and variance $\sigma^2$. If we let $F$ denote the cumulative distribution function of the population, then $F(x) = \Pr(x_i < x)$. In this notation, each $x_i$ is a random variable having the cumulative distribution $F$, which is abbreviated $x_i \sim F$. Very often the population is assumed to be Gaussian (or normal), in which case $F(x)$ is the function that appears in tables at the back of many statistics texts.

The sample-to-sample variation of the sample average is well known. If $\bar{x} = \Sigma \, x_i/n$ denotes the sample mean, then its variance is

$$\text{VAR}(\bar{x}) = \Sigma \, \text{VAR} \, (x_i) \, / \, n^2 = \sigma^2 / \, n.$$

When $\sigma^2$ is not known, the sample variance $s^2 = \Sigma(x_i-\bar{x})^2/(n-1)$ replaces it, giving the familiar estimator $\text{var}(\bar{x}) = s^2/n$. How well $\text{var}(\bar{x})$ estimates $\text{VAR}(\bar{x})$ depends on how close the distribution of the $x_i$ is to being Gaussian with variance $\sigma^2$; the distribution does not need to drift far for $\text{var}(\bar{x})$ to perform poorly.[1] Notice the notation: "VAR" written in upper case denotes the true variance, whereas "var" in lower case denotes an estimator of "VAR."

The bootstrap approach to estimating VAR($\bar{x}$) is suggested by thinking about what var($\bar{x}$) estimates: the variability of $\bar{x}$ across samples from the population with distribution $F$. In a *utopian setting* in which many samples from the population are available, formulas like that for var($\bar{x}$) are unnecessary because one could compute the mean of many samples and estimate its variability directly. Many samples from the same population are seldom available, however, for a variety of reasons ranging from temporal changes to financial hurdles (see Finifter, 1972, which also refers to resampling as bootstrapping). Although it is not possible to get many samples from the population described by $F$, it is possible to get repeated samples from a population whose distribution approximates $F$. This is the idea behind the bootstrap: Replace the unknown function $F$, which describes a population that cannot be resampled, with an estimator of $F$, which describes a population that can be sampled repeatedly.

Given a minimum of assumptions, the optimal estimator of $F$ is the *empirical distribution function* (EDF). For a sample of size $n$, the EDF is denoted $F_n$, and it is the cumulative distribution of the sample,

$$F_n(x) = \#(x_i \leq x)/n$$

where $\#(x_i \leq x)$ is the number of times that the inequality holds as $i$ ranges from 1 to $n$. Thus, $F_n(10)$ is the proportion of the $n$ sample observations that are less than or equal to 10. Unlike smooth distributions, such as the Gaussian, an empirical distribution has a "jump" at each observed value. For example, if the sample $X$ consists of the five observations (1, 3, 4, 5.5, 8), then $F_5(0.5) = 0$, because none of the $x_i$ are less than or equal to 0.5, and $F_5(5.5) = 4/5$. The jumps reflect the fact that only $n$ distinct values are possible from this approximation to the true population $F$. Figure 8.1 shows the empirical distribution and the underlying population distribution for a sample of 25 Gaussian observations. Generally, $F_n$ resembles $F$, but the jumps make it "rougher."

Given our willingness to approximate the population distribution $F$ by the empirical distribution $F_n$ two avenues are available for finding bootstrap variances. One is based on mathematics similar to those leading to var($\bar{x}$), and the second relies on simulation. The latter computational approach to the bootstrap is a Monte Carlo simulation in which a multitude of samples are drawn from the observed data rather

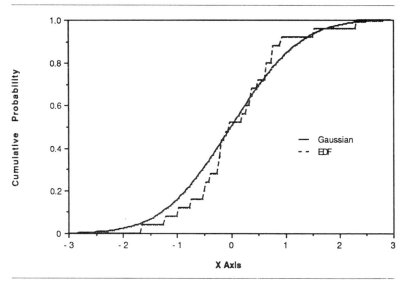

Figure 8.1  The empirical distribution of a sample of 25 observations tracks
the cumulative Gaussian but is rougher.

than from some hypothetical distribution. One draws repeated samples
of the same size as the observed sample *with replacement* from the data,
computes the mean of each such *bootstrap sample*, and then calculates
the variance of this set of means. This variance estimate replaces $\text{var}(\bar{x})$.
Because each bootstrap sample consists of $n$ observations that are drawn
with replacement from the data, each bootstrap sample typically omits
several observations and has multiple copies of others. If $n$ is 5, for
example, two bootstrap samples are $(x_4, x_1, x_3, x_4, x_2)$ and $(x_3, x_1, x_1,$
$x_5, x_3)$. In the following algorithm, a superscript "*" distinguishes
bootstrap quantities, as in $\text{var}^*$ and $\bar{x}^*$. The superscript b always ranges
from 1 to $B$, indexing the bootstrap samples. The bootstrap algorithm
for estimating the variance of $\bar{x}$ is:

(1) Use a random number generator to create *bootstrap samples of size n* by
    sampling *with replacement* from the observations. The $b$th bootstrap sample
    is denoted

$$X^{*(b)} = (x_1^{*(b)}, x_2^{*(b)}, \ldots, x_n^{*(b)})$$

where each $x_i^{*(b)}$ is a random selection from the original sample.

(2) Compute the mean $\bar{x}^{*(b)}$ from each of the bootstrap samples

$$\bar{x}^{*(b)} = \sum_{i=1}^{n} x_i^{*(b)}/n$$

(3) Use the B bootstrap means $\bar{x}^{*(1)}, \ldots, \bar{x}^{*(B)}$ to calculate the simulated *bootstrap variance estimate*

$$\mathrm{var}_B^*(\bar{x}) = \sum_{b=1}^{B} |\bar{x}^{*(b)} - \mathrm{avg}(\bar{x}^{*(b)})|^2/(B-1)$$

where
$$\mathrm{avg}(\bar{x}^{*(b)}) = \sum_{b=1}^{B} \bar{x}^{*(b)}/B$$

The number of bootstrap replications $B$ depends on the application, but for standard error estimates, $B \approx 100$ is generally sufficient. Because one can seldom draw every possible bootstrap sample, $\mathrm{var}_B^*(\bar{x})$ estimates the bootstrap variance of the mean, $\mathrm{VAR}^*(\bar{x})$, that we would get if $B$ were infinitely large.[2]

In the setting of the sample mean, we can mathematically derive $\mathrm{VAR}^*(\bar{x})$ without a computer simulation. Computer simulation is no more needed to find $\mathrm{VAR}^*(\bar{x})$ than to determine $\mathrm{VAR}(\bar{x})$. The mathematics are just like those leading to $\mathrm{VAR}(\bar{x}) = \sigma^2/n$, once we accept replacing the theoretical distribution $F$ with the empirical distribution $F_n$. In as much as the bootstrap samples are drawn with replacement from the observed sample, the empirical distribution function $F_n$ defined by the original data *is* the cumulative distribution of the bootstrap samples. Rather than having samples in which $x_i \sim F$, we have bootstrap samples in which $x_i^* \sim F_n$. Thus, the population distribution is known for the bootstrap samples, and various theoretical calculations are possible. For example, the expectation of an observation from the population with distribution $F$ is $E(x_i) = \mu$. Because $F$ is not known, we do not know this expectation. On the other hand, let $E^*$ denote expectation with respect to the bootstrap population that is defined by $F_n$. Because $F_n$ is known, we can find expectations such as $E^*(x_i^*)$.

To evaluate $E^*(x_i^*)$, recall that the expectation of a random variable is a weighted average of the possible values, with weights given by the probability of that value occurring. Under bootstrap resampling from $F_n$, each of the observed values $x_i, \ldots, x_n$ is equally likely to occur with probability $1/n$. Thus the expected value of a random draw from the population defined by $F_n$ (which is just a random draw from the original observations) is the sample mean

$$E^*(x_i^*) = x_1(1/n) + x_2(1/n) + \ldots + x_n(1/n) = \bar{x}$$

Just as $\mu$ is the mean of the theoretic population, $\bar{x}$ is the mean of the bootstrap population. Because the variance is also defined as an expectation, it too is a weighted average

$$VAR^*(x_i^*) = E^*\left[x_i^* - E^*(x_i^*)\right]^2$$

$$= (x_1 - \bar{x})^2(1/n) + (x_2 - \bar{x})^2 + \ldots + (x_n - \bar{x})^2(1/n)$$

$$= s_n^2$$

which is $n/(n-1)$ times the usual variance estimator.[3] The $x_i^*$ are drawn from the observations with replacement, so the $x_i^*$ are independent of each other, and the bootstrap variance of the sample mean is

$$VAR^*(\bar{x}^*) = \Sigma\, VAR^*(x_i^*)/n^2 = s_n^2/n,$$

which is almost the classical estimate of variance. For a large class of familiar statistics which includes certain regression models, simulation is not needed to obtain bootstrap variance estimates. (See the section on bootstrapping a regression model.)

Whether the bootstrap estimate is obtained by mathematics or simulation, the validity of bootstrap variance estimates requires that a key analogy holds for the statistic of interest. The key step of the bootstrap approach is to replace utopian sampling from the population defined by $F$ with bootstrap resampling from the data, the population defined by $F_n$.[4] When is this a reasonable thing to do? Clearly, it depends on $F_n$ being a good estimator of $F$. Without making other assumptions about the nature of the population, such as symmetry, $F_n$ is about the best we can do.[5] The key analogy is that the *resampling* properties of $\bar{x}^* - \bar{x}$ must be similar to the *sampling* properties of $\bar{x} - \mu$. This analogy does not hold for every statistic. Because the bootstrap does not always give the correct answer, it is important to recognize the limits of this methodol-

**Table 8.1** **Summary of Simulated Lengths and Coverages of 90% Confidence Intervals for the Mean Using 1,000 Samples of Size 20 from a Standard Gaussian Population**

| Method | Length | | Coverage |
|---|---|---|---|
| | *Average* | *Standard Deviation* | |
| Classical *t* | 0.761 | 0.12 | 0.90 |
| BS Percentile | | | |
| (*B* = 19) | 0.795 | 0.20 | 0.87 |
| (*B* = 99) | 0.719 | 0.13 | 0.88 |
| (*B* = 499) | 0.710 | 0.12 | 0.88 |

ogy, and some examples where it fails appear in the final section of this chapter.

### Bootstrap Distributions and Confidence Intervals

The utility of a variance estimate depends upon how well we can use that estimate to measure the uncertainty in a statistic. For example, a common approximation uses the interval [estimator ± 2(standard error of estimator)] as a confidence interval. Under certain conditions — such as the statistic being unbiased with a symmetric distribution, e.g., the Gaussian — this interval approximates a 95% confidence interval. Whether we obtain the standard error via traditional methods or the bootstrap, the interval requires certain assumptions.

The bootstrap distribution of the statistic permits a more direct approach. The idea is to use percentiles of the *bootstrap distribution* of $\bar{x}^*$, $G^*(x) = \mathrm{Pr}^*(\bar{x}^* \leq x)$ to determine a confidence interval. The 90% bootstrap percentile interval for $\mu$ is the interval that contains the middle 90% of the $B$ bootstrap means. Symbolically, this interval is $[G^{*-1}(0.05), G^{*-1}(0.95)]$, where $G^{*-1}(p)$ denotes the $p$th quantile of the distribution of $\bar{x}^*$.[6] Whereas $G^*$ is usually approximated by a simulation, we estimate it with $G_B^*(t) = \#\{\bar{x}^{*(b)} \leq t\}/B$. Again, $B$ denotes the number of simulated bootstrap samples. The approximate bootstrap interval is then $[G_B^{*-1}(0.05), G_B^{*-1}(0.95)]$, the interval formed by the $5^{th}$ and $95^{th}$ percentiles of the $B$ bootstrap means $\bar{x}^{*(1)}, \ldots, \bar{x}^{*(B)}$.

Table 8.1 compares the bootstrap 90% confidence intervals for the mean to the usual *t* interval. The population is Gaussian so that the *t* interval [ $\bar{x}+t(.05, n-1)$ $s/\sqrt{n}$, $\bar{x}+t(.95, n-1)s/\sqrt{n}$ ] is correct, where

$t(p,df)$ is the $p$th percentile of a $t$ distribution with $df$ degrees of freedom. The bootstrap interval is based on either $B = 19, 99,$ or $499$ bootstrap samples. The results in the table are from 1,000 simulated samples of size 20 from a standard Gaussian distribution with $\mu = 0$ and $\sigma = 1$. The coverage column for each interval is the proportion of the 1,000 intervals that included the true mean 0. Even with only 19 bootstrap samples, the bootstrap intervals nearly obtain the performance of the best interval in this case, that given by *knowing* that the data are from a Gaussian distribution. Because the standard error of the coverage estimates is roughly $\{(.1)(.9)/1000\}^{1/2} \approx 0.01$, the percentile intervals have coverage significantly less than 0.9. Increasing the number of bootstrap replications $B$ does little to improve the coverage, although it does lead to a shorter interval whose length is more stable from sample to sample. The slight lack in coverage and more variable length are the price we pay for not assuming a Gaussian distribution — a small cost given that data are seldom from a Gaussian distribution.

## Relationship to the Jackknife

Sample re-use methods such as the bootstrap are not entirely new, and perhaps the most well-known predecessor is the jackknife. The jackknife shares the goal of easily obtained, trustworthy variance estimates, but it relies on a less demanding computational algorithm. Rather than compute the statistic for a large collection of bootstrap samples from the original data, the jackknife relies on dividing the sample observations into, say, $S$ disjoint subsets, each having the same number of observations. The statistic of interest is then computed $S$ times, each time omitting one of the subsets. Rather than having perhaps 100 repetitions of the statistic, the jackknife requires at most $n$ when each subset consists of a single observation. Many overviews of the jackknife exist, such as that of Miller (1974) and the applications of Mosteller and Tukey (1977). A recent study of the theoretical properties of the jackknife and related methods appears in Wu (1986).

To illustrate the jackknife, consider again the problem of estimating the variance of $\bar{x}$. For this example, let each subset consist of one observation. Begin by computing the mean of $(x_2, x_3, \ldots, x_n)$, the $n-1$ observations left after removing $x_1$. Label the mean of these $n-1$ observations $\bar{x}_{(-1)}$. Then compute $\bar{x}_{(-2)}$, the mean of $(x_1, x_3, \ldots, x_n)$. Continuing in this fashion, the procedure leads to n "leave-one-out" means $\bar{x}_{(-1)}, \ldots, \bar{x}_{(-n)}$. The jackknife combines these to obtain its variance estimate. Unlike the bootstrap values $\bar{x}^{*(b)}$, which are independent of each other (conditional on the observed sample), the jackknife replicates $\bar{x}_{(-i)}$ are highly correlated; every pair of jackknife means has $n-2$ observations in common. By comparison, given the values in the sample, the bootstrap replicates $\bar{x}^*$ are conditionally independent of each other; two bootstrap samples may have no values in common. A further difference from the bootstrap lies in the sample size. The jackknife "samples" are of size $n-1$ rather than $n$. As a result, the jackknife variance expression includes an adjustment factor of $(1-1/n)$. The jackknife variance estimate is

$$\text{var}_{JK}(\bar{x}) = \frac{n-1}{n} \sum_{i=1}^{n} (\bar{x}_{(-i)} - \bar{x}_{(\cdot)})^2,$$

where $\bar{x}_{(\cdot)}$ is the average of $\bar{x}_{(-1)}, \ldots, \bar{x}_{(-n)}$.

Efron (1982) presents the bootstrap as a generalized framework encompassing the jackknife. For example, he shows that the jackknife estimate of variation is an approximation to the bootstrap estimate and agrees with the bootstrap in large samples for statistics such as the mean. Although such an embedding is possible, the jackknife takes a fundamentally different view of the possible replicates of the statistic. The jackknife treats them as a finite collection, whereas bootstrap resampling assumes that the replicates are a sample from a population of infinite size. As a result, the jackknife only uses at most $n$ values of the statistic, whereas the bootstrap considers a much larger collection.

The degree to which the bootstrap outperforms the jackknife (or vice versa) seems to depend on the degree to which the data are really independent observations from the same population. If some complex structure or correlation exists among the observations, a grouped jackknife may be more appropriate (Tukey, 1987). Notice also that the jackknife was never intended to be a method for estimating a distribution. The usual procedure for getting confidence intervals from the jackknife is to use the jackknife standard error in a modified $t$ interval, as described in the initial abstract of Tukey (1958).

### The Role of Mathematics

Most of the mathematical results about the bootstrap describe how it performs as the sample size grows. For example, one can show that the bootstrap variance estimates in regression approach the correct value as the sample size becomes arbitrarily large (Freedman, 1981). *Asymptotic*, or large sample, properties of a statistic are important theoretical results, but they are not always indicative of the performance of a statistic in applications. No one wants to use an estimator that is not consistent, and asymptotics are needed to determine such large sample properties. For data analysis, however, asymptotics are a guide that can often be unreliable when confronted with small samples and outlying values. Most asymptotic results describe how a statistic behaves under the best of circumstances: unlimited growth of the number of independent observations from the same population.

These assumptions suggest two questions to ask when assessing the relevance of asymptotics. First, How large a sample size is needed for the asymptotics to be useful? Some asymptotic results, such as the familiar Central Limit Theorem, are relevant even when the sample has only 30 observations. In fact, until recently, a commonly used method of using computers to generate samples from a normal distribution was to take the average of 12 uniformly distributed observations. Other asymptotic results require larger samples. For example, the asymptotics that lead to the standard error estimates in the section on applications in robust regression require larger samples than the 20 observations used there. The second question asks: Can a large sample really consist of independent observations from the same population? Such an abstraction is needed for the mathematics, but is unusual in practice. If it requires six months to gather the data for a large survey, then the underlying population may have changed over the course of the data collection (see Cook & Campbell, 1976).

## Overview of the Remaining Sections

The following section illustrates the bootstrap in regression and constitutes the bulk of this chapter. The section on bootstrap confidence intervals describes bootstrap confidence intervals in detail. The fourth section, on computing bootstrap estimates, contains advice, including deciding on how large to set the number of replications $B$. Finally, the fifth section suggests where resampling methodology is moving, including some adventurous applications. Other reviews of the bootstrap tend to focus on the question, Does the bootstrap work? (e.g., Diaconis & Efron, 1983; Efron, 1979b; Efron, 1982; Efron & Gong, 1983; Efron & Tibshirani, 1986). With some exceptions, this review begins with the premise that the bootstrap is a good idea and focuses on how to use it in data analysis, particularly regression.

## APPLICATIONS OF BOOTSTRAP RESAMPLING IN REGRESSION

Regression models remain at the heart of applied statistics. Robust estimation strategies and residual diagnostics have improved the usefulness of these techniques, and the bootstrap adds another dimension. After a quick review of the basic regression model, we describe two methods of bootstrap resampling. The nature of the data determines which alternative is appropriate. Modeling assumptions are very important with the regression model, and heteroscedasticity and serial correlation present problems that the bootstrap, if properly used, often handles better than classical methods. Once the model is chosen, the bootstrap also allows us to compare different estimation strategies, such as robust regression estimates to least squares. Some problems in structural equations also are easily handled with the bootstrap.

### Bootstrapping a Regression Model

In the usual regression model, $\mathbf{Y} = (y_1, y_2, \ldots, y_n)'$ denotes the $n \times 1$ vector of the response, and the $n \times k$ matrix of regressors is $\mathbf{X} = (\mathbf{x}_1, \mathbf{x}_2, \ldots, \mathbf{x}_n)'$, where the $k \times 1$ vector $\mathbf{x}_i$ denotes the regressors for the $i$th observation. The usual linear model is then

$$\mathbf{Y} = \mathbf{X}\,\beta + \varepsilon \text{ or } y_i = \mathbf{x}_i'\beta + \varepsilon_i, i = 1, \ldots, n \qquad (8.1)$$

where $\varepsilon$ is an $n \times 1$ vector of uncorrelated error terms having mean 0 and variance $\sigma^2$. The $k \times 1$ vector $\beta$ holds the unknown parameters, for which the ordinary least squares (OLS) estimator is

$$\hat{\beta} = (\mathbf{X}'\mathbf{X})^{-1}\,\mathbf{X}'\mathbf{Y} = \beta + (\mathbf{X}'\mathbf{X})^{-1}\mathbf{X}'\varepsilon. \qquad (8.2)$$

It follows that $\text{VAR}(\hat{\beta}) = \sigma^2\,(\mathbf{X}'\mathbf{X})^{-1}$. Because $\sigma^2$ is not usually known, $\text{VAR}(\hat{\beta})$ is estimated by

$$\text{var}(\hat{\beta}) = s^2(\mathbf{X}'\mathbf{X})^{-1} \qquad (8.3)$$

where $s^2$ is the unbiased variance estimator provided by the residuals $e_i = y_i - x_i' \hat{\beta}$, $i = 1, \ldots, n$

$$s^2 = (y_i - x_i' \hat{\beta})^2 /(n-k) = \Sigma\, e_i^2/(n-k).$$

Throughout this section, $s^2$ denotes this variance estimator, not the sample variance estimator of the introduction. A general reference on the theory of least squares estimation is Fox (1984).

Two methods exist for bootstrapping the regression model, and the choice of which to use depends upon the regressors. If the regressors are *fixed*, as in a designed experiment, then bootstrap resampling must preserve that structure. Each bootstrap sample should have the same regressors. On the other hand, regression models built from survey data typically have regressors that are as random as the response, and bootstrap samples should also possess this additional variation.

*Resampling with random regressors.* Bootstrapping regression models with *random* regressors follows the strategy of the introduction. Let the $(k+1) \times 1$ vector $z_i = (y_i, x_i')'$ denote the values associated with the $i$th observation. Just as in the case for bootstrapping $\bar{x}$, one samples with replacement from the observations. Only in this case, the set of observations are the vectors $(z_1, \ldots, z_n)$ rather than a set of scalar values. The three steps of the random regressor algorithm are:

(1r) Draw a bootstrap sample $(z_1^{*(b)}, z_2^{*(b)}, \ldots z_n^{*(b)})$ from the observations and label the elements of each vector

$$z_i^{*(b)'} = (y_i^{*(b)}, x_i^{*(b)'})'.$$

From these form the vector $Y^{*(b)} = (y_1^{*(b)}, y_2^{*(b)}, \ldots, y_n^{*(b)})'$ and the matrix $X^{*(b)} = (x_1^{*(b)'}, x_2^{*(b)'}, \ldots, x_n^{*(b)'})$.

(2r) Calculate the OLS coefficients from the bootstrap sample:

$$\hat{\beta}^{*(b)} = (X^{*(b)'}X^{*(b)})^{-1}\ X^{*(b)'}Y^{*(b)}$$

In a very small sample, the matrix $(X^{*(b)'}X^{*(b)})$ might be singular and would necessitate drawing a new sample.

(3r) Repeat steps 1 and 2 for $b = 1, \ldots, B$, and use the resulting bootstrap estimates $\hat{\beta}^{*(1)}, \hat{\beta}^{*(2)}, \ldots, \hat{\beta}^{*(B)}$ to estimate variances or confidence intervals. The bootstrap estimate of the covariance matrix of $\hat{\beta}$ is

$$\text{var}_B{}^*(\hat{\beta}^*) = \sum_{b=1}^{B} d_b{}^* d_b{}^{*'}/(B-1) \tag{8.4}$$

where the vector of deviations is $d_b{}^* = \hat{\beta}^{*(b)} - \text{avg}(\hat{\beta}^{*(b)})$, $b = 1, \ldots, B$.

The effect of sampling the $z_i$ is to keep the response $y_i$ of a given observation paired with the regressors $x_i$ of that observation.[7]

*Resampling with fixed regressors.* When the regression model has fixed regressors, the resampling should preserve the structure of the design matrix. For example, suppose $X$ defines a balanced two-way analysis of variance for an experiment or consists of polynomial time trends. If random resampling is used, $X^*$ would not likely possess the needed structure: The ANOVA design would be unbalanced and the polynomial time trends would have gaps and clusters. In regression models in which $X$ is fixed, each utopian sample has the same design. Bootstrap samples need this same characteristic. The algorithm that produces this behavior is not as straightforward as that for the random design and relies on regression residuals. It is, however, more computationally efficient. The change in the preceding algorithm occurs in the first step, which defines how the bootstrap samples are generated. The second step reveals the computational advantage. The steps are:

(1f) Compute the bootstrap samples by adding *resampled residuals* onto the least squares regression fit, holding the regression design fixed:

$$Y^{*(b)} = X \hat{\beta} + e^{*(b)}$$

where the $n \times 1$ vector $e^{*(b)} = (e_1{}^{*(b)}, e_2{}^{*(b)}, \ldots, e_n{}^{*(b)})'$, and each $e_i{}^{*(b)}$ is a random draw from the set of n regression residuals.

(2f) Obtain least squares estimates from the bootstrap sample:

$$\hat{\beta}^{*(b)} = (X'X)^{-1}X'Y^{*(b)}$$
$$= \hat{\beta} + (X'X)^{-1}X'e^{*(b)}.$$

Because $(X'X)^{-1}$ appears in every $\hat{\beta}^{*(b)}$, only one matrix inverse is needed. Also, the second line shows that one need never explicitly form $Y^*$.

(3f) Repeat steps (1) and (2) for $b = 1, \ldots, B$, and proceed as in (3r).

In contrast to the random regressor model, this resampling approach generates $Y^*$ by adding samples of the residuals to the fitted equation $X \hat{\beta}$ rather than by resampling from the actual data.

The introduction of residuals raises important issues. Residuals are the product of a model imposed upon the data; their values depend upon the model that we choose. Ideally, one would like to be able to sample from the true population of errors. Because this population is unknown, the bootstrap resamples the residuals, even though least squares residuals are rather different from the true errors. In particular, residuals are neither independent nor identically distributed, even if the regression model is correct. The covariance matrix of the residual vector $\mathbf{e}$ is

$$VAR(\mathbf{e}) = VAR\{(\mathbf{I}-\mathbf{H})\varepsilon\} = \sigma^2(\mathbf{I}-\mathbf{H})$$

where the $\mathbf{I}$ is the $n \times n$ identity matrix and the projection or "hat" matrix $\mathbf{H}$ is

$$\mathbf{H} = \mathbf{X}(\mathbf{X}'\mathbf{X})^{-1}\mathbf{X}'. \tag{8.5}$$

Typically, $\mathbf{I}-\mathbf{H}$ has substantial off-diagonal elements and a nonconstant diagonal. Hence, in place of independent, constant variance errors, the bootstrap samples correlated heteroscedastic residuals.[8] The bootstrap succeeds in spite of these differences between residuals and true errors. The bootstrap vector $\mathbf{e}^*$ consists of independent errors with constant variance, *regardless* of the properties of the residuals. Bootstrap resampling from the residuals gives independent error terms with variance $(1-k/n) \, s^2$.[9] Inasmuch as the variance of the population defined by the residuals is too small, one can "fatten" the residuals by dividing each by a factor of $(1-k/n)^{1/2}$. Tukey (1987) heartily recommends such "degree-of-freedom" corrections, and these modifications are useful in contexts such as prediction intervals (Stine, 1985).

As in the case of the sample mean, we do not need simulation to find the bootstrap variance of $\hat{\beta}$ in the fixed regressor model. The mathematical derivation of the bootstrap variance mimics the usual derivation of $VAR(\hat{\beta})$. For models with fixed regressors, the bootstrap variance is (Efron, 1982, p. 36)

$$VAR^*(\hat{\beta}^*) = (1-k/n) \, s^2 \, (\mathbf{X}'\mathbf{X})^{-1},$$

differing only by a scale factor from $var(\hat{\beta})$. In fact, for any *linear statistic*, one can compute the bootstrap variance without computer simulation.[10]

### Effects of Outliers

So how do these resampling methods compare, how are they useful in data analysis, and which is better to use? The choice of which to use is easy to determine: Bootstrap resampling should always resemble the

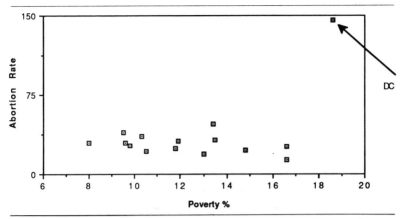

**Figure 8.2** Abortion rates and poverty in the east, with the District of Columbia being a large outlier.

original sampling procedure. Models having a fixed design lead naturally to bootstrapping with fixed regressors; those with a random design lead to random resampling. Although these two methods of resampling differ, it has been proven that the resulting differences become small as the sample size grows (Freedman, 1981). But with small samples, important differences emerge that must be understood if one is to make practical use of the bootstrap. In particular, because these methods differ in how they bind $y_i$ to $x_i$, they react differently to outliers.

Some ideas from regression diagnostics are needed for this discussion. The *leverage* of an observation in a regression model is a measure of how sensitive $\hat{\beta}$ is to changes in the response at that point. The leverage values $h_i, i = 1, \ldots, n$ are the diagonals of the projection matrix $\mathbf{H}$ (8.5) and $0 \leq h_i \leq 1$. A related measure is the *influence* of an observation, which indicates how much $\hat{\beta}$ changes when an observation is removed from the data. Influence combines the leverage and residual for an observation; the change in $\hat{\beta}$ when the ith observation is removed is $(\mathbf{X}'\mathbf{X})^{-1} x_i e_i /(1-h_i)$ (e.g., Fox, 1984, and Chapter 6, this volume).

An example illustrates the different effects of outliers. The scatterplot of Figure 8.2 shows the abortion rate per 1,000 women aged 18-44 versus the proportion of the population below the poverty level in the 14 Eastern coastal states as well as the District of Columbia. (The data are from Tables 104 and 712 of *The Statistical Abstract of the U.S., 1988.*) The outlier is the District of Columbia, which had an abortion rate of approximately 146 per 1,000 women in 1985. This observation

**Table 8.2  Estimated Least Squares and Robust Estimates with *t* values for a Linear Regression Model Fit to the Abortion Rate Data in Figure 8.2**

| Estimation Method | Intercept | Slope |
|---|---|---|
| Least squares, all data | −21.4 (−0.7) | +4.6  (1.8) |
| Lease squares, excluding DC | +41.8  (3.8) | −1.1 (−1.3) |
| Biweight, all data | +42.3  (4.5) | −1.2 (−1.7) |

is very influential in a simple regression of the abortion rate on the poverty percentage because it combines a large residual with high leverage. The high leverage is the result of D.C. having the largest poverty percentage (18.6%). Least squares and robust estimates for a simple linear model appear in Table 8.2. The least squares slope is positive if the outlier is included, suggesting to the hasty data analyst that higher poverty leads to higher abortion rates. Dropping D.C. suggests the opposite conclusion, although not very strongly. The robust fit resembles the least squares fit that omits D.C.

The two regression resampling methods differ considerably when applied to these data. Because the poverty percentage in these states is random and not experimentally controlled, random resampling is the correct method. When it is used, D.C. appears in about 64% of the bootstrap samples.[11] Because samples containing the District of Columbia give a positive slope and those without this observation usually give a negative slope, the estimates of the slope from bootstrap samples are sometimes positive and sometimes negative. The histogram of the bootstrap slopes based on $B = 500$ bootstrap samples in Figure 8.3 shows the resulting bimodal shape, with most of the slopes being positive.[12] In contrast, the method of fixed regressors samples the residuals and adds them to the least squares regression fit. Thus, the large residual for D.C. could appear at any (or even several) of the 15 observations in a bootstrap sample. By severing the tie between the large residual and high leverage point, residual resampling produces slope estimates whose histogram (also in Figure 8.3) is quite normal in appearance.

Neither bootstrap scheme "cures" the outlier problem, and they give different impressions of the effect of an outlier. Residual resampling spreads the effect of the outlier about the design, whereas random resampling keeps it localized as in the observed sample. Because the regressor in this problem is random, random resampling is appropriate. So then how are we to react to the bimodal shape of the histogram for

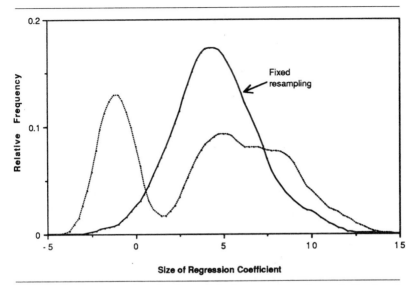

**Figure 8.3  Bootstrap distributions of the least squares slope via fixed and random resampling.**

the slope? It draws our attention to a problem in the regression model, and reveals how outliers affect the distribution of $\hat{\beta}$.[13]

### Bootstrapping with Heteroscedasticity

Because an outlier can be viewed as an observation with large variance, the preceding example suggests that the two resampling methods react differently in the presence of heteroscedasticity. If the errors are heteroscedastic and fixed resampling is used, random resampling of the residuals leads to bootstrap samples that are homoscedastic. Taking random draws from the residuals scatters the residuals around the design, giving bootstrap data sets that show no sign of heteroscedasticity. Random resampling of the observations preserves the heteroscedasticity. If $\text{VAR}(\varepsilon) = \sigma^2 \mathbf{D}$, where $\mathbf{D}$ is an $n \times n$ diagonal matrix with varying entries that reflect the presence of heteroscedasticity, then residual resampling leads to the variance estimate

$$\text{VAR}^*_{\text{fixed}}(\hat{\beta}) = v^2 (\mathbf{X}'\mathbf{X})^{-1}$$

where $nv^2 = E(\mathbf{e'e}) = \sigma^2$ trace $(\mathbf{I-H})\mathbf{D}$. Random resampling preserves the heteroscedasticity, and its bootstrap variance is approximately the correct answer

$$\text{VAR}^*_{\text{random}}(\hat{\beta}) \approx \sigma^2(\mathbf{X'X})^{-1}(\mathbf{X'DX})(\mathbf{X'X})^{-1}.$$

An extensive discussion of the effects of uncorrected heteroscedasticity on the bootstrap appears in Wu (1986, especially the discussion).

Now suppose that we have recognized the presence of heteroscedastic errors and want to do something about it. The broad validity of random resampling makes it preferable to the usual approach of estimating the variance of weighted least squares (WLS) estimators, assuming that the regressors of the bootstrap sample possess the sampling characteristics of those in the original data. If we continue with the assumption $\text{VAR}(\varepsilon) = \sigma^2\mathbf{D}$, then the optimal WLS estimator and its variance are (e.g., Fox 1984)

$$\hat{\beta}_W = (\mathbf{X'D^{-1}X})^{-1}\mathbf{X'D^{-1}Y}, \qquad (8.6)$$

$$\text{VAR}(\hat{\beta}_W) = \sigma^2(\mathbf{X'D^{-1}X})^{-1}.$$

In practice, however, one often uses estimators such as

$$\hat{\mathbf{b}}_W = (\mathbf{X'\hat{D}^{-1}X})^{-1}\mathbf{X'\hat{D}^{-1}Y}$$

for which the obvious variance estimator corresponding to (8.6) is

$$\text{var}(\hat{\mathbf{b}}_W) = s^2(\mathbf{X'\hat{D}^{-1}X})^{-1} \qquad (8.7)$$

where $\hat{\mathbf{D}}$ is estimated from the data. Thus $\hat{\beta}_W$ is the WLS estimator that requires that we know the variance structure in the matrix $\mathbf{D}$; $\hat{\mathbf{b}}_W$ is a practical approximation to $\hat{\beta}_W$ based on an estimate of $\mathbf{D}$. Unfortunately, the common variance estimator (8.7) is more an estimator of the variance of $\hat{\beta}_W$ than of $\text{VAR}(\hat{\mathbf{b}}_W)$ because it does not incorporate the estimation of $\mathbf{D}$, which is needed in $\hat{\mathbf{b}}_W$.

Bootstrap methods capture more of the uncertainty induced by the estimation of error variance structure. As an example, suppose that our data have several observations at each value of the regressor, and the variance increases with the regressor. The book-price data (from Table 369

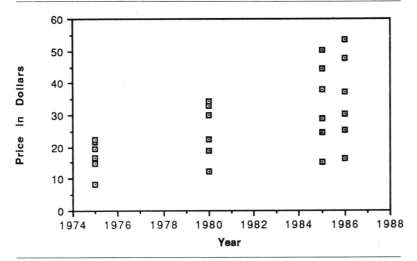

**Figure 8.4  Book prices are increasing and becoming more variable over time.**

of the *Statistical Abstract of the U.S., 1988*) in Figure 8.4 have this form. The average and variance of price increase over time. One model for these data is to assume that $\mathbf{D} = \text{diag}(d_1, d_1, d_1, d_1, d_1, d_1, d_2, d_2, \ldots, d_4)$. Because the error variances depend in some unknown fashion upon year, an iterative estimation strategy is needed:

(1) Use OLS to obtain residual estimates, $\mathbf{e} = \mathbf{Y} - \mathbf{X}\hat{\beta}$.
(2) Estimate the variance of the residuals at each value of the regressor, and estimate $\mathbf{D}$ with

$$\hat{d_i} = \sum_{j=1}^{6} (e_{ij} - \bar{e}_i)^2/5$$

where $e_{ij}$ is the $j$th residual at the $i$th design point and $\bar{e}_i$ is the average of the six residuals in that group.
(3) Form the estimator $\hat{b}_W = (\mathbf{X}'\hat{\mathbf{D}}^{-1}\mathbf{X})^{-1} \mathbf{X}'\hat{\mathbf{D}}^{-1}\mathbf{Y}$.
(4) If the difference of $\hat{b}_W$ from the previous estimate of $\beta$ is small, terminate the calculations. Otherwise, continue with step 5.
(5) Compute the residuals associated with the most recent estimate of $\beta$, $\mathbf{e} = \mathbf{Y} - \mathbf{X}\hat{b}_W$, and return to step 2.

Each iteration attempts to obtain more accurate error estimates and use these to get a better idea of the error covariances. Applying this procedure to the book-price data gives the slope estimate 1.62. The nominal WLS variance estimator $s^2(X'\hat{D}^{-1}X)^{-1}$ on the first line of Table 8.3 ignores the estimation of $D$, and one suspects that this estimate is too small. By comparison, the bootstrap variance on line two of the table is 23% larger. Because the bootstrap estimate of variance incorporates the estimation of $D$, it seems to be a better estimate of variation than that from the traditional procedure. This bootstrap variance is obtained by repeating the preceding algorithm on 20 bootstrap samples using the following variant of random resampling. Inasmuch as errors in different years have different variances, we resample within each group. Each bootstrap sample thus has six observations at each of four years, preserving this structural feature of the original data.

It remains to be determined whether either of these variance estimates is accurate, and the bootstrap is one of three approaches to answering this question. Mathematical expressions would be best, but the iterative nature of $\hat{b}_W$ suggests that this approach is unlikely to yield easily interpreted results without a host of assumptions. Alternatively, we could perform a simulation in which we estimate the variation of $\hat{b}_W$ across simulated samples, and compare this variation to the average of the nominal variance estimates (8.7). However, we have to decide what distribution to sample. But the bootstrap is a procedure for evaluating statistics, and the bootstrap variance estimate is a statistic. So why not bootstrap the bootstrap? The amount of calculation becomes intimidating, but the strategy of using the bootstrap to evaluate itself is appealing and avoids the troublesome choice of what distribution to sample. Keep in mind that the bootstrap estimate of the variance of $\hat{b}_W$ is a statistic like any other, although it takes a bit more calculation to obtain. The nested computations proceed as follows:

(1)  Draw $B_1$ bootstrap samples $(Y^*, X^*)^{(j)}, j = 1, \ldots, B_1$, from the original data. For each sample, estimate the variance of $\hat{b}_W$ using the WLS expression (8.7). Denote these estimates $\text{var}_{wls}^{(j)}, j = 1, \ldots, B_1$.

(2)  For each of the $B_1$ initial bootstrap samples:

    (2a)  Draw $B_2$ bootstrap samples from $(Y^*, X^*)^{(j)}$ and label these $(Y^{**}, X^{**})^{(jb)}, b = 1, \ldots, B_2$.

    (2b)  Estimate $\hat{b}_w^{**(jb)}$ from each of the $B_2$ samples $(Y^{**}, X^{**})^{(jb)}$. Compute the variance of the collection $\hat{b}_W^{**(jb)}$ as in (4), and denote this variance estimate $\text{var}_{B2}^{*(j)}$.

**Table 8.3  Standard Error Estimates for the Slope of the Regression Line Fit to the Heteroscedastic Book-Price Data of Figure 8.4**

| Method of Estimation | Standard Error |
|---|---|
| (1) WLS estimate $s^2 (\mathbf{X}'\hat{\mathbf{D}}^{-1}\mathbf{X})^{-1}$ | 0.39 |
| (2) Bootstrap, $B = 20$ | 0.48 |
| (3) Iterated WLS | 0.36 |
| (4) Iterated bootstrap | 0.47 |

(3)  Compare the average WLS estimate to the average bootstrap estimate:

$$\text{average nominal WLS std. error: } \{\Sigma_j \text{ var}_{wls}^{(j)}/B_1\}^{1/2},$$

$$\text{average bootstrap std. error: } \{\Sigma_j \text{ var}_{B2}^{*(j)}/B_1\}^{1/2}.$$

Because we are sampling the population defined by the observed sample, the correct answer *is* the original bootstrap estimate given on line 2 of Table 8.3; that is, 0.48 *is* the standard error of the slope estimate when sampling from the population defined by the original data. The results of step 3 are on lines 3 and 4 of Table 8.3 with $B_1 = 100$ and $B_2 = 20$. The average 0.36 of the WLS estimates is too small; the estimation of **D** adds a substantial amount to the variance of the slope estimator. On the other hand, the average of the bootstrap samples 0.47 is quite close to the target value, 0.48.[14]

### Applications in Robust Regression

The notion of using the bootstrap to estimate variances of iterative estimators such as $\hat{\mathbf{b}}_W$ suggests applications in robust regression. Bootstrap methods share the intent of robust statistics, albeit with a different slant. Robust statistical methods provide nearly optimal parameter estimates under a variety of broad conditions. Bootstrap methods reduce the need for tenuous assumptions, but concentrate on evaluating an estimator rather than defining it. Bootstrapping does not produce robust estimators, but it can suggest how robust an estimator is. For a well-motivated introduction and overview of robust methods, see Hampel et al. (1986; Chapter 7, this volume).

In robust regression, outlying observations are downweighted so that the regression captures the pattern in the majority of data rather than tracks outliers. The downweighting is accomplished by using an iterative reweighting scheme not too different from that used to obtain $\hat{\mathbf{b}}_W$.

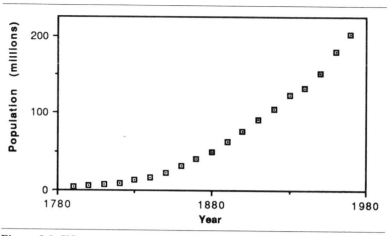

Figure 8.5   US population shows quadratic growth.

The weights are chosen by a variety of schemes, such as the *biweight* used here. Asymptotic methods exist for estimating the variances of robust regression coefficients, and one must take care to allow for the variability in the weighting process (Street et al., 1988). The bootstrap is also a valid procedure for estimating the variance of common robust estimators (Shorack, 1982).

Our example of bootstrapping a robust regression utilizes a quadratic model for the growth of the U.S. population, which appears in Figure 8.5. Despite a high $R^2$, the last few observations do not fit this model well and have relatively large, highly leveraged residuals. (This deviation from the model suggests the presence of specification error: A variable that is not included in this simple model assumes an important role in the later data.) These later points lead to the difference shown in Table 8.4 between the coefficients of the OLS fit and a robust fit. In both quadratic models, the regressor (time) is centered and rescaled to run from −1 to 1. The slope estimates are similar, but the differences are large relative to the estimated standard errors. The difference between the coefficients of the linear term in the model is 1.8, which is more than four standard errors of the robust estimator. Also, the robust estimator claims a standard error that is less than half that of the least squares estimator.

Table 8.4  Coefficients of Quadratic Models for the U.S. Population Growth Shown in Figure 8.5, Estimated by Least Squares and Robust Methods

|           | Coefficient | | |
| Estimator | Constant | Linear | Quadratic |
| --- | --- | --- | --- |
| OLS | 50.7 (0.96) | 97.1 (1.05) | 51.4 (1.93) |
| Robust | 51.1 (0.37) | 98.9 (0.40) | 52.8 (0.74) |

Table 8.5  Average and Standard Error of Bootstrap Replicates of the Least Squares and Robust Coefficients in Models for U.S. Population Growth (*B*=500).

|           | Coefficient | | |
| Estimator | Constant | Linear | Quadratic |
| --- | --- | --- | --- |
| OLS | 50.7 (0.90) | 97.0 (0.97) | 51.4 (1.79) |
| Robust | 51.1 (0.58) | 98.9 (0.73) | 52.6 (1.33) |

The bootstrap gives a different sense of how these estimators behave. We must use fixed resampling in this model because the regressors are time and time squared. Random resampling would yield bootstrap data sets with several observations at one year, and none at others. Fixed resampling preserves the rigid time progression of the original data and is the appropriate method. The average and standard error of the bootstrap results with $B = 500$ are in Table 8.5. The bootstrap results suggest that both coefficient estimators are unbiased for their expectations because the averages of the bootstrap coefficients approximate the original estimates. The bootstrap estimates of standard error are about the same as the usual OLS estimates. In fixed resampling, the bootstrap estimates of standard error of the coefficient estimators approach the usual least-squares values as $B$ grows large. The bootstrap estimates of standard error in Table 8.5, however, are much larger than asymptotic standard error estimates for the robust coefficients in Table 8.4; the sample size is perhaps too small for the asymptotics to be accurate. In both cases, however, the robust estimator has smaller variance than the OLS estimator.[15] The bootstrap distributions of the OLS and robust

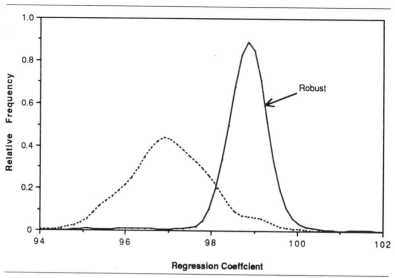

**Figure 8.6** Bootstrap distributions of estimated linear coefficients in OLS and robust regression fits.

linear coefficients in Figure 8.6 confirm these impressions: The distribution of the robust estimator is much more tightly concentrated than that of the OLS estimator.

A closer look at the bootstrap distribution of the robust estimator also suggests why its bootstrap standard error is so much larger than the asymptotic estimate. The bootstrap distribution of the robust estimator in Figure 8.6 is very peaked, but this figure conceals the tails of the distribution. The Gaussian quantile comparison plot in Figure 8.7 reveals that the tails of this distribution are much heavier than those of the Gaussian distribution. The asymptotic standard error is based on a Gaussian approximation to a sampling distribution. Because the robust estimator has a long-tailed distribution, this approximation is not very accurate. It is ironic that one typically sees such Gaussian properties as standard error applied to estimators like the biweight that do not show Gaussian behavior in small samples, an observation I owe to John Fox. A better comparison of these estimators would be in terms of a more robust estimator of variation, such as the hinge-spread. On the other hand, once standard errors are surrendered, it becomes quite hard to draw comparisons to traditional results.

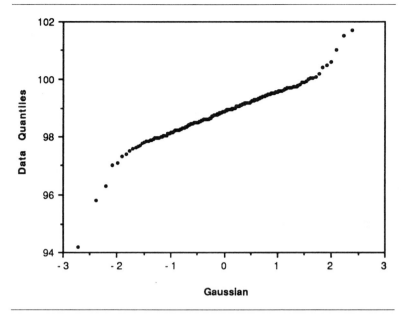

Figure 8.7 Quantile comparison plot of the bootstrap replications of the robust slope estimator reveals heavy tails.

## Structural Equation Models and the Bootstrap

Some of the more interesting features of path models are indirect effects. These measure the effect that one variable has upon another through other factors in the model. Because estimates of indirect effects are products of several regression coefficients, one cannot apply the usual least squares formulas. Some applications of indirect effects appear in Fox (1984).

One approach to estimating the distribution of an estimated indirect effects is to combine the *delta method* with a normal approximation. The delta method (Bishop et al., 1975) is based on the observation that it is easy to compute the variance of linear functions of statistics, such as $a+b\hat{\theta}$. The idea behind the delta method is to find a linear approximation to a statistic, and use this approximation to estimate the variance. Suppose $g(\hat{\theta})$ is a nonlinear function of the statistic $\hat{\theta}$, for example, $g(\hat{\theta}) = \log(\hat{\theta})$. To approximate the variance of $g(\hat{\theta})$, we estimate the variance of the linear approximation based on the derivative of $g$ at $\hat{\theta}$.

This approximation to $g(\hat{\theta})$ is $g(\theta)$ plus a slight change to reflect replacing $\theta$ by $\hat{\theta}$. The change in $g$ as the parameter changes from $\theta$ to $\hat{\theta}$ is estimated by the derivative of $g$ at $\theta$, $g'(\theta)$. The resulting approximation to $g(\hat{\theta})$ is then

$$g(\hat{\theta}) \approx g(\theta) + g'(\theta)(\hat{\theta} - \theta). \qquad (8.8)$$

For $g(\hat{\theta}) = \log(\hat{\theta})$, this approximation is $\log(\hat{\theta}) \approx \log(\theta) + (\hat{\theta} - \theta)/\theta$ because $g'(\theta) = 1/\theta$. In as much as $g(\theta)$ and $g'(\theta)$ are constants, the variance of $g(\hat{\theta})$ is approximately

$$\text{VAR}\{g(\hat{\theta})\} \approx g'(\theta)^2 \, \text{VAR}(\hat{\theta}). \qquad (8.9)$$

In practice, (8.9) is not useful because it requires evaluating the derivative at the true parameter and finding $\text{VAR}(\hat{\theta})$, both of which are usually unknown. Substituting $\hat{\theta}$ for $\theta$ and $\text{var}(\hat{\theta})$ for $\text{VAR}(\hat{\theta})$ in (8.9), one is led to the delta method variance approximation

$$\text{var}\{g(\hat{\theta})\} \approx g'(\hat{\theta})^2 \, \text{var}(\hat{\theta}). \qquad (8.10)$$

The accuracy of $\text{var}\{g(\hat{\theta})\}$ depends on three factors: the distance of $\hat{\theta}$ from $\theta$, the smoothness of the derivative that permits the switch from $g'(\theta)$ to $g'(\hat{\theta})$, and the accuracy of the initial approximation (8.8). In the simulations of Efron (1982: Table 5.2), standard errors from the delta method are too small, particularly for statistics such as the correlation.

Applying the delta method to indirect effects is not as easy as in the scalar case described above because $\hat{\theta}$ now consists of a vector of regression coefficients. As a result, the linear approximations (8.8), (8.9), and (8.10) require vector calculus. For example, if $\hat{\theta}$ denotes the vector of coefficient estimates from our model, then $g(\hat{\theta})$ is typically a product such as $\hat{\theta}_2$, $\hat{\theta}_4$, $\hat{\theta}_5$, and the scalar derivative becomes a vector of partial derivatives; details appear in Sobel (1982).

The bootstrap can also be applied to indirect effects. One simply forms the coefficient estimates from the various equations of the model and computes the indirect effect. Each equation in the model is bootstrapped $B$ times using the *same B* bootstrap samples for all of the equations. In the simple case of a recursive model (i.e., one with no feedback), the collection of bootstrap indirect effects is just the product of the bootstrapped regression coefficients from the several equations. Because the bootstrap regression estimates are based on the same $B$

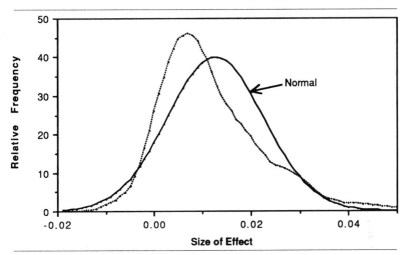

**Figure 8.8  Bootstrap and normal approximations to the distribution of an indirect effect in a small path model.**

bootstrap samples, the coefficient estimates are correlated across the equations, as they should be.

In general, the delta method and bootstrap give similar results for indirect effects. Bootstrap standard errors are generally larger than those from the delta method, with the size of the difference depending on the sample size. More importantly, however, the bootstrap can reveal skewness in the distribution of an estimated indirect effect. Because the delta method is teamed with a Gaussian distribution, it does not reveal asymmetries. The distributions in Figure 8.8 are the smoothed bootstrap and delta-method approximations to the distribution of an indirect effect in a small, recursive path model estimated from a sample of 50 observations (Bollen & Stine, 1988). The two distributions are similar, but the bootstrap suggests asymmetry that the normal approximation associated with the delta method cannot capture. In the same model with a larger sample size ($n=172$), the differences are quite small.

## BOOTSTRAP CONFIDENCE INTERVALS

A substantial body of recent research in statistics concerns bootstrap confidence intervals. Rather than bury the reader in the details of the most recent advances, this section displays the key ideas that underlie this research. This section begins with a quick overview of bootstrap $t$ intervals, which are a variation of intervals based on the classic $t$ statistic. Treatment of percentile intervals follows. Percentile intervals are closely related to the smoothed histograms of the bootstrap replications shown in the regression examples.

### Bootstrap t Intervals

Bootstrap $t$ intervals share the form of the classic $t$ interval, but do not require the Gaussian populations or the use of a $t$ table for critical values. Essentially, a new table constructed using bootstrap replications replaces the familiar $t$ table in each application. The case of a confidence interval for the mean of a Gaussian population illustrates the ideas.

The usual 90% confidence interval for the mean $\mu$ of a normal population based on a sample of size n is $[\bar{x} \pm t(.05, n-1) \, s/\sqrt{n}\,]$, where $t(\alpha, df)$ is the $\alpha$ percentile of Student's $t$ distribution with $df$ degrees of freedom and $s$ is the sample standard deviation. The validity of this interval (i.e., the reason that it really is a 90% confidence interval for $\mu$) relies upon the fact that

$$\Pr\{\sqrt{n}(\bar{x}-\mu)/s \leq t(\alpha, df)\} = \alpha, \quad 0<\alpha<1. \qquad (8.11)$$

The usual interpretation of the probability in (8.11) implies that the ratio $\sqrt{n}(\bar{x}-\mu)/s$ is less than the critical value $t(\alpha, df)$ in $100\alpha\%$ of the utopian collection of samples from the Gaussian population. The bootstrap $t$ interval is based in the same logic, and seeks an analogous value $t^*(\alpha; n)$ such that[16]

$$\Pr^*\{\sqrt{n}(\bar{x}^*-\bar{x})/sd_B^*(\bar{x}^*) \leq t^*(\alpha;n)\} = \alpha, \quad 0<\alpha<1 \qquad (8.12)$$

In (8.12) probabilities associated with bootstrap sampling from the data replace probabilities associated with sampling from the true population. This change replaces "Pr" in (8.11) with "Pr\*," which denotes the probability induced by bootstrap resampling from the empirical distribution $F_n$. Also, $sd_B^*(\bar{x}^*)$ is the bootstrap estimate of the standard deviation of the sample mean based on $B$ replications $\bar{x}^{*(1)}, \ldots, \bar{x}^{*(B)}$. Rather than find a percentile from the $t$ table, the bootstrap approach is to find it directly from the distribution of the ratio $(\bar{x}^*-\bar{x})/sd_B^*(\bar{x}^*)$. For example, the 90% bootstrap $t$ interval for $\mu$ is

$$[\bar{x}+t^*(.05; n) \times sd_B{}^*(\bar{x}^*),\ \bar{x}+t^*(.95; n) \times sd_B{}^*(\bar{x}^*)].$$

Finding $t^*(\alpha;n)$ requires simulation, as the mathematics quickly become intractable. Hall (1986a) gives an example of the mathematics involved.

To find $t^*(\alpha;n)$ requires a nested bootstrap simulation. Each iteration of the outer loop of the simulation generates a bootstrap replication of the pivot $R^* = (\bar{x}^*-\bar{x})/sd_B{}^*(\bar{x}^*)$. The required value of $t^*(\alpha;n)$ is the $\alpha$ percentile of the simulated collection of pivots. The inner loop is needed to find the bootstrap standard error estimate. The algorithm is:

(1) Draw $B_1$ bootstrap samples from the original observations and denote these by $X^{*(j)} = (x_1{}^{*(j)}, \ldots, x_n{}^{*(j)}), j = 1, \ldots, B_1$.
(2) For each of these $B_1$ bootstrap samples, estimate the standard deviation of the mean by bootstrapping:

    (2a) Draw $B_2$ bootstrap samples from $X^{*(j)}$ and label these

$$X^{*(jb)} = (x_1{}^{*(jb)}, \ldots, x_n{}^{*(jb)}), b = 1, \ldots, B_2$$

where $x_i{}^{*(jb)}$ is sampled with replacement from the observations in the sample $X^{*(j)}$.

    (2b) Estimate the mean $\bar{x}^{*(jb)}$ of each of the $B_2$ bootstrap samples $X^{*(jb)}$

    (2c) Compute $sd_{B2}{}^{*(j)}$ from the collection of bootstrap means

$$sd_{B2}{}^{*(j)}(\bar{x}^*) = [\sum_{b=1}^{B_2} (\bar{x}*^{(jb)} - \bar{x}*^{(j.)})^2 /(B_2 - 1)]$$

where $\bar{x}*^{(j.)}$ is the average of the $B_2$ bootstrap means.

(3) Form the bootstrap pivot $R^{*(j)} = (\bar{x}^{*(j)}-\bar{x}) / sd_{B2}{}^{*(j)}(\bar{x}^*)$ for each of the $B_1$ initial bootstrap samples.
(4) Use the collection of bootstrap pivots to obtain the desired percentiles

$$t^*(\alpha;n) = \alpha \text{ quantile of the } R^{*(j)}.$$

At the cost of much more calculation, one gains the freedom of not having to know the distribution of $\sqrt{n}\ (\bar{x}-\mu)/s$.[17]

Fortunately, only a relatively small simulation is needed to obtain the optimal level of accuracy. If the number of bootstrap samples $B_1$ in the outer loop of this nested simulation is roughly equal to the sample size, then the difference in coverage from performing an infinite amount of resampling is very slight. Such accuracy requires careful choice of the level $\alpha$. Because $B_1$ replications of the ratio $R^*$ divide the line into $B_1+1$ segments, $\alpha$ and $B_1$ should be chosen so that $\alpha = k/(B_1+1)$ for some positive integer $k$. For example, to get a 90% interval, the smallest satisfactory number of replications $B_1$ is 19 because these divide the line into 20 segments, each holding 5% of the probability. If $R_{(1)}^* \leq R_{(2)}^* \leq \ldots R_{(19)}^*$ are the ordered $R^{*(j)}$'s, then the lower endpoint of the bootstrap interval is $\bar{x} + R_{(1)}^* sd_B^*(\bar{x}^*)$ and the upper is $\bar{x} + R_{(19)}^* sd_B^*(\bar{x}^*)$. The cost of doing so little resampling lies in the length of the interval. Although the coverage accuracy of the interval is hardly affected by $B_1$, the length of the interval is. Doing too little resampling generally leads to intervals that are unnecessarily long (Hall, 1986b).

### Confidence Intervals for the Correlation

Building a confidence interval for the correlation of two random variables is neither so simple nor obvious as doing so for the mean. Many of the problems are suggested by the bootstrap distribution of the correlation of the law school data shown in Figure 8.9. These data appear in many of the Efron references (e.g., Efron, 1982) and are grade-point averages (GPA) and law school aptitude test (LSAT) scores from 15 U.S. law schools. The sample correlation is rather large, $r = 0.776$. The bootstrap distribution of the correlation ($B=1000$) shown in Figure 8.10 is skewed. Consequently, symmetric $t$ intervals are inaccurate. For example, an approximation to the standard error of $r$ is $SE(r) \approx (1-r^2)/(n-2)^{1/2}$, so that an approximate 90% interval for the population correlation $\rho$ is

$$[0.776 \pm 1.645 \times 0.115] = [0.776 \pm 0.189] = [0.587, 0.965].$$

The interval gives no indication of the skewness revealed in the bootstrap distribution and relies upon an unrealistic Gaussian approximation. In fact, the upper endpoint of the 95% interval (replace 1.645 with 1.96) is greater than 1. The approximation to $SE(r)$ also reveals a further complication: The variability of r depends on the value of $\rho$. The larger $\rho$ becomes, the less variable r is. Getting a better interval depends, in part, on how well one can transform the correlation into a statistic that has a normal distribution whose variance does not depend on the underlying parameter.

The required transformation in this case is Fisher's $z$ transformation, $\phi(r) = (1/2) \, ln\{(1+r)/(1-r)\}$. This transformation maps the range of the correlation $[-1, +1]$ onto the whole line, $-\infty < \phi(r) < +\infty$. In so doing, it removes much of the asymmetry seen in Figure 8.10. Also, the variance of $\phi(r)$ is approximately $1/(n-3)$, which does not depend upon $\rho$.

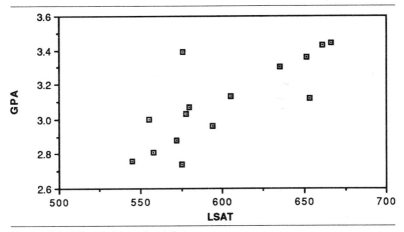

**Figure 8.9** Efron's law school data.

Because the distribution of $\phi(r)$ is more nearly a Gaussian distribution, we can construct a $t$ interval for $\phi(\rho)$. We can then use this interval to get one for $\rho$. The idea, then, is to form an interval on a transformed scale where the usual strategy of [estimate $\pm t \times$ std. err.] is roughly correct. Then we reverse, or *invert*, the transformation to get back to the original scale and finish with an asymmetric interval.

An example using the law school data illustrates these ideas. Using Fisher's transformation gives $\phi(0.776) = (1/2)ln(1.776/0.224) = 1.035$, and an approximate 90% confidence interval for $\phi(\rho)$ is

$$[1.035 \pm 1.645 \times 0.289] = [0.560, 1.510].$$

To get an interval for $\rho$, note that if $\phi(r) = z$, then solving for r in terms of $z$ gives $r = (e^z - e^{-z})/(e^z + e^{-z}) = \tanh(z)$, a function found on some hand calculators. Applying this transformation to the endpoints of the interval for $\phi(\rho)$ yields the desired interval for $\rho$

$$[0.508, 0.907] = [0.776 - 0.268, 0.776 + 0.131].$$

This interval is asymmetric and cannot include values outside the range $-1$ to $+1$.

Bootstrap percentile intervals automatically accomplish much of what Fisher's $z$ transformation does. Intervals for the correlation based on Fisher's $z$ transformation work rather well even for fairly large

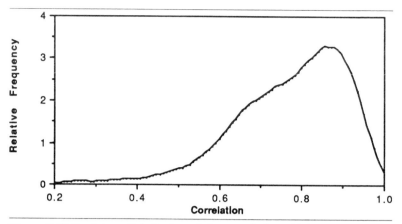

**Figure 8.10** Bootstrap distribution of the correlation of LSAT and GPA.

values of $\rho$, but their use requires that we know about this transformation. Generally, it is rather hard to find a transformation for an arbitrary statistic that works as well as $\phi$ works for the sample correlation, although some recent work seeking to automate this search shows promise (Tibshirani, 1988). Bootstrap percentile intervals are more direct. Suppose that we computed $B$ bootstrap replications of the sample correlation $r^{*(1)}, r^{*(2)}, \ldots, r^{*(B)}$. In this case, $B$ will need to be rather large — on the order of 1000. As with random resampling in regression, we resample from the pairs (LSAT$_i$, GPA$_i$) so as to preserve the relationship between the two variables. The 90% bootstrap percentile interval is then $[r^*(0.05), \ r^*(0.95)]$, where $r^*(p)$ $(0<p<1)$ is the $100p$th percentile of the bootstrap distribution of the correlation. That is, we merely sort the bootstrap replicates, find the one greater than 5% of the $r^*$'s, and use it for the lower endpoint. Similarly, the replicate that is greater than 95% of the $r^*$'s becomes the upper endpoint.

The key property of percentile intervals is that, in a sense, they automatically make use of Fisher's transformation. Suppose that we knew of the skewness in the distribution of the sample correlation and used Fisher's $z$ transformation *with* the bootstrap. Instead of looking at 1000 replications of $r$, we instead would compute 1000 replications of $\phi(r)$. The resulting bootstrap percentile interval for $\phi(\rho)$ would then be formed from the 5th and 95th percentiles of the collection of $\phi(r^*)$'s. When this interval is inverted to give an interval for $\rho$, however, we get the same interval that we would have gotten without the transformation.

This invariance occurs because $\phi$ is a monotone function (it steadily increases). Thus, it preserves the order of the bootstrap replications. The 5th percentile of the transformed values $\phi(r^*)$ is simply $\phi$ applied to the 5th percentile of the $r^*$'s. When the percentile interval $[\phi\{r^*(0.05)\}, \phi\{r^*(0.95)\}]$ is inverted back to the original scale, we obtain the same interval as before, $[r^*(0.05), r^*(0.95)]$. How well this automatic transformation performs depends on some key assumptions laid out in the next section.

### *Percentile and Bias Corrected Percentile Intervals*

The validity of the percentile interval stems from the existence of a normalizing transformation. Suppose that we want a confidence interval for some population parameter $\theta$ that has been estimated by the statistic $\hat{\theta}$. The simplest, but most restrictive assumption that guarantees that percentile intervals give the correct coverage is to assume

$$\frac{(\hat{\theta}* - \hat{\theta})}{(\hat{\theta} - \theta)} \sim N(0, \sigma^2). \tag{8.A1}$$

That is, the bootstrap analogy holds and both deviations from "true" values have a normal distribution with mean 0. Of course, the bootstrap distribution of $\hat{\theta}^*$ is discrete and cannot be normal, so we interpret (8.A1) to mean that the bootstrap distribution becomes very close to normal as the sample size increases.

To see why (8.A1) implies that percentile intervals give the correct coverage, we have to compare the usual Gaussian interval for $\theta$ with the bootstrap percentile interval and show that they are the same. Begin by noting that if $\sigma$ is known, then a $1-2\alpha$ confidence interval for $\theta$ is $[\hat{\theta}+z(\alpha)\sigma, \hat{\theta}+z(1-\alpha)\sigma]$. Again, $z(\alpha)$ is the $\alpha$ percentile of the Gaussian distribution; for example, $z(.05) = -1.645$ and $z(.95) = 1.645$. Under bootstrap resampling, the probability of a bootstrap replicate $\hat{\theta}^*$ being less than the lower endpoint of this interval is

$$G*\{\hat{\theta} + z(\alpha)\sigma\} = \mathrm{Pr}*\{\hat{\theta}* \leq \hat{\theta} + z(\alpha)\sigma\}$$

$$= \mathrm{Pr}*\{(\hat{\theta}* - \hat{\theta})/\sigma \leq z(\alpha)\}$$

$$= \alpha$$

because (8.A1) implies that $(\hat{\theta}^* - \hat{\theta})/\sigma$ has a standard normal distribution. Thus, the value that cuts off the lower $100\alpha\%$ of the bootstrap distribution of $\hat{\theta}^*$, the lower endpoint of the bootstrap interval, is also the lower endpoint of the standard interval. As a result, the bootstrap interval $[G^{*-1}(\alpha), G^{*-1}(1-\alpha)]$ has the correct coverage.[18]

Assumption (8.A1) is rather restrictive, and the first generalization allows for a transformation to normality. The statistic $\hat{\theta}$ is allowed to have a non-Gaussian distribution, and it is assumed that an invertible transformation to normality exists, like Fisher's transformation of the correlation. If this normalizing transformation is labelled "h," then the generalization of (8.A1) is to assume

$$\frac{(h(\hat{\theta}^*) - h(\hat{\theta}))}{(h(\hat{\theta}) - h(\theta))} \sim N(0, \sigma^2) \qquad (8.A2)$$

Under (8.A2), the usual $1-2\alpha$ interval for $h(\theta)$ is

$$[h(\hat{\theta}) + z(\alpha)\sigma, \, h(\hat{\theta}) + z(1-\alpha)\sigma].$$

Using the existence of the inverse transformation $h^{-1}$ (tanh in the case of Fisher's $z$ transformation), the interval for $\theta$ is $[h^{-1}\{h(\hat{\theta}) + z(\alpha)\,\sigma\}, h^{-1}\{h(\hat{\theta}) + z(1-\alpha)\,\sigma\}]$. To arrive at this interval requires knowing $h$, $h^{-1}$, and $\sigma$. Again, the percentile interval arrives at the same endpoints without requiring so much a priori information. Arguing as before, the probability of $\hat{\theta}^*$ being less than the lower endpoint of the desired interval is

$$\mathrm{Pr}^*\{\hat{\theta}^* \leq h^{-1}(h(\hat{\theta}) + z(\alpha)\sigma)\} = \mathrm{Pr}^*\{h(\hat{\theta}^*) - h(\hat{\theta}))/\sigma \leq z(\alpha)\}$$
$$= \alpha$$

and the percentile interval gets the correct coverage *without* having to be told the normalizing transformation.

As broad as assumption (8.A2) first appears, it does not obtain in some common situations, particularly in the presence of bias. To get a sense for why the percentile interval fails, consider what happens if it is used with a biased estimator. Suppose that the estimator $\hat{\theta}$ is biased for the true parameter $\theta$ and tends to be too small — say $\hat{\theta}$ is on average 2 less than $\theta$, $E(\hat{\theta}-\theta) = -2$. If the bootstrap analogy holds, then the bootstrap replicates $\hat{\theta}^*$ are also biased for the true parameter of the bootstrap population, $\hat{\theta}$. Thus, the bootstrap replicates used to form the endpoints of the percentile interval are shifted to the left of $\hat{\theta}$, when in fact they should be shifted to the right toward $\theta$.

Fortunately, a diagnostic method exists that measures discrepancies from assumption (8.A2) and provides the means to correct the problem. This diagnostic is to check that the probability of $\hat{\theta}^*$ being less than $\hat{\theta}$ is 1/2; that is, half of the bootstrap values $\hat{\theta}^*$ should be less than the observed statistic $\hat{\theta}$, a condition known as median unbiased. Under (8.A2), half of the $\hat{\theta}^*$'s should be less than $\hat{\theta}$ because it is assumed that $h(\hat{\theta}^*)$ is normally distributed about $h(\hat{\theta})$. Using the notation of bootstrap distributions, we need to check that $G^*(\hat{\theta}) = \Pr^*(\hat{\theta}^*\leq\hat{\theta}) = 0.5$. For the law school data, only 446 of the 1000 bootstrap replications of the correlation are less than the observed correlation, $G_{1000}^*(r) = 0.446$. Because $G_{1000}^*$ is an estimate of $G^*$, we need to decide whether the observed deviation from 0.5 is indicative of a problem or merely the result of sampling fluctuations. In other words, we need to test the null hypothesis $H_0$: $G^*(r) = 0.5$. Under $H_0$, the number of the 1000 bootstrap replicates $r^*$ that are less than $r$ has a binomial distribution with mean 500 and standard deviation $0.5\times1000^{1/2} = 15.8$. Because the observed count is well over 3 standard deviations from 500, assumption (8.A2) does not hold.

*Bias-corrected percentile intervals* allow for the presence of bias and consequently lead to a more general bootstrap confidence interval. Rather than require that $h(\hat{\theta}^*) - h(\hat{\theta})$ and $h(\hat{\theta}) - h(\theta)$ both be centered on 0, these intervals allow for some bias. The assumed behavior is

$$(h(\hat{\theta}^*)-h(\hat{\theta}))$$

$$\sim N(-Z_0\sigma, \sigma^2) \qquad (8.A3)$$

$$(h(\hat{\theta})-h(\theta))$$

where the bias is expressed as a constant, $-Z_0$, number of multiples of the standard deviation $\sigma$. Because (8.A3) implies that the mean of $h(\hat{\theta})$ is $h(\theta) - Z_0\sigma$, it follows that

$$\{h(\hat{\theta})-h(\theta) +Z_0\sigma\}/\sigma \sim N(0,1)$$

and the standard $(1-2\alpha)$ interval for $\theta$ is

$$[h^{-1}\{h(\hat{\theta})+Z_0\sigma +z(\alpha)\sigma\}, h^{-1}\{h(\hat{\theta})+Z_0\sigma+ z(1-\alpha)\sigma\}].$$

This interval requires that we know the transformation h, its inverse $h^{-1}$, *and* both $Z_0$ and $\sigma$. But again, if we consider the probability of $\hat{\theta}*$ being less than the lower endpoint of the desired interval, we find that the lower endpoint of the normal-theory interval is related to a percentile of the bootstrap distribution

$$G*\left\{h^{-1}(h(\hat{\theta})+Z_0\sigma+z(\alpha)\sigma)\right\} = \text{Pr*}\left\{h(\hat{\theta}*) \le h(\hat{\theta}) + Z_0\sigma+z(\alpha)\sigma\right\}$$

$$= \text{Pr*}\left\{(h(\hat{\theta}*) - h(\hat{\theta}) + Z_0\sigma)/\sigma \le 2Z_0 + z(\alpha)\right\}$$

$$= \Phi(2Z_0+z(\alpha))$$

where $\Phi(x)$ is the cumulative normal distribution, $\Phi(x) = \text{Pr}\{N(0,1) \le x\}$. The presence of the bias implies that the percentile interval constructed using the $\alpha$ and $1-\alpha$ percentiles is no longer correct. Instead the lower endpoint of the bias-corrected bootstrap interval needs to be the $\Phi(2Z_0 + z(\alpha))$ percentile, which suggests that we still need to know the bias factor $Z_0$. However, the same diagnostic that suggests the need for a bias adjustment gives an estimate of $Z_0$. The proportion of bootstrap replicates $\hat{\theta}*$ that are less than $\hat{\theta}$ is the proportion of the normal distribution less than $Z_0$

$$G^*(\hat{\theta}) = \text{Pr*} \{(h(\hat{\theta}) - h(\theta) + Z_0\sigma )/\sigma \le Z_0\} = \Phi(Z_0).$$

Thus, $Z_0 = \Phi^{-1}\{G^*(\hat{\theta})\}$, the z value corresponding to $\text{Pr*}\{\hat{\theta}*\le \hat{\theta} \}$. Notice that the bias corrected interval reduces to the usual percentile interval if $\hat{\theta}*\le\hat{\theta}$ in half of the samples. In this case, $Z_0 = 0$ because $\Phi^{-1}(0.5) = 0$.

Bias correction makes a slight difference in the interval for the correlation. The effect of bias correction in this example is subtle because

$$Z_0 = \Phi^{-1} \text{ (proportion of BS correlations less than } r)$$

$$= \Phi^{-1}(0.446) = -0.13.$$

**Table 8.6 Several 90% Bootstrap Confidence Intervals for the Correlation of the Law School Data of 15 Observations with Sample Correlation 0.776.**

| Method | Interval |
|---|---|
| Classical | |
| without Fisher's z | [0.56, 0.99] |
| with Fisher's z | [0.49, 0.90] |
| Bootstrap ($B = 1000$) | |
| percentile | [0.55, 0.94] |
| BC percentile | [0.52, 0.93] |
| accelerated percentile | [0.43, 0.92] |

For the lower endpoint, $\Phi\{2Z_0+z(0.05)\} = \Phi\{2(-0.13)-1.65\} = 0.028$. Thus, the value cutting off the lower 2.8% of the bootstrap distribution of $r^*$ becomes the lower endpoint of the 90% interval, rather than the 5% point. For the upper endpoint, the 91.8% point of $G^*$ is used. Although the interval endpoints appear to imply that the coverage is no longer 0.9 (because 0.918−0.028=0.89), the interval is nonetheless an estimated 90% confidence interval. Table 8.6 summarizes the several types of intervals. Fisher's transformation produces an asymmetric interval; the direct normal approximation does not. The bootstrap intervals become progressively more skewed as one moves down the table.

### Accelerated Bootstrap Intervals

Efron (1987) proposes *accelerated percentile intervals* as further enhancement of percentile intervals. As illustrated in Table 8.6, accelerated intervals can be much more asymmetric than the bias-corrected interval. For some familiar statistics, including the sample variance $s^2$, the transformation needed for the bias-corrected interval does not exist because the variance of the normal approximation depends on the value of $\theta$ (Schenker, 1985; Efron, 1987). Simulations of an interval for the variance $\sigma^2$ based on samples of 35 Gaussian observations (Schenker, 1985) revealed that the coverage of the 90% percentile interval was much too small, only 82%, and the coverage of the bias-corrected percentile interval was not much better − only 85%.

Like the bias-corrected interval, accelerated bootstrap intervals alter the percentiles of the bootstrap distribution that are used for the endpoints of the bootstrap interval. For the correlation in the law school data, the bias-corrected percentile interval is too far to the right. Accelerated intervals remedy much of this problem by using as endpoints the 1st and 89th percentiles of the bootstrap distribution of the correlation, as compared to the 3rd, and 92nd used in the bias-corrected interval. The accelerated interval thus reaches farther into the tail of the distribution. Unfortunately, the computation of the accelerated intervals is more involved than that of the percentile intervals and will not be covered further here. Details of the calculations appear in Efron (1987) and DiCicco and Tibshirani (1987).

### Bootstrap Prediction Intervals

A variation on utopian sampling suggests how to use the bootstrap to find confidence intervals for predictions. Having estimated the regression model (1), we frequently forecast the values of new observations $y_f = x_f'\beta + \varepsilon_f$ with the predictor $x_f'\hat{\beta}$. To construct an interval that measures the uncertainty of this forecast, the standard approach is to assume that the errors in the regression model possess a Gaussian distribution. If $k$ regressors are used in the model, then a prediction interval with coverage $1-2\alpha$ for $y_f$ is $I_G(f) = [x_f'\hat{\beta}+t(\alpha; n-k)s_f, x_f'\hat{\beta}+t(1-\alpha; n-k)s_f]$ where $s_f$ is the standard error of the forecast, $s_f^2 = s^2(1+x_f'(X'X)^{-1}x_f)$.[19]

The idea behind bootstrap prediction intervals is to replicate the entire sampling process and directly observe the prediction error. This procedure consists of generating bootstrap replicates of the observations $Y^*$ and $X^*$, using the fitted model to obtain a future value $y_f^* = x_f'\hat{\beta} + e_f^*$, and measuring the observable prediction error $PE_f^* = y_f^* - x_f'\hat{\beta}^*$. Here, $e_f^*$ is a random draw from the empirical distribution of the residuals, which is independent of the resampling used to generate $Y^*$ and $X^*$. The resulting interval resembles a percentile interval; the percentiles of the bootstrap prediction errors are added to the original prediction rather than a parameter estimate. If we let $H^{*-1}(\alpha)$ denote the $100\alpha$ percentile of $PE_f^{*(1)}$, ..., $PE_f^{*(B)}$, then a $1-2\alpha$ coverage bootstrap prediction error for $y_f$ is $I_{BS}(f) = \{x_f'\hat{\beta} + H^{*-1}(\alpha), x_f'\hat{\beta} + H^{*-1}(1-\alpha)]$.

Table 8.7 contrasts the coverage probabilities of the bootstrap prediction intervals with the usual normal theory intervals. Although the coverage of $I_{BS}$ is slightly less than 0.8, the coverage is consistent for all three distributions. One can prove in special cases that the distribution of the coverage of $I_{BS}$ is asymptotically distribution-free: The coverage of the bootstrap intervals does not depend on the shape of the

**Table 8.7  Coverage of Bootstrap and Normal Theory Prediction Intervals for Regression Models with Errors from Several Distributions**

| Error Distribution | Bootstrap | Normal Theory |
|---|---|---|
| Gaussian | 0.78 | 0.80 |
| Logistic | 0.79 | 0.81 |
| Student's $t$ (4 $df$) | 0.78 | 0.83 |

NOTE: The nominal coverage is 0.80 and the sample size is 24 (Stine, 1985).

underlying population. In contrast, the coverage of the normal theory interval deviates further from the nominal amount as the distribution becomes more long-tailed. Further details and a computational enhancement appear in Stine (1985); similar methods for time-series models appear in Stine (1987).

## COMPUTING BOOTSTRAP ESTIMATES

It would be convenient at this point to be able to direct the reader to a well-developed commercial software package that included bootstrap procedures. But because such a package does not exist, it is useful to remember some computational issues that arise in resampling. The bootstrap calculations that appear in this chapter were prepared using a collection of APL programs written by the author. It is also possible to use the SAS macrolanguage to write special routines to do bootstrap calculations. One can write such a bootstrapping macro in any statistical package that permits the user to make function calls to statistical routines and supports random number generation.

### Some General Points to Remember

Most interesting applications of the bootstrap, such as confidence intervals, require simulation. Although no rules exist to always give the best computing strategy, a few general points deserve emphasis. Some have already been mentioned, but are repeated here.

(1) *Simulation is not always necessary.* The bootstrap is not a collection of simulation algorithms. Rather, the bootstrap is a methodology based on substituting the sample for the unknown population. Often, simple mathemat-

ics can replace simulation, as in the example of computing the variance of the sample average.

(2) *Improve naive bootstrap methods with substantive knowledge.* The naive bootstrap prediction intervals of the earlier section are intuitive, but the resulting computational strategy is not computationally efficient. A basic understanding of the structure of predictions leads to an algorithm that produces more accurate intervals with less resampling (Stine, 1985).

(3) *Avoid iterating nonlinear statistics.* Many nonlinear estimators, including robust regression, begin at some starting point and sequentially improve the solution. Although these are often iterated "until convergence," one step of such a method is generally sufficient because one step from a consistent initial estimate is asymptotically efficient (Zacks, 1971, sec. 5.5). Related ideas appear in Jorgensen (1987).

(4) *Use the same bootstrap samples when comparing estimators.* To make the most of bootstrap comparisons, use the same bootstrap samples for both estimators. If different bootstrap samples are used for comparing two estimators, some of the differences between the estimators will be due to differences in the bootstrap samples. Using the same samples induces correlation, which helps comparisons.

## How Many Bootstrap Samples Are Necessary

One of the most common questions about using the bootstrap is, How many bootstrap samples are needed? The answer depends upon the problem, but $B$ on the order of 100 is typically needed for standard error estimates, whereas $B \approx 1000$ or larger is typically necessary for estimating a percentile of a distribution. Even with an infinite number of bootstrap replications, the bootstrap standard error is still a random variable. If $B$ is chosen by these rough guidelines, sample-to-sample variation in the bootstrap standard error is typically much larger than the variation induced by limiting the size of the simulation. Tibshirani (1985) gives a precise description of how to determine $B$ when estimating standard errors and percentiles, and further ideas appear in Efron (1987, sec. 9).

## FUTURE DIRECTIONS

Several recent applications of bootstrap methods reach beyond straightforward applications in variance estimation and confidence intervals. One can expect to see further extensions along these lines. Finally, a

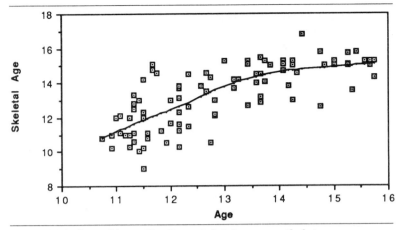

**Figure 8.11** Smoothing spline fit to skeletal age growth data.

closing warning shows that the bootstrap need not give the correct answer, especially when the model imposed on the data is incorrect.

### Nonparametric Regression Methods

Inexpensive computing resources have renewed interest in nonparametric regression. In nonparametric regression, the conditional expectation of the response $Y$ is not restricted to the linear form of model (8.1), but is instead permitted to be an arbitrary function of $X$. Several methods exist for fitting such functions, and one is based on smoothing splines. The usual spline function is a smooth curve that interpolates the data; a smoothing spline is a related function, but it does not pass through every observation. As an example, Figure 8.11 shows a smoothing spline fit to the age and skeletal age of 100 black male adolescents in a study of hypertension in blacks (Katz et al., 1980). Skeletal age is a measure of maturation based on interpreting x-rays of the hand and wrist. What is interesting in the figure is the location of the bend in the curve between 13 and 14 years of age. Does the location of the kink really fall in this interval or are we being misled by sampling variation?

The bootstrap offers one approach to answering this question. Simply generate bootstrap samples from the 100 observations, fit smoothing splines to each, and see how the location of the kink varies. Figure 8.12 shows smoothing splines fit to five bootstrap samples. Although considerable variation exists in the fitted splines before age

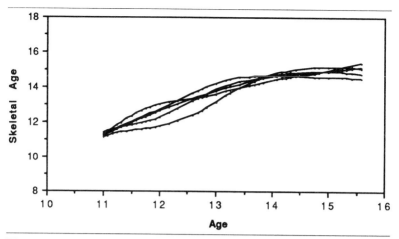

**Figure 8.12**  Replications of the smoothing spline from five bootstrap samples of the growth data.

14, the curves come together at about age 14 and all flatten out. Maturation, as measured by skeletal age, appears to stop in this sample after age 14. Further details on smoothing splines appear in Silverman (1985), and other examples of nonparametric regression appear in Gasser et al. (1984).

### Model Assessment and Error Rates

The bootstrap is a useful tool for evaluating overall model fit. Summaries such as $s^2$ and $R^2$ use deviations of the data from the fitted model to measure the success of the model. Such criteria are often "optimistic" because the same data that generated the model are used to assess the model. Models based on one sample often fit new data poorly. Adjustments for degrees of freedom offer some improvement, but the bootstrap suggests how to go further. Efron (1983) uses the bootstrap to estimate how optimistic the standard estimates of goodness-of-fit are.

The basic idea is simple: Evaluate models constructed from bootstrap samples based on how well they fit the bootstrap population, the original sample. One begins by constructing a predictive model from a bootstrap sample. The model could be logistic regression, discriminant analysis, or even linear regression. These models provide an estimate of how well they can predict future observations from the same population, such as the classification error rate in discriminant analysis.

Because the bootstrap population is known, we can see how well the estimated model predicts the population. By comparing the actual accuracy to the model's claimed accuracy, we get an idea of how well the goodness-of-fit measure performs. Once it is known that the model is never so accurate as it claims to be, we can inflate the size of the expected error by an amount suggested by the bootstrap.

## Confidence Intervals

Confidence intervals in very small samples remain a problem. When the data supply little information, the data analyst has to impose some form of external structure. Rather than appeal to the existential transformation of bootstrap percentile intervals, handle skewness by finding a normalizing (or at least symmetrizing) transformation. The bootstrap can help in this search: Use the bootstrap distribution of the statistic to judge the effectiveness of a given transformation. The methods of exploratory data analysis are also useful in this search, noting that now one is seeking to symmetrize the distribution of a statistic rather than the distribution of the sample.

The confidence intervals described in the section on bootstrap confidence intervals apply to scalar-valued statistics. What if we want to form a simultaneous confidence region? For example, it is common in regression to form a confidence region for several of the slope parameters simultaneously. Bootstrap intervals are not so well established in this area. Once we look simultaneously at several parameters, it becomes hard to generate enough bootstrap replications to get reasonable percentile intervals, a problem that is similar to density estimation over the plane (Silverman, 1986). Also, it is not clear just how we should define a bootstrap confidence region. Some recent work on this problem appears in Hall (1987).

## Hybrid Estimators

The bootstrap comparison of the robust and least-squares estimators suggests constructing a new hybrid estimator. A hybrid estimator is a mixture of several estimators, such as least-squares and robust estimators. When the bootstrap standard errors reveal that the OLS estimator is more stable, then the hybrid is the least-squares estimator. If the robust estimator seems more stable, then it is to be the value of the hybrid. An early example of this idea is Switzer's adaptive trimmed mean. This estimate of location selects the amount of trimming by minimizing the *jackknife* estimate of variance. (See Efron (1982, p. 28) for further discussion of this estimator and comparisons to other techniques.)

### Other Topics

The bootstrap has found applications in virtually every area of statistics. For example, censored data occur when we do not observe the actual value of some variable, but only know that it exceeds some known cutoff. Such data problems appear in event-history analysis. Efron (1981) showed how to use the bootstrap to estimate sampling properties of the Kaplan-Meier estimator, which appears in the analysis of censored data, and further applications appear in Akritas (1986). Applications in time-series analysis are less common, primarily because serial correlation requires assumptions about the structure of the data. Freedman (1984) describes bootstrapping in very complex econometric models and includes proofs of the large sample validity of the bootstrap in this setting. Examples of bootstrapping with time-series models appear in Efron and Tibshirani (1986), Swanepoel and Van Wyck (1985), and Stine (1987). The bootstrap is also useful in multivariate analysis, with applications ranging from the variation of principal component weights (Diaconis & Efron, 1983) to error rates in discriminant analysis (Efron, 1983).

All of our applications have treated the data as if they are a simple random sample. Real data are seldom so simple, and are often gathered through complex sampling designs. In these cases, naive bootstrap methods do not replicate the actual sampling structure of the data, and they give incorrect results. Rao and Wu (1988) address these issues for a variety of sampling designs, including stratified cluster sampling and two-stage cluster sampling.

### Problems in Paradise:
### A Situation in Which the Bootstrap Fails

The bootstrap does not always yield the correct standard error estimator, particularly if the resampling scheme does not parallel the structure of the actual sampling mechanism. The presence of correlated observations presents a case in which it is easy to misuse the bootstrap and obtain misleading results. Once the assumption of independence is dropped, the bootstrap requires that the dependence be properly modelled.

Recall our original problem of estimating the variance of a sample mean. Only now, suppose that, unknown to the data analyst, the observations $(x_1, \ldots, x_n)$ are correlated. For example, assume that all of the observations have equal correlation $\rho$ with one another

$$\text{Cov}(x_i, x_j) \begin{cases} = \sigma^2 & (i = j) \\ = \rho\sigma^2 & (i \neq j) \end{cases}$$

If the correlation is ignored, the introduction shows that the bootstrap estimate of the variance of $\bar{x}$ is $\Sigma(x_i - \bar{x})^2/n$. However, the actual variance of $\bar{x}$ is rather different: VAR $(\bar{x}) = \sigma^2\{1 + \rho(n-1)\}/n \approx \rho\sigma^2$. A careless application of the bootstrap based on the wrong sampling procedure provides incorrect results. A multivariate example in which the obvious bootstrap approach fails appears in Beran and Srivastava (1985).

The bootstrap also gives misleading results for certain types of statistics. In general, such failures occur when the statistic of interest depends on a narrow feature of the original sampling process that bootstrap sampling cannot reproduce. For example, the bootstrap overcomes the well-publicized failure of the jackknife estimate of the standard error of the median, but fails for the maximum. Tukey (1987) gives a detailed heuristic argument, and a technical discussion appears in Bickel and Freedman (1981). Statistics such as the maximum that lack a normal sampling distribution require more caution than the usual weighed-average estimators so common in practice. Babu (1984) gives results for bootstrapping statistics that are asymptotically $\chi^2$.

## NOTES

1. The estimator var($\bar{x}$) can fail for a variety of reasons. Mosteller and Tukey (1977, chap. 7) point out the existence of other sources of variation, and the robustness literature (e.g., Hampel et al., 1986) contains many alternative estimators that perform better than $s^2$ if the population that has been sampled is not normal.

2. A finite total of $n^n$ possible bootstrap samples exist, because any one of the $n$ observations could be drawn first, any of the $n$ could be second, and so forth. Not all of these samples give a distinct value for $\bar{x}^*$ because the mean ignores the ordering of the data. If we computed $\bar{x}^*$ for each of these $n^n$ samples, we would obtain the true bootstrap variance of the sample mean, but such extreme computation is wasteful and unnecessary in this case.

3. The maximum likelihood estimator of $\sigma^2$ under a Gaussian population is $s_n^2$. Maximum likelihood estimators frequently are biased and lack corrections for degrees of

freedom. Like maximum likelihood, the bootstrap typically leads to divisors of n rather than $n-1$. In a sense, the bootstrap *is* maximum likelihood, but with respect to the empirical distribution function.

4. The population defined by $F_n$ is infinite in size, but only the observed set of values $(x_1, \ldots, x_n)$ are possible. Sampling with replacement from the observed data is equivalent to sampling from this infinite population.

5. With additional assumptions, one can obtain better estimates of the population distribution. For example, the parametric bootstrap uses an estimate of $F$ that is a member of a particular parametric family, such as the Gaussian (Efron, 1982). The parametric bootstrap requires the rather strong assumption that we know the shape of the distribution of the population, and so we have chosen to stay with the basic scheme using $F_n$. The parametric approach does allow more detailed mathematical analysis of the technique.

6. The use of $G^{*-1}$ to denote a quantile is standard in the statistics literature. This notation comes from recognizing that a quantile is really just a value of the inverse of a distribution function. Whereas a distribution function takes any value as an argument and returns a probability, the inverse of a distribution takes a probability and returns the associated quantile.

7. If the pairing given by sampling the $z_i$ is removed, $Y^*$ and $X^*$ will be independent in the bootstrap simulation and $\hat{\beta}^*$ will be distributed about 0, with the exception of the constant. Nonparametric tests use this very idea. In these tests, all possible pairings (or a large sampling of pairings) of the regressors with the response are considered and the size of the observed effect is judged relative to this collection (see Lehmann & D'Abrera, 1975).

8. The residuals that are resampled must have an average of zero. If the residuals do not, as can occur when the regression model lacks a constant term, the bootstrap *fails* to give consistent variance estimates (Freedman, 1981).

9. Independence in the context of bootstrap resampling is always to be interpreted as conditional independence given the values of the observed data. This independence is a consequence of sampling with replacement from the original observations. The variance of the bootstrap population defined by the residuals is

$$\text{VAR}\,(e_i{}^*) = \sum_{i=1}^{n} e_i^2/n = \frac{n-k}{n}s^2.$$

10. A linear statistic is a nonrandom linear combination of random variables. Thus, $\hat{\beta}$ is a linear statistic when the design is fixed. When the design is random, $\hat{\beta}$ is no longer linear because the weights of the linear combination vary with $X$.

11. The probability of not getting a particular observation in a bootstrap sample is the probability of choosing all $n$ bootstrap observations from the remaining $n-1$ points, an event with probability $(1-1/n)^n \approx 0.36$.

12. The histograms of the bootstrap estimates have been smoothed using a *kernel density estimator*. The kernel density estimator smooths the random irregularities of the familiar histogram, removes some of the subjective choice of bin location and width, and gives a better visual impression of the shape of the distribution. Silverman (1986) gives an excellent overview of this technique. Further ideas on using kernel smoothing to improve bootstrap estimates appear in Silverman and Young (1987).

13. This naive illustrative model also suffers from specification error. The District of Columbia combines a high poverty percentage with a high average income, so that the poverty percentage may not be a good indicator of economic well-being.

14. An extensive discussion of problems caused by heteroscedasticity in regression appears in Carroll and Ruppert (1988). A more complex application of these ideas appears in Freedman and Peters (1982), who used the bootstrap to examine an econometric model that includes lagged endogenous variables. They found that the usual standard error was about one third of the true standard error. The bootstrap standard error was also too small, but much better than the usual WLS estimator (about 80% of the correct value).

15. That the robust estimator has smaller variation than the least squares estimator does not contradict the Gauss-Markov theorem. This theorem only applies to linear statistics, and the robust estimator is *not* linear because its weights are determined iteratively from the data.

16. The notation for $t^*(\alpha;n)$ differs from the usual $t$ interval because the bootstrap is not making use of the notion of degrees of freedom, and only requires the sample size $n$.

17. As shown in the introduction, it is known that $VAR^*\bar{x} = (n-1)s^2/n^2$. Thus, we could improve the bootstrap interval and reduce the calculations by making use of this fact and replace the bootstrap estimate $sd_B^*$ by the true value, $(n-1)^{1/2}s/n$. In general, however, $VAR^*$ is seldom known and must be estimated by simulation. If one performs the simulations using $\sqrt{n}\ (\bar{x}^*-\bar{x})/s$, lacking $s^*$ in the denominator, then the bootstrap interval does not give the desired coverage.

18. One can replace the normal distribution in assumption (8.A1) and those that follow by some other distribution (and $z(\alpha)$ by the correct percentile), but the large sample distribution of most statistics is Gaussian, and this choice is thus most broad. Also, these calculations are in terms of the true bootstrap distribution, not the simulated estimate of $G_B^*$ from $B$ replications. Generally, $B \approx 1000$ is necessary to get a good estimate of $G^*$.

19. The coverage of a prediction interval is the expected probability that the interval captures the future observation. Because the value being predicted is random, the situation differs from that with the usual confidence interval. A confidence interval either does or does not contain the sought parameter. A prediction interval, however, captures a fraction of the distribution of the predicted value. The average of this fraction over many samples is the coverage of the interval.

# REFERENCES

Akritas, M. G. (1986). Bootstrapping the Kaplan-Meier estimator. *Journal of the American Statistical Association, 81,* 1032-1038.

Babu, G. J. (1984). Bootstrapping statistics with linear combinations of chi-squares as weak limit. *Sankhya, Series A, 46,* 85-93.

Beran, R., & Srivastiva, M. S. (1985). Bootstrap tests and confidence regions for functions of a covariance matrix. *Annals of Statistics, 13,* 95-115.

Bickel, P., & Freedman, D. (1981). Some asymptotic theory for the bootstrap. *Annals of Statistics, 9,* 1196-1217.

Bishop, Y., Feinburg, S., & Holland, P. (1975). *Discrete multivariate analysis.* Cambridge: MIT Press.

Bollen, K. A., & Stine, R. A. (1988). *Bootstrapping indirect effects in structural equation models.* Unpublished manuscript.

Carrol, R. J., & Ruppert, D. (1988). An asymptotic theory for weighted least-squares with weights estimated by replication. *Biometrika, 75,* 35-44.

Cook, T. D., & Campbell, D. T. (1976). The design and conduct of quasi-experiments and true experiments in field settings. In M. Dunnette, (Ed.), *Handbook of industrial and organization psychology.* New York: Rand-McNally.

Diaconis, P., & Efron, B. (1983). Computer intensive methods in statistics. *Scientific American, 248*(5), 116-130.

Dicicco, T., & Tibshirani, R. (1987). Bootstrap confidence intervals and bootstrap approximations. *Journal of the American Statistical Asociation, 82,* 163-170.

Efron, B. (1979a). Computers and the theory of statistics: Thinking the unthinkable. *Siam Review, 21,* 460-480.

Efron, B. (1979b). Bootstrap methods: Another look at the jackknife. *Annals of Statistics, 7,* 1-26.

Efron, B. (1981). Censored data and the bootstrap. *Journal of the American Statistical Association, 76,* 312-319.

Efron, B. (1982). *The jackknife, the bootstrap, and other resampling plans.* Philadelphia: Society for Industrial and Applied Mathematics.

Efron, B. (1983). Estimating the error rate of a prediction rule: Improvement on cross-validation. *Journal of the American Statistical Association, 78,* 316-331.

Efron, B. (1987). Better bootstrap confidence intervals. *Journal of the American Statistical Association, 82,* 171-200.

Efron, B., & Gong, G. (1983). A leisurely look at the bootstrap, the jackknife, and cross-validation. *American Statistician, 37,* 36-48.

Efron, B., & Tibshirani, R. (1986). Bootstrap methods for standard errors, confidence intervals, and other measures of statistical accuracy. *Statistical Science, 1,* 54-75.

Finifter, B. M. (1972). The generation of confidence: Evaluating research findings by random subsample replication. In H. L. Costineau (Ed.), *Sociological methodology* (pp.112-175). San Francisco: Jossey-Bass.

Fox, J. (1984). *Linear statistical models and related methods.* New York: John Wiley.

Freedman, D. A. (1981). Bootstrapping regression models. *Annals of Statistics, 9,* 1218-1228.

Freedman, D. A. (1984). On bootstrapping two-stage least squares estimates in stationary linear models. *Annals of Statistics, 12,* 827-842.

Freedman, D. A., & Peters, S. C. (1982). Bootstrapping a regression equation: Some empirical results. *Journal of the American Statistical Association, 79,* 97-106.

Gasser, T., Kohler, W., Muller, H. G., Kneip, A., Larjo, R., Molinari, L., & Prader, A. (1984). Velocity and acceleration of height growth using kernel estimation. *Annals of Human Biology, 11,* 397-411.

Hall, P. (1986a). On the bootstrap and confidence intervals. *Annals of Statistics, 14,* 1431-1452.

Hall, P. (1986b). On the number of bootstrap simulations required to construct a confidence interval. *Annals of Statistics, 14,* 1453-1462.

Hall, P. (1987). On the bootstrap and likelihood-based confidence regions. *Biometrika, 74,* 481-493.

Hampel, F. R., Ronchetti, E. M., Rousseeuw, P. J., & Stahel, W. A. (1986). *Robust statistics.* New York: John Wiley.

Hardle, W., & Bowman, A. W. (1988). Bootstrapping in nonparametric regression: Local adaptive smoothing and confidence bands. *Journal of the American Statistical Association, 83,* 102-110.

Jorgensen, M. A. (1987). Jackknifing fixed points of iterations. *Biometrika, 74,* 207-211.

Katz, S. H., Hediger, M. L., Schall, J. I., Bowers, I. J., Barker, W. F., Aurand, S., Eveleth, P. B., Gruskin, A. B., & Parks, J. S. (1980). Blood pressure, growth, and maturation from childhood through adolescence. *Hypertension, 2*(Supp. 1), I55-I69.

Lehman, E. L., & D'Abrera, H. J. M. (1975). *Nonparametrics.* San Francisco: Holden-Day.

Loh, W. Y. (1987). Calibrating confidence coefficients. *Journal of the American Statistical Association, 82,* 155-162.

Miller, R. G. (1974). The jackknife: A review. *Biometrika, 61,* 1-15.

Mosteller, F., & Tukey, J. W. (1977). *Data analysis and regression.* Reading, MA: Addison-Wesley.

Rao, J.N.K., & Wu, C.F.J. (1988). Resampling inference with complex survey data. *Journal of the American Statistical Association, 83,* 231-245.

Schenker, N. (1985). Qualms about bootstrap confidence intervals. *Journal of the American Statistical Association, 80,* 360-361.

Shorack, G.R. (1982). Bootstrapping robust regression. *Communication in Statistics, A11,* 961-972.

Silverman, B. W. (1985). Some aspects of the spline smoothing approach to non-parametric regression curve fitting. *Journal of the Royal Statistical Society, B47,* 1-52.

Silverman, B. W. (1986). *Density estimation for statistics and data analysis.* London: Chapman & Hall.

Silverman, B. W., & Young, G. A. (1987). The bootstrap: To smooth or not to smooth? *Biometrika, 74,* 469-480.

Sobel, M. E. (1982). Asymptotic confidence intervals for indirect effects in structural equation models. In H. L. Costineau (Ed.), *Sociological methodology* (pp.290-312). San Francisco: Jossey-Bass.

Stine, R. A. (1985). Bootstrap prediction intervals for regression. *Journal of the American Statistical Association, 80,* 1026-1031.

Stine, R. A. (1987). Estimating properties of autoregressive forecasts. *Journal of the American Statistical Association, 82,* 1072-1078.

Street, J. O., Carroll, J. J., & Ruppert, D. (1988). A note on computing robust regression estimates via iteratively reweighted least squares. *American Statistician, 42,* 152-154.

Swanepoel, J.W.H., & Van Wyk, J.W.J. (1986). The bootstrap applied to power spectral density function estimation. *Biometrika, 73,* 135-142.

Tibshirani, R. (1985). *How many bootstraps?* (Tech. rep. no. 362). Stanford, CA: Stanford University, Department of Statistics.

Tibshirani, R. (1988). Variance stabilization and the bootstrap. *Biometrika, 75,* 433-444.

Tukey, J. W. (1958). Bias and confidence in not-quite large samples. *Annals of Mathematical Statistics, 29,* 614.

Tukey, J. W. (1986). Sunset salvo. *American Statistician, 40,* 72-76.

Tukey, J. W. (1987). Kinds of bootstraps and kinds of jackknives, discussed in terms of a year of weather related data. (Tech. rep. no. 292). Princeton, NJ: Princeton University, Department of Statistics.

Wu, C.F.J. (1986). Jackknife, bootstrap and other resampling methods in regression analysis. *Annals of Statistics, 14,* 1261-1350.

Zacks, S. (1971). *The theory of statistical inference.* New York: John Wiley.

# 9

## THE ANALYSIS OF
## SOCIAL SCIENCE DATA
## WITH MISSING VALUES

Roderick J. A. Little
Donald B. Rubin

### The Problem

Many social science data sets suffer from missing values. For example, surveys may be incomplete due to either refusal of some respondents to answer certain questions or the editing out of inappropriate values; panel surveys suffer from incompleteness due to attrition; times of life events may be missing due to censoring by the date of interview. In this article, we discuss the analysis of incomplete data of the form displayed in Figure 9.1a, which displays an $(n \times K)$ matrix $\mathbf{X} = (x_{ij})$ of data on $K$ variables $X_1, \ldots, X_K$ for a sample of $n$ observations. We assume that if all the values were recorded, the data would be analyzed by some standard statistical method — for example, forming the sample mean and covariance matrix (e.g., if $X_1, \ldots, X_K$ are interval-scaled), fitting a loglinear model (e.g., if $X_1, \ldots, X_K$ are categorical), or computing the regression of one variable on the others. The problem we address is the modification of complete-data analysis to handle data sets with some of the values (the question marks in Figure 9.1a) missing.

Some missing-data methods are designed to handle any pattern of missing data. Others apply only to certain *special patterns* of missing data, such as those illustrated in Figure 9.1b. *Univariate* missing data

AUTHORS' NOTE: This research was supported by grants MH 37188 from the U.S. National Institute of Mental Health and SES 880453 from the U.S. National Science Foundation. We thank J. Scott Long and John Fox for a number of useful comments.

a) General Pattern

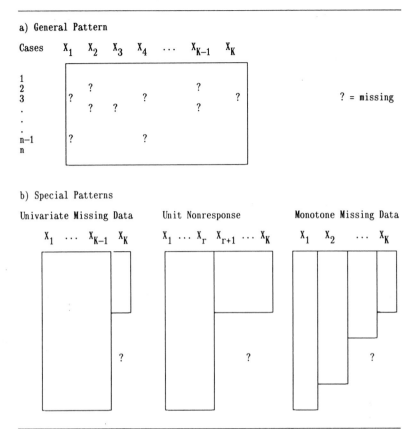

Figure 9.1  **Patterns of missing data.**

occur when missing values are confined to a single variable and the others are fully recorded. The pattern labelled *"unit nonresponse"* illustrates data where a block of variables is missing for the same set of cases, and the remaining variables are all complete. The label reflects the fact that unit nonresponse in a survey is a special case of this pattern, where the fully observed variables are survey design variables, the incompletely observed variables are the variables actually recorded during the survey, and the latter are missing for individuals not interviewed due to refusal or noncontact. The third pattern illustrates *monotone* missing data, where the variables can be arranged so that for $j=1, \ldots, K-1$, $X_j$ is observed whenever $X_{j+1}$ is observed. Attrition from a panel survey leads to data of this form.

### Three Strategies

Three general strategies for analyzing incomplete data can be distinguished: *imputation, weighting*, and *direct analysis of the incomplete data*. We begin by outlining these approaches and their basic characteristics. Later we illustrate them on a simple missing-data structure, and outline extensions to more general problems.

*Imputation* replaces missing values by suitable estimates and then applies standard complete-data methods to the filled-in data. The method is attractive to practitioners because the resulting completed data can be handled using standard software for rectangular data sets. Imputation retains data in incomplete cases that would be discarded if analysis were restricted to the complete cases. These data values are useful not only for analyses directly involving them, but also for imputing the values of correlated missing variables; indeed, an important characteristic of a good imputation method is that it makes good use of information in the incomplete cases.

Imputation is an attractive idea, but it has pitfalls. The main one is that analyses of the filled-in data treat the imputed data as if they were real, and thus overstate precision. For example, 95% confidence intervals for parameters computed from the filled-in data may in fact cover the true parameter value only 80% or 90% of the time, and tests with nominal significance level of 5% may have a true significance level of 10% or 20% (multivariate tests from filled-in data are particularly misleading, as we shall see later—for example, 5% tests with a true significance level of 50%). Later, we consider an extension of imputation—namely, *multiple imputation* (Rubin, 1987)—that corrects this problem and yields appropriate tests and interval estimates for parameters.

Even with the limited objective of point estimation, the imputation method needs to be carefully considered and appropriate for the analysis intended. For example, imputing the best estimate of a missing value can be optimal for estimating the mean of the variable, but is generally inappropriate for estimating the median or a measure of spread, or regression coefficients from a regression for which the imputed variable is a regressor. See Little (1988a) and Rubin (1987, sec. 4.2-4.3) for properties of a good imputation method.

*Weighting* methods discard the incomplete cases and assign a new weight to each complete case to compensate for the dropped cases. These weights are incorporated in subsequent analyses; for example, estimates of means, variances, and covariances are based on weighted sums, sums of squares, and sums of cross-products. The most common application is to unit nonresponse in surveys, with weights proportional to the inverse of the response rates in adjustment cells formed by combinations of survey design variables. Weighting can be a useful technique for reducing the bias that arises from restricting analyses to the complete cases. However, the method is strictly only applicable to monotone patterns of missing data, and the derivation of appropriate standard errors from the weighted analysis is a difficult enterprise.

The simplest form of the weighting approach is *complete-case analysis*, where the complete cases are all given the same nonresponse weight. Complete-case analysis is often the default analysis when data with missing values are input to a statistical package for analysis. Its main advantage is simplicity. Defects include the obvious loss of information from discarding the incomplete cases, and the fact that the resulting analysis will in general be biased unless the complete cases form a random subsample of the original sample. This is often not the case; for example, in a panel survey with attrition, the individuals who remain to the end often differ systematically from the individuals who drop out.

*Direct analysis of the incomplete data* analyzes all the data using a method that does not require rectangular data. Two forms of this approach are available-case analysis and maximum likelihood. *Available-case analysis* replaces components in complete-data statistics by corresponding quantities calculable from the available data. For example, univariate statistics such as means and variances are calculated using the set of cases for which each variable is observed, and covariances (or correlations) are computed using the set of cases for which both variables in the pair are observed. Although simple and intuitively appealing, available-case analysis does not constitute a reliable general approach, sometimes even providing estimates that are less efficient than estimates from complete cases.

In our view, the most useful general approach to missing-data problems is to base inferences on a model for the data and missing-data mechanism. We focus on two variants of this approach that have received most attention in the literature — namely, direct analysis of the incomplete data by the method of maximum likelihood, and multiple imputation based on explicit and implicit models. These two methods are introduced in the context of monotone missing data with a bivariate normal model; more advanced applications are considered later. To help motivate these procedures, we begin by considering the other methods introduced above for a relatively simple missing-data problem.

## CASE STUDY: MONOTONE DATA ON $K = 2$ VARIABLES

### Example 1

The following simple missing-data problem illustrates many important issues. Consider monotone data with $K = 2$ variables $X_1$ and $X_2$, with $X_1$ observed for all $n$ cases and $X_2$ observed for $m < n$ cases. For convenience, arrange the data so that the first m cases are complete and the remaining $n - m$ have $X_1$ only. Suppose $X_1$ and $X_2$ are continuous variables and the objective is to estimate the mean vector $(\mu_1, \mu_2)$, variances $(\sigma_{11}, \sigma_{22})$, and covariance $\sigma_{12}$. We may also be interested in functions of these parameters such as the difference in means, the regression slope of $X_2$ on $X_1$ or $X_1$ on $X_2$, or the correlation $\rho$.

### Complete-Case and Available-Case Analysis

Let

$$\bar{x}_j = \sum_{i=1}^{m} x_{ij} / m, \qquad s_{jk} = \sum_{i=1}^{m} (x_{ij} - \bar{x}_j)(x_{ik} - \bar{x}_k)/m, \quad 1 \le j, k \le 2 \qquad (9.1)$$

denote the sample means, variances, and covariance of $X_1$ and $X_2$ from the $m$ complete cases. Here, the usual small sample correction of $m-1$ for $m$ in the denominator of $s_{jk}$ has been omitted to keep expressions simple. A complete-case analysis of these data uses these estimates for their population analogs. The inefficiency of complete-case estimates of $\mu_1$ and $\sigma_{11}$ is clear, because $n-m$ values of $X_1$ are ignored. Intuitively, the complete-case estimates of $\mu_2$ and $\sigma_{22}$ are not fully efficient, because incomplete cases contain information about $\mu_2$ and $\sigma_{22}$ when $X_1$ and $X_2$ are correlated. Is $s_{12}$ the "best" estimate of $\sigma_{12}$? An answer is given in the section on maximum likelihood and bivariate normality.

Available-case analysis yields the same estimates of $\mu_2$ and $\sigma_{22}$, because $X_2$ is only recorded in the complete cases. However, $\mu_1$ and $\sigma_{11}$ are estimated by the sample mean and variance of $X_1$ from all n cases, which we denote as $\hat{\mu}_1$ and $\hat{\sigma}_{11}$. The obvious available-case estimate of $\sigma_{12}$ is $s_{12}$, because $X_1$ and $X_2$ are both observed only when the data are complete, although other estimates are plausible. For example, we might replace $\bar{x}_1$ in the expression for $s_{12}$ (equation 9.1) by the more precise estimate $\hat{\mu}_1$, arguing that this makes better use of the available data. Alternatively, suppose we write

$$\sigma_{12} = \rho\sqrt{\sigma_{11}\sigma_{22}} \qquad (9.2)$$

and substitute available-case estimates for the parameters on the right side. Then $\rho$ and $\sigma_{22}$ would be estimated from the complete cases and $\sigma_{11}$ from all the cases, yielding a different estimate than $s_{12}$. Similarly, $\rho$ might be estimated directly from complete cases or by estimating $\sigma_{12}$ and $\sigma_{22}$ from complete cases, $\sigma_{11}$ from all cases, and substituting these in (9.2), solving for $\rho$.

From this brief discussion, it is clear that ad hoc arguments can yield a variety of estimates that make use of all the available data in apparently plausible ways. Some of these choices have undesirable properties — in particular, it is easy to see that the last method for estimating $\rho$ can yield values outside the range $(-1,1)$ (for example, suppose $s_{12} = .9$, $s_{11} = s_{22} = .95$, and $\hat{\sigma}_{11} = .7$). More generally, a $K{\times}K$ correlation matrix built up by available-case methods is not necessarily positive definite, because the entries are in general derived from different sets of cases. This inconsistency can easily lead to trouble when these matrices are used to compute regressions or other forms of multivariate analysis.

Available-case analysis seems better than complete-case analysis for estimating means: $\hat{\mu}_1$ is clearly preferable to $\bar{x}_1$, and both methods estimate $\mu_2$ by $\bar{x}_2$. However, which is the better estimate of $\delta = \mu_2 - \mu_1$: the available-case estimate $\hat{\delta}_A = \bar{x}_2 - \hat{\mu}_1$, or the complete-case estimate $\hat{\delta}_C = \bar{x}_2 - \bar{x}_1$?

The answer depends on the *missing-data mechanism*, and, in particular, on whether missingness depends on the values of $X_1$ and $X_2$. Suppose first that the data are *missing completely at random (MCAR)*, which means that missingness of $X_2$ does not depend on the values of $X_1$ or $X_2$; in other words, the complete cases are a random subsample of all the cases. Then both $\hat{\delta}_A$ and $\hat{\delta}_C$ are unbiased, and

$$\operatorname{var}(\hat{\delta}_A) = \frac{\sigma_{11}}{m} + \frac{1}{n}\left[\frac{\sigma_{22}}{\sigma_{11}} - 2\rho\sqrt{\frac{\sigma_{22}}{\sigma_{11}}}\right]; \quad \operatorname{var}(\hat{\delta}_C) = \frac{\sigma_{11}}{m} + \frac{1}{m}\left[\frac{\sigma_{22}}{\sigma_{11}} - 2\rho\sqrt{\frac{\sigma_{22}}{\sigma_{11}}}\right].$$

Comparing variances,

$$\text{var}(\hat{\delta}_A) < \text{var}(\hat{\delta}_C) \quad \text{if } \rho < \frac{1}{2}\sqrt{\sigma_{22}/\sigma_{11}}, \text{ and}$$

$$\text{var}(\hat{\delta}_A) > \text{var}(\hat{\delta}_C) \quad \text{if } \rho > \frac{1}{2}\sqrt{\sigma_{22}/\sigma_{11}}.$$

Thus, for comparing means, available-case analysis is *less* efficient than complete-case analysis if the correlation is large, despite the impression that it makes better use of the available data.

If the data are not MCAR — that is, if missingness *is* related to the values of $X_1$ and/or $X_2$ — then both complete-case and available-case analysis are not only subject to inefficiency but also may be biased. This is clear for complete-case analysis because the complete cases are no longer a random sample of all the cases. Available-case analysis is good for estimating the distribution of $X_1$ because it uses the full sample, but it can yield biased estimates of other parameters. In fact, for inference about the difference in means, available-case analysis tends to have a larger bias than complete-case analysis, so it is even less attractive than that method. (For more discussion, see Little & Su, 1989).

## Imputation

We now consider methods for imputing the $n-m$ missing values of $X_2$ in Example 1. A simple and common expedient is *unconditional mean imputation* in which missing values are imputed by the unconditional sample mean $\bar{x}_2$. The method achieves little except the illusion of progress. Estimates of means are the same as for available cases. The covariance matrix from the filled-in data is positive definite, but the estimates of $|\sigma_{12}|$ and $\sigma_{22}$ are too small by a factor $m/n$; slopes of $X_2$ on $X_1$ and of $X_1$ on $X_2$ are also biased. Multiplying the 12 and 22 entries of the matrix by $n/m$ to remove the bias leads to available-case estimates with their attendant problems. Standard errors from the filled-in data are much too low, because (a) variability of $X_2$ values is underestimated, and (b) sample size is overstated. Here and in many more complex situations, we think it is better to leave missing values blank than to impute unconditional means.

An improvement is *conditional mean imputation*, where an estimate of the mean of the conditional distribution of $X_2$ given $X_1$ is imputed. A common choice is *regression imputation*, where the regression of $X_2$ on $X_1$ is estimated from the $m$ complete cases, and the resulting prediction equation used to impute the conditional mean of the missing $X_2$

values. Another approach is to classify cases into adjustment cells based on similar values of $X_1$, and then impute the within-cell mean of $X_2$. This procedure can be viewed as regression imputation, with regressors that are dummy variables indicating the cells. It is a natural choice when $X_1$ is in fact a categorical variable.

Regression imputation is a plausible method, particularly when most of the variation of $X_2$ is explained by $X_1$ (in other words, when $\sigma_{22.1}$, the residual variance of $X_2$ given $X_1$ is small). The estimate of $\mu_2$ from the filled-in data is reasonable, but the marginal distribution of $X_2$ is still distorted because the imputations do not reflect variation in the distribution of $X_2$ given $X_1$. (If this is not obvious, consider the case where $X_1$ is not predictive of $X_2$, and the method essentially imputes $\bar{x}_2$.) Hence, $\sigma_{22}$ is underestimated, as is the slope of the regression of $X_1$ on $X_2$. Standard errors of estimates from the filled-in data are underestimated, particularly when $\sigma_{22.1}$ is substantial.

Mean imputation (unconditional or conditional) can yield satisfactory estimates of aggregate means but leads to distorted estimates of variation and covariation. For all-purpose use, we prefer methods that impute a *value* from the predictive distribution, rather than a mean. An example is *stochastic regression imputation*. A missing $x_{i2}$ is replaced by

$$\tilde{x}_{i2} = \hat{x}_{i2} + r_i$$

where $\hat{x}_{i2}$ is the prediction from the regression of $X_2$ on $X_1$, and $r_i$ is a normal deviate with mean 0, variance $\hat{\sigma}_{22.1}$, or alternatively the regression residual from a randomly selected complete case. Another example is *hot-deck* imputation, where adjustment cells are formed based on values of $X_2$ and a missing $X_2$ is replaced by an observed value of $X_2$ from a randomly chosen respondent in the same adjustment cell. For an empirical comparison of these methods in the more complex setting of income imputation in the Current Population Survey, see David et al. (1986). An extensive discussion of hot-deck and alternative nonresponse adjustment methods for surveys is given in Madow et al. (1983).

These methods sacrifice some efficiency in estimating means, but provide better estimates of marginal distributions of variables. Also, estimates of covariation between variables are improved, providing the imputations condition on observed variables in each case (Kalton & Kasprzyk, 1982). Standard errors of estimates from the filled-in data are less biased than those from mean imputation, but nevertheless remain too optimistic.

A solution to this problem is to draw more than one value from the predictive distribution of the missing values, and then repeat analyses with different imputes substituted. A formal development of this method of multiple imputation is provided after considering maximum likelihood estimation.

### Maximum Likelihood Assuming Bivariate Normality

Better estimates of the parameters can be obtained by applying the ML approach to this problem. ML estimation requires that we (a) specify a model for the joint distribution of $X_1$ and $X_2$; (b) compute the *likelihood* of the observed data under that model, where the likelihood is simply the probability density of the data regarded as a function of the parameters for the fixed observed data; and (c) estimate the parameters to maximize the likelihood. In particular, suppose we make the assumption that the data in Example 1 are an incomplete random sample from the bivariate normal distribution with means $(\mu_1,\mu_2)$, variances $(\sigma_{11},\sigma_{22})$, and covariance $\sigma_{12}$. Then, writing $\theta = (\mu_1, \mu_2, \sigma_{11}, \sigma_{12}, \sigma_{22})$ for the parameters, the probability density of the observed data (say $\mathbf{X}_{obs}$) has the form

$$f(\mathbf{X}_{obs}|\theta) = \prod_{i=1}^{m} N_2(x_{i1},x_{i2}|\theta) \prod_{i=m+1}^{n} N_1(x_{i1}|\mu_1,\sigma_{11}) \qquad (9.3)$$

where $N_1$ and $N_2$ denote the univariate and bivariate normal densities, respectively; the first product is over the $m$ complete observations $\{(x_{i1}, x_{i2}): i=1, \ldots, m\}$ and the second product is over the $n-m$ incomplete observations $\{x_{i1}: i=m+1, \ldots, n\}$.

The likelihood of $\theta$ is (9.3) regarded as a function of $\theta$, and ML estimates are obtained by maximizing this function with respect to $\theta$. The process is simplified in this example by applying the method of *factored likelihoods* (Anderson, 1957; Rubin, 1974; Little & Rubin, 1987, chap. 6). The likelihood is reexpressed as the product of two complete-data likelihoods, one for the parameters of the marginal distribution of $X_1$ based on all $n$ cases, and one for the parameters of the conditional distribution of $X_2$ given $X_1$ based on the $m$ complete cases. Under the normal model, the sets of parameters in these two factors are distinct, so the factors can be maximized separately, yielding a combination of available-case analysis for the parameters of the distribution of $X_1$ and complete-case analysis for the parameters of the distribution of $X_2$ given $X_1$. The former analysis yields ML estimates $\hat{\mu}_1$ for $\mu_1$ and $\hat{\sigma}_{11}$ for $\sigma_{11}$. ML estimates of $\mu_2$, $\sigma_{12}$, and $\sigma_{22}$ are found by combining estimates from these available-case and complete-case analyses, using the fact that ML estimates of one-to-one functions of parameters are the functions evaluated at the ML estimates. This yields ML estimates

$$\hat{\mu}_2 = \bar{x}_2 + b_{21}(\hat{\mu}_1 - \bar{x}_1) \tag{9.4}$$

$$\hat{\sigma}_{12} = s_{12}(\hat{\sigma}_{11} / s_{11}) \tag{9.5}$$

$$\hat{\sigma}_{22} = s_{22} + b_{21}^2(\hat{\sigma}_{11} - s_{11}) \tag{9.6}$$

for $\mu_2$, $\sigma_{12}$, and $\sigma_{22}$, where $b_{21} = s_{12}/s_{11}$. The statistic $\hat{\mu}_2$ is called the *regression estimate* of $\mu_2$ and is easily seen to be the average of the observed and imputed values of $X_2$, where imputed values are the predictions from the least-squares linear regression of $X_2$ on $X_1$, computed from the complete cases (that is, the regression imputation method of the previous section). The ML estimates of $\sigma_{12}$ and $\sigma_{22}$ are reasonable, but subtle, modifications of the complete-case estimates $s_{12}$ and $s_{22}$. The estimates are not associated with any scheme for single imputations, but, as noted in the next section, are associated with an appropriate multiple-imputation scheme.

Why do we prefer these estimates to the others discussed in this chapter? First, the ML estimates are consistent and efficient if the model is correct. In particular, $\hat{\mu}_2 - \hat{\mu}_1$ is unbiased for $\mu_2 - \mu_1$ with a large-sample variance that is uniformly smaller than that of $\bar{x}_2 - \bar{x}_1$ or $\bar{x}_2 - \hat{\mu}_1$. ML estimates of $\sigma_{22}$ and $\sigma_{12}$ avoid the biases of estimates from regression imputation, and are more efficient than estimates from complete cases.

Second, ML estimates remain consistent and efficient for certain non-MCAR missing-data mechanisms, where missingness depends on the data. If missingness depends on observed values in the data matrix **X** but not on missing values, the missing data are called *missing at random (MAR)*. On the other hand, if missingness depends on missing (and possibly observed) values in **X**, the missing data are not MAR.

ML estimation based on the marginal distribution of $\mathbf{X}_{obs}$ remains valid if the missing data are MAR. In particular, in our example suppose that missingness of $X_2$ depends on the value of $X_1$ but not on the value of $X_2$; that is

$$p(X_{i2} \text{ missing}|X_{i1}, X_{i2}) = p(X_{i2} \text{ missing}|X_{i1}), \text{ for all } X_{i2}$$

Because $X_{i1}$ is always observed, the data are MAR, and ML estimates (9.4)-(9.6) are valid. On the other hand, if missingness depends on the value of $X_2$ rather than $X_1$, then the data are not MAR (because $X_2$ is missing in some observations), and (9.4)-(9.6) are in general biased. The theory underlying these statements is outlined in the section on ML estimation. In practice, it is often hard to decide from the data whether the MAR assumption is appropriate; however ML often reduces non-response bias even when the MAR assumption is not strictly valid.

Third, large-sample standard errors and associated tests and interval estimates can be obtained by applying standard ML theory. In particular, the asymptotic covariance matrix of the parameter estimates is obtained by inverting the negative matrix of second derivatives of the loglikelihood (the observed information matrix) or its expected value (the expected or Fisher information matrix). Because these information matrices are based only on the observed data, the resulting standard errors take into account the missing data, unlike standard errors computed from imputed data sets. Standard errors for Example 1 are discussed in Little and Rubin (1987, sec. 6.3). Fourth, ML for this simple problem provides guidance on harder problems, such as those considered in the section on estimation.

Some might argue that ad hocery in the formation of estimates has been replaced by ad hocery in the assumptions of the model. However, the multivariate normal is a natural baseline model for estimation based on the mean and covariance matrix, and ML estimates under normality seem to do better than available-case and complete-case methods even when the model is misspecified (for example, Azen & Van Guilder, 1981; Little, 1988b). Also, the model can be refined in particular circumstances. For example, we might include a quadratic term in $X_1$ for the regression of $X_2$ on $X_1$, or model heterogeneity of the residual variance as a function of $X_1$. Such issues of model specification arise even when the data are complete, of course, and an advantage of the ML approach is that it builds on modeling experience developed with complete data.

An important assumption of the model is that the missing data are MAR. In particular, if missingness of $X_2$ depends on the value of $X_2$, then the MAR assumption is not correct and the estimates (9.4)-(9.6) will be biased. For example, suppose $X_2$ is income and individuals with large incomes are less likely to respond than others. As another example, if individuals with $X_2 = 0$ have a greater tendency to fail to report, then the probability of response is smaller for $X_2 = 0$ than for other values, and the missing-data mechanism is again not MAR. The ML approach can still be applied in such cases, but it requires the inclusion of an additional factor in the likelihood modeling the missing-data mechanism as discussed later. The correct specification of these nonrandom selection terms is difficult because our knowledge of the form of the missing-data mechanism is often soft to nonexistent, and results are sensitive to misspecification errors that the data themselves are unable to detect (see Little & Rubin, 1987, chap. 11).

Where possible, studies should be designed to limit the impact of nonrandom missing-data mechanisms. For income nonresponse, for example, measurable covariates that correlate with income should be collected, such as owner/renter status, square footage of house, number of cars owned, income above or below \$40,000. In some cases, zeros and missing values are liable to be confounded, a situation that needs to be avoided by clearly distinguishing zeros and missing values during data collection.

### Multiple Imputation

We have seen that ML yields the same estimates of $\mu_1$ and $\mu_2$ as that from regression imputation, but has the advantage of yielding consistent estimates of the other parameters. In this section, we introduce *multiple imputation*, a method that retains the practical advantages of imputation and also yields valid large-sample inferences about all the parameters. The basic feature of the method is that instead of creating a single impute for each missing value, $M \geq 2$ imputed values are created from the predictive distribution of each missing value. The resulting multiply-imputed data set supplements the original units by variables matrix with a matrix of multiple imputations, each row corresponding to a missing value in the original data (see Figure 9.2).

For the data in Example 1, a crude version of multiple imputation is a simple extension of stochastic regression imputation: The $M$ imputed values for $x_{i2}$ take the form

$$\hat{x}_{i2} + r_{il}, \quad l = 1, \ldots, M \tag{9.7}$$

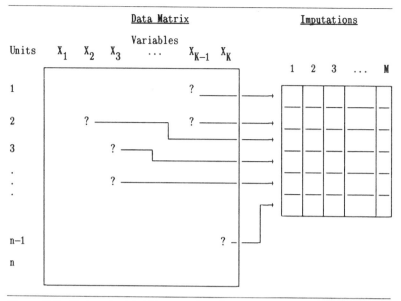

**Figure 9.2    Data set with $M$ imputations for each missing datum.**

where $\hat{x}_{i2}$ is the predicted mean from the regression of $X_2$ on $X_1$, and $r_{i1}, \ldots, r_{iM}$ are randomly drawn residuals from the complete cases. A better version incorporates uncertainty in the estimation of the regression parameters by replacing $\hat{x}_{i2}$ in (7) by

$$\hat{x}_{i2}^{(l)} = \alpha_{21}^{(l)} + \beta_{21}^{(l)} x_{i1}$$

where the intercept $\alpha_{21}^{(l)}$ and the slope $\beta_{21}^{(l)}$ are drawn from a distribution that reflects their sampling variability. This is an important adjustment when the fraction of missing data is large, but subtle relative to the improvements afforded by multiple rather than single imputation.

Under normal assumptions, the regression parameters can be drawn using the following three steps:

(i)   First, draw the residual variance of $X_2$ given $X_1$, $\sigma_{22.1}$:

$$\sigma_{22.1}^{(l)} = \sum_{i=1}^{m} (x_{i2} - \hat{x}_{i2})^2 / \chi_{m-2}^{2(l)}$$

where $\chi^{2(l)}_{m-2}$ is a chi-squared random variable on $m-2$ degrees of freedom.

(ii) Given the drawn value of $\sigma_{22.1}$, draw the slope of $X_2$ on $X_1$, $\beta_{21}$:

$$\beta^{(l)}_{21} = b_{21} + \frac{\sigma^{(l)}_{22.1}}{ms^2_1} Z_l$$

where $Z_l$ is a standard normal deviate.

(iii) Given the drawn values of $\sigma_{22.1}$ and $\beta_{21}$, draw the intercept $\alpha_{21}$:

$$\alpha^{(l)}_{21} = \bar{y}_1 - \beta^{(l)}_{21}\bar{x}_1 + \frac{1}{m} \sigma^{(l)}_{22.1} Z'_l$$

where $Z'_l$ is an independent normal deviate.

The $M$ sets of imputed values for the missing values $(x_{m+1, 2}, \ldots, x_{n, 2})$ are used to create $M$ completed data matrices, each of which is analyzed by standard complete-data methods. The first set of imputed values creates the first complete-data analysis, and so forth. The $M$ complete-data analyses are then combined to create one inference. For example, consider the parameter $\mu_2$; its estimate with complete data would be the mean of the $n$ observations of $X_2$, with associated squared standard error $SE^2 = s^2_2/n$ where $s^2_2$ is the sample variance of the $n$ observations of $X_2$. Let $\bar{x}_2^{(l)}$, $SE^{(l)}$ $l = 1, \ldots, M$ be the $M$ values of these complete-data statistics across the $M$ completed data sets. These statistics vary because they depend on the imputed values, which vary. The resultant estimate of $\mu_2$ is the average value of $\bar{x}_2^{(l)}$

$$\hat{\mu}^*_2 = \sum_{l=1}^{M} \bar{x}_2^{(l)}/M$$

and the associated standard error

$$SE^* = \left[\bar{U} + \frac{M+1}{M} B\right]^{1/2}$$

involves the average within-imputation variability

$$\overline{U} = \sum_{l=1}^{M} \frac{SE^{(l)2}}{M}$$

and the between-imputation variability

$$B = \sum_{l=1}^{M} \frac{(\overline{X}^{(l)} - \hat{\mu}_2^*)^2}{(M-1)}$$

The estimate $\hat{\mu}_2^*$ with associated standard error $SE^*$ provides essentially valid inferences for $\mu_2$. For example, for large $M$ and large samples, $\hat{\mu}_2^*$ equals $\hat{\mu}_2$, the ML estimate, and $SE^2$ gives the large sample variance of $(\hat{\mu}_2 - \mu_2)$, so interval estimates will have their nominal coverages and tests will have their nominal significance levels. In practice, minor adjustments discussed later allow valid inferences with M as low as 2 or 3, even with large fractions of missing data (e.g., 50%).

If there is concern that the missing data are not MAR, the above procedure can be repeated using a model that reflects hypothesized differences between respondents and nonrespondents, thereby leading to one inference for $\mu_2$ that assumes missing data are MAR and a second inference that assumes missing data are not MAR. The comparison of these two inferences exposes sensitivity of inference to the missing-data process. A very simple method of deriving the non-MAR inference is simply to distort systematically the imputations from the MAR model. For example, if there is concern that the missing $X_2$ values may be systematically higher than expected, as possibly with income nonresponse, all imputed $X_2$ values from the MAR model might be increased by some plausible amount (for example, 20%). More discussion of the uses and properties of multiple imputation is given after considering ML estimation for more complex missing-data problems.

## ML ESTIMATION FOR
## MORE COMPLEX MISSING-DATA PROBLEMS

### *ML Theory*

The ML approach illustrated previously in the context of bivariate normality allows us to tackle systematically problems with more than two variables, arbitrary missing-data patterns, and more ambitious forms of analysis. The parametric form of the modeling argument can be summarized as follows. Let $\mathbf{X}$ denote the complete ($n{\times}K$) data matrix, and assume a model that specifies a distribution for $\mathbf{X}$ with density $f(\mathbf{X}|\theta)$ indexed by unknown parameters $\theta$. In Example 1 with ML estimation, $f$ was the density of a size $n$ bivariate normal random sample, and $\theta$ represented the mean and covariance matrix. With no missing data, ML would estimate $\theta$ to maximize the likelihood of $\theta$, which is simply $f(\mathbf{X}|\theta)$ regarded as a function of $\theta$. With missing values, let $\mathbf{X}_{obs}$ denote the observed components of $\mathbf{X}$, and $\mathbf{X}_{mis}$ the missing components. The marginal distribution of $\mathbf{X}_{obs}$ is obtained by integrating $f(\mathbf{X}|\theta) = f(\mathbf{X}_{obs}, \mathbf{X}_{mis}|\theta)$ over the missing values $\mathbf{X}_{mis}$:

$$f(\mathbf{X}_{obs}|\theta) = \int f(\mathbf{X}_{obs}, \mathbf{X}_{mis}|\theta)d\mathbf{X}_{mis}. \qquad (9.8)$$

Equation (9.3) illustrates the form of this density for Example 1; as in most applications, the density of $\mathbf{X}_{obs}$ can be written down without carrying out the integration on the right side of (9.8). The ML estimate of $\theta$ is the value that maximizes the likelihood of $\theta$ given $\mathbf{X}_{obs}$ — namely, $f(\mathbf{X}_{obs}|\theta)$ regarded as a function of $\theta$. Furthermore, the asymptotic covariance matrix of $\hat{\theta} - \theta$ can be computed using standard likelihood tools, such as $\mathbf{I}^{-1}(\hat{\theta}|\mathbf{X}_{obs})$, where

$$\mathbf{I}(\theta|\mathbf{X}_{obs}) = -\frac{\partial^2 \ln f(\mathbf{X}_{obs}|\theta)}{\partial\theta\partial\theta} \qquad (9.9)$$

is the observed information, or $\mathbf{J}^{-1}(\hat{\theta})$, where $\mathbf{J}(\theta)$ is the expected value of $\mathbf{I}(\theta|\mathbf{X}_{obs})$. As noted earlier when discussing monotone data, these estimates of precision take into account the fact that some values in $\mathbf{X}$ are missing.

Rubin (1976) showed that inference based on (9.8) and (9.9) in effect assumes that the missing data are MAR, which means that missingness can depend on variables observed in the data set but not on variables that are missing. To formalize this idea, we introduce an ($n{\times}K$) missing-data indicator matrix $\mathbf{R}$, with $(i, j)$th entry $r_{ij} = 1$ if $x_{ij}$ is present and $r_{ij} = 0$ if $x_{ij}$ is missing. The missing-data mechanism is then modeled by treating $\mathbf{R}$ as a stochastic matrix. Let $f(\mathbf{R}|\mathbf{X},\varphi)$ denote the density of the distribution of $\mathbf{R}$ given $\mathbf{X}$, indexed by unknown parameters $\varphi$. Then, the missing data are MAR if

$$f(\mathbf{R}|\mathbf{X},\varphi) = f(\mathbf{R}|\mathbf{X}_{obs},\varphi) \quad \text{for all } \mathbf{X}_{mis} \qquad (9.10)$$

that is, the distribution of $\mathbf{R}$ given $\mathbf{X}$ evaluated at the observed values does not depend on the missing data $\mathbf{X}_{mis}$ (although it may depend on the observed data $\mathbf{X}_{obs}$). We say the data are MCAR if

$$f(\mathbf{R}|\mathbf{X},\varphi) = f(\mathbf{R}|\varphi) \quad \text{for all } \mathbf{X}$$

which implies that missingness does not depend on the values of $\mathbf{X}$, missing or observed. Note that the MCAR assumption is stronger than MAR.

A general form of the likelihood approach combines the model for $\mathbf{X}$ with the model for $\mathbf{R}$ given $\mathbf{X}$ to yield the joint density of $\mathbf{R}$ and $\mathbf{X}$:

$$f(\mathbf{R},\mathbf{X}|\theta,\varphi) = f(\mathbf{X}|\theta)f(\mathbf{R}|\mathbf{X},\varphi) \qquad (9.11)$$

The distribution of the observed data $(\mathbf{R}, \mathbf{X}_{obs})$ is then

$$f(\mathbf{R},\mathbf{X}_{obs}|\theta,\varphi) = \int f(\mathbf{R},\mathbf{X}_{obs},\mathbf{X}_{mis}|\theta,\varphi) \ d\mathbf{X}_{mis} \qquad (9.12)$$

obtained by integrating (9.11) over the missing data $\mathbf{X}_{mis}$. The full likelihood of $\theta$ and $\varphi$ is given by (9.12), treated as a function of $\theta$ and $\varphi$. Rubin calls the missing-data mechanism *ignorable* if likelihood inference for $\theta$ based on (9.12) is equivalent to likelihood inference based on (9.8), and showed that this was the case if the data are MAR and $\theta$ and $\varphi$ are distinct (in the sense that their parameter spaces are disjoint, and, if prior distributions are defined, the parameters are a priori independent). MAR is the key condition, because if MAR holds but $\theta$ and $\varphi$ are not distinct, inferences based on (9.8) have appropriate repeated-sampling properties but are not necessarily fully efficient. For a recent account of this theory, see Little and Rubin (1987, chap. 5).

The ML approach provides useful solutions to missing-data problems, both in relatively simple settings such as Example 1 and in more complex problems where ad hoc approaches guided by intuition are generally inadequate. Limitations stem from the fact that ML is basically a large-sample inferential approach. With small or moderate-sized data sets, the likelihood may have a highly nonnormal shape, possibly with local maxima, and asymptotic theory may not work well. In particular, standard errors based on an information matrix may not yield reliable inferences. One approach to small sample problems is to add a prior and analyze the data by Bayesian methods; see, for example, Little and Rubin (1987, sec. 6.3.2).

Another disadvantage of ML methods for incomplete-data problems is that the likelihoods tend to be complicated and require iterative maximization algorithms. Considerable progress has been made on this topic. Standard numerical maximization algorithms such as Newton-Raphson and scoring have been successfully applied to incomplete-data loglikelihoods (see, for example, Hartley & Hocking, 1971; Greenlees et al., 1982; Jennrich & Schluchter, 1986). Another algorithm particularly tuned to missing-data problems, the *Expectation-Maximization* or *EM algorithm* (Dempster et al., 1977), has been extensively used. It is often easy to code and provides instructive links with imputation methods. We provide a brief description here, and apply it to some examples. Little and Rubin (1987) provide more theory and many more applications.

### The EM Algorithm

The EM algorithm was given its name by Dempster et al. (1977), who presented general theory for the algorithm and a large range of examples. Orchard and Woodbury (1972) first noted the general applicability of the underlying idea, calling it the "missing information principle." Applications of the algorithm date back at least to McKendrick (1926). We describe the EM algorithm for maximizing the likelihood (9.8) ignoring the missing-data mechanism — the extension to nonignorable likelihoods is straightforward (Little & Rubin, 1987, chap. 11).

Let $l(\theta|\mathbf{X}_{obs},\mathbf{X}_{mis})$ denote the loglikelihood of $\theta$ based on the hypothetical complete data $\mathbf{X} = (\mathbf{X}_{obs},\mathbf{X}_{mis})$. Let $\theta^{(t)}$ denote an estimate of $\theta$ at iteration $t$ of the algorithm. Iteration $t+1$ consists of an E-step and an M-step. The E-step consists of taking the expectation of $l(\theta|\mathbf{X}_{obs},\mathbf{X}_{mis})$ over the conditional distribution of $\mathbf{X}_{mis}$ given $\mathbf{X}_{obs}$, evaluated at $\theta = \theta^{(t)}$. That is, the expected loglikelihood

$$Q(\theta|\theta^{(t)}) = \int l(\theta|\mathbf{X}_{obs},\mathbf{X}_{mis})f(\mathbf{X}_{mis}|\mathbf{X}_{obs},\theta = \theta^{(t)})d\mathbf{X}_{mis}$$

is formed.

The M-step determines $\theta^{(t+1)}$ by maximizing this expected loglikelihood:

$$Q(\theta^{(t+1)}|\theta^{(t)}) \geq Q(\theta|\theta^{(t)}), \quad \text{for } all\ \theta.$$

The new estimate $\theta^{(t+1)}$ then replaces $\theta^{(t)}$ in the next iteration. It can easily be shown that each step of EM increases the likelihood of $\theta$ given $X_{obs}$. Also under quite general conditions, EM converges to the maximum of this function. In particular, if a unique finite ML estimate of $\theta$ exists, EM will find it.

EM is particularly useful when the M-step is noniterative or available using existing software. Note that the algorithm avoids computing and inverting an information matrix at each iteration. This feature can be useful in problems with many parameters, because the information matrix is square with dimension equal to the number of parameters. Standard errors based on the inverted information matrix, however, are not an automatic output of EM and hence, if required, need a separate computation. The SEM algorithm (Meng & Rubin, 1989) obtains the asymptotic variance-covariance matrix using only code for the E and M steps and code for the complete-data variance-covariance matrix. (Other methods of computing standard errors, such as profile likelihood or sample reuse methods, do not rely on the information matrix and may be preferable with moderate-sized samples.) Although EM is reliable in that it increases the likelihood at each iteration, it can be painfully slow to converge in problems where the fraction of missing information (defined in terms of eigenvalues of the information matrix) is large.

### EM for Multivariate Normal Data

*Example 2. Bivariate Normal Data with Missing Values.* For the monotone bivariate normal data of Example 1, we have seen that explicit ML estimates are available, so EM is unnecessary. Nevertheless, it is instructive to see how EM works for this problem. The complete-data loglikelihood is linear in the following sufficient statistics:

$$T_1 = \sum_{i=1}^{n} x_{i1}, \quad T_2 = \sum_{i=1}^{n} x_{i2}, \quad T_{11} = \sum_{i=1}^{n} x_{i1}^2, \quad T_{12} = \sum_{i=1}^{n} x_{i1}x_{i2}, \quad (9.13)$$

$$\text{and} \quad T_{22} = \sum_{i=1}^{n} x_{i2}^2$$

Suppose initial estimates $\theta^{(0)}$ of the parameters are computed from the complete cases: $\mu_j^{(0)} = \bar{x}_j$, $\sigma_{jk}^{(0)} = s_{jk}$, for $j,k = 1,2$. The first E-step computes the expected values of the sufficient statistics (9.13):

$$T_1^{(1)} = \mathrm{E}(T_1|\mathbf{X}_{\mathrm{obs}}, \theta^{(0)}) = T_1, \quad \text{and} \quad T_{11}^{(1)} = \mathrm{E}(T_{11}|\mathbf{X}_{\mathrm{obs}}, \theta^{(0)}) = T_{11}$$

because all the values $x_{i1}$ are observed;

$$T_2^{(1)} = \mathrm{E}(T_2^{(1)}|\mathbf{X}_{\mathrm{obs}}, \theta^{(0)}) = \sum_{i=1}^{m} x_{i2} + \sum_{i=m+1}^{n} \hat{x}_{i2}$$

$$T_{12}^{(1)} = E(T_{12}|\mathbf{X}_{\mathrm{obs}}, \theta^{(0)}) = \sum_{i=1}^{m} x_{i1}x_{i2} + \sum_{i=m+1}^{n} x_{i1}\hat{x}_{i2}$$

where $\hat{x}_{i2} = \mathrm{E}(x_{i2}|x_{i1}, \theta^{(0)})$ is the predicted value of $x_{i2}$ from the regression of $X_2$ on $X_1$, with parameters $\theta^{(0)}$ based on the complete cases; and finally

$$T_{22}^{(1)} = \mathrm{E}(T_{22}|\mathbf{X}_{\mathrm{obs}}, \theta^{(0)}) = \sum_{i=1}^{m} x_{i2}^2 + \sum_{i=m+1}^{n} (\hat{x}_{i2}^2 + \sigma_{22.1}^{(0)})$$

where $\sigma_{22.1}^{(0)}$ is the estimated residual variance of $X_2$ given $X_1$ from the regression on complete cases. The M-step computes new estimates from these expected sufficient statistics:

$$\mu_1^{(1)} = T_1^{(1)} / n$$

$$\mu_2^{(1)} = T_2^{(1)} / n$$

$$\sigma_{11}^{(1)} = T_{11}^{(1)} / n - \left(\mu_1^{(1)}\right)^2 \qquad (9.14)$$

$$\sigma_{12}^{(1)} = T_{12}^{(1)} / n - \mu_1^{(1)}\mu_2^{(1)}$$

$$\sigma_{22}^{(1)} = T_{22}^{(1)} / n - \left(\mu_2^{(1)}\right)^2.$$

Some algebraic manipulation shows that these are in fact the ML estimates previously given in the section on bivariate normality. Note the link with imputation here: $\mu_2^{(1)}$ and $\sigma_{12}^{(1)}$ are the estimates obtained from the filled-in data with $\hat{x}_{i2}$ imputed for missing values of $x_{i2}$. The same remark would apply to $\sigma_{22.1}^{(1)}$, except for the fact that $T_{22}^{(1)}$ includes terms $\sigma_{22.1}^{(0)}$, that would be omitted if $T_{22}^{(1)}$ were computed from the filled-in data. These additional terms correct for the underestimation of variance from imputing the conditional means $\hat{x}_{i2}$.

These estimates do not change in subsequent iterations of EM. If we had started with different initial values (for example, from available cases) the results of the first iteration would not be ML, but EM would eventually converge to the ML estimates (9.14).

*Example 3. Multivariate Normal Data with Missing Values.* Suppose additional observations on $X_2$ alone are added to the data of the previous example, yielding a nonmonotone missing-data pattern with $K = 2$ variables. Explicit expressions for the ML estimates are no longer available, and EM is iterative: It does not converge in a single iteration. The M-step equations are the same as before. The E-step is similar, but contributions from the additional observations on $X_2$ need to be added to the expected sufficient statistics. These involve predictions of $x_{i1}$ and $x_{i1}^2$ from the regression of $X_1$ on $X_2$: For the first iteration, $E(x_{i1}|x_{i2}, \theta^{(0)}) = \hat{x}_{i1}$ and $E(x_{i1}^2|x_{i2}, \theta^{(0)}) = \hat{x}_{i1}^2 + \sigma_{11.2}^{(0)}$ where $\sigma_{11.2}^{(0)}$ estimates the residual variance of $X_1$ given $X_2$. In subsequent iterations $\theta^{(0)}$ is replaced by the current estimate of $\theta$.

This algorithm generalizes in a natural way to the K-variate normal distribution with mean $\mu$, covariance matrix $\Sigma$, and an arbitrary pattern of missing values. The sufficient statistics (9.13) generalize to the sums, sums of squares, and sums of cross-products of the variables over all $n$ cases, and the M-step is the direct extension of (9.14) to $K$ variables; in practice, the M-step can be computed accurately with one pass through the data using standard updating methods. The E-step estimates the sufficient statistics, with contributions from each incomplete case based on the regression of the missing variables on the observed variables for that case, computed using current estimates of the parameters. The necessary regressions are easily computed using the SWEEP operator. For more details on the computations and a discussion of standard errors, see Little and Rubin (1987, Section 8.2). This EM algorithm is available as the BMDPAM program in the BMDP statistical package (Dixon, 1988), and in a recently released GAUSS module (Schoenberg, 1988).

*Example 4. Missing Data in Multiple Regression.* If $\hat{\theta}$ is the ML estimate of $\theta$, then the ML estimate of a function $g(\theta)$ is simply $g(\hat{\theta})$ — that is, the function evaluated at $\hat{\theta}$. In particular, parameters of the regression of $X_K$ on $X_1, \ldots, X_{K-1}$ are well known functions of $\mu$ and $\Sigma$, the mean and covariance matrix of $X_1, \ldots, X_K$. Hence, ML estimates of the regression parameters are obtained by evaluating these functions with ML estimates $\hat{\mu}$ and $\hat{\Sigma}$ from Example 3 substituted for $\mu$ and $\Sigma$. Computations are easily accomplished using the SWEEP operator.

## Other Examples of ML for Incomplete Data

Extensions of the multivariate normal model that place special structure on the mean and covariance matrix yield a variety of models of interest to social scientists. EM can be applied to these models to provide ML estimates from incomplete data. Important examples include ML for factor analysis, robust estimation, and repeated-measures analysis (see, for example, Little & Rubin, 1987, Example 8.2 and Sections 8.5 and 10.5). ML repeated-measures analysis from incomplete data has attracted the attention of software developers; in particular, the algorithms of Jennrich and Schluchter (1986) have been implemented in the BMDP package in the program BMDP5V (Dixon, 1988), and SAS has a program under development. Allison (1987) and Muthen et al. (1987) discuss ML estimation for structural equation models with latent variables using the LISREL package.

ML methods can also be applied to models involving discrete data. Because loglinear models for contingency tables are popular in the social sciences, a brief description of EM for this model seems worthwhile.

*Example 5. Contingency Tables with Supplemental Margins.* If variables are discrete, incomplete data as in Figure 9.1 can be rearranged as a K-way contingency table with supplemental margins. For example, suppose that $K = 2$, and $X_1$ takes $I$ and $X_2$ takes $J$ values. Then, fully observed cases can be classified into the $I \times J$ contingency table defined by joint levels of $X_1$ and $X_2$. Cases with $X_1$ observed and $X_2$ missing form a supplemental $X_1$ margin with $I$ entries, and cases with $X_2$ observed and $X_1$ missing form a supplemental $X_2$ margin with $J$ entries.

Complete-data analysis of contingency tables is often based on a multinomial model for the cell counts. That is, if the contingency table has $C$ cells with count $n_c$ in cell $c$, $\{n\} = \{n_1, \ldots, n_C\}$ is assumed to be

**Table 9.1  A 2 × 2 Table with Supplemental Margins for Both Variables**

(1) Classified by $X_1$ and $X_2$

| | | $X_2$ | | |
|---|---|---|---|---|
| | | 1 | 2 | Total |
| $X_1$ | 1 | 100 | 50 | 150 |
| | 2 | 75 | 75 | 150 |
| Total | | 175 | 125 | 300 |

(2) Classified by $X_1$

| | | |
|---|---|---|
| $X_1$ | 1 | $30^a$ |
| | 2 | $60^b$ |
| Total | | 90 |

(3) Classified by $X_2$

| | $X_2$ | +, | |
|---|---|---|---|
| | 1 | 2 | Total |
| | $28^c$ | $60^d$ | 88 |
| | , | | |
| | , | | |

NOTE: The superscripts $a$, $b$, $c$, and $d$ refer to the partially classified cells and are used in Table 9.2.
SOURCE: Little (1982). Reprinted by permission of the American Statistical Association.

multinomially distributed with index $n_+ = \Sigma_c n_c$ and probabilities $\{\pi\} = \{\pi_1, \ldots, \pi_C\}$, where $\Sigma_c \pi_c = 1$. The complete-data likelihood is

$$L(\{\pi\}|\{n\}) = \prod_{c=1}^{C} \pi_c^{n_c} \qquad (9.15)$$

and the ML estimate of $\pi_c$ is simply $n_c/n_+$, the proportion of cases in cell $c$.

With supplemental margins representing partially observed data, ML estimation is readily accomplished using the EM algorithm. Because the logarithm of the complete-data likelihood (9.15) is linear in the cell counts $\{n\}$, the E-step simply estimates these complete-data counts given the data and current estimates of the cell probabilities. The effect is to classify counts in the supplemental margins into the full table according to current estimates of the cell probabilities. The M-step performs complete-data ML estimation on the filled-in contingency table: that is, the estimated probability in a cell is the proportion of observed and fractionally allocated supplemental counts in that cell (Chen & Fienberg, 1974).

Table 9.2 displays three iterations of this algorithm for the 2×2 table with $C = 4$ cells and supplemental margins given in Table 9.1. Initially, cell probabilities are estimated from the completely classified table. These probabilities are then used to allocate the partially classified observations as indicated. For example, the 28 partially classified cases with $X_2 = 1$ have $X_1 = 1$ with probability $100/(100+75)$ and $X_1 = 2$ with probability $75/(100+75)$. Thus, of the 28 cases, in effect $(28)(100)/175 = 16$ are allocated to $X_1 = 1$ and $(28)(75)/175 = 12$ are allocated to $X_1 = 2$. In the next step, new probabilities are found from the filled-in data, and

**Table 9.2 The EM Algorithm for Data in Table 9.1, Ignoring the Missing Data Mechanism**

*Estimated Probabilities*

*Fractional Allocation of Units*

Step 1

|  |  | $X_2$ | | |  |  | $X_2$ | | |
|---|---|---|---|---|---|---|---|---|---|
|  |  | 1 | 2 |  |  |  | 1 | | |
| $X_1$ | 1 | 100/300 | 50/300 | | $X_1$ | 1 | $100 + 20^a + 16^c$ | $50 + 10^a + 24^d$ | $30^a$ |
|  | 2 | 75/300 | 75/300 | |  | 2 | $75 + 30^b + 12^c$ | $75 + 30^b + 36^d$ | $60^b$ |
|  |  |  |  |  |  |  | $28^c$ | $60^d$ | |

Step 2

|  |  |  |  |  |
|---|---|---|---|---|
| 136/478 | 84/478 | | $100 + 18.6 + 15.1$ | $50 + 11.4 + 22.4$ |
| 117/478 | 141/478 | | $75 + 27.2 + 12.9$ | $75 + 32.8 + 37.6$ |

Step 3

|  |  |  |  |  |
|---|---|---|---|---|
| .28 | .18 | | $100 + 18.4 + 15.1$ | $50 + 11.6 + 21.9$ |
| .24 | .30 | | $75 + 26.5 + 12.9$ | $75 + 33.5 + 38.1$ |

Step 4

|  |  |
|---|---|
| .28 | .17 |
| .24 | .31 |

NOTE: The superscripts in the top right panel indicate the partially classified cells in Table 9.1. For example, of 28 units with $X_2 = 1$ (superscript c), 16 are allocated to $X_1 = 1$, and 12 are allocated to $X_1 = 2$. SOURCE: Little (1982). Reprinted by permission of the American Statistical Association.

the procedure iterates to convergence; fractional counts are allowed and create no problems. Final ML estimates are $\hat{\pi}_{11} = 0.28$, $\hat{\pi}_{12} = 0.17$, $\hat{\pi}_{21} = 0.24$, and $\hat{\pi}_{22} = 0.31$.

As with models for continuous data, it is often useful to modify the model by placing special structure on the cell probabilities. In particular, loglinear models decompose the logarithm of the cell probabilities as the sum of a constant, main effects, and higher-order associations, and then set some of the terms in the decomposition to zero. (See, for example, Bishop et al., 1975.) EM can also be used to estimate loglinear models from data with supplemental margins (Dempster, et al., 1977; Fuchs, 1982). The E-step allocates the partially classified cases using probabilities calculated from the current parameter estimates, as before. The M-step computes new parameter estimates by fitting the loglinear model to the filled-in data. This step is itself iterative for loglinear models that do not have explicit ML estimates from complete data. This may not be of major concern, however, because statistical software for fitting loglinear models to complete data is readily available. For more details, see Little and Rubin (1987, chap. 9).

## MULTIPLE IMPUTATION FOR
## MORE COMPLEX MISSING-DATA PROBLEMS

### Advantages and Disadvantages of
### Imputation, Single and Multiple

In addition to the obvious advantage of allowing complete-data methods of analysis, imputation performed by the data collector (e.g., a census bureau) also has the important advantage of allowing the use of information available to the data collector but not available to an external data analyst such as a university social scientist analyzing a public-use file. This information may involve detailed knowledge of interviewing procedures and reasons for nonresponse that are too cumbersome to place on public-use files, or may be facts, such as street addresses of dwelling units, that cannot be placed on public-use files because of confidentiality constraints.

A third advantage of imputation by the data-base constructor is that the missing-data problem is handled once, rather than many times, by the users. This implies consistency of the data-bases across users, and a consequent consistency of answers from identical analyses. Too often, the same analysis (e.g., least-squares regression) when applied to the same data base will result in different outcomes because of differences in the way that users and programs handle missing data. This process leads to unnecessary confusion and wasted resources.

Just as there are obvious advantages to imputing one value for each missing value, there are obvious disadvantages of this procedure arising from the fact that the one imputed value cannot itself represent any uncertainty about which value to impute: If one value were really adequate, then that value would not be missing. Hence, analyses that treat imputed values just like observed values generally underestimate uncertainty, even assuming the precise reasons for nonresponse are known. Equally serious, single imputation cannot represent any additional uncertainty that arises when the reasons for nonresponse are not known.

Multiple imputation, first proposed in Rubin (1977, 1978), retains the three major advantages of single imputation and can rectify its major disadvantages. Multiple imputations ideally should be drawn according to the following general scheme. For each model being considered, the $M$ imputations of the missing values, $\mathbf{X}_{mis}$, are $M$ repetitions from the posterior predictive distribution of $\mathbf{X}_{mis}$, each repetition being an independent drawing of the parameters and missing values under appropriate Bayesian models for the data and the posited response mechanism.

More explicitly, $M$ imputations are created under one model by repeating the following steps $M$ independent times. First, draw a value of the parameters from their posterior distribution. Second, treating the values of the parameters drawn in the first step as true, draw the missing values from their predictive distribution.

Drawing imputations following such a two-step prescription, or a good approximation to it, rectifies the disadvantages of single imputation while retaining its advantages. The first major advantage of single imputation is retained with multiple imputation because standard complete-data methods are used to analyze each completed data set. The second major advantage of imputation — that is, the ability to utilize data collectors' knowledge in handling the missing values — is not only retained but also enhanced. In addition to allowing data collectors to use their knowledge to make point estimates for imputed values, multiple imputation allows data collectors to reflect their uncertainty as to which values to impute. This uncertainty is of two types: sampling variability assuming the reasons for nonresponse are known, and variability due to uncertainty about the reasons for nonresponse. Under each posited model for nonresponse, two or more imputations are created to reflect sampling variability under the model; imputations under more than one model for nonresponse reflect uncertainty about the reasons for nonresponse. The multiple imputations within one model are called repetitions and can be combined to form a valid inference under that model; the inferences under different models can be contrasted to reveal sensitivity of answers to posited reasons for nonresponse. Thus, multiple imputation rectifies both disadvantages of single imputation. The third advantage of single imputation — consistency of answers across users — is also retained, because the same set of multiple imputations is passed on to all users, and all users applying one analysis method will obtain the same answer.

### The Repeated Imputation Inference for
### Point and Interval Estimation

Let $\hat{\theta}_l$, $\mathbf{U}_l$, $l = 1, \ldots, M$ be $M$ complete-data estimates and their associated variances for a parameter $\theta$, calculated from the $M$ data sets completed by repeated imputations under one model for nonresponse. For instance, for a regression analysis, $\theta = \beta$, $\hat{\theta}_l$ = the least-squares estimate of $\beta$, and $\mathbf{U}_l$ = (residual mean square) $\times$ $(\mathbf{X}^T\mathbf{X})^{-1}$, in the standard notation. The final estimate of $\theta$ is

$$\bar{\theta} = \sum_{l=1}^{M} \hat{\theta}_l / M$$

The variability associated with this estimate has two components: the average within-imputation variance,

$$\bar{\mathbf{U}} = \sum_{l=1}^{M} \mathbf{U}_l / M$$

and the between-imputation component

$$\mathbf{B} = \sum (\hat{\theta}_l - \bar{\theta})^2 / (M-1)$$

where, when $\theta$ is a vector, $(\bullet)^2$ is replaced by $(\bullet)^T(\bullet)$. The total variability associated with $\bar{\theta}$ is then

$$\mathbf{T} = \bar{\mathbf{U}} + (1+M^{-1})\mathbf{B}$$

where $(1+M^{-1})$ is an adjustment reflecting the variability of $\bar{\theta}$. With scalar $\theta$, the approximate reference distribution for interval estimates and significance tests is a t distribution:

$$(\theta - \bar{\theta})T^{-1/2} \, t_v$$

where the degrees of freedom

$$v = (M-1)\{1+[(1+M^{-1})B \, / \bar{U} \, ]^{-1}\}^2$$

is based on a Satterthwaite approximation. In particular, a 95% interval estimate of θ is given by

$$\bar{\theta} \pm CT^{1/2}$$

where $C$ is the upper 2.5% point of the $t$ distribution on $v$ degrees of freedom. The within-to-between ratio $r = \bar{U}/B$ estimates the population quantity $(1-\gamma)/\gamma$, where $\gamma$ is the fraction of information about θ missing due to nonresponse. In the case of ignorable nonresponse with no covariates, $\gamma$ equals the fraction of data values that are missing, but typically $\gamma$ is less than this because of dependence between variables with the attendant ability to improve prediction of missing values from observed values.

### Significance Levels for Multicomponent θ

For θ with $k > 1$ components, significance levels for null values of θ can be obtained from $M$ repeated complete-data estimates, $\hat{\theta}_l$, and variance-covariance matrices, $U_l$ using multivariate analogues of the previous expressions. Several alternative procedures are given in Rubin (1987, chaps. 3 and 4).

An excellent choice is to let the $p$-value for the null value $\theta_0$ of θ be given by

$$\text{Prob}\{F_{k,w} > \tilde{D}\}$$

with

$$\tilde{D} = (\theta_0 - \bar{\theta}_0)\bar{U}^{-1}(\theta_0 - \bar{\theta})^T / [(1+r)k]$$

Here, $F_{k,w}$ is an $F$ random variable, $r = (1+M^{-1})$ trace $(B\bar{U}^{-1})/k$, and the denominator degrees of freedom $w$ are given by

$$w = 4 + [k(M-1)-4]\left[1 + r^{-1}\frac{k(M-1)-2}{k(M-1)}\right]$$

when $k(M-1) > 4$ as in Li et al. (1989), and by $(M-1)(k+1)(1+r^{-1})^2/2$, as in Rubin (1987), when $k(M-1)\leq 4$.

With large data sets and large models, such as occur often with multiway contingency tables in social science research, a complete-data analysis may only produce the $p$-value or equivalently the $\chi^2$ statistic

**Table 9.3 Actual Large Sample Coverages of Confidence Intervals Based on Single ($M$=1) and Multiple ($M$=3) Imputation with 30% Missing Information**

| $M$ | *Nominal Coverage* | | |
| --- | --- | --- | --- |
| | *90%* | *95%* | *99%* |
| 1 | 77 | 85 | 94 |
| 3 | 90 | 95 | 99 |

on each completed data set, for example, likelihood ratio statistics or Wald statistics of the form:

$$d_l = (\theta_0 - \theta_l)\mathbf{U}_l^{-1}(\theta_0 - \theta_l)^T$$

The problem of directly combining the $(d_l, l=1, \ldots, M))$ is very tricky because each $d_l$ typically leads to a $p$-value that is too extreme (i.e., too significant). At present, the simplest consistent procedure (Rubin, 1987, sec. 3.5 and improved by Li et al. [1989]) is to let the $p$-value be given by

$$\text{Prob}\left\{ F_{k,w'} > \hat{D} \right\}$$

with

$$\hat{D} = \frac{\dfrac{\bar{d}}{k} - \left(1 - \dfrac{1}{m}\right) v(\sqrt{d})}{1 + \left(1 + \dfrac{1}{m}\right) v(\sqrt{d})}$$

where $\bar{d}$ is the average $d_l$, $v(\sqrt{d})$ is the variance of the $\sqrt{d_l}$ and the denominator degrees of freedom, $w'$, are given approximately by $w/k^{3/M}$, where $r$ in the expression for $w$ is replaced by $(1-1/M)v(\sqrt{d})$.

## Some Frequency Evaluations

Under a correctly specified model, multiple imputation inferences with infinite $M$ are fully efficient. An important question is, How much is lost by basing inferences on a finite number $M$ of imputations?

**Table 9.4 Actual Large Sample Levels of Tests Based on Single (*M*=1) and Multiple (*M*=3) Imputation with 30% Missing Information and a Ten-Component Hypothesis Being Tested (that is, *k*=10)**

|  | Nominal Level | | |
|---|---|---|---|
| *M* | *10%* | *5%* | *1%* |
| 1 | 57 | 45 | 25 |
| 3, using $\overline{D}$ | 10 | 5 | 1 |
| 3, using $\hat{D}$ | 10 | 6 | 2 |

The large sample relative efficiency of the finite-M multiple-imputation estimator using proper imputation methods relative to the infinite-M estimator, in units of standard errors is

$$(1+\gamma/M)^{-1/2}$$

Even for relatively large γ, modest values of *M* result in estimates of θ that are nearly fully efficient. For example, for γ = 30% (usually an extreme case) and *M* = 3 (a reasonable choice for many applications), the relative efficiency of $\overline{\theta}$ is approximately 95%.

In large samples, the confidence coverage of proper imputation methods using the *t* reference distribution can be tabulated as a function of *M*, γ, and the nominal level, 1−α. With single imputation, the between component of variance is automatically set to zero, because it cannot be estimated, and the reference distribution is the normal, because *v* cannot be estimated without *B*. Table 9.3 gives illustrative values for the improvements when going from single to multiple imputation with γ = 30%. Three repeated imputations yield essentially valid confidence coverages, which is in striking contrast to coverages using only one imputation. Even worse coverages for single imputation would have been obtained using best prediction methods, such as "fill in the conditional mean."

Table 9.4 indicates the tremendous improvements that can accrue when using multiple rather than single imputation for significance testing. The test based on $\tilde{D}$ is essentially perfect for the values of γ, *k*, and *M* presented. Not only are the levels of $\tilde{D}$ correct to the accuracy of the table, but also results presented in Li et al. (1988) show that typically very little power is lost as well.

When the $\hat{\theta}$ and $\mathbf{U}_l$ are not available, $\hat{D}$ can be used, and, although not perfect, still affords a dramatic improvement over single imputation; the improvement would be even more dramatic if a "best prediction" method had been used for single imputation. Improved procedures are being developed and evaluated.

## Extensions to Nonignorable Nonresponse

When nonresponse is nonignorable, unless follow-up information is available from the nonrespondents, some assumptions must be made that are not directly testable from the data at hand. The most acceptable approach is to make the scientifically most plausible assumptions. Multiple imputation can be a valuable tool for investigating this sensitivity, because two or more imputations can be made under both a nonignorable and ignorable model, thereby displaying sensitivity to modeling assumptions.

One possible assumption is about distributional shape, such as to claim that the distribution of values is normal in the population. Under such an assumption, if the observed data deviate from normality, we would essentially fill in the missing data to make the resultant completed data more normal. We do not find such assumptions plausible in most applications, yet they do play a role in some econometric selection models; for a recent review, see Amemiya (1984). A more important role in these selection models is played by so-called instrumental variables, whose main effects (regression coefficients) are assumed to be positive in determining response but exactly zero in determining the outcome variable (Heckman, 1976). We do not find these methods appealing because results are liable to be sensitive to minor deviations of the coefficients from zero; such deviations seem to us highly likely in practice.

More plausible are assumptions that the higher-order interactions are zero (Baker & Laird, 1988) or, even more plausible, that higher-order interactions are typically smaller than lower-order interactions and main effects (Rubin et al., 1988). This area is attracting attention currently, and so should be better developed in a few years.

A final point to emphasize when nonignorable missing data are of concern is the desirability of obtaining follow-up data to desensitize inference. Whenever possible, follow-up data should be obtained from a sample of the nonrespondents. Likelihood-based methods can be applied to the resulting data by including a variable that indicates initial response/nonresponse strata. Multiple imputation can be easily implemented using the follow-up nonrespondents data to create imputations for non-follow-up nonrespondents, and may be an easier path to follow in many cases, especially when there is a need to create shared data bases (see Rubin, 1987, sec. 6.6 and 6.7; and Glynn et al., 1986).

## The Use of Implicit Models

Multiple imputation can be difficult to apply with large data sets if explicit models that are realistic need to be used. In such cases, implicit imputation models can be preferable.

For example, full models for imputation of income items in the Current Population Survey are hard to formulate because they need to model both recipiency and amount of income sources, and also need to be multivariate to account for correlations between different income types and between incomes of family members. The U.S. Census Bureau's hot-deck imputation method for income fields, which imputes missing values from respondents in flexibly defined adjustment cells, has some undesirable features (Lillard et al., 1982), but nevertheless in practice appears to make reasonably good use of covariate information on nonrespondents (David et al., 1986). It is a single-imputation method, however, and hence has the limitations noted earlier. A simple extension, providing two or more matched respondents for each incomplete case, would yield multiple imputations for each missing value and allow imputation variance to be assessed (Oh & Schueren, 1980; Herzog & Rubin, 1983). Predictive mean matching (Rubin, 1986; Little, 1988a) is an alternative implicit-modeling technique that resolves some of the limitations of the adjustment-cell method.

Another example of implicit modeling is the analysis of interval-censored data in event histories, where time to an event for some individuals is only known to lie in a finite interval; for example, suppose that the year of a birth is reported but not the month. Full ML estimation for interval-censored data tends to involve complicated likelihood functions that are hard to compute and maximize. A common approach in practice is to impute the midpoint of the interval and analyze the filled-in data. Some idea of the variability from interval-censoring is obtained by imputing $M \geq 2$ uniformly distributed draws within the interval, and then analyzing the M resulting imputed data sets using the methods described earlier. Provided the intervals are not too wide, this method can be expected to approximate ML estimates from a fully specified model quite well (Heitjan & Rubin, 1986; Little, in press).

## CONCLUDING ADVICE

Given current knowledge and technology, what should a social scientist do when faced with data with missing values? We conclude with some remarks that seem important to us.

1. *Formulate a strategy for complete data before worrying about missing data.* We find it useful to separate the formulation of a complete-data strategy from the problem of how to deal with missing values.
2. *Formulate a strategy to minimize the effects of nonresponse.* Consider both data-collection techniques and the measurement of covariates that predict outcome variables likely to be missing.
3. *Be wary of naive fixes,* such as available case methods or mean-imputation methods. These methods may not improve on an analysis that discards incomplete cases.
4. *Consider the missing-data mechanism in both data collection and data analysis.* What is the process that leads to missing values? Can it be considered ignorable? If not, follow up some nonrespondents when feasible, or try to assess sensitivity of answers to plausible departures from ignorability.
5. *Consider ML estimation under a suitable model for the data and missing-data mechanism.* Software for a variety of models is becoming available, and in other problems (for example, loglinear modeling of contingency tables with supplemental margins), the EM algorithm is straightforward to implement.
6. *Consider multiple imputation,* whenever imputation is contemplated. We have emphasized the value of multiple imputation as a method for reflecting the uncertainty due to nonresponse and hence for yielding better inferences.
7. *Consider approximate methods based on implicit imputation models.* ML or multiple imputation under a fully specified model may be difficult for complex problems. Multiple imputation based on less efficient but simpler implicit models may be a more realistic option in such cases.

# REFERENCES

Allison, P. D. (1987). Estimation of linear models with incomplete data. In H. L. Costineau (Ed.), *Sociological methodology* (pp.3-61). San Francisco: Jossey-Bass.

Amemiya, T. (1984). Tobit models: A survey. *Journal of Econometrics, 24*, 3-61.

Anderson, T. W. (1957). Maximum likelihood estimation for the multivariate normal distribution when some observations are missing. *Journal of the American Statistical Association, 52*, 200-203.

Azen, S., & Van Guilder, M. (1981). Conclusions regarding algorithms for handling incomplete data. In *Proceedings of the survey research methods section* (pp. 53-56). Arlington, VA: American Statistical Association.

Baker, S. G., & Laird, N. M. (1988). Regression analysis for categorical variables with outcome subject to nonignorable nonresponse. *Journal of the American Statistical Association, 81*, 29-41.

Bishop, Y.M.M., Fienberg, S. E., & Holland, P. W. (1975). *Discrete multivariate analysis: Theory and practice.* Cambridge: MIT Press.

Chen, T., & Fienberg, S. E. (1974). Two-dimensional contingency tables with both completely and partially classified data. *Biometrics, 30*, 629-642.

David, M., Little, R.J.A., Samuhel, M. E., & Triest, R. K. (1986). Alternative methods of CPS income imputation. *Journal of the American Statistical Association, 81*, 29-41.

Dempster, A. P., Laird, N. M., & Rubin, D. B. (1977). Maximum likelihood from incomplete data via the EM algorithm. *Journal of the Royal Statistical Society, B39*, 1-38.

Dixon, W. J. (Ed.). (1988). *BMDP statistical software.* Los Angeles: University of California Press.

Fuchs, C. (1982). Maximum likelihood estimation and model selection in contingency tables with missing data. *Journal of the American Statistical Association, 77*, 270-278.

Glynn, R., Laird, N. M., & Rubin, D. B. (1986). Selection modeling versus mixture modeling with nonignorable nonresponse. In H. Wainer (Ed.), *Drawing inferences from self-selected samples* (pp.119-146). New York: Springer-Verlag.

Greenlees, J. S., Reece, W. S., & Zieschang, K. O. (1982). Imputation of missing values when the probability of response depends on the variable being imputed. *Journal of the American Statistical Association, 77*, 251-261.

Hartley, H. O., & Hocking, R. R. (1971). The analysis of incomplete data. *Biometrics, 14*, 174-194.

Heckman, J. (1976). The common structure of statistical models of truncation, sample selection, and limited dependent variables and a simple estimator for such models. *Annals of Economic and Social Measurement, 5*, 475-492.

Heitjan, D. F., & Rubin, D. B. (1986). Inference from coarse data using multiple imputation. In T. J. Boardman (Ed.), *Computer science and statistics: Proceedings of the 18th Symposium on the Interface* (pp. 138-143). Arlington, VA: American Statistical Association.

Herzog, T. N., & Rubin, D. B. (1983). Using multiple imputations to handle nonresponse in sample surveys. In W. G. Madow, I. Olkin, & D. B. Rubin (Eds.), *Incomplete data in sample surveys. Vol. 2: Theory and bibliographies* (pp. 210-248). New York: Academic Press.

Jennrich, R. I., & Schluchter, M. D. (1986). Unbalanced repeated-measures models with structured covariance matrices. *Biometrics, 42*, 800-820.

Kalton, G., & Kaspryzk, D. (1982). Imputing for missing survey responses. In *Proceedings of the survey research methods section* (pp. 22-31). Arlington, VA: American Statistical Association.

Li, K. H., Meng, X. L., Raghunathan, T. E., & Rubin, D. B. (1989). *Significance levels from repeated p-values with multiply imputed data*. Research report, Harvard University, Department of Statistics.

Li, K. H., Raghunathan, T. E., & Rubin, D. B. (1989). *Large sample significance levels from multiply imputed data using moment-based statistics and an F reference distribution*. Research report, Harvard University, Department of Statistics.

Lillard, L., Smith, J. P., & Welch, F. (1982). What do we really know about wages: The importance of nonreporting and census imputation. *Journal of Political Economy, 94,* 489-506.

Little, R.J.A. (1982). Models for nonresponse in sample surveys. *Journal of the American Statistical Association, 77,* 237-250.

Little, R.J.A. (1988a). Missing data adjustments in large surveys. *Journal of Business and Economic Statistics, 6,* 1-15.

Little, R.J.A. (1988b). Robust estimation of the mean and covariance matrix from data with missing values. *Applied Statistics, 37,* 23-38.

Little, R.J.A. (in press). *Incomplete data in event history analysis*. In J. Trussell (ed.), *Demographic Applications in Event History Analysis*. Oxford: Oxford University Press.

Little, R.J.A., & Rubin, D. B. (1987). *Statistical analysis with missing data*. New York: John Wiley.

Little, R.J.A., & Su, H. L. (1989). Item nonresponse in panel surveys. In D. Kasprzyk, G. Duncan, & M. P. Singh (Eds.), *Panel surveys* (pp. 400-425). New York: John Wiley.

Madow, W. G., Nisselson, H., Olkin, I., & Rubin, D. B. (Eds.). (1983). *Incomplete data in sample surveys* (Vols. 1-3). New York: Academic Press.

McKendrick, A. G. (1926). Applications of mathematics to medical problems. *Proceedings of the Edinburgh Mathematics Society, 44,* 98-130.

Meng, X. L., & Rubin, D. B. (1989). Obtaining asymptotic variance-covariance matrices in missing-data problems using EM. In *Proceedings of the Statistical Computing Section, American Statistical Association*. Arlington, VA: American Statistical Association.

Muthen, B., Kaplan, D., & Hollis, M.(1987). On structural equation modeling with data that are not missing completely at random. *Psychometrika, 52,* 431-462.

Oh, H. L., & Schueren, F. E. (1980). Estimating the variance impact of missing CPS income data. In *Proceedings of the survey research methods section* (pp. 408-415). Arlington, VA: American Statistical Association.

Orchard, T., & Woodbury, M. A. (1972). A missing information principle: Theory and applications. *Proceedings of the Sixth Berkeley Symposium on Mathematical Statistics and Probability, 1,* 697-715.

Rubin, D. B. (1974). Characterizing the estimation of parameters in incomplete data problems. *Journal of the American Statistical Association, 69,* 467-474.

Rubin, D. B. (1976). Inference and missing data. *Biometrika, 63,* 581-592.

Rubin, D. B. (1977). Formalizing subjective notions about the effect of nonrespondents in sample surveys. *Journal of the American Statistical Association, 72,* 538-543.

Rubin, D. B. (1978). Multiple imputations in sample surveys—A phenomenological Bayesian approach to nonresponse. In *Proceedings of the survey research methods section* (pp. 20-34). Arlington, VA: American Statistical Association.

Rubin, D. B. (1983). Iteratively reweighted least squares. *Encyclopedia of the Statistical Sciences, 4,* 272-275.

Rubin, D. B. (1986). Statistical matching and file concatenation with adjusted weights and multiple imputations. *Journal of Business and Economic Statistics, 4,* 87-94.

Rubin, D. B. (1987). *Multiple imputation for nonresponse in surveys.* New York: John Wiley.

Rubin, D. B., Schafer, J. L., & Schenker, N. (1988). Imputation strategies for estimating the undercount. In *Bureau of the Census Fourth Annual Research Conference* (pp. 151-159). Washington, DC: Department of Commerce.

Rubin, D. B., & Schenker, N. (1986). Multiple imputation for interval estimation from simple random samples with ignorable nonresponse. *Journal of the American Statistical Association, 81,* 366-374.

Schoenburg, R. S. (1988). *MISS: A program for missing data.* GAUSS Programming Language. Aptech Systems Inc. [P.O. Box 6487, Kent, WA 98064]

# 10

## SELECTION BIAS IN
## LINEAR REGRESSION,
## LOGIT AND PROBIT MODELS

Jeffrey A. Dubin
Douglas Rivers

### INTRODUCTION

Most empirical work in the social sciences is based on observational data that are incomplete. Often, data are missing for reasons other than that the investigator (or other collector of the data) did not record certain measurements. A much more common cause of missing data is that the subjects themselves act in a way that makes it impossible to obtain measurements on certain variables. For example, in political surveys, we do not have data on how some respondents voted for the simple reason that some respondents *chose* not to vote. Restricting data analysis to the sample of voters leaves us with a *self-selected* sample. If our interest is in the relationship between demographic characteristics and political preferences in the population as a whole, the subsample of nonmissing observations is likely to produce misleading conclusions.

In the voting example above, one solution would be to ask nonvoters which candidate they would have voted for, but this "solution" is not very practical for secondary analysts who lack control over data collection. In other situations, it is hard to envision how the missing data could be collected even if we had abundant resources. For example, in analyzing the relationship between schooling and earnings, we only have earnings data for those who are employed. Labor-force participation is voluntary. Some people choose not to work, others are unable to find work they considerable acceptable. The employed sample is unlikely to be a random subset of the entire population and there is no reliable way to impute earnings to those who are unemployed.

In recent years, a good deal of work has been devoted to missing data problems. (The book by Little and Rubin, 1987, is a good summary; see also their chapter in this volume for an alternative approach to handling missing data.) The method developed by Heckman (1979) for correcting for selectivity bias in linear regression models with normal errors has found many applications in econometrics and is now a standard tool for empirical workers. Little, however, is known about the treatment of missing data in probit and logit models. These models have attained considerable popularity in the social sciences for analyzing discrete-choice and other qualitative data. Unfortunately, there is no simple analog to the Heckman method for discrete-choice models, even though the same basic conceptual framework carries over in a natural way. In this article we adapt the Heckman framework to logit and probit models and discuss various methods of estimation in this context.

To provide background material for readers who may be unfamiliar with the standard econometric approach to selectivity, a brief exposition of selection bias in linear regression models is presented in the next section. We restrict our attention to cases where only observations on the dependent variable are missing. The simplest case is the well-known Tobit model of Tobin (1958) in which the censoring is governed by the value of the dependent variable itself. A simple geometric argument makes the nature of the bias apparent and the maximum likelihood estimator is very simple to develop in this context. We then consider Heckman's (1979) adaptation of the Tobit model to situations in which there is a separate mechanism governing the censoring.

In the following three sections, we adapt the Heckman setup to probit and logit analysis with selectivity. Analogous to the Heckman method, there is both a two-step estimator and a maximum likelihood estimator. The computational advantages of two-step estimation are less here than in Heckman's case, as they still require specialized software. We also propose a simple score test for selection bias that does not require computation of the full model. The sixth section contains estimates of a voting model that have been corrected for selection bias. All but the simplest derivations have been placed in the Appendix.

## SELECTION BIAS IN LINEAR REGRESSION MODELS

In this section, we briefly review the symptoms and treatment of selection bias in linear regression models. In this case, selection bias turns out to be a garden variety specification error similar to omitting a variable. The obvious solution — including the omitted variable — is an effective cure. The linear regression model is a convenient starting place for the subsequent development.

Our primary interest concerns a linear regression model of the form:

$$y_i = \beta' x_i + u_i . \qquad (10.1)$$

Equation (10.1) is a "structural model" that is intended to represent some behavioral process. In econometric applications, (10.1) might arise from an optimization problem. For example, $y_i$ might denote the quantity consumed of some good, and the vector $x_i$ would include the prices of various goods and characteristics of the consumer (including income). Equation (10.1) could be obtained by specifying a "representative" utility function for each consumer (depending upon the quantity consumed of each good and the consumer's demographic characteristics). The quantity consumed, $y_i$, is assumed to maximize the consumer's utility subject to a budget constraint. At some point in the derivation, the error term $u_i$ is introduced to capture unmeasured variables in the utility function or, perhaps, errors of optimization.

The key point is that equation (10.1) is assumed to hold independent of how any data might be collected. It is this aspect of the econometric approach that often causes statisticians difficulty. The regression in (10.1) is not an empirical relation, but a theoretical one. At the outset, we are willing to commit to a model specification that is derived from an economic or other social scientific theory. The purpose of estimation is not to learn what process generates the observed variables — this is taken to be known in advance of any data analysis — but to learn the parameters of this process (such as price elasticities).

It should be obvious that (10.1) alone does not determine the distribution of the observed variables $(x_i, y_i)$. This will depend on two things: the distribution of the errors and how the data were collected. We discuss each in turn.

In most applications, the error term $u_i$ is introduced because the theory, as represented by the rest of (10.1), is not completely adequate. One should be reluctant to make too many assumptions about the errors that, admittedly, represent theoretical ignorance. But, to the degree that we have confidence in our theory, observations with large errors are unusual because they are not accounted for by the model. In this sense, the errors represent failures of the model. Being realists, we are willing to tolerate such failures as long as they have no systematic pattern. The customary assumptions are that nothing systematic has been omitted from the model ($x_i$ and $u_i$ are independent) and that, on average, the model is correct (the mean of $u_i$ is zero). Again, these assumptions appear to be largely a theoretical matter. If one believes the theory, then one should be willing to make the necessary assumptions.

Data collection is an altogether different matter. One can believe the theory implied by (10.1) in its entirety and yet not expect a sample to yield regression estimates resembling (10.1). The sampling procedure may be such that it over- or underrepresents specific types of individuals. This causes no serious problems if the sampling fractions are purely a function of the explanatory variables. Nor is it a problem when the sampling fractions are independent of the errors. The source of the problem is sample selection *related* to the errors. When this happens, the assumed theoretical model fails in a *systematic* way: The errors occurring in the sample no longer have a zero mean because the sampling procedure has picked out observations that are, in terms of the theory, "unusual."

### The Tobit Model

The simplest case of selection bias arises when certain observations on the dependent variable $y_i$ have been "censored." In a classic paper, Tobin (1958) analyzed automobile purchases. In this application, $y_i$ denotes the amount a household would like to spend on new cars. If the least expensive car costs $c$, households whose desired level of automotive expenditures is less than $c$ will be unable to transact. In this case, we would not observe the amount $y_i$ that they would like to spend. Their actual expenditures would be zero, but this would not be indicative of their desired expenditures, which the regression is intended to explain. For any given level of $x_i$, the sample would overrepresent those households with large positive errors.

It might be tempting in this situation to go ahead and regress $y_i$ on $x_i$ and a constant using only those households who purchased cars. In Figure 10.1, solid dots indicate households for which $y_i \geq c$; these are households whose desired level of expenditures was sufficiently high

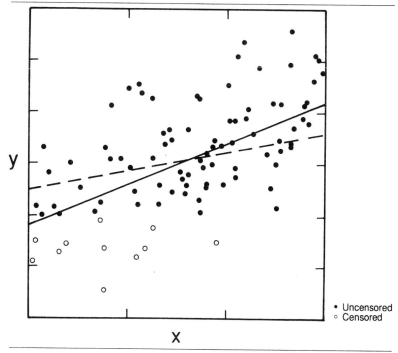

y

X

**Figure 10.1   Bias of least squares in the tobit model.**

that a transaction occurred. Empty circles indicate households with zero expenditures – i.e., those for which $y_i < c$. It is apparent from Figure 10.1 that use of the truncated sample can lead to severe bias. The estimated regression line (dashed) is less steep than the true regression line (solid).

How general is this result? A slightly more formal treatment is instructive. For simplicity, suppose (10.1) contains a single regressor and a constant term, as in Figure 10.1:

$$y_i = \alpha + \beta x_i + u_i . \qquad (10.2)$$

What happens when we apply least squares to (10.2), omitting those observations for which $y_i < c$? Let $\hat{\beta}$ denote the least-squares estimator of $\beta$ based on those observations satisfying the sample selection rule $y_i \geq c$. We will analyze the probability limit of $\hat{\beta}$ and will show that under rather general conditions $\hat{\beta}$ is attenuated — i.e., $|E\hat{\beta}| < |\beta|$. That is, the least-squares estimator based on the truncated sample will be attenuated; it will tend to underestimate the true impact of $x_i$ on $y_i$.

The relationship between $x_i$ and $y_i$ in the sample will reflect the impact of conditioning on the sample selection rule $y_i \geq c$. The basic idea is that the relation between $x_i$ and $y_i$ in the sample takes the form:

$$E(y_i|x_i, y_i \geq c) = \alpha + \beta x_i + E(u_i|x_i, y_i \geq c)$$
$$= \alpha + \beta x_i + E(u_i|u_i \geq c - \alpha - \beta x_i, x_i) \quad (10.3)$$

The last term in (10.3) varies from one observation to another, depending on the value of $x_i$. To simplify the notation, define:

$$\xi_i = E(u_i|u_i \geq c - \alpha - \beta x_i, x_i). \quad (10.4)$$

Letting $\tilde{u}_i = u_i - \xi_i$ (10.3) can be rewritten as:

$$y_i = \alpha + \beta x_i + \xi_i + \tilde{u}_i . \quad (10.5)$$

Equation (10.5) is in the form of a regression equation with a constant term and two regressors — $x_i$ and $\xi_i$.

Equation (10.5) provides the basis for a consistent estimation method in the presence of censoring. If the additional "regressor" $\xi_i$ were available, ordinary least squares could be applied to (10.5) to obtain estimates of $\alpha$ and $\beta$. For this regression to be consistent, it is necessary for the errors *in the subsample of uncensored observations* to have a mean of zero and to be uncorrelated with the regressors. The subsample of uncensored observations are those for which $y_i \geq c$. Thus, the relevant condition to ensure consistency of the regression is that $\tilde{u}_i$ have a mean of zero and be uncorrelated with the regressors *conditional* upon $y_i \geq c$.

To see that the expectation of $\tilde{u}_i$ in the sample is zero, we take the expectation of $\tilde{u}_i$ conditional on the sample selection rule $y_i \geq c$:

$$E(\tilde{u}_i|y_i \geq c) = E(u_i - \xi_i|y_i \geq c) \quad (10.6)$$
$$= E(E(u_i|y_i \geq c, x_i) - \xi_i|y_i \geq c)$$
$$= 0$$

by the law of iterated expectations[1] and equation (10.5). A similar argument shows that $\tilde{u}_i$ is uncorrelated with $x_i$ and $\xi_i$ in the sample:

$$E(x_i, \tilde{u}_i | y_i > c) = E(\xi_i, \tilde{u}_i | y_i > c) = 0 \qquad (10.7)$$

If observations on $\xi_i$ were available, then least squares could be applied to equation (10.5) to obtain unbiased and consistent estimates of $\alpha$ and $\beta$.

Least squares applied to the truncated sample is inconsistent because a variable $-\xi_i-$ is omitted from the estimating equation. Heckman (1979) observed that the direction of the bias could be found by applying the standard omitted variables formula (Theil, 1957; Griliches, 1957). We supply the details below.

Estimating equation (10.2) amounts to estimating a misspecified version of equation (10.5). The omitted variables formula can be used to analyze the nature and direction of the resulting biases. The omitted variables formula states that, aside from sampling variation, the estimated coefficient of a variable in a regression with an omitted variable equals the true coefficient of that variable plus the coefficient of the omitted variable times the coefficient of the included variable in an "auxiliary regression" of the omitted variable on the included variables. In the present context, the coefficient of the omitted variable $\xi_i$ is equal to one, so the usual specification bias formula reduces to:

$$\plim_{n \to \infty} \hat{\beta} = \beta + \pi \qquad (10.8)$$

where $\pi$ is the coefficient of $x_i$ if $\xi_i$ were regressed on $x_i$ and a constant; i.e.,

$$\pi = \frac{\text{Cov}(x_i, \xi_i | y_i \geq c)}{\text{Var}(x_i | y_i \geq c)} . \qquad (10.9)$$

The direction of the bias depends upon the sign of $\pi$. In Appendix A, we show that the sign of $\pi$ is the opposite of that of $\beta$:

$$\pi \begin{matrix} < \\ = \\ > \end{matrix} 0 \quad \text{if} \quad \beta \begin{matrix} > \\ = \\ < \end{matrix} 0. \qquad (10.10)$$

From (10.10), it follows that plim $\hat{\beta} < \beta$ if $\beta > 0$ and plim $\hat{\beta} > \beta$ if $\beta < 0$. Thus, selection biases the estimated coefficient toward zero.[2]

Because the results above indicate that a direct application of least squares is unsuitable to a truncated sample, alternative estimation procedures must be sought. Tobin (1958), in his classic paper, suggested assuming a normal distribution for $u_i$ and estimating $\alpha$ and $\beta$ by maximum likelihood. We assume that $u_i$ has a $N(0,\sigma^2)$ distribution and either that the explanatory variables in (10.1) are fixed or the analysis is conditional upon the $x$'s.[3] For censored observations $(y_i < c)$, the likelihood is given by:

$$\Pr(y_i < c|x_i) = \Pr(u_i < c - \beta'x_i) = \Phi\left(\frac{c - \beta'x_i}{\sigma}\right) \qquad (10.11)$$

where $\Phi(\bullet)$ denotes the cumulative distribution function (cdf) of a standard normal random variable. For the uncensored observations $(y_i \geq c)$, the distribution of $y_i$ is the same as that of $u_i$ except for its expectation (because the Jacobian of the transformation from $u_i$ to $y_i$ is unity), and is given by the density:

$$f_Y(y_i) = f_u(y_i - \beta'x_i) = \frac{1}{\sigma}\phi\left(\frac{y_i - \beta'x_i}{\sigma}\right). \qquad (10.12)$$

Let $d_i$ be a dummy variable indicating whether an observation was censored $(d_i = 0$ if $y_i < c)$ or not $(d_i = 1$ otherwise$)$. Combining (10.11) and (10.12), we obtain the log-likelihood function:

$$L(\beta,\sigma) = \sum_{i=1}^{n} d_i \log \Phi\left(\frac{c - \beta'x_i}{\sigma}\right) + (1 - d_i) \log \frac{1}{\sigma}\phi\left(\frac{y_i - \beta'x_i}{\sigma}\right). \qquad (10.13)$$

The ML estimates $\tilde{\beta}$ and $\tilde{\sigma}$ are obtained by maximizing (10.13) with respect to $\beta$ and $\sigma$. We will not go into the details here, except to mention that computer software is available for this problem.[4]

It is also possible to estimate the Tobit model using a two-step procedure. The first stage is a probit analysis, and the second stage is a linear regression. To simplify the notation, suppose the model includes only a constant and a single regressor. In the first stage, define a dummy variable $d_i$ that equals zero if the observation is censored $(y_i < c)$ and equals one otherwise. Let $\alpha^* = (\alpha - c)/\sigma$ and $\beta^* = \beta/\sigma$. Because

$$\Pr(d_i = 1|x_i) = \Phi(\alpha^* + \beta^* x_i) \tag{10.14}$$

a probit analysis with $d_i$ as the dependent variable and $x_i$ and a constant as independent variables gives consistent estimates of $\alpha^*$ and $\beta^*$. Denote these estimates by $\hat{\alpha}^*$ and $\hat{\beta}^*$, respectively. Under the assumption of normality, the mean of $u_i$ for a censored observation is given by

$$\xi_i = \sigma\lambda(\alpha^* + \beta^* x_i) \equiv \sigma\lambda_i \tag{10.15}$$

where

$$\lambda(t) = \frac{\phi(t)}{1 - \Phi(t)} \tag{10.16}$$

is the reciprocal of the Mills ratio, also called the hazard rate. (A similar formula holds when $u_{1i}$ has a nonnormal distribution; see the Appendix for further discussion.) An estimate of $\lambda_i$ is available from the first stage of the procedure:

$$\hat{\lambda}_i = \phi(\hat{\alpha}^* + \hat{\beta}^* x_i). \tag{10.17}$$

Substituting (10.15) into (10.5) and replacing $\lambda_i$ by $\hat{\lambda}_i$ yields

$$y_i = \alpha + \beta x_i + \sigma\hat{\lambda}_i + \tilde{u}_i + \sigma(\lambda_i - \hat{\lambda}_i). \tag{10.18}$$

In the second stage, $\alpha$, $\beta$, and $\sigma$ can be estimated by applying least squares to (10.18). There are two sources of inefficiency to this procedure. The first stage estimates of $\lambda_i$ do not fully exploit the sample information (by neglecting the values of $y_i$ for uncensored observations). Second, the errors in (10.18) are heteroscedastic (whether or not $\lambda_i$ is estimated), so ordinary least squares is inefficient. In principle, the efficiency of the two-step procedure could be improved by using weighted least squares, but in practice it is simpler to resort to the ML estimator, which is fully efficient.

### Heckman's Selectivity Model

The simple Tobit model is only applicable when the sample selection rule depends solely on the value of the dependent variable. In other situations, the selection criterion may be correlated with the dependent variable, but other factors also affect whether a value is censored. The approach to selection bias that we pursue here involves a further specification of the sample selection mechanism. This requires a slight shift in notation. Rewrite the structural equation (10.1) that we want to estimate as

$$y_{1i} = \beta_1' x_{1i} + u_{1i} \qquad (10.19)$$

where $y_{1i}$ is only partially observable — i.e., some observations on $y_{1i}$ are censored. In this context, equation (10.19) is sometimes called the *outcome equation* to distinguish it from the *selection equation* defined below. Let $y_{2i}$ be a dummy variable indicating whether $y_{1i}$ is observed ($y_{2i} = 1$) or not ($y_{2i} = 0$). It is necessary to specify how $y_{2i}$ is determined. Because $y_{2i}$ is dichotomous, a regression model would be ill-suited for this purpose. Instead, we introduce an auxiliary latent variable $y_{2i}^*$ which is determined by the selection equation

$$y_{2i}^* = \beta_2' x_{2i} + u_{2i} . \qquad (10.20)$$

When the latent index $y_{2i}^*$ is positive, $y_{1i}$ is observed; otherwise $y_{1i}$ is censored. Once a distribution is chosen for the errors, the model defined by equations (10.19) and (10.20) is fully determined.

A concrete example may help to motivate the specification in (10.19) and (10.20). Heckman (1974) analyzed female labor supply using this setup. The market wage level for a female worker ($y_{1i}$) depends upon various observable characteristics of the worker (education, age, and experience — denoted by the vector $x_{1i}$) as well as various unobservable characteristics (represented by $u_{1i}$). However, many married women choose not to work outside the home, so any data on the wages of female workers is subject to considerable self-selection. Heckman modeled the labor-force participation decision using a standard reservation wage model. Each woman sets a reservation wage level: If the woman finds an employer willing to offer a wage higher than the reservation wage, the woman accepts the wage offer and is employed. Let $y_{2i}^*$ denote the difference between the market wage offered to worker $i$ and her reservation wage. Presumably $y_{2i}^*$ would be affected by any variable affecting the market wage $y_{1i}$ as well as some factors irrelevant to the worker's productivity (marital status is one possible factor of this type), so $x_{2i}$ would include the elements of $x_{1i}$ as well as some additional variables. When $y_{2i}^*$ is positive (or, equivalently, when $y_{2i} = 1$), then the market wage exceeds the reservation wage, the woman is employed, and her wage is observable. When $y_{2i}^*$ is negative, the woman is unemployed and $y_{1i}$ is censored.

Estimating (10.19) by applying least squares to the uncensored observations results in biased estimates for the same reasons that least squares fails in the Tobit model. That is, in the subsample of uncensored observations, the errors $u_{1i}$ have a nonzero mean, which can be shown to be:

$$E(u_{1i}|x_{1i}, x_{2i}, y_{2i}^* > 0) = \frac{\sigma_{12}}{\sigma_2}\lambda\left(\frac{\beta_2' x_{2i}}{\sigma_2}\right) \equiv \frac{\sigma_{12}}{\sigma_2}\lambda_i^*. \qquad (10.21)$$

Equation (10.21) is a generalization of (10.15) that allows the censoring to be governed by a separate equation. It reduces to (10.15) when $y_{2i}^* = y_{1i}$.

To estimate the system of equations (10.19) and (10.20) by maximum likelihood methods requires a specification for the joint distribution of $(u_{1i}, u_{2i})$. It is conventional to assume that $(u_{1i}, u_{2i})$ are independent identically distributed with a bivariate normal distribution with mean zero, variances $\sigma_1^2$ and $\sigma_2^2$, and covariance $\sigma_{12}$. Because $y_{2i}^*$ in (10.20) is latent, we define the dummy variable $y_{2i} = 1$ if $y_{2i}^* > 0$ and $y_{2i} = 0$ otherwise. That is, $y_{1i}$ is observed if $y_{2i} = 1$ and otherwise is censored.

The model, as written, is not identified, because (10.20) can be multiplied by any positive number without affecting any of the observables. For example, divide (10.20) by $\sigma_2$:

$$\frac{y_{2i}^*}{\sigma_2} = \left(\frac{\beta_2}{\sigma_2}\right)' x_{2i} + \frac{u_{2i}}{\sigma_2}. \qquad (10.22)$$

The sign of $y_{2i}^* / \sigma_2$ is the same as that of $y_{2i}^*$ so the implied value of $y_{2i}$ is unaffected. Insofar as the observable variables $y_{2i}$ and $x_{2i}$ are concerned, equations (10.20) and (10.21) are indistinguishable. Thus, the variance $\sigma_2^2$ is unidentified and can be set to any arbitrary value. A convenient normalization is $\sigma_2^2 = 1$. Then, the probability that an observation is not censored (conditional on $x_{2i}$) is:

$$Q_i(\beta_2) = \Phi(\beta_2' x_{2i}) \qquad (10.23)$$

while the component of the likelihood for an uncensored observation is

$$P_i(\beta_1, \beta_2, \sigma_1^2, \sigma_{12}) = \frac{1}{\sigma_1} \phi \left( \frac{y_{1i} - \beta_1' x_{1i}}{\sigma_1} \right)$$

$$\times \Phi \left( \frac{\beta_2' x_{2i} + \sigma_{12}(y_{1i} - \beta_1' x_{1i}) / \sigma_1^2}{\sqrt{1 - \sigma_{12}/\sigma_1^2}} \right) \quad (10.24)$$

It follows that the log-likelihood function is given by

$$L(\beta_1, \beta_2, \sigma_1^2, \sigma_{12}) = \sum_{i=1}^{n} y_{2i} \log P_i(\beta_1, \beta_2, \sigma_1^2, \sigma_{12})$$

$$+ (1 - y_{2i}) \log Q_i(\beta_2) \quad (10.25)$$

Thus the likelihood function is relatively simple and only requires the numerical evaluation of a one-dimensional normal integral $\Phi(\cdot)$ for which there are several good algorithms. Further discussion may be found in Griliches et al. (1978).

Heckman (1979) proposed a simple two-step procedure for estimating the model in (10.19) and (10.20) that avoids some of the complications of full ML estimation. In the first step of the Heckman procedure, $\beta_2$ is estimated by applying probit analysis to the selection equation alone. That is, one maximizes the marginal likelihood function for $y_{2i}$:

$$L_2(\beta_2) = \sum_{i=1}^{n} y_{2i} \log \Phi(\beta_2' x_{2i}) + (1 - y_{2i}) \log(1 - \Phi(\beta_2' x_{2i})). \quad (10.26)$$

Denote the first stage estimate of $\beta_2$ by $\hat{\beta}_2$. Heckman then suggests estimating $\lambda_i^*$ by:

$$\hat{\lambda}_i^* = \lambda(\hat{\beta}_2' x_{2i}). \quad (10.27)$$

For the uncensored observations, we have from (10.21) and the normalization $\sigma_2 = 1$:

$$y_{1i} = \beta'_1 x_{1i} + \sigma_{12}\hat{\lambda}_i^* + (u_{2i} - \sigma_{12}\hat{\lambda}_i^*).  \qquad (10.28)$$

The error in (10.28) is heteroscedastic, but (asymptotically) uncorrelated with the righthand side variables. Hence, applying least squares to (10.28) provides a consistent, although somewhat inefficient, estimator of $\beta_1$. Heckman (1979) explains how to obtain standard errors for the coefficients.

### Nonnormal Error Distributions

Our discussion has so far relied upon specifications in which the errors are assumed to have a normal distribution. The econometric approach to selection bias is sometimes criticized for its dependence upon normality assumptions, but, in fact, normality is not an essential assumption. A variety of alternate parametric methods have been proposed to relax the normality assumption. Amemiya and Boskin (1974) considered the estimation of the Tobit model (10.2) when the errors have a log-normal rather than a normal distribution. Dubin and McFadden (1984) consider estimation of the Heckman selectivity model (10.19) and (10.20) under the assumption that $u_{2i}$ has a logistic rather than a normal distribution. The selection equation then is of the logit rather than the probit form (see the next section). Further discussion of selection bias with parametric nonnormal distributions is given in Lee (1982).

The estimation of the system of equations represented by (10.19) and (10.20) has generally relied on an assumed parametric form of the likelihood for the bivariate distribution of $(u_{1i}, u_{2i})$. However, several researchers (Arabmazar & Schmidt, 1981, and Goldberger, 1983), have pointed out that maximum likelihood estimation methods will yield inconsistent estimates of the parameters of interest if the parametric form of the error distribution is misspecified (whether it is assumed to be normal, log-normal, or logistic). Such misspecification may arise due to nonnormality of the disturbance or if maximum likelihood procedures are naively applied to aggregate data without consideration of heteroscedasticity. Because theory may not always suggest the proper parametric specification of the random disturbances, recent research in econometrics has focused on semiparametric methods.

Semiparametric methods seek identification and consistent estimation of the parameters of interest ($\beta_1$ in (10.19)) without a full-information specification of the selection equation. The bulk of the literature on semiparametric estimation of econometric models has considered the class of single-disturbance models such as that presented in equation (10.2). Because these models involve only one error term, identification of the parameters of interest can proceed under rather weak conditions, such as symmetry of the error distribution (see Chamberlain, 1986). One simple semiparametric estimator for the censored regression model is Powell's (1984) least absolute deviations (LAD) estimator. The logic of the LAD estimator is fairly simple. Consider equation (10.2) with only a constant term and no regressors. In this case, the LAD estimator is the median of the $y_i$'s (with censored observations replaced by zeros). The least-squares estimator is the mean of the $y_i$'s (again with censored observations replaced by zeros). So long as less than half of the observations are censored, the median will be a consistent estimator of $\alpha$, while the sample mean will be downwardly biased. Powell shows that the same estimator is consistent when there are regressors.

Semiparametric estimation of the class of bivariate selection models given by (10.19) and (10.20) is not as well developed as that for the censored regression model (10.2). Heckman and Robb (1985) have proposed a method of moments estimator, while Powell (1987) has extended recent work on semiparametric estimation of discrete choice models to this context. Estimation proceeds in two steps. First, an estimate of $\hat{\beta}_2$ is computed by applying semiparametric methods to the selection equation alone. (Cosslett, 1984; Stoker, 1986; and others have suggested consistent estimators in this case.) In the second step, $\beta_1$ is estimated using semiparametric regression methods. The essential idea is that the conditional distribution of the errors $u_{1i}$ in equation (10.19), given the selection mechanism (10.20), depends only on $x_{2i}$ through the index $\beta_2' x_{2i}$. In the second step, the parameters of interest are identified through a comparison of pairs of observations for which the indices $\hat{\beta}_2' x_{2i}$ and $\hat{\beta}_2' x_{2j}$ are "close." See Powell (1987) for further discussion.

The development of semiparametric methods is still at an early stage, and we do not have much practical experience in the application of such methods. There is obviously a tradeoff between robustness and efficiency in the use of parametric and semiparametric methods. We focus primarily on parametric methods that make fairly strong distributional assumptions, but it is mistaken to believe that the econometric approach to selectivity necessarily requires such assumptions.

## SELECTION BIAS IN BINARY CHOICE MODELS

Heckman's method provides a useful framework for handling linear regression models when the data are subject to an endogenous selection mechanism. Many applications in the social sciences, however, involve discrete dependent variables for which linear models are inappropriate. In this section, we discuss how the Heckman selection model can be adapted to models for dichotomous dependent variables. The most popular models of this sort are the logit and probit models. Before discussing selectivity corrections for these models, we briefly review the logit and probit specifications without the complications of censoring.

The most frequent occurrence of dichotomous variables in the social sciences involves situations in which a decision maker faces a choice between two alternatives. The conventional model of choice in economics and other social sciences ascribes an unobservable level of utility $\tilde{U}_{ij}$ to alternative $j$ for decision maker $i$. The primary purpose of most empirical studies of choice is to determine how various factors influence the attractiveness of the alternatives to different types of individuals. Although utility levels are unobservable (being analytical devices, rather than empirical measures), a regression-like framework provides a convenient model for relating the attributes of the alternatives and decision makers to utility levels:

$$\tilde{U}_{ij} = \beta_1' \tilde{x}_{ij} + \varepsilon_{ij} \quad (j=1, 2) \tag{10.29}$$

where $\tilde{x}_{ij}$ usually includes the cost of alternative $j$ and other factors thought to affect choice. If utilities were observable, then regression methods could be applied directly to (10.29).

To estimate (10.29) it is necessary to invoke the hypothesis of utility maximization. A rational decision maker should choose the alternative that maximizes his or her utility. Let $y_{1i}^*$ denote the difference between the utility of the first alternative and the second for decision maker $i$:

$$y_{1i}^* = \tilde{U}_{i1} - \tilde{U}_{i2} = \beta_1' x_{1i} + u_{1i} \tag{10.30}$$

where $x_{1i} = \tilde{x}_{i1} - \tilde{x}_{i2}$ and $u_{1i} = \varepsilon_{i1} - \varepsilon_{i2}$. If $y^*_{1i} > 0$, the first alternative yields higher utility and is selected; otherwise, the second alternative is selected. Define a dummy variable, $y_{1i}$, denoting which alternative was selected:

$$y_{1i} = \begin{cases} 1, & \text{if } y_{1i}^* > 0 \\ 0, & \text{otherwise} \end{cases} \tag{10.31}$$

At this point, a convenient distribution is usually specified for the errors $\varepsilon_{1i}$ and $\varepsilon_{2i}$, and then the distribution of $y_{1i}$ is derived. From this point, it is straightforward to obtain the maximum likelihood estimator for this model. (See Amemiya, 1984, for further discussion.)

The logit and probit models arise from different assumptions about the distribution of $\varepsilon_{i1}$ and $\varepsilon_{i2}$. If $\varepsilon_{i1}$ and $\varepsilon_{i2}$ are assumed to have independent type I extreme value distributions,[5] then it can be shown that $u_{1i} = \varepsilon_{i1} - \varepsilon_{i2}$ has a *logistic distribution* with cdf

$$F(u) = \frac{1}{1 + e^{-u}}. \tag{10.32}$$

Alternatively, $\varepsilon_{i1}$ and $\varepsilon_{i2}$ can be assumed to have a joint normal distribution, each with mean zero, in which case the density of $u_{1i}$ is given by

$$F(u) = \Phi(u/\sigma) = \frac{1}{\sqrt{2\pi\sigma^2}} \int_{-\infty}^{u} e^{-t^2/2\sigma^2} dt \tag{10.33}$$

where $\sigma^2 = \text{Var}(\varepsilon_{i1} - \varepsilon_{i2})$. There is not much to choose between the two specifications. Both the logistic and normal distributions are symmetric and unimodal and, aside from different scale factors, differ only in their tails. Both have generalizations to choice models for more than two alternatives, but these will not concern us here.

There is no reason to believe that selection bias is any less of a problem in logit and probit models than in linear regression models. However, its treatment is more difficult—at least computationally, if not conceptually—than in the linear model, so the possibility is frequently ignored. The remainder of this article is devoted to the treatment of selection bias in binary choice models. From a conceptual point of view, the development is entirely straightforward. One specifies a selection equation, resulting in a bivariate model that can, with appropriate distributional assumptions, be estimated by maximum likelihood.

We examine the form of the likelihood equations and derive expressions for the information matrix. In the fourth and fifth sections, we specialize to the case of selection models of the probit and logit forms, respectively.

For binary choice models subject to selectivity, the specification is entirely analogous to the linear regression model of equations (10.19) and (10.20), except that the observable dependent variable in the outcome equation (10.19) is replaced by the latent variable formulation of equation (10.30). Following equation (10.20), we again specify a selection equation of the form

$$y_{2i}^* = \beta_2' x_{2i} + u_{2i} \tag{10.34}$$

so that $y_{1i}$ is observed if and only if $y_{2i}^* > 0$. The corresponding indicator of whether $y_{1i}$ is observed or censored is again denoted $y_{2i}$:

$$y_{2i} = \begin{cases} 1, & \text{if } y_{2i}^* > 0 \\ 0, & \text{if } y_{2i}^* \leq 0 \end{cases}. \tag{10.35}$$

The specification of (10.30) and (10.34) is the natural way to adapt Heckman's selection model to a binary choice situation.

In the case of the linear regression model with censoring described in the second section, a bivariate normal distribution is usual for the errors $u_{1i}$ and $u_{2i}$. The same assumption applied to the binary choice model (10.30) with selection equation (10.34) leads to a probit model with censoring. This case is covered in some detail in the next section. Alternatively, if we assume that $u_{1i}$ and $u_{2i}$ have a bivariate logistic distribution, then we obtain the logit model with the censoring in the fifth section. The logit case is less clear-cut than the probit, because there are several possible choices for a bivariate logistic model. The parameterization we propose is flexible and computationally tractable.

Before specializing to particular distributions, we consider the ML estimator for the case of an arbitrary bivariate distribution of $u_{1i}$ and $u_{2i}$. The following assumptions will be made:

**A1.** $(x_{1i}, x_{2i})$ is independent of $(u_{1i}, u_{2i})$. The cumulative distribution function of $(u_{1i}, u_{2i})$ is $F(u_{1i}, u_{2i})$.

**A2.** The observations $(x_{1i}, x_{2i}, u_{1i}, u_{2i})$ are independently and identically distributed.

Assumption A1 is that the explanatory variables be exogenously determined. Lee (1981) discusses estimation of selection models with endogenous regressors. Assumption A2 is that, aside from the censoring of some observations according to the selection rule (10.35), the observations were obtained by random sampling from some population. As most selectivity models are applied to cross-sectional survey data, this assumption should be satisfied at least approximately.

The choice of $F$, as emphasized above, is more a matter of computational convenience than anything else. $F$ should be sufficiently flexible to capture plausible forms of dependence between $u_{1i}$ and $u_{2i}$, but if this requirement is satisfied, a simple parameterization should be the main concern. We will impose two restrictions on $F$. First, note that the location and scale parameters for $u_{1i}$ and $u_{2i}$ can be normalized to convenient values by appropriate shifts and rescalings of $y_{1i}^*$ and $y_{2i}^*$ as in the usual binary choice situation. Thus, there is little loss of generality in requiring that $F$ have identical marginal distributions for $u_1$ and $u_2$. Second, we will restrict ourselves to one parameter families for $F$ and will denote the parameter by $\rho$. In the normal case, $\rho$ will be the correlation between $u_{1i}$ and $u_{2i}$, while in the logit case the relationship is somewhat more complicated. To summarize, the joint cdf takes the form $F(u_1, u_2; \rho)$ and has marginal distributions $H(u_1) \equiv F(u_1, \infty; \rho)$ and $F(\infty, u_2; \rho) \equiv H(u_2)$, which do not depend on $\rho$.[6]

Next, we calculate the probability of the three possible outcomes: a censored observation ($y_{2i} = 0$), an uncensored success ($y_{1i} = 1$ and $y_{2i} = 1$), and an uncensored failure ($y_{1i} = 0$ and $y_{2i} = 1$). This requires some additional notation. Let $G(\cdot, \cdot; \rho)$ denote the upper tail probability of $F(\cdot, \cdot; \rho)$; i.e.,

$$G(u_1, u_2; \rho) = \Pr(u_{1i} > u_1, u_{2i} > u_2) \qquad (10.36)$$
$$= 1 - H(u_1) - H(u_2) + F(u_1, u_2; \rho).$$

Then the probability of an observation *not* being censored is given by

$$Q_i(\beta_2) = \Pr(y_{2i} = 1 | x_{1i}, x_{2i}) = \Pr(y_{2i}^* > 0) = 1 - H(-\beta_2' x_{2i}). \qquad (10.37)$$

The probability of an uncensored success is given by:

$$P_i(\beta_1, \beta_2, \rho) = \Pr(y_{1i} = 1, y_{2i} = 1 | x_{1i}, x_{2i}) \qquad (10.38)$$

$$= \Pr(y^*_{1i} > 0, y^*_{2i} > 0 | x_{1i}, x_{2i})$$

$$= G(-\beta'_1 x_{1i}, -\beta'_2 x_{2i}).$$

Finally, the probability of an uncensored failure is given by

$$Q_i(\beta_2) - P_i(\beta_1, \beta_2, \rho). \qquad (10.39)$$

Combining (10.37), (10.38), and (10.39), we obtain the log-likelihood function

$$L(\beta_1, \beta_2, \rho) = \sum_{i-1}^{n} y_{2i}(y_{1i} \log P_i(\beta_1, \beta_2, \rho)$$

$$+ (1 - y_{1i}) \log(Q_i(\beta_2) - P_i(\beta_1, \beta_2, \rho))$$

$$+ (1 - y_{2i}) \log(1 - Q_i(\beta_2)). \qquad (10.40)$$

The ML estimator of $\theta = (\beta_1, \beta_2, \rho)$ is obtained by maximizing (10.40) with respect to $\theta$. This is a somewhat more difficult maximization problem than the usual binary choice problem because $P_i(\beta_1, \beta_2, \rho)$ requires the computation of a bivariate integral. It is possible, however, to obtain some simplification of the optimization problem as shown below.

The first-order conditions for the ML estimator are

$$\frac{\partial L}{\partial \beta_1} = \sum_{i=1}^{n} y_{2i} \frac{y_{1i} Q_i(\beta_2) - P_i(\beta_1, \beta_2, \rho)}{P_i(\beta_1, \beta_2, \rho)(Q_i(\beta_2) - P_i(\beta_1, \beta_2, \rho))}$$

$$\times \frac{\partial P_1(\beta_1, \beta_2, \rho)}{\partial \beta_1} = 0 \qquad (10.41)$$

$$\frac{\partial L}{\partial \beta_2} = \sum_{i=1}^{n} \frac{y_{2i} - Q_i(\beta_2)}{Q_i(\beta_2)(1 - Q_i(\beta_2))} \frac{\partial Q_i(\beta_2)}{\partial \beta_2}$$

$$- \sum_{i=1}^{n} \frac{y_{2i}}{Q_i(\beta_2) - P_i(\beta_1, \beta_2, \rho)} \left[ \left( 1 - \frac{y_{1i} Q_i(\beta_2)}{P_i(\beta_1, \beta_2, \rho)} \right) \frac{\partial P_i(\beta_1, \beta_2, \rho)}{\partial \beta_2} \right.$$

$$\left. + \left( y_{1i} - \frac{P_i(\beta_1, \beta_2, \rho)}{Q_i(\beta_2)} \right) \frac{\partial Q_i(\beta_2)}{\partial \beta_2} \right] = 0 \qquad (10.42)$$

$$\frac{\partial L}{\partial \rho} = \sum_{i=1}^{n} y_{2i} \frac{y_{1i} Q_i(\beta_2) - P_i(\beta_1, \beta_2, \rho)}{P_i(\beta_1, \beta_2, \rho)(Q_i(\beta_2) - P_i(\beta_1, \beta_2, \rho))}$$

$$\times \frac{\partial P_i(\beta_1, \beta_2, \rho)}{\partial \rho} = 0 \qquad (10.43)$$

Some insight into the first-order conditions (10.41), (10.42), and (10.43) can be obtained by noting that

$$\frac{y_{1i} Q_i(\beta_2) - P_i(\beta_1, \beta_2, \rho)}{P_i(\beta_1, \beta_2, \rho)(Q_i(\beta_2) - P_i(\beta_1, \beta_2, \rho))} = \frac{y_{1i} - R_i(\beta_1, \beta_2, \rho)}{R_i(\beta_1, \beta_2, \rho)(1 - R_i(\beta_1, \beta_2, \rho))} \qquad (10.44)$$

where $R_i(\beta_1, \beta_2, \rho) = P_i(\beta_1, \beta_2, \rho) / Q_i(\beta_2)$ is the conditional probability $y_{1i} = 1$ given $y_{2i} = 1$. Thus, the first-order conditions essentially "fit" the uncensored observations on $y_{1i}$ to their conditional expectation $R_i(\beta_1, \beta_2, \rho)$.

Equations (10.41), (10.42), and (10.43) are a system of nonlinear equations that can be difficult to solve numerically, although the computational requirements are not impossible. An alternative two-step estimation procedure is available that allows some simplification in computation at the cost of a reduction of the efficiency of the resulting estimators. The first line of equation (10.42) is the first-order condition from a binary choice model without censoring. The term inside the square brackets on the second and third lines of (10.42) has expectation zero conditional on $x_{1i}$, $x_{2i}$, and $y_{2i} = 1$. Thus, if we neglect this term, we can obtain a consistent estimator of $\beta_2$ by solving

$$\sum_{i=1}^{n} \frac{y_{2i} - Q_i(\hat{\beta}_2)}{Q_i(\hat{\beta}_2)\left(1 - Q_i(\hat{\beta}_2)\right)} \frac{\partial Q_i(\hat{\beta}_2)}{\partial \beta_2} = 0 \qquad (10.45)$$

for $\hat{\beta}_2$. This amounts to either a logit or probit analysis of the selection equation *alone*. In the second step of the estimation procedure, one then solves equations (10.41) and (10.43) for $\beta_1$ and $\rho$ after replacing $\beta_2$ by $\hat{\beta}_2$. Notice that equations (10.41) and (10.43) only involve the uncensored observations and have a structure similar to that of the usual binary choice problem. The standard errors obtained in the second step must be corrected for the estimation of $\hat{\beta}_2$ in the first step. (See Vuong, 1985, or Duncan, 1987, for details.)

## ESTIMATION IN THE NORMAL CASE

The results in the previous section are easily specialized to the case where the errors have a standardized bivariate normal distribution with correlation coefficient $\rho$. In the censored probit model, the joint cdf of $u_{1i}$, $u_{2i}$ is assumed to be

$$F(u_{1i}, u_{2i}; \rho) = \frac{1}{2\pi\sqrt{1-\rho^2}} \tag{10.46}$$

$$\times \int_{-\infty}^{u_{1i}} \int_{-\infty}^{u_{2i}} \exp\left[-\frac{1}{2(1-\rho^2)}(u_1^2 - \rho u_1 u_2 + u_2^2)\right] du_1 du_2.$$

The probability of an observation being uncensored (conditional on $x_{1i}$ and $x_{2i}$) is given by

$$Q_i(\beta_2) = \Phi(\beta_2' x_{2i}) \tag{10.47]}$$

and the probability of an uncensored success is given by:

$$P_i(\beta_1, \beta_2, \rho) = F(\beta_1' x_{1i}, \beta_2' x_{2i}, \rho) \tag{10.48]}$$

where we have used the fact that $\Phi(x) = 1 - \Phi(-x)$ and $G(x, y, \rho) = F(-x, -y, \rho)$. The gradients in the probit case also take a fairly simple form:

$$\frac{\partial P_i(\beta_1, \beta_2, \rho)}{\partial \beta_1} = \phi(\beta_1' x_{1i}) \Phi\left(\frac{\beta_2' x_{2i} - \rho\beta_1' x_{1i}}{\sqrt{1-\rho^2}}\right) x_{1i} \qquad (10.49)$$

$$\frac{\partial P_i(\beta_1, \beta_2, \rho)}{\partial \beta_2} = \phi(\beta_2' x_{2i}) \Phi\left(\frac{\beta_1' x_{1i} - \rho\beta_2' x_{2i}}{\sqrt{1-\rho^2}}\right) x_{2i} \qquad (10.50)$$

$$\frac{\partial Q_i(\beta_2)}{\partial \beta_2} = \phi(\beta_2' x_{2i}) x_{2i} \qquad (10.51)$$

$$\frac{\partial P_i(\beta_1, \beta_2, \rho)}{\partial \rho} = (1 - \rho^2)^{-1/2}\phi(\beta_1' x_{1i}) \phi\left(\frac{\beta_2' x_{2i} - \rho\beta_1' x_{1i}}{\sqrt{1-\rho^2}}\right). \qquad (10.52)$$

Substituting (10.49) through (10.52) into (10.41) through (10.43) and solving provides ML estimates for the probit model with selectivity.

Computation of the ML estimates is a nontrivial problem. It would be convenient to have a way of testing for the presence of selection bias without having to compute the ML estimates. The null hypothesis of no selection bias is $H_0 : \rho = 0$. There are a variety of ways of testing this hypothesis that have the same asymptotic properties. Wald's method, for instance, would require that we estimate $\rho$ by maximum likelihood and compute the statistic

$$W = \hat\rho^2/\hat{V}(\hat\rho) \qquad (10.53)$$

which has an approximate chi-square distribution with one degree of freedom under the null hypothesis. (The statistic in (10.53) is the square of the usual $t$-statistic for testing $\rho = 0$.) The likelihood ratio statistic compares the value of the likelihood function at the ML and constrained ML estimates. The constrained ML estimates are easily obtained because, when $\rho = 0$,

$$P_i(\beta_1, \beta_2, 0) = \Phi(\beta_1' x_{1i}) Q_i(\beta_2' x_{2i}). \qquad (10.54)$$

In this case, the constrained ML estimates can be obtained from two univariate probit analyses. First, estimate the outcome equation (using the nonmissing observations) to obtain the constrained ML estimate $\tilde\beta_1$.

Second, estimate the selection equation by probit analysis to obtain the constrained ML estimates $\tilde{\beta}_2$. The value of the log likelihood evaluated at the constrained ML estimates, denoted $L(\tilde{\beta}_1, \tilde{\beta}_2, 0)$, is the sum of the log likelihoods from the two univariate probit analyses. The $LR$ statistic for testing $\rho = 0$ is

$$LR = -2(L(\tilde{\beta}_1, \tilde{\beta}_2, 0) - L(\hat{\beta}_1, \hat{\beta}_2, \hat{\rho})) \qquad (10.55)$$

which also has an approximate chi-square distribution with one degree of freedom.

The disadvantage of the Wald and likelihood ratio statistics is that both require computation of the full ML estimates. We have shown, however, that the constrained ML estimates are easily obtained and do not require specialized software. An easier method that avoids computation of the full model is the score test procedure (Rao, 1973, pp. 417-418). If $\rho = 0$, the gradients (10.41), (10.42), and (10.43) simplify to

$$\frac{\partial L}{\partial \beta_1} = \sum_{i=1}^{n} y_{2i} x_{1i} \hat{u}_{1i} \qquad (10.56)$$

$$\frac{\partial L}{\partial \beta_2} = \sum_{i=1}^{n} x_{2i} \hat{u}_{2i} \qquad (10.57)$$

$$\frac{\partial L}{\partial \rho} = \sum_{i=1}^{n} \hat{u}_{1i} \hat{u}_{2i} \qquad (10.58)$$

where $\hat{u}_{1i}$ and $\hat{u}_{2i}$ are "generalized residuals" (Gourieroux et al., 1987):

$$\hat{u}_{1i} = \frac{\phi(\tilde{\beta}_1' x_{1i})}{\Phi(\tilde{\beta}_1' x_{1i})(1 - \Phi(\tilde{\beta}_1' x_{1i}))} (y_{1i} - \Phi(\tilde{\beta}_1' x_{1i})) \qquad (10.59)$$

$$\hat{u}_{2i} = \frac{\phi(\tilde{\beta}_2' x_{2i})}{\Phi(\tilde{\beta}_2' x_{2i})(1 - \Phi(\tilde{\beta}_2' x_{2i}))} (y_{2i} - \Phi(\tilde{\beta}_2' x_{2i})). \qquad (10.60)$$

If the null hypothesis is correct, the gradients (10.56), (10.57), and (10.58) should be close to zero. The score statistic is a quadratic form in the gradients with the information matrix (or a consistent estimate) as weighting matrix. A convenient method for obtaining the score statistic is to perform an "artificial regression" in which the dependent variable equals one for all observations and the independent variables are $y_{2i}x_{1i}\hat{u}_{1i}$, $x_{2i}\hat{u}_{2i}$, and $\hat{u}_{1i}\hat{u}_{2i}$. Computed in this way, the score statistic is

$$S = nR^2 \tag{10.61}$$

where the $R^2$ is obtained from the artificial regression described above.

## ESTIMATION IN THE LOGISTIC CASE

The main task in specializing to the logistic case is to choose a bivariate logistic distribution. The usual suggestions for a bivariate logistic distribution allow only very restricted forms of correlation (see Johnson & Kotz, 1972, pp. 291-294). We propose an alternative bivariate logistic distribution that is an improvement by this criterion:

$$F(u_1, u_2, \rho) = \frac{1}{1 + (e^{-u_i/\rho} + e^{-u_2/\rho})^\rho} \tag{10.62}$$

where the parameter $\rho$ can only take positive values. $F$ is, in fact, a bivariate logistic distribution as its marginals are of the logistic form; e.g.,

$$H(u_1) = \lim_{u_2 \to \infty} F(u_1, u_2) = \frac{1}{1 + e^{-u_1}}. \tag{10.63}$$

It can be shown that for $0 < \rho \le \sqrt{2}$ that $\text{corr}(u_1, u_2) = 1 - \rho^2/2$ so the case $\rho = \sqrt{2}$ corresponds to no correlation between $u_1$ and $u_2$. A zero correlation between $u_1$ and $u_2$, however, does not imply that they are independent; in fact, for no value of $\rho$ will $u_1$ and $u_2$ be independent. With these reservations noted, we proceed to develop a logit model with selection.

From equations (10.36), (10.37), and (10.38), substituting (10.62) and (10.63), we obtain the necessary probabilities to form the likelihood

$$Q_i(\beta_2) = \frac{1}{1 + e^{-\beta_2 x_{2i}}} \qquad (10.64)$$

$$P_i(\beta_2) = 1 - \frac{1}{1 + e^{-\beta_1' x_{1i}}} - \frac{1}{1 + e^{-\beta_2' x_{2i}}} + \frac{1}{1 + (e^{\beta_1' x_{1i}/\rho} + e^{\beta_2' x_{2i}/\rho})^{1/\rho}}. \quad (10.65)$$

The probabilities in (10.64) and (10.65) are somewhat easier to compute than in the normal case, but the expressions for the derivatives are more complex:

$$\frac{\partial P_i(\beta_1, \beta_2, \rho)}{\partial \beta_1} = \left(H(\beta_1' x_{1i})(1 - H(\beta_1' x_{1i})) - \rho^{-2} \frac{e^{\beta_1' x_{1i}/\rho}}{e^{\beta_1' x_{1i}} + e^{\beta_2' x_{2i}}}\right. \qquad (10.66)$$
$$\left. \times F(-\beta_1' x_{1i}, -\beta_2' x_{2i})(1 - F(-\beta_1' x_{1i}, -\beta_2' x_{2i}))\right) x_{1i}$$

$$\frac{\partial P_i(\beta_1, \beta_2, \rho)}{\partial \beta_2} = \left(H(\beta_2' x_{2i})(1 - H(\beta_2' x_{2i})) - \rho^{-2} \frac{e^{\beta_2' x_{2i}/\rho}}{e^{\beta_1' x_{1i}} + e^{\beta_2' x_{2i}}}\right. \qquad (10.67)$$
$$\left. \times F(-\beta_1' x_{1i}, -\beta_2' x_{2i})(1 - F(-\beta_1' x_{1i}, -\beta_2' x_{2i}))\right) x_{2i}$$

$$\frac{\partial P_i(\beta_1, \beta_2, \rho)}{\partial \rho} = \frac{1}{\rho^2}\left(1 + \log(e^{\beta_1' x_{1i}/\rho} + e^{\beta_2' x_{2i}/\rho})\right) \qquad (10.68)$$
$$\times F(\beta_1' x_{1i}, \beta_2' x_{2i}, \rho)(1 - F(\beta_1' x_{1i}, \beta_2' x_{2i}, \rho))$$

$$\frac{\partial Q_i(\beta_2)}{\partial \beta_2} = H(\beta_2' x_{2i})(1 - H(\beta_2' x_{2i})) x_{2i}. \qquad (10.69)$$

Once more, substituting (10.66) through (10.69) into (10.41) through (10.43) and solving provides ML estimates for the logit model with selectivity.

## EMPIRICAL APPLICATION: TURNOUT AND VOTING BEHAVIOR

As an application of the methods described in the preceding sections, we consider the analysis of political preferences using voting data. Voting behavior has been of interest not only to political scientists, but also to sociologists, psychologists, and economists because voting reflects a variety of social, psychological, and economic concerns. As diverse as these approaches are, they share a common structure: The characteristics of voters determine their group memberships, attitudes, or preferences, and vote choices are taken to be a measure of such memberships, attitudes, or preferences. Our purpose here is not to engage in a debate over which approach to voting analysis is superior, but only to point out that virtually *all* such analyses are subject to selection problems.

Empirical voting research is primarily concerned with the relation between various political, demographic, and psychological characteristics and political preferences. In two-candidate elections, vote and candidate preference are synonymous (unlike multicandidate elections, where strategic factors may make it in a voter's interest to vote for someone other than his or her most preferred candidate), so there appears to be little point in distinguishing between vote and preference. Nonvoters, however, also have preferences, but they do not vote. If preference is measured by vote, then data on preference are missing for nonvoters.

In the U.S. voting literature, vote equations are invariably interpreted in terms of preferences and attitudes. Presumably, the same model of preference applies to nonvoters as well as voters. If turnout and preference are unrelated, there should be no bias in estimating a model of preference based on the subsample of voters whose preference is observed. To the degree that there are common factors determining both turnout and preference, turnout is a source of selection bias.

The customary practice in voting studies has been to analyze turnout and vote choice separately. The voting electorate, however, is not a random subsample of the voting age population. Voters are known to be older, more educated, and more likely to be married than nonvoters (Wolfinger and Rosenstone, 1980). The effects of race and gender are less clear. Blacks vote at lower rates than whites, but it has been argued that black turnout is as high or higher than white turnout after controlling for education and income (Wolfinger and Rosenstone, 1980: 90-91; Verba and Nie, 1972: 170-171). In the 1950s, male turnout was approximately 10 points higher than female turnout (Campbell et al., 1960: 485-489), but the gender gap in turnout has eroded considerably since (Wolfinger and Rosenstone, 1980: 41-44) to the point that women may now participate at slightly higher levels than men. Registration laws tend to reduce turnout rates among the more mobile segments of the population (Squire, et al., 1987). On the other hand, Wolfinger and Rosenstone (1980: 109-113) argue that there are no significant ideological differences between voters and nonvoters.

Some of the variables that appear in turnout studies are clearly relevant to preference. Blacks vote overwhelmingly Democratic. The gender gap in Republican support has been widely discussed, as have generational differences. Other variables that influence voting rates, such as education or residential mobility, do not correspond very closely to any current cleavage in American politics and can be safely omitted from a vote equation.

Data from the 1984 U.S. National Election Study (NES) were used to estimate probit models of vote and turnout. The outcome variable is whether the respondent voted for Ronald Reagan and is missing for nonvoters. In this case, the selection equation is a standard turnout equation. In the NES survey, there is some overreporting of turnout. After the postelection interview, public voting records were examined to determine whether respondents who claimed to have voted actually did, and thus our analysis is based on the "validated" turnout variable. Estimating a vote equation using only validated voters should produce results similar to those based on an exit poll.

For purposes of comparison, we present in Table 10.1 separate probit analyses of vote and turnout. The vote equation in the first column of Table 10.1 includes 1347 validated voters. Blacks, women, union households, persons over 55 years old, and self-classified liberals were less likely to vote for Reagan, although gender was insignificant and age only marginally significant. Estimates for the turnout equation are presented in the second column of Table 10.1. Respondents who have lived at their current address for less than a year were classified as "new residents" and were found to turn out at much lower rates, as were younger voters and blacks. Respondents who had attended college, were married, either read a newspaper or watched network evening news on a daily basis, or belonged to a labor household were more likely to turn out. Women were slightly more likely to vote than men.

Are the estimates of the vote equation in Table 10.1 subject to selection bias? The score test described in the fourth section was performed and the null hypothesis could be rejected ($X^2$ = 4.32 with one degree of freedom, $p < 0.01$). The likelihood ratio and Wald statistics were 3.78 and 5.24, respectively.

The model in Table 10.1 was reestimated using the bivariate normal selection model of the fourth section. Maximum likelihood estimates

**Table 10.1  Probit Estimates of Vote and Turnout**

| Variable | Outcome Equation (Reagan vote) | Selection Equation (turnout) | Sample Mean (voters only) |
|---|---|---|---|
| Constant | 0.18 | -0.29 | |
| | (0.09) | (0.09) | |
| Black | -1.37 | -0.27 | 0.08 |
| | (0.18) | (0.09) | |
| Female | -0.09 | 0.14 | 0.57 |
| | (0.07) | (0.06) | |
| Union | -0.51 | 0.20 | 0.24 |
| | (0.09) | (0.07) | |
| Under 30 | 0.03 | -0.22 | 0.21 |
| | (0.10) | (0.07) | |
| Over 55 | -0.19 | 0.18 | 0.33 |
| | (0.09) | (0.07) | |
| Liberal | -0.40 | — | -0.19 |
| | (0.10) | | |
| Conservative | 0.52 | — | 0.32 |
| | (0.08) | | |
| New resident | — | -0.53 | 0.14 |
| | | (0.07) | |
| College | — | 0.62 | 0.49 |
| | | (0.07) | |
| Married | — | 0.26 | 0.62 |
| | | (0.06) | |
| TV/newspaper usage | — | 0.32 | 0.70 |
| | | (0.06) | |
| Log likelihood | -817 | -1344 | |
| $n$ | 1347 | 2237 | |

are presented in Table 10.2. The estimated turnout equation in the second column of Table 10.2, for all practical purposes, is identical to that in Table 10.1, as should be the case if the bivariate model is correctly specified. The estimated coefficients in the outcome equation, however, do change after the correction for self-selection. The largest differences between Tables 10.1 and 10.2 are in the age coefficients. After correcting for turnout, we find a much stronger relationship between age and Reagan preference (with younger voters more likely to prefer Reagan) and the estimated gender gap is larger and significant (for a one-tailed test with a 0.05 significance level). The coefficients of the ideology dummies are slightly smaller than those reported in Table 10.1.

**Table 10.2  Bivariate Normal Selection Model**

| Variable | Outcome Equation (Reagan vote) | Selection Equation (turnout) | Sample Mean (voters only) |
|---|---|---|---|
| Constant | 0.49 | −0.29 | |
| | (0.11) | (0.09) | |
| Black | −1.22 | −0.27 | 0.11 |
| | (0.20) | (0.09) | |
| Female | −0.11 | 0.14 | 0.56 |
| | (0.07) | (0.06) | |
| Union | −0.55 | 0.20 | 0.21 |
| | (0.08) | (0.07) | |
| Under 30 | 0.14 | −0.22 | 0.28 |
| | (0.10) | (0.07) | |
| Over 55 | −0.24 | 0.19 | 0.29 |
| | (0.08) | (0.07) | |
| Liberal | −0.36 | — | −0.18 |
| | (0.09) | | |
| Conservative | 0.49 | — | 0.29 |
| | (0.08) | | |
| New resident | — | −0.53 | 0.21 |
| | | (0.07) | |
| College | — | 0.62 | 0.41 |
| | | (0.06) | |
| Married | — | 0.28 | 0.57 |
| | | (0.06) | |
| TV/newspaper usage | — | 0.31 | 0.62 |
| | | (0.06) | |
| $\rho$ | | −0.41 | |
| | | (0.14) | |
| Log Likelihood | | −2159 | |
| $n$ | | 2237 | |

The estimated correlation between the errors in the turnout and vote equations is −0.41, which implies that, after controlling for measured characteristics, nonvoters were more likely to prefer Reagan than voters. Our estimates suggest that the Democratic loss in 1984 is not attributable to low turnout. Note also that the estimated intercept increases substantially after correcting for self-selection.

## CONCLUSION

Missing data problems are pervasive in the social sciences. The econometric approach to selectivity, pioneered by Heckman (1979), provides a useful framework for modeling self-selection mechanisms. The econometric approach relies on an economic or other social scientific theory for guidance in modeling the selection process, but if one is willing to subscribe to some specification — as we suspect most social scientists are willing to do — it allows most missing data problems to be overcome. The main contribution of this chapter was to indicate how the Heckman model could be extended to probit and logit models. The test for selection bias in the probit model (described in the fourth section) is suggested as a useful diagnostic for situations when the selection problem is not the primary focus of attention.

## APPENDIX A

### *Derivation of Equation (10.10)*

It is fairly straightforward to prove that the sign of $\pi$ is the opposite of that of $\beta$. First, a bit of notation. Let $F$ denote the cumulative distribution function (cdf) of $u_i$ and assume that $F$ is continuously differentiable with density $f = F'$. Let $g$ denote the density of $x_i$ and assume $x_i$ and $u_i$ are independent. To avoid unnecessary technical details, suppose that $f(u) > 0$ for all $u$. Define:

$$\xi(t) = E(u_i | u_i > t) = \frac{1}{1-F(t)} \int_t^\infty u f(u) du. \qquad (10.A1)$$

Note that

$$\xi'(t) = \frac{f(t)}{(1 - F(t))^2} \int_t^\infty u f(u) du - \frac{t f(t)}{1 - F(t)} \qquad (10.A2)$$

$$= h(t)(\xi(t) - t)$$

where $h(t) = f(t) / (1 - F(t))$ is the *hazard function*. (An interpretation of the hazard function is that $h(x)dx$ is the conditional probability of a random variable $X$ with density $f(x)$ falling in the interval $(x, x + dx)$ given that $X > x$.) It follows from (10.A2) that $\xi'(t) \geq 0$ for all $t$.

Because $x$ and $u$ are assumed to be independent (in the full sample), it follows that

$$\xi_i = \xi(c - \alpha - \beta x_i). \qquad (10.A3)$$

Let $u = E(x_i|y_i \geq c)$. Then, expanding $\xi(t)$ around the point $t = c - \alpha - \beta\mu$, by the mean value theorem there exists $z(x)$ between $x$ and $\mu$ such that

$$\xi_i = \xi(c - \alpha - \beta\mu) - \beta(x - \mu)\xi'(c - \alpha - \beta z(x)). \tag{10.A4}$$

Hence,

$$\text{Cov}(x_i, \xi_i|y_i > c) = \int (x - \mu)\xi(c - \alpha - \beta x)g(x|y \geq c)dx \tag{10.A5}$$

$$= \xi(c - \alpha - \beta\mu)\int(x - \mu)g(x|y \geq c)dx$$

$$-\beta\int(x - \mu)^2\xi'(c - \alpha - \beta z(x))g(x|y \geq c)dx$$

$$= -\beta\int(x - \mu)^2\xi'(c - \alpha - \beta z(x))g(x|y \geq c)dx$$

using (10.A2). The integrand on the last line of (10.A5) is nonnegative, so the sign of $\text{Cov}(x_i, \xi_i)$ is the opposite of $\beta$ except, of course, when $\beta = 0$ and the covariance is zero.

## NOTES

1. The law of iterated expectations states that if $X$ is a random variable and $A$ and $B$ are events, then $E(X|A) = E[E(X|A \cap B)|A]$. See, for example, Billingsley (1987, Theorem 34.4).

2. Note, however, that plim $\hat{\beta} = \beta$ if $\beta = 0$, so the usual t-test of the hypothesis $\beta = 0$ is consistent.

3. If the marginal distribution of the $x$'s does not involve either $\beta$ or $\sigma^2$, the conditional and full ML estimates will coincide, as they will for the normal linear regression model.

4. Estimators for the models in this article have been implemented in version 2.0 of Statistical Software Tools (Dubin and Rivers, 1989).

5. The type I extreme value distribution has a cdf of the form $F(t) = \exp\{-e^{-t}\}$. See Johnson and Kotz (1970, chap. 21) for further discussion.

6. Mardia (1970) discusses a general method for forming bivariate distributions with specified marginal distributions.

## REFERENCES

Amemiya, T. (1984). Tobit models: A survey. *Journal of Econometrics, 24*(1), 3-61.

Amemiya, T., & Boskin, M. (1974). Regression analysis when the dependent variable is truncated lognormal, with an application to the determinants of the duration of welfare dependency. *International Economic Review, 15,* 485-496.

Arabmazar, A., & Schmidt, P. (1981). Further evidence on the robustness of the Tobit estimator to heteroscedasticity. *Journal of Econometrics, 17,* 253-258.

Billingsley, P. (1987). *Probability and measure* (2nd ed.). New York: John Wiley.

Campbell, A., Converse, P. E., Miller, W. E., & Stokes, D. E. (1960). *The American voter.* New York: John Wiley.

Chamberlain, G. (1986). Asymptotic efficiency in semiparametric models with censoring. *Journal of Econometrics, 32,* 189-218.

Cosslett, S. R. (1984). Distribution-free maximum likelihood estimator of the binary choice model. *Econometrica, 51,* 765-782.

Dubin, J. A., & McFadden, D. L. (1984). Econometric analysis of residential electric appliance holdings and consumption. *Econometrica, 52*(2), 345-362.

Dubin, J. A., & Rivers, R. D. (1989). *Statistical software tools* (2nd ed.). Pasadena, CA: Dubin/Rivers Research.

Duncan, G. M. (1987). A simplified approach to M-estimation with application to two-stage estimators. *Journal of Econometrics, 34,* 373-390.

Goldberger, A. S. (1983). Abnormal selection bias. In S. Karlin et al. (Eds.), *Studies in econometrics, time series, and multivariate statistics.* New York: Academic Press.

Gourieroux, C., Monfort, A., Renault, E., & Trognon, A. (1987). Generalized residuals. *Journal of Econometrics, 34,* 5-32.

Griliches, Z. (1957). Specification bias in estimates of production functions. *Journal of Farm Economics, 39,* 8-20.

Griliches, Z., Hall, B. H., & Hausman, J. A. (1978). Missing data and self-selection in large panels. *Annales de L'Insee,* 30-31.

Heckman, J. J. (1974). Shadow prices, market wages, and labor supply. *Econometrica, 42,* 679-694.

Heckman, J. J. (1979). Sample selection bias as a specification error. *Econometrica, 47*(1), 153-162.

Heckman, J. J., & Robb, R. (1985). Alternative methods for evaluating the impact of interventions. In J.J. Heckman & B. Singer (Eds.), *Longitudinal analysis of labor market data* (pp.156-246). New York: Cambridge University Press.

Johnson, N. L., & Kotz, S. (1970). *Distributions in statistics: Continuous univariate distributions—I.* New York: John Wiley.

Johnson, N. L., & Kotz, S. (1972). *Distributions in statistics: Continuous multivariate distributions.* New York: John Wiley.

Lee, L. F. (1981). Simultaneous equations models with discrete endogenous and censored variables. In C.F. Manski & D. McFadden (Eds.), *Structural analysis of discrete data with econometric applications* (pp.346-364). Cambridge: MIT Press.

Lee, L. F. (1982). Some approaches to the correction of selectivity bias. *Review of Economic Studies, 49,* 355-372.

Little, R.J.A., & Rubin, D. B. (1987). *Statistical analysis with missing data.* New York: John Wiley.

Mardis, K. V. (1970). *Families of bivariate distributions.* London: Hafner.

Powell, J. L. (1984). Least absolute deviations estimation for the censored regression model. *Journal of Econometrics, 25,* 303-325.

Powell, J. L. (1987). *Semiparametric estimation of bivariate latent variable models.* Working paper No. 8704. Social Systems Research Institute, University of Wisconsin.

Rao, C. R. (1973). *Linear statistical inference and its applications* (2nd ed.). New York: John Wiley.

Squire, P., Wolfinger, R. E., & Glass, D. P. (1987). Residential mobility and voter turnout. *American Political Science Review, 81,* 45-65.

Stoker, T. M. (1986). Consistent estimation of scaled coefficients. *Econometrica, 54,* 1461-1481.

Theil, H. (1957). Specification errors and the estimation of economic relationships. *Review of the International Statistics Institute, 25,* 41-51.

Tobin, J. (1958). Estimation of relationships for limited dependent variables. *Econometrica, 26,* 24-36.

Verba, S., & Nie, N. H. (1971). *Participation in America: Political democracy and social equality.* New York: Harper & Row.

Vuong, Q. H. (1985). *Two-stage conditional maximum likelihood estimation of econometric models.* Unpublished manuscript.

Wolfinger, R. E., & Rosenstone, S. J. (1980). *Who votes?* New Haven, CT: Yale University Press.

# ABOUT THE EDITORS

JOHN FOX is Professor of Sociology at York University in Toronto, where he is also Coordinator of Statistical Consulting at the Institute for Social Research. His research interests include the political economy of Canada and various topics in social statistics. He is the author of *Linear Statistical Models and Related Methods*.

J. SCOTT LONG is Professor of Sociology at Indiana University. His most recent book is *Common Problems/Proper Solutions*. He has contributed to many journals, including *American Sociological Review*, *Social Forces*, and *Sociological Methods and Research* (for which he is also Editor). Dr. Long is completing a major research project funded by the National Science Foundation to study sex differences in scientific careers.

# ABOUT THE CONTRIBUTORS

RICHARD A. BERK is Professor in the Department of Sociology and Program in Social Statistics at the University of California, Los Angeles. He is Chair of the Methodology Section of the American Sociological Association, Vice Chair on the Board of Directors of the Social Science Research Council, and a Fellow of the American Association for the Advancement of Science. His research is typically applied with recent publications on criminal justice, the environment, and AIDS.

KENNETH A. BOLLEN is Associate Professor of Sociology at the University of North Carolina at Chapel Hill. His major research interests are in international development and statistics. He is the author of *Structural Equations with Latent Variables*.

RICHARD D. De VEAUX (Ph.D., Stanford University) is Assistant Professor of Civil Engineering and Operations Research, Program in Statistics and Operations Research at Princeton University. He has worked as Research Associate for the Analysis Center, the Wharton School, University of Pennsylvania, and was Lecturer and Assistant Professor in the Department of Statistics, also at the Wharton School.

JEFFREY A. DUBIN (Ph.D., Massachusetts Institute of Technology) is Associate Professor of Economics at the California Institute of Technology. He is the author of *Consumer Durable Choice and the Demand for Electricity* and articles in the *American Economic Review*, *Econometrica*, and *Journal of Econometrics*.

COLIN GOODALL (Ph.D., Harvard University) is Assistant Professor in the Program of Statistics and Operations Research at Princeton University. He joined Princeton University after an extended stay at Stanford University and one year at New York's Rockefeller University. Along with a lengthy involvement at Harvard and Princeton in robust and exploratory data analysis, Dr. Goodall's interests are in the statistics of shapes and health care financing.

ROBERT W. JACKMAN is Professor of Political Science at the University of California, Davis. His research interests are in comparative politics and political sociology. He is author of *Politics and Social Equality* and coauthor of *Class Awareness in the United States*.

STEPHAN LEWANDOWSKY is Research Associate in the Department of Psychology at the University of Toronto. His research interests include the cognitive processing of statistical graphs and distributed memory models.

RODERICK J.A. LITTLE (Ph.D., Imperial College, London University) is Professor of Biomathematics at the University of California, Los Angeles. After postdoctoral work at the University of Chicago, he worked for the World Fertility Survey and the U.S. Environmental Protection Agency, and spent a year at the U.S. Census Bureau as an ASA/NSF/Census Research Fellow. Dr. Little is a Fellow of the American Statistical Association, a member of the International Statistical Institute, and Associate Editor of the *Journal of the American Statistical Association*. An active statistical consultant and author, his research interests include the analysis of incomplete data, survey data, and Bayesian methods.

GEORGES MONETTE (Ph.D., Toronto University) is Associate Professor in the Mathematics Department at York University. He acts as a statistical consultant in the Institute for Social Research. His research has centered on the foundations of inference, and recently, he has been interested in the visualization of statistical concepts.

DOUGLAS RIVERS (Ph.D., Harvard University) is Professor in the Political Science Department at Stanford University. He has contributed articles to the *American Political Science Review*, *American Journal of Political Science*, and *Journal of Econometrics*.

DONALD B. RUBIN (Ph.D., Harvard University) is Professor and Chairman of the Department of Statistics at Harvard University. He has been Director of the Statistics Group at the Educational Testing Service and Professor of Statistics and Education at the University of Chicago. A Fellow of the Institute of Mathematical Sciences, the American Statistical Association, and the American Association for the Advancement of Science, he has served as Associate Editor for several journals and as Coordinating and Applications Editor of the *Journal of the American Statistical Association*. A prolific writer on statistics, Dr. Rubin's current research interests include missing data, Bayesian statistics, causal inference, sample surveys, and applied statistics in general.

IAN SPENCE is Professor in the Department of Psychology at the University of Toronto. His research interests are in psychometrics, psychophysics, and the perception of statistical graphs.

ROBERT A. STINE (Ph.D., Princeton University) is Assistant Professor of Statistics at the Wharton School, University of Pennsylvania. His current research interests include resampling methods, time series analysis, and statistical computing. In each case, his work addresses problems that arise in data analysis, particularly the analysis of data related to energy resources and consumption and to biomedical problems.